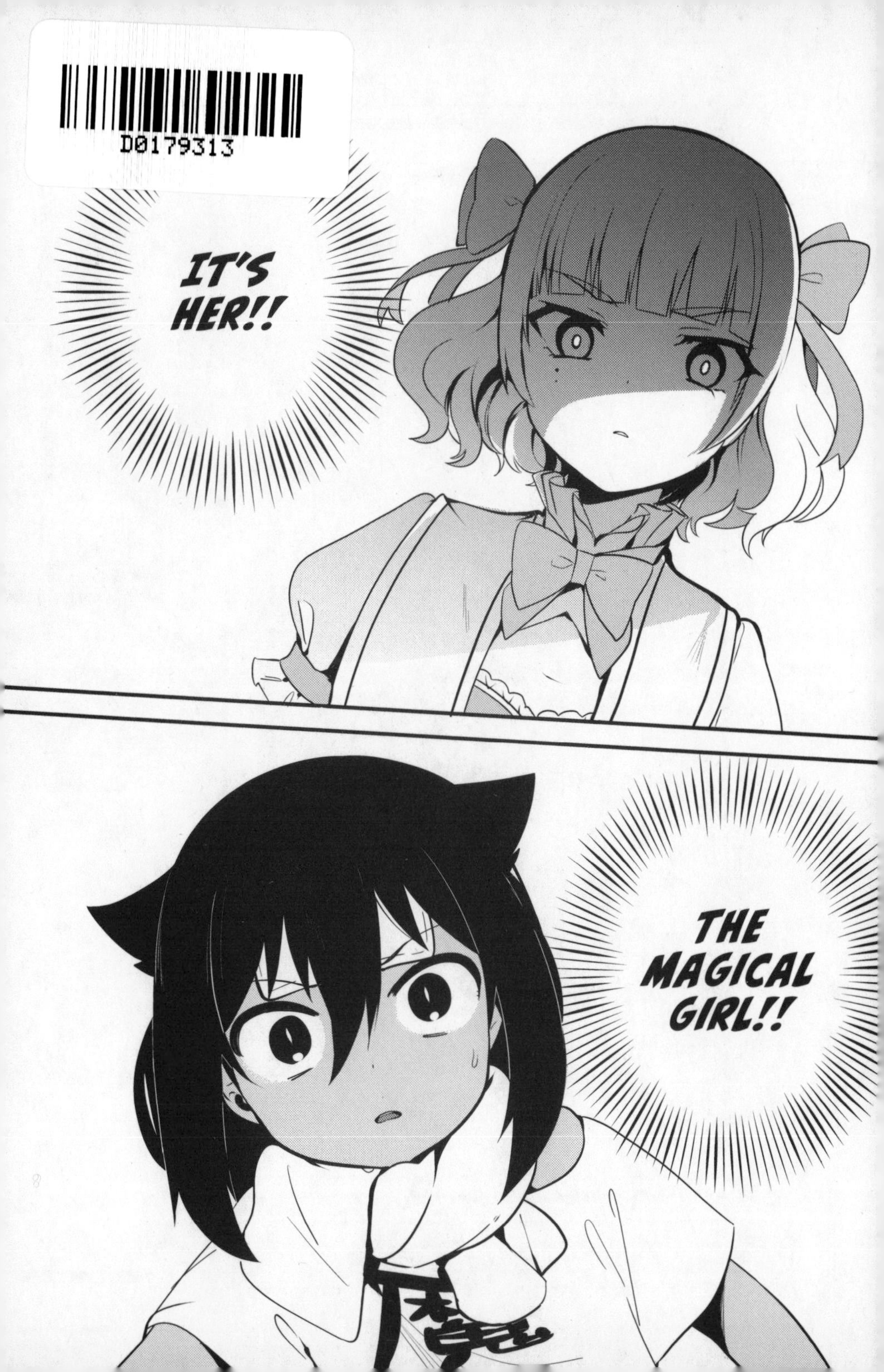
IT'S HER!!
THE MAGICAL GIRL!!

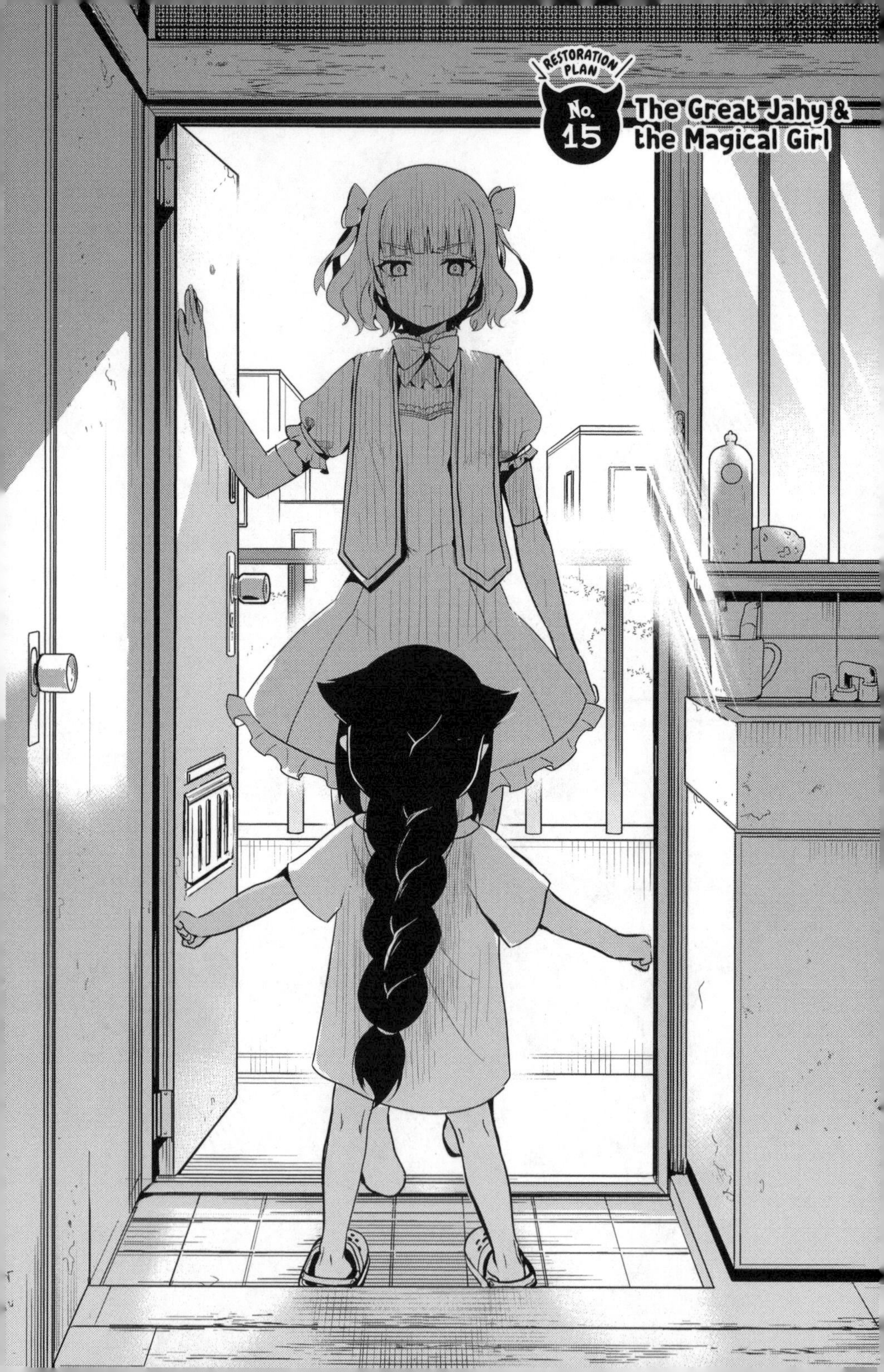
RESTORATION PLAN
No. 15
The Great Jahy & the Magical Girl

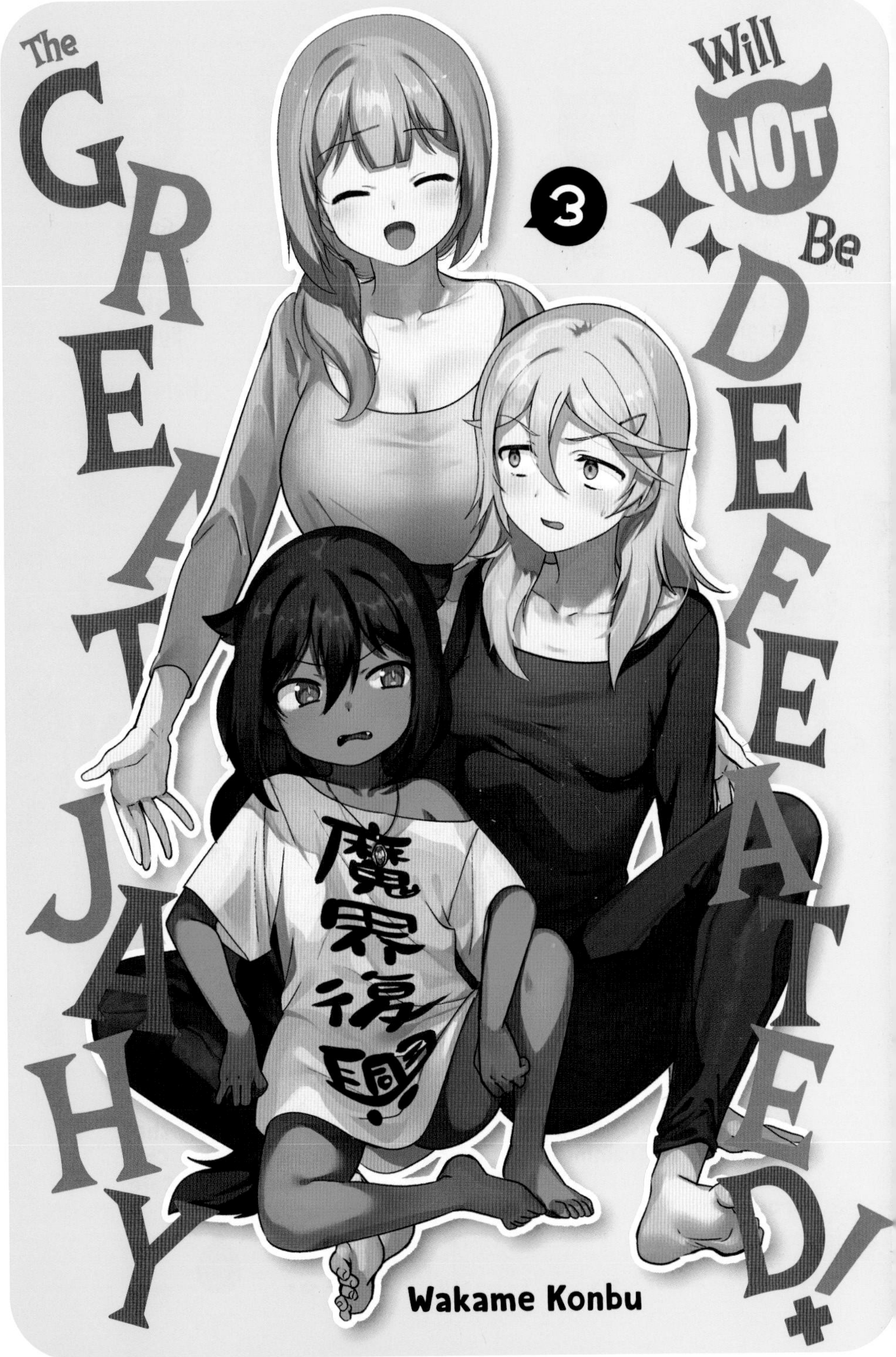

The GREAT JAHY Will NOT Be DEFEATED!
3
魔界復興!
Wakame Konbu

The GREAT JAHY will NOT Be DEFEATED!

CONTENTS

RESTORATION PLAN

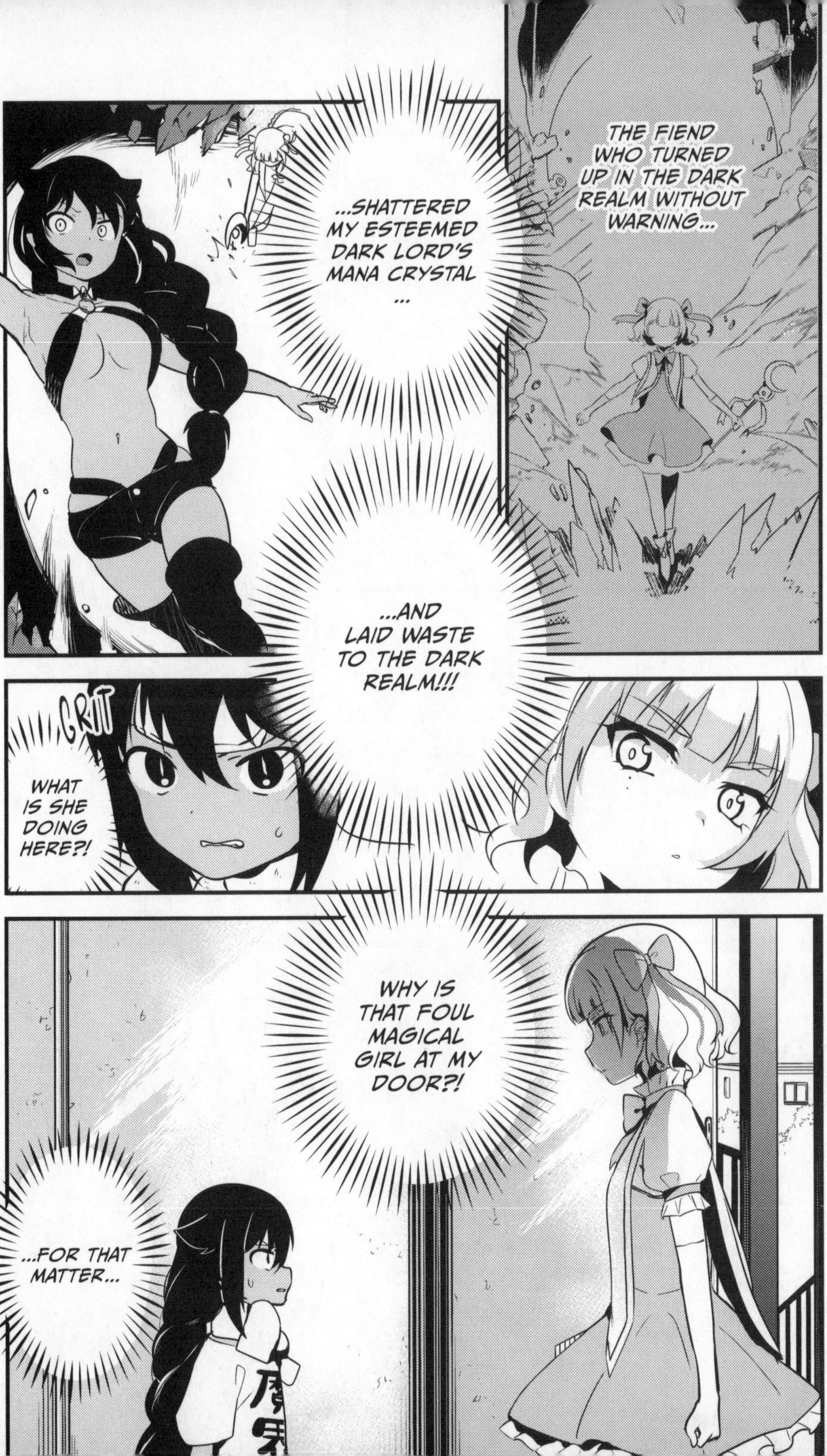
THE FIEND WHO TURNED UP IN THE DARK REALM WITHOUT WARNING...
...SHATTERED MY ESTEEMED DARK LORD'S MANA CRYSTAL ...
...AND LAID WASTE TO THE DARK REALM!!!
GRIT
WHAT IS SHE DOING HERE?!
WHY IS THAT FOUL MAGICAL GIRL AT MY DOOR?!
...FOR THAT MATTER...

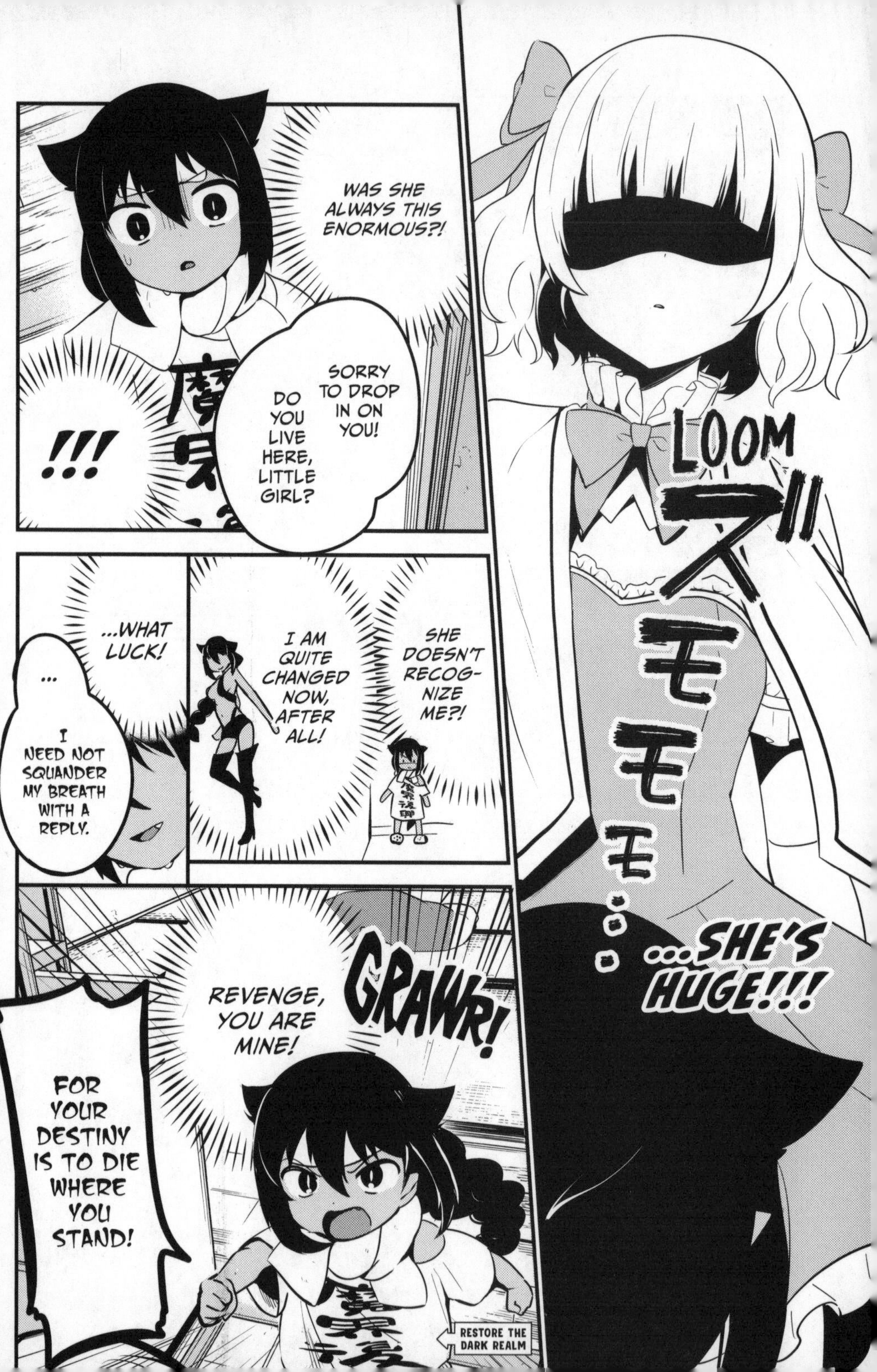
LOOM
ズモモモ…
...SHE'S HUGE!!!
WAS SHE ALWAYS THIS ENORMOUS?!
!!!
SORRY TO DROP IN ON YOU!
DO YOU LIVE HERE, LITTLE GIRL?
SHE DOESN'T RECOG-NIZE ME?!
I AM QUITE CHANGED NOW, AFTER ALL!
...WHAT LUCK!
...
I NEED NOT SQUANDER MY BREATH WITH A REPLY.
GRAWR!
REVENGE, YOU ARE MINE!
FOR YOUR DESTINY IS TO DIE WHERE YOU STAND!
RESTORE THE DARK REALM

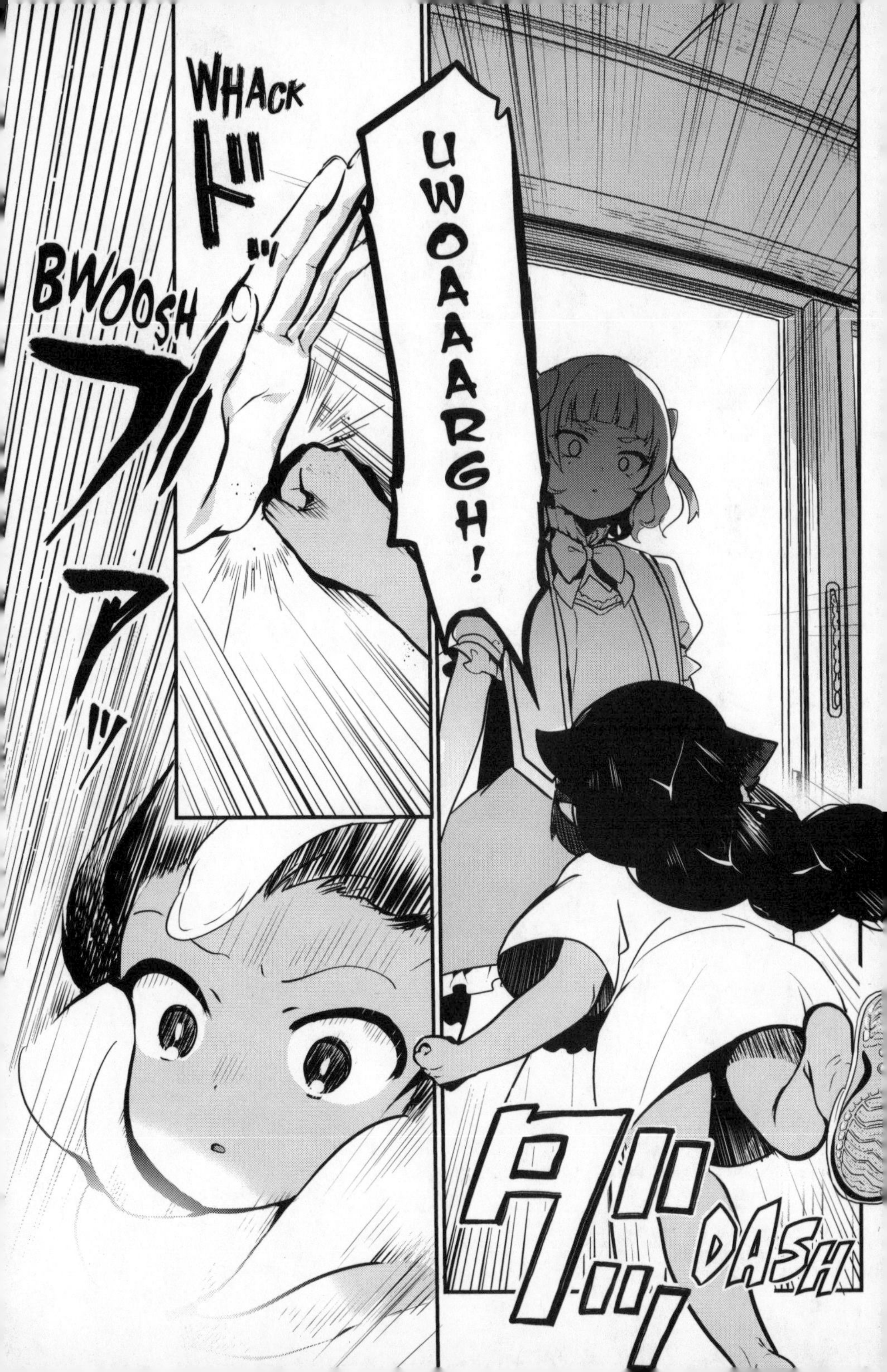
UWOAAARGH!
WHACK
BWOOSH
DASH

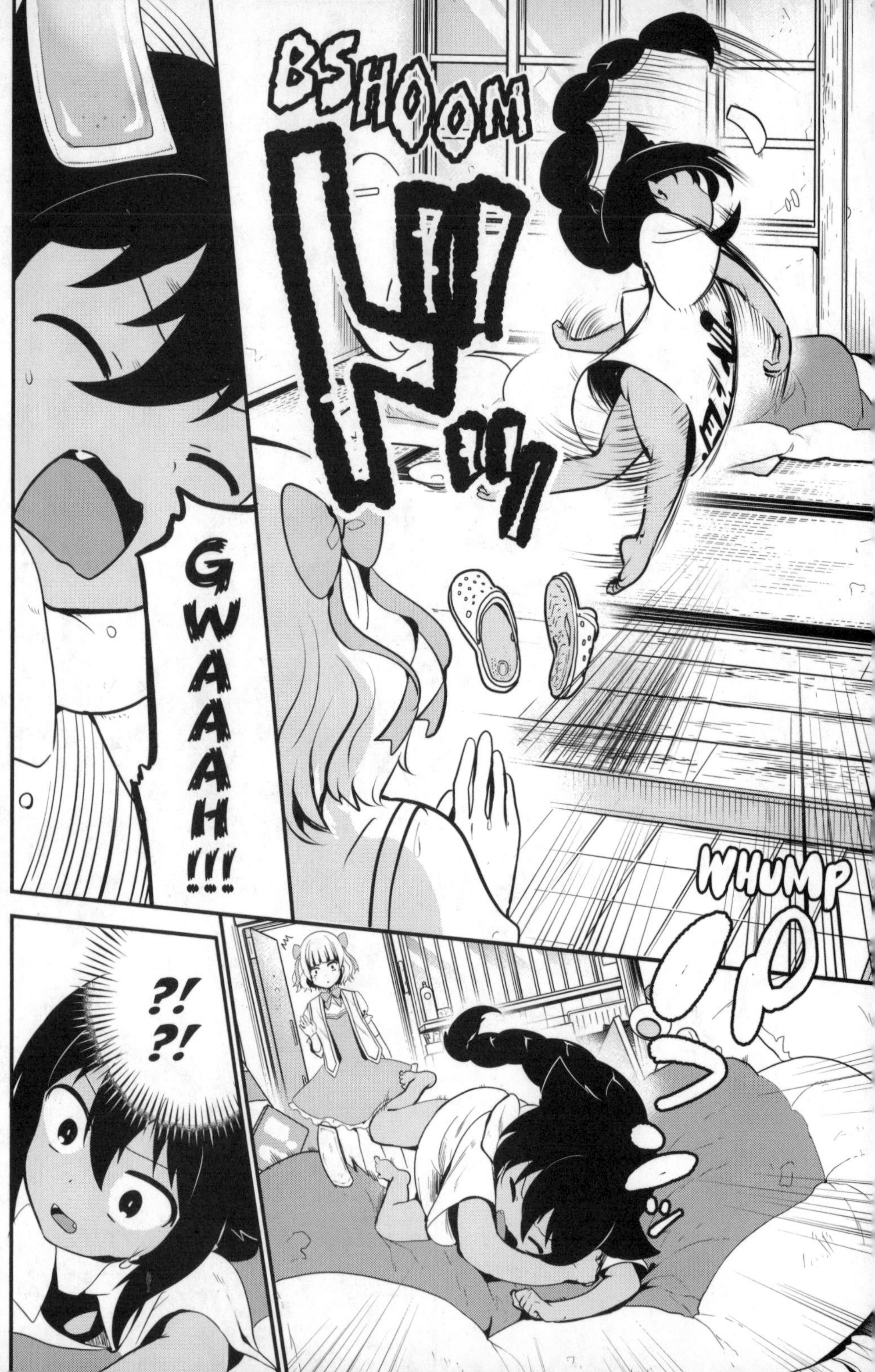
BSHOOM
WHUMP
GWAAAH!!!
?!
?!

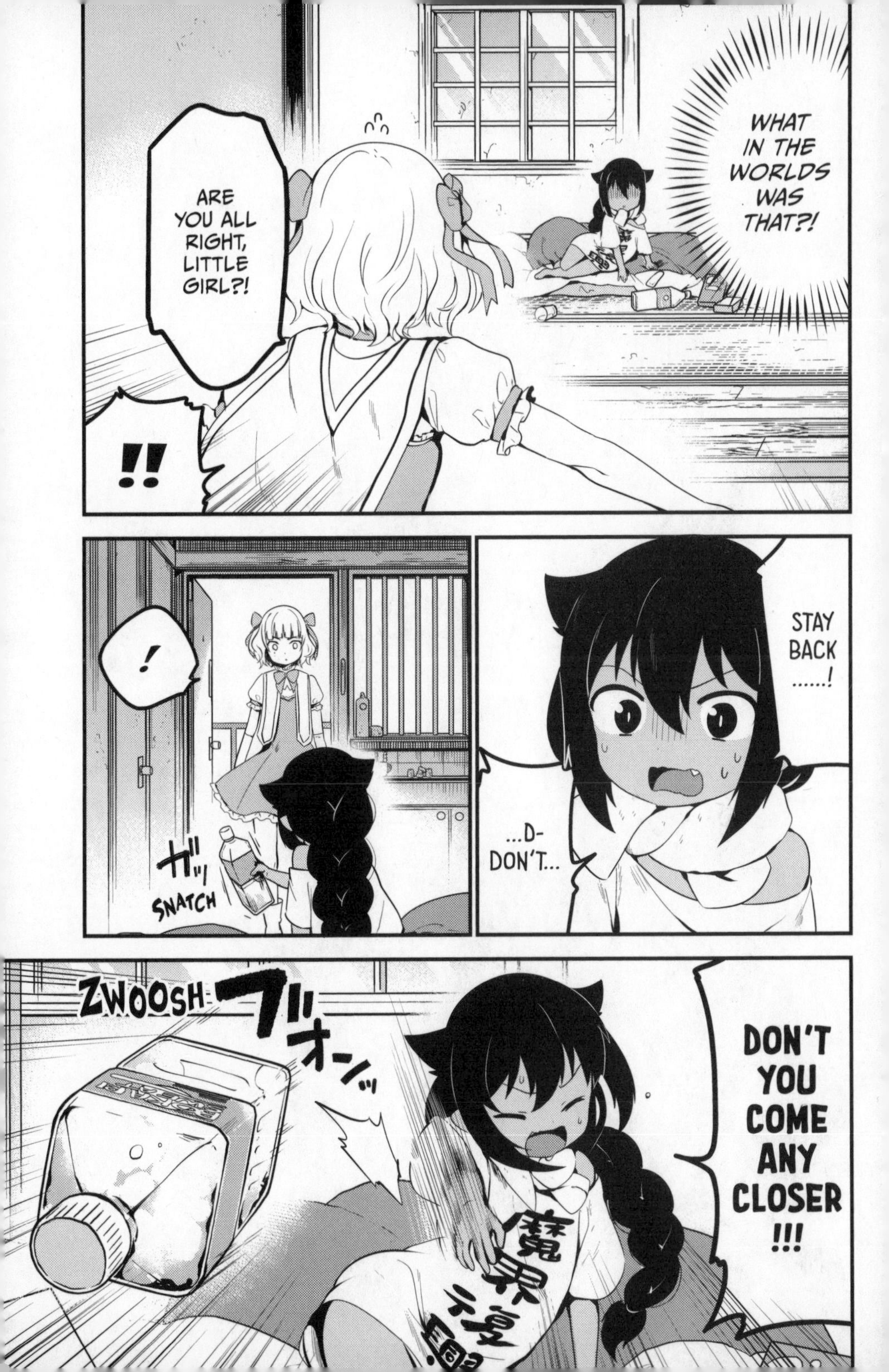
WHAT IN THE WORLDS WAS THAT?!
ARE YOU ALL RIGHT, LITTLE GIRL?!
!!
STAY BACK ......!
...D- DON'T...
!
ガッ
SNATCH
DON'T YOU COME ANY CLOSER !!!
ZWOOSH
ブオンッ

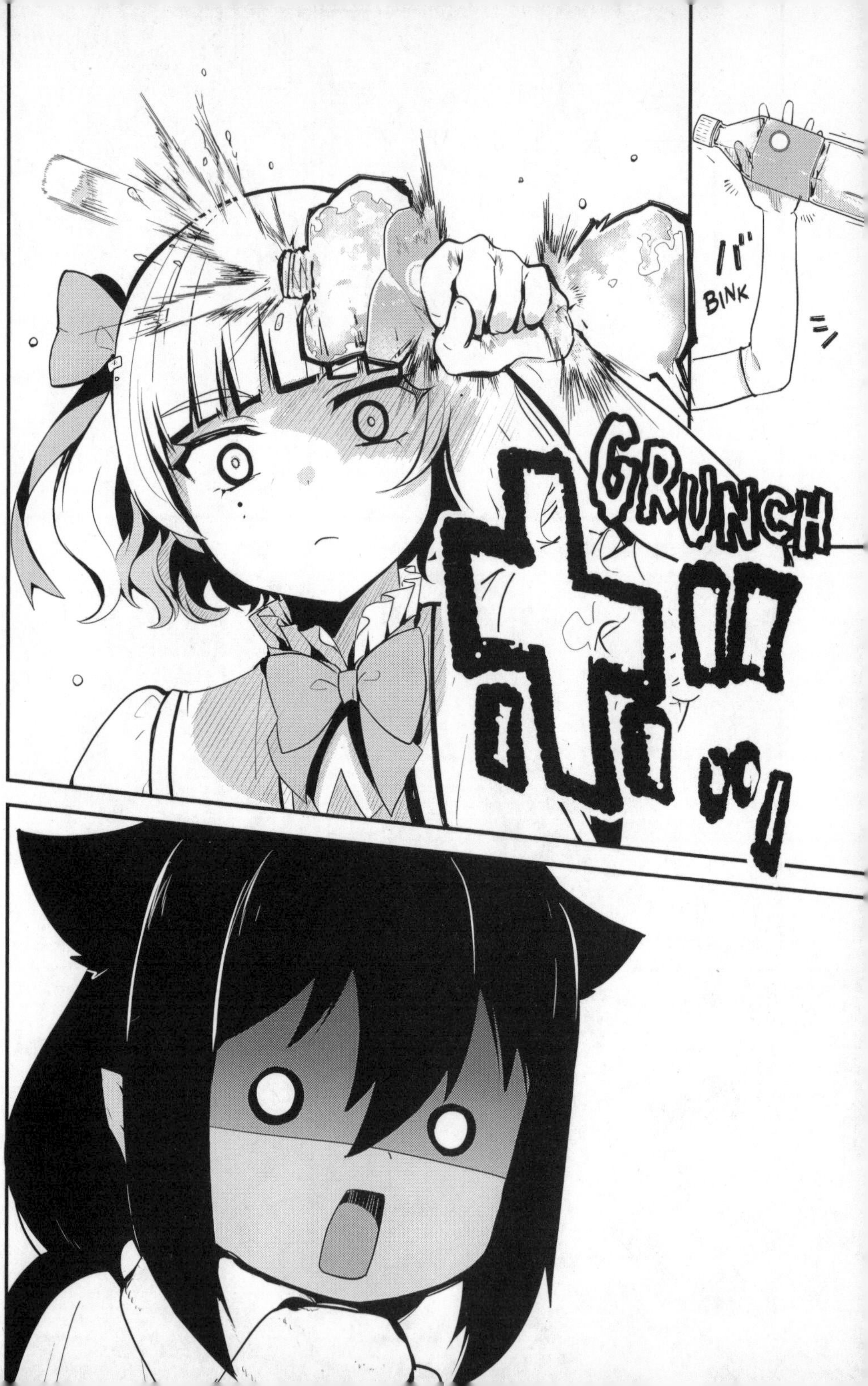BINK
GRUNCH

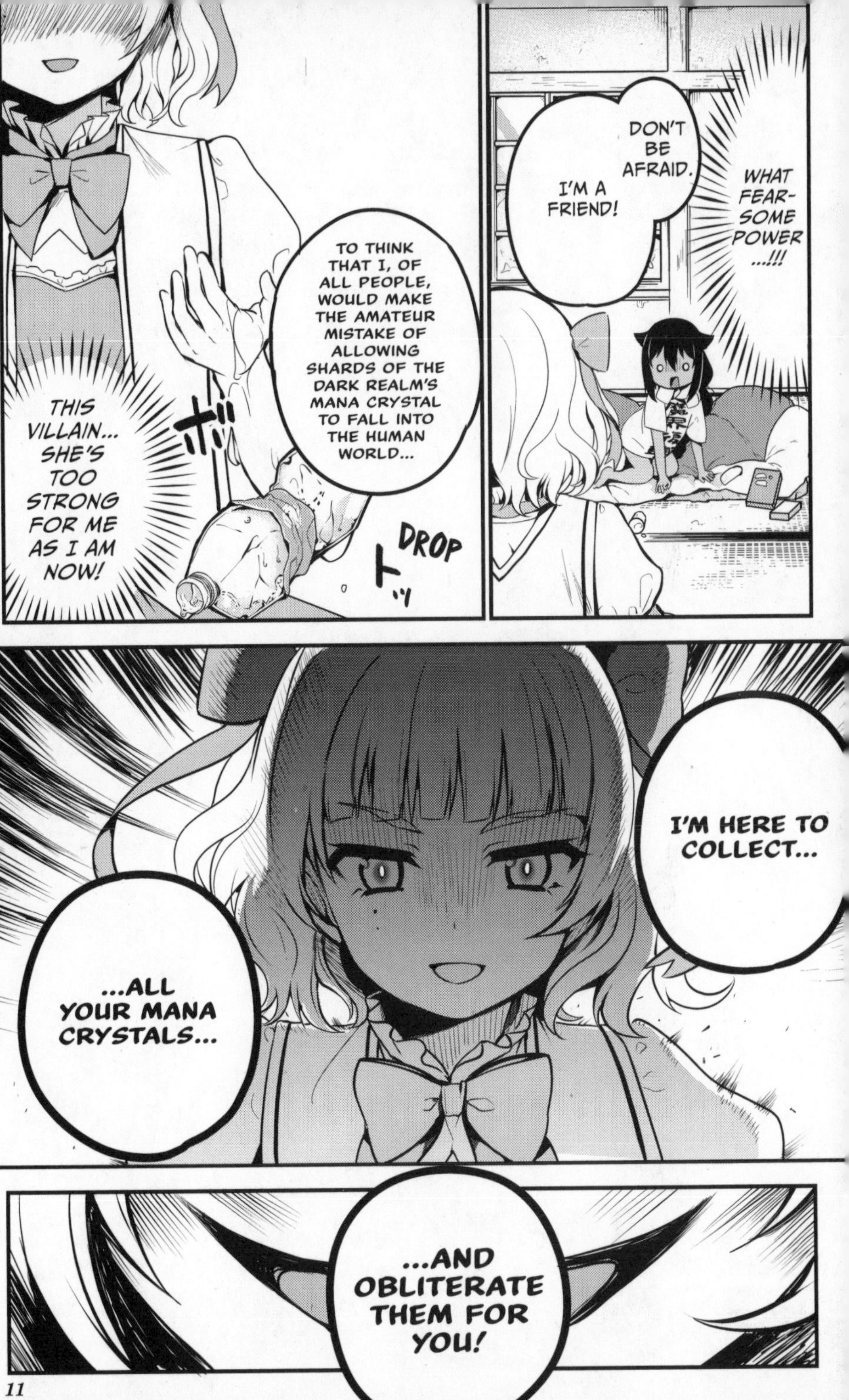
DON'T BE AFRAID.
I'M A FRIEND!
WHAT FEAR-SOME POWER ...!!!
TO THINK THAT I, OF ALL PEOPLE, WOULD MAKE THE AMATEUR MISTAKE OF ALLOWING SHARDS OF THE DARK REALM'S MANA CRYSTAL TO FALL INTO THE HUMAN WORLD...
THIS VILLAIN... SHE'S TOO STRONG FOR ME AS I AM NOW!
DROP
トッ
I'M HERE TO COLLECT...
...ALL YOUR MANA CRYSTALS...
...AND OBLITERATE THEM FOR YOU!

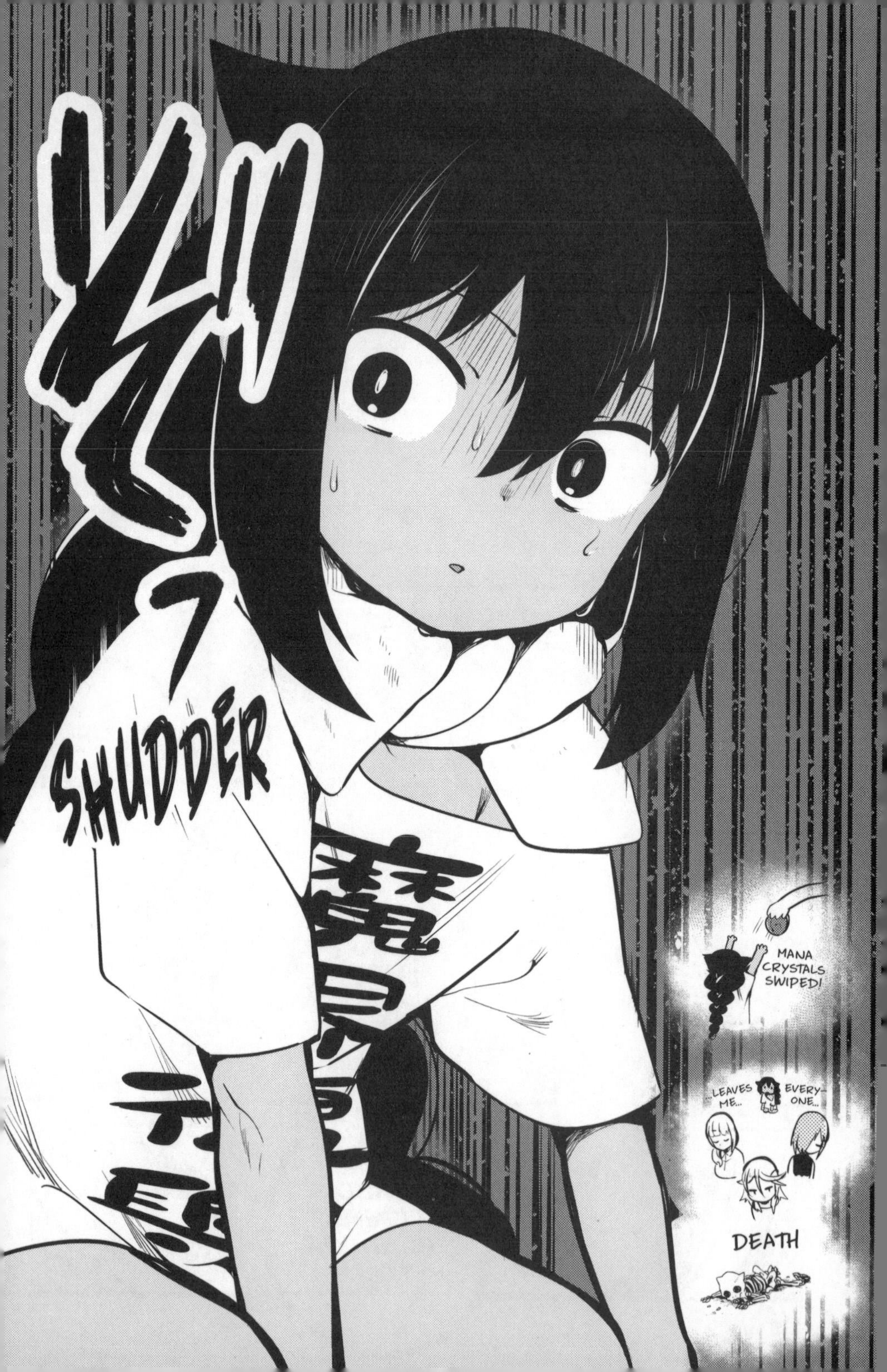
SHUDDER
MANA CRYSTALS SWIPED!
EVERY-ONE...
...LEAVES ME...
DEATH

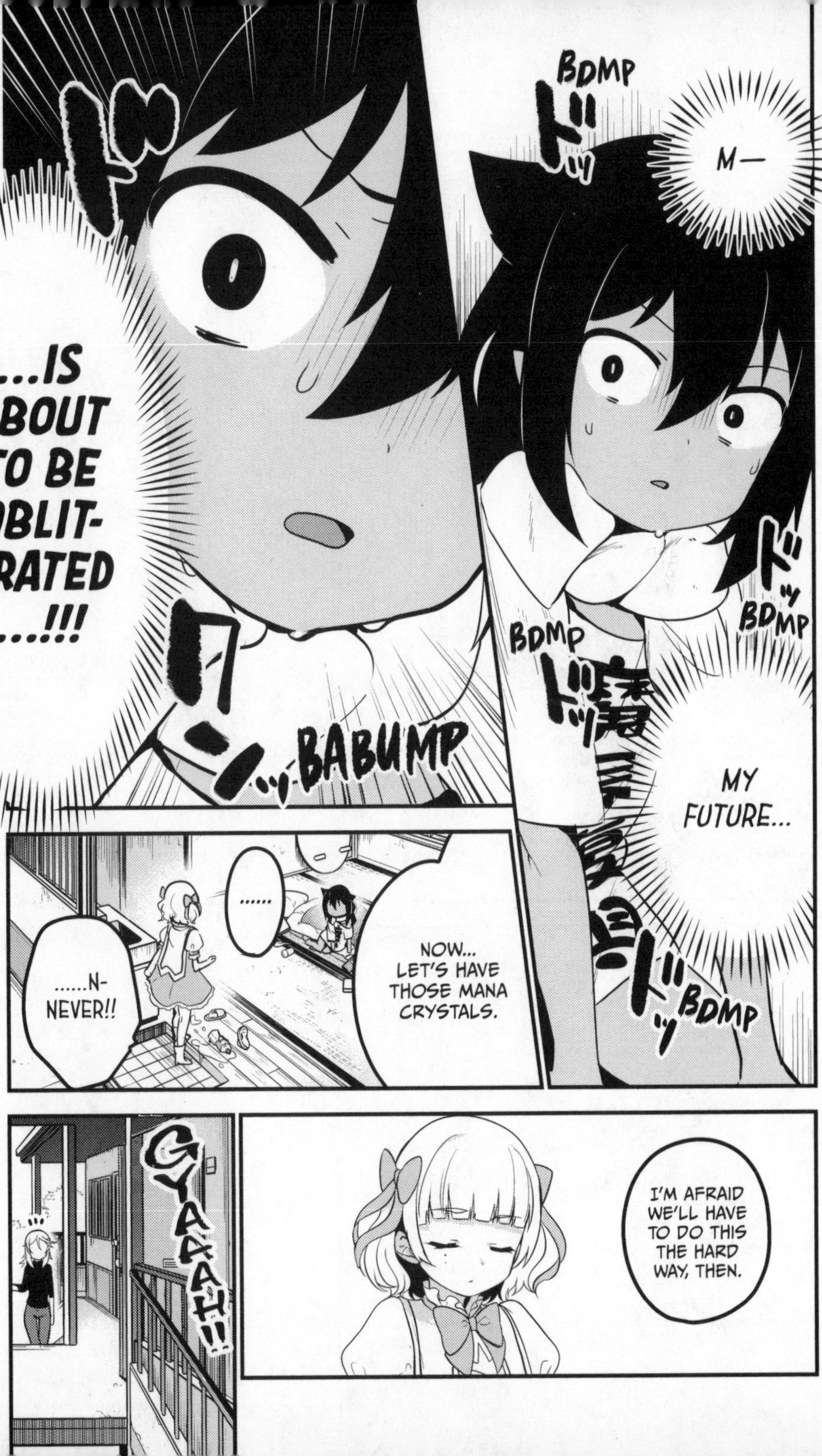
BDMP
M—
BDMP
BDMP
MY FUTURE...
BDMP
...IS ABOUT TO BE OBLIT-ERATED ....!!!
BABUMP
NOW... LET'S HAVE THOSE MANA CRYSTALS.
......
......N- NEVER!!
I'M AFRAID WE'LL HAVE TO DO THIS THE HARD WAY, THEN.
GYAAAAH!!

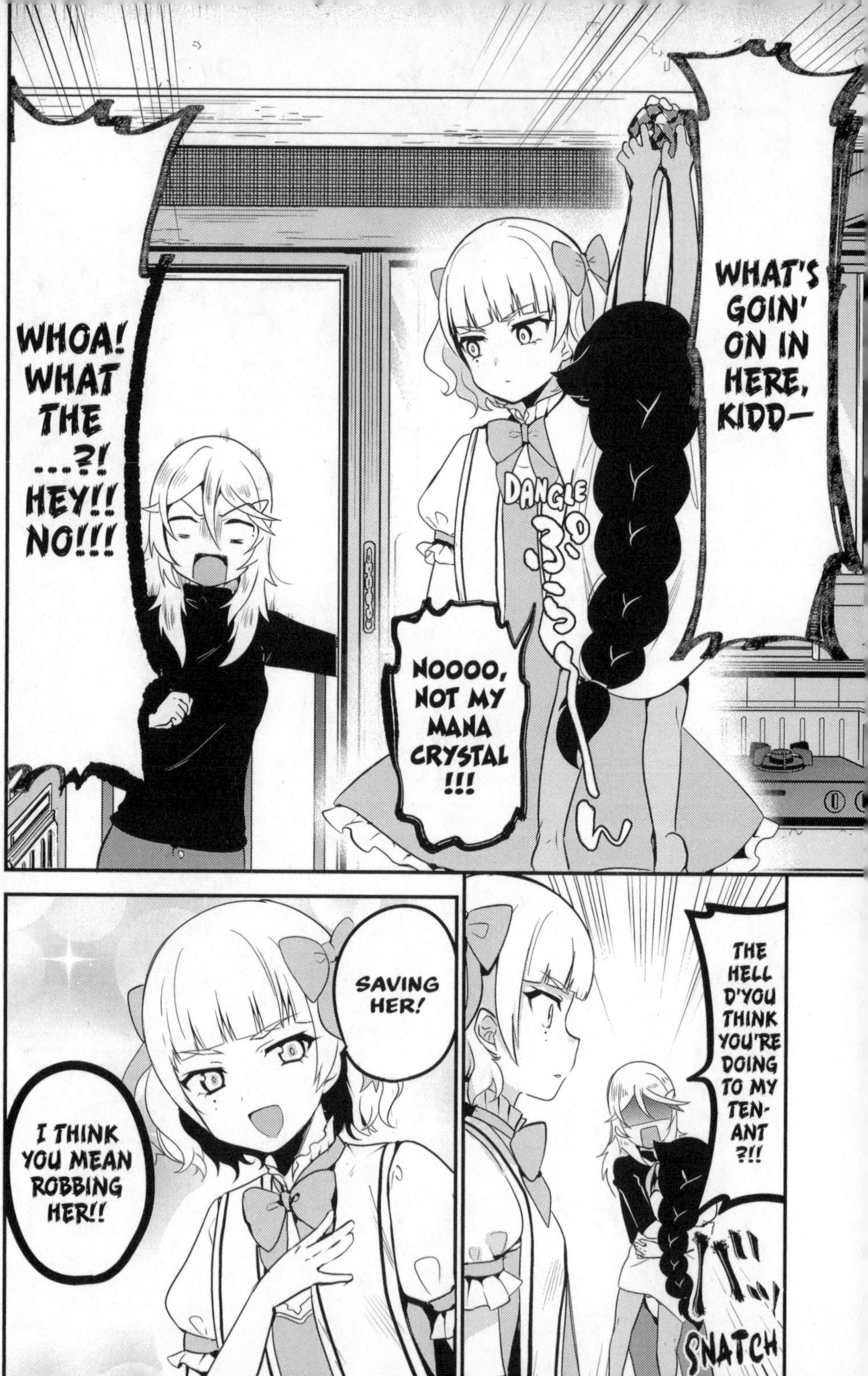
WHAT'S GOIN' ON IN HERE, KIDD—
WHOA! WHAT THE ...?! HEY!! NO!!!
DANGLE
NOOOO, NOT MY MANA CRYSTAL!!!
THE HELL D'YOU THINK YOU'RE DOING TO MY TEN-ANT?!!
SNATCH
SAVING HER!
I THINK YOU MEAN ROBBING HER!!

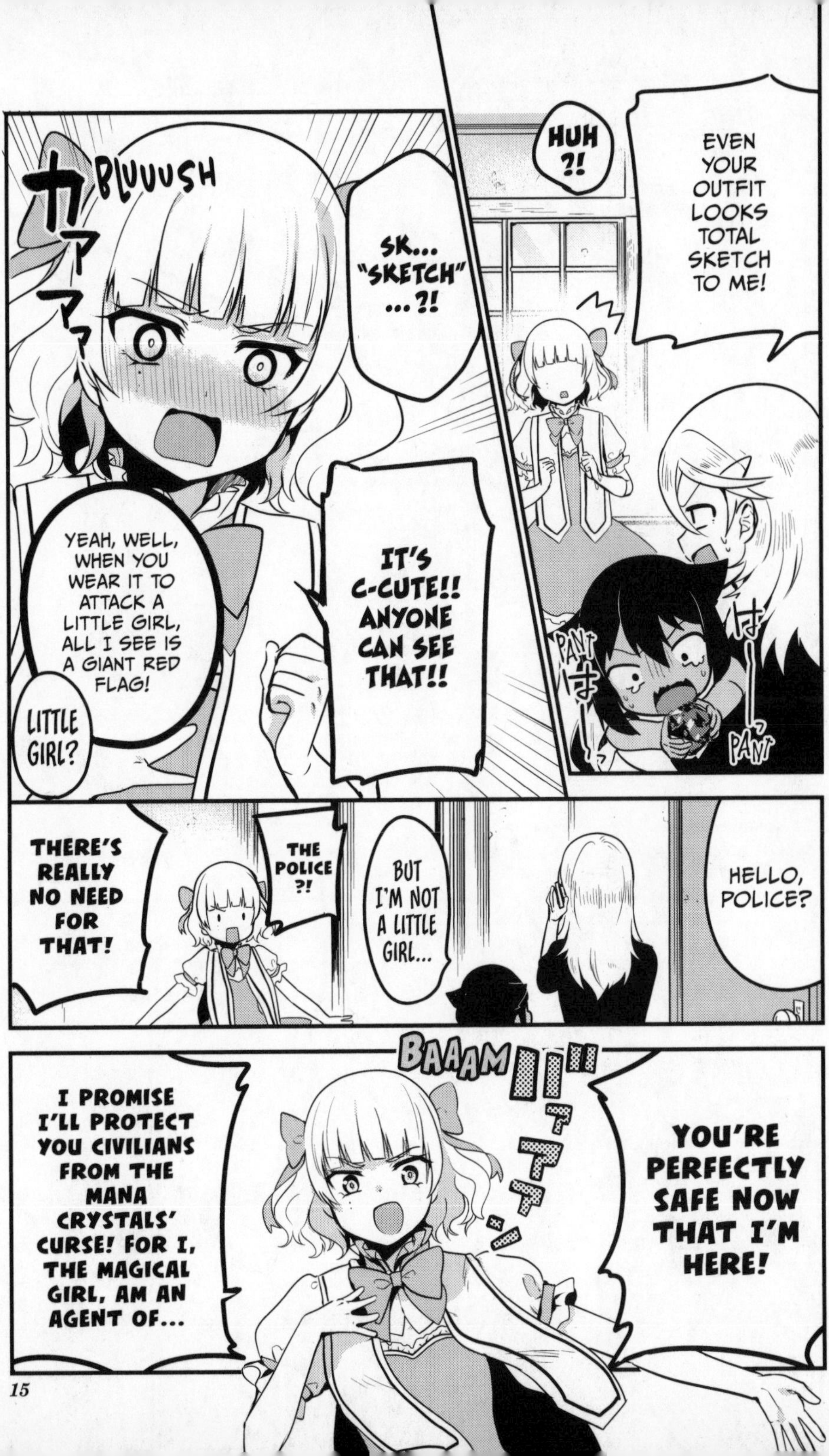
EVEN YOUR OUTFIT LOOKS TOTAL SKETCH TO ME!
HUH ?!
はーはー PANT PANT
カァァァ BLUUUSH
SK... "SKETCH" ...?!
IT'S C-CUTE!! ANYONE CAN SEE THAT!!
YEAH, WELL, WHEN YOU WEAR IT TO ATTACK A LITTLE GIRL, ALL I SEE IS A GIANT RED FLAG!
LITTLE GIRL?
HELLO, POLICE?
BUT I'M NOT A LITTLE GIRL...
THE POLICE ?!
THERE'S REALLY NO NEED FOR THAT!
バァァァン BAAAM
YOU'RE PERFECTLY SAFE NOW THAT I'M HERE!
I PROMISE I'LL PROTECT YOU CIVILIANS FROM THE MANA CRYSTALS' CURSE! FOR I, THE MAGICAL GIRL, AM AN AGENT OF...

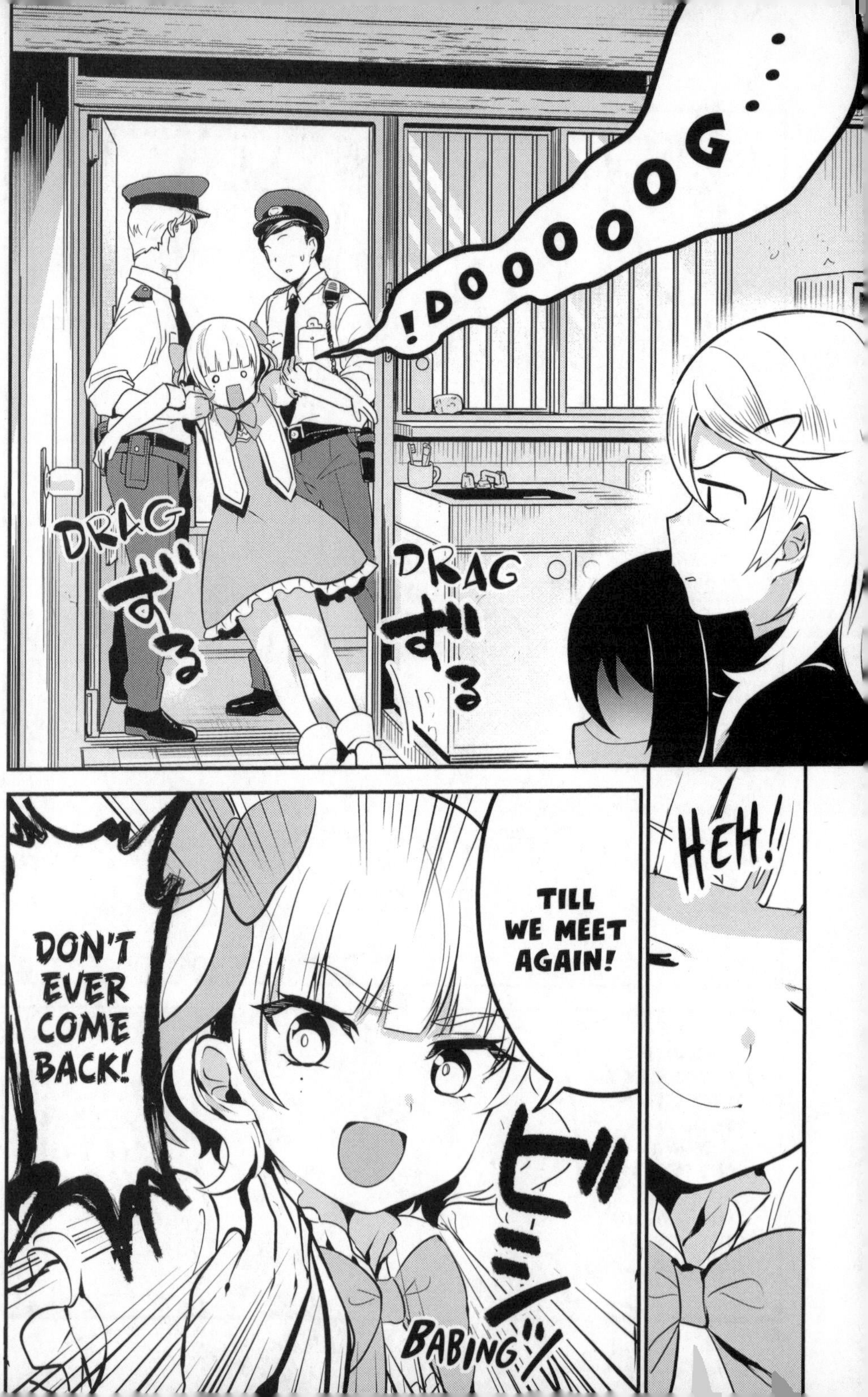
!DOOOOOG...
DRAG
ずる
DRAG
ずる
HEH!
TILL WE MEET AGAIN!
DON'T EVER COME BACK!
BABING!!

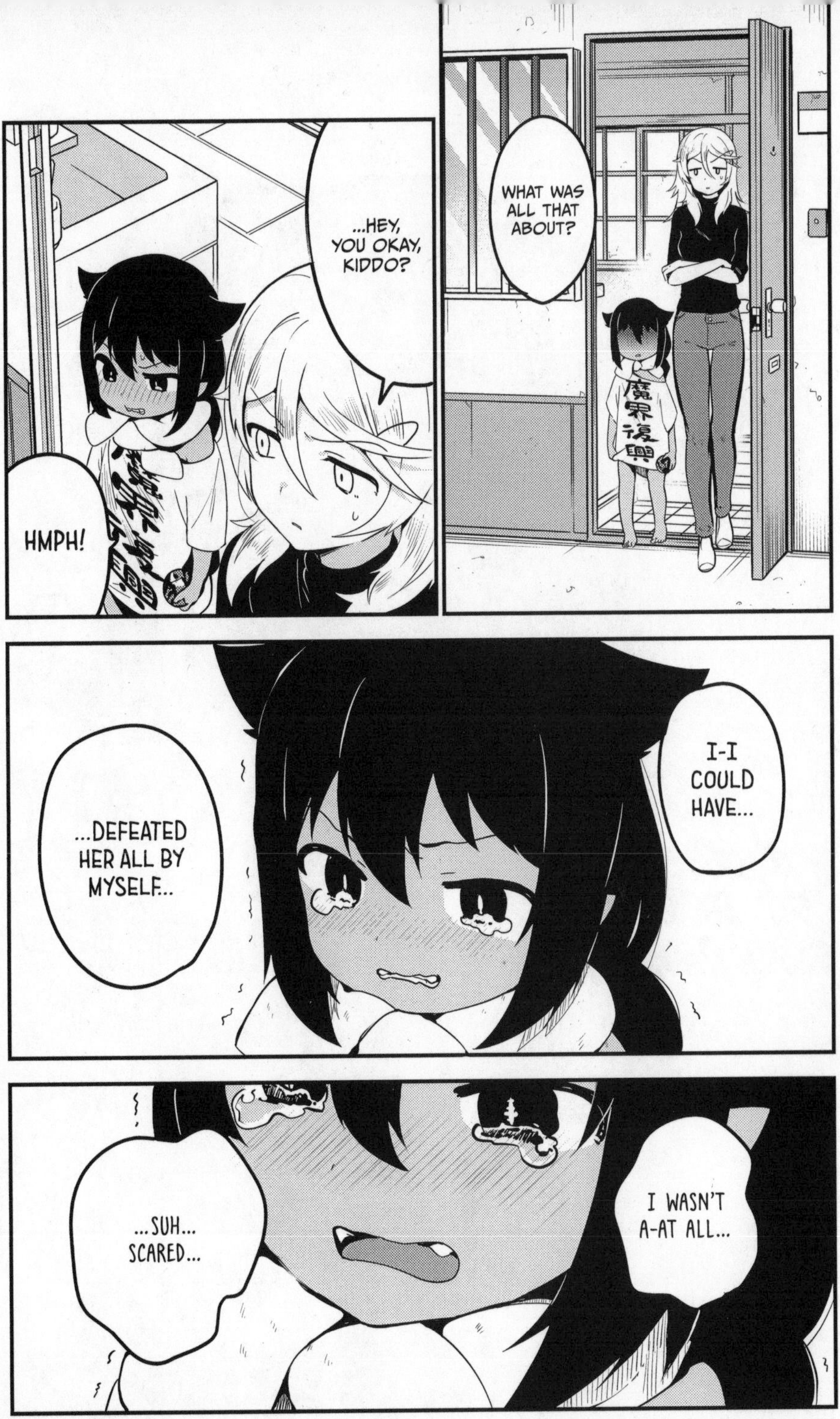
WHAT WAS ALL THAT ABOUT?
魔界復興
...HEY, YOU OKAY, KIDDO?
HMPH!
I-I COULD HAVE...
...DEFEATED HER ALL BY MYSELF...
I WASN'T A-AT ALL...
...SUH... SCARED...

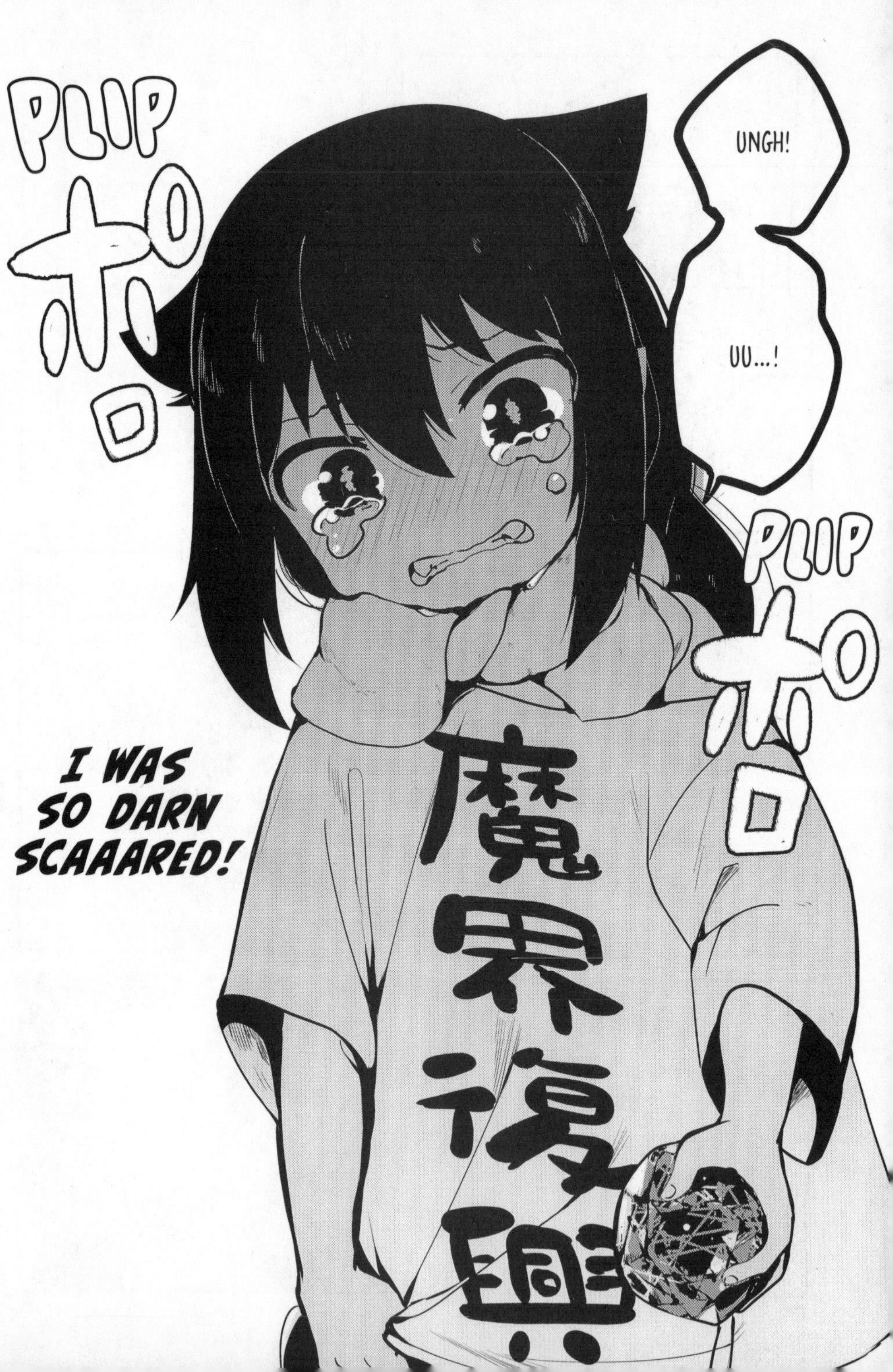
UNGH!
UU...!
PLIP
ポロ
PLIP
ポロ
I WAS SO DARN SCAARED!
魔界復興

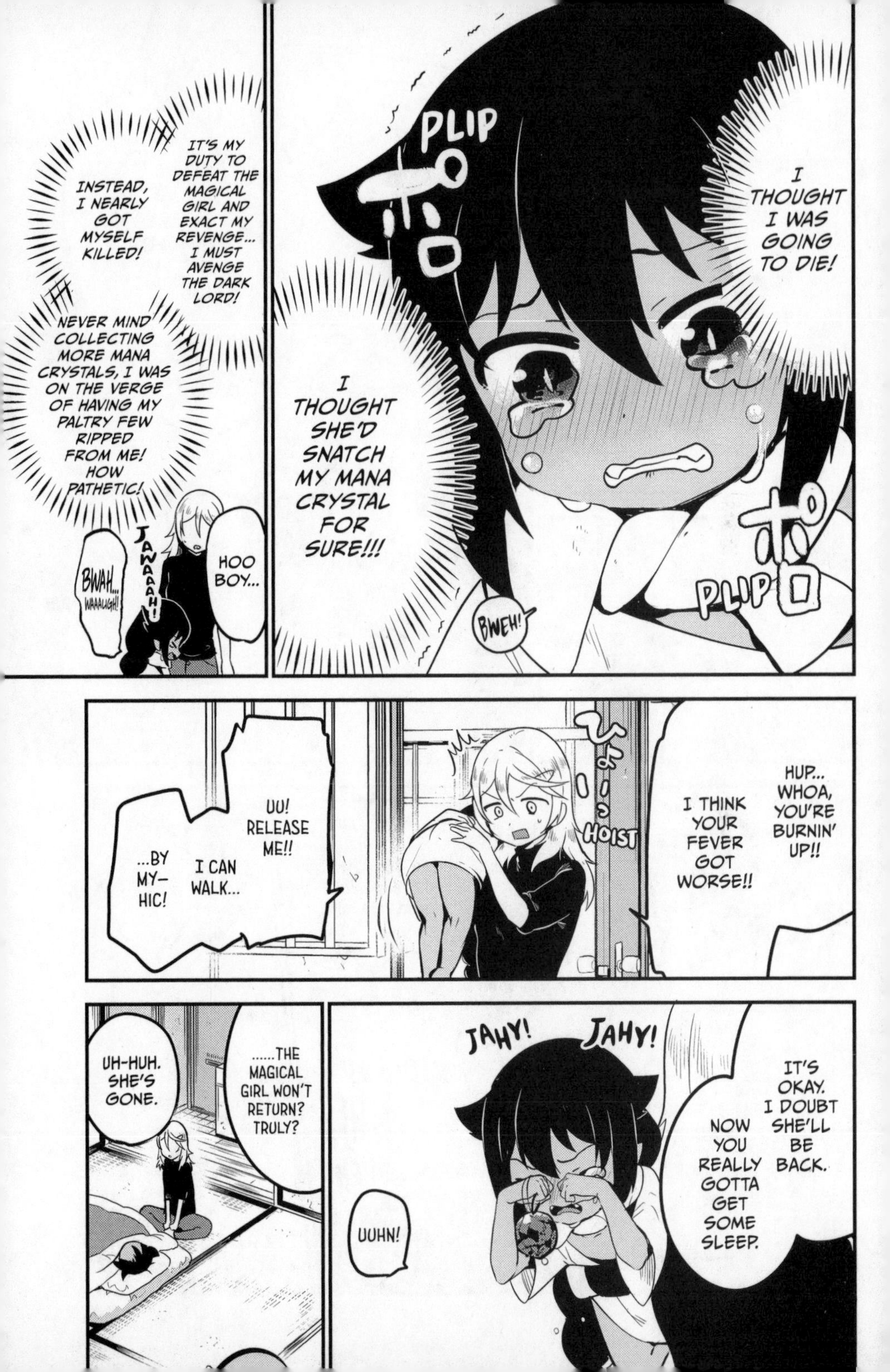

I THOUGHT I WAS GOING TO DIE!
PLIP
I THOUGHT SHE'D SNATCH MY MANA CRYSTAL FOR SURE!!!
PLIP
BWEH!
IT'S MY DUTY TO DEFEAT THE MAGICAL GIRL AND EXACT MY REVENGE... I MUST AVENGE THE DARK LORD!
INSTEAD, I NEARLY GOT MYSELF KILLED!
NEVER MIND COLLECTING MORE MANA CRYSTALS, I WAS ON THE VERGE OF HAVING MY PALTRY FEW RIPPED FROM ME! HOW PATHETIC!
HOO BOY...
JAWAAAAH!
BWAH... WAAAUGH!
HUP... WHOA, YOU'RE BURNIN' UP!!
I THINK YOUR FEVER GOT WORSE!!
HOIST
UU! RELEASE ME!!
I CAN WALK...
...BY MY— HIC!
JAHY! JAHY!
IT'S OKAY. I DOUBT SHE'LL BE BACK.
NOW YOU REALLY GOTTA GET SOME SLEEP.
UUHN!
......THE MAGICAL GIRL WON'T RETURN? TRULY?
UH-HUH. SHE'S GONE.

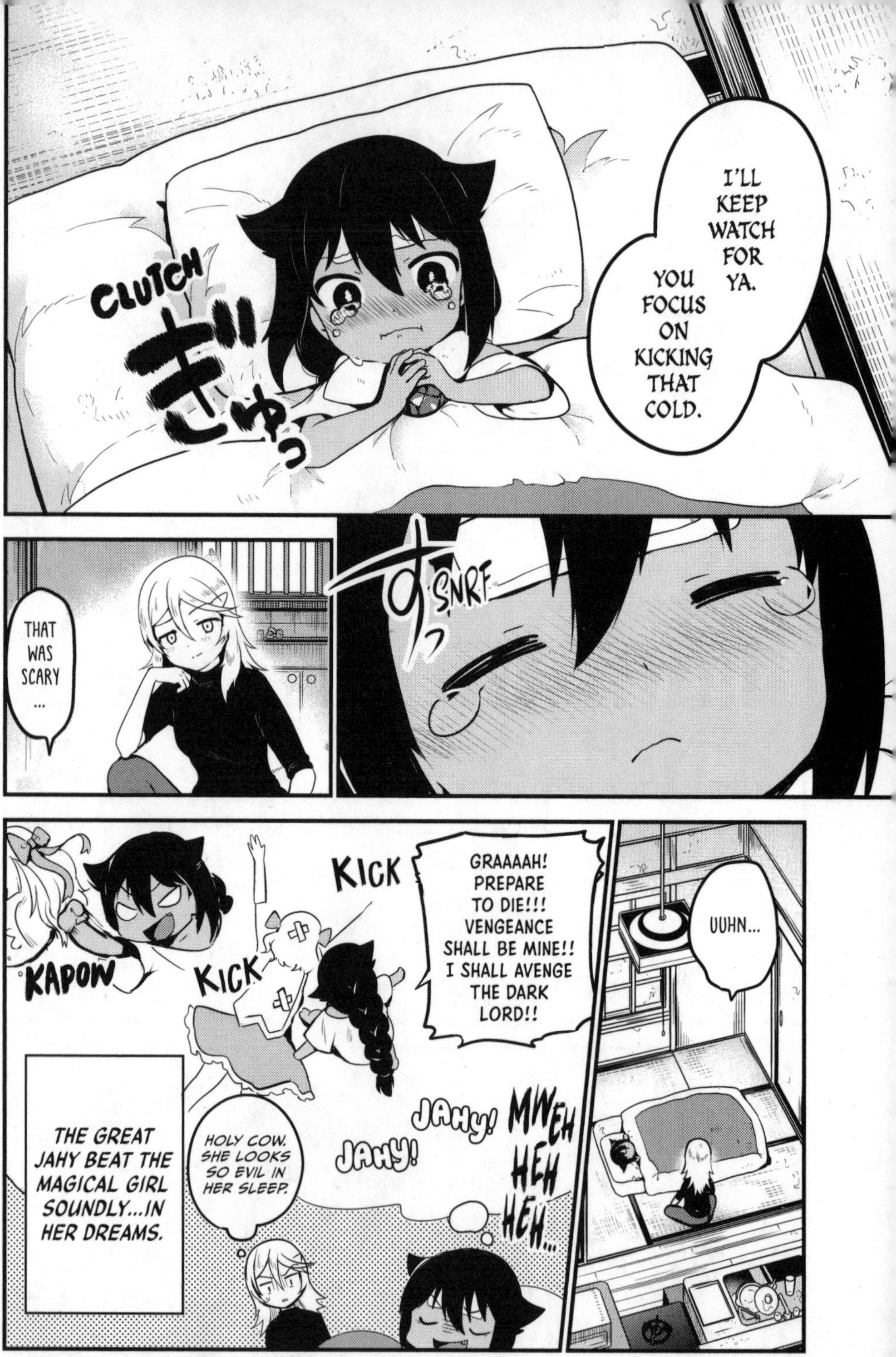

I'LL KEEP WATCH FOR YA. YOU FOCUS ON KICKING THAT COLD.
CLUTCH
ぎゅっ
すっ
SNRF
THAT WAS SCARY...
UUHN...
GRAAAAH! PREPARE TO DIE!!! VENGEANCE SHALL BE MINE!! I SHALL AVENGE THE DARK LORD!!
KICK
KICK
KAPOW
MWEH HEH HEH HEH...
JAHY!
JAHY!
HOLY COW. SHE LOOKS SO EVIL IN HER SLEEP.
THE GREAT JAHY BEAT THE MAGICAL GIRL SOUNDLY...IN HER DREAMS.

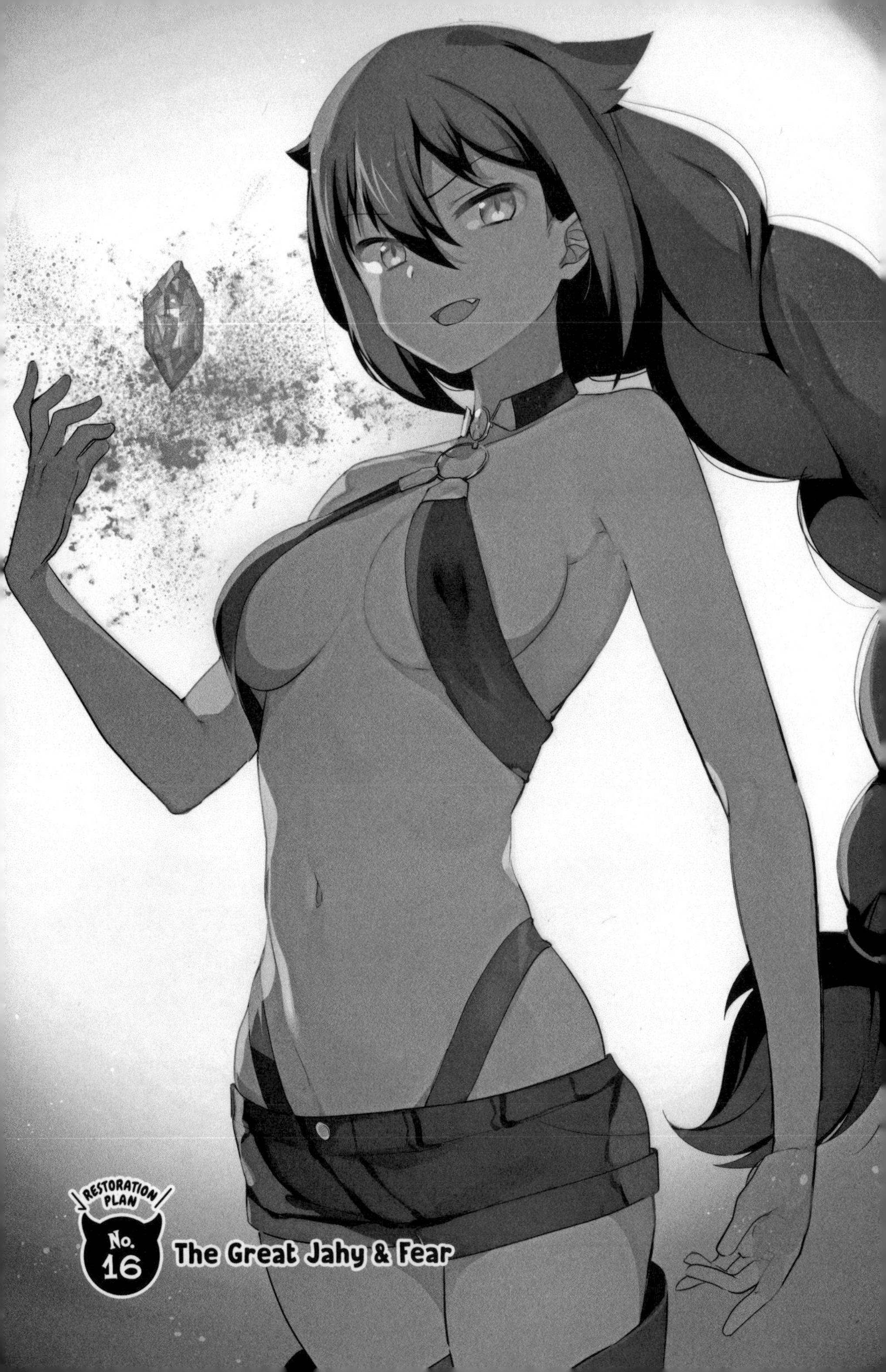

RESTORATION PLAN No. 16
The Great Jahy & Fear

The GREAT JAHY Will NOT Be DEFEATED!

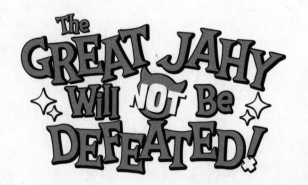

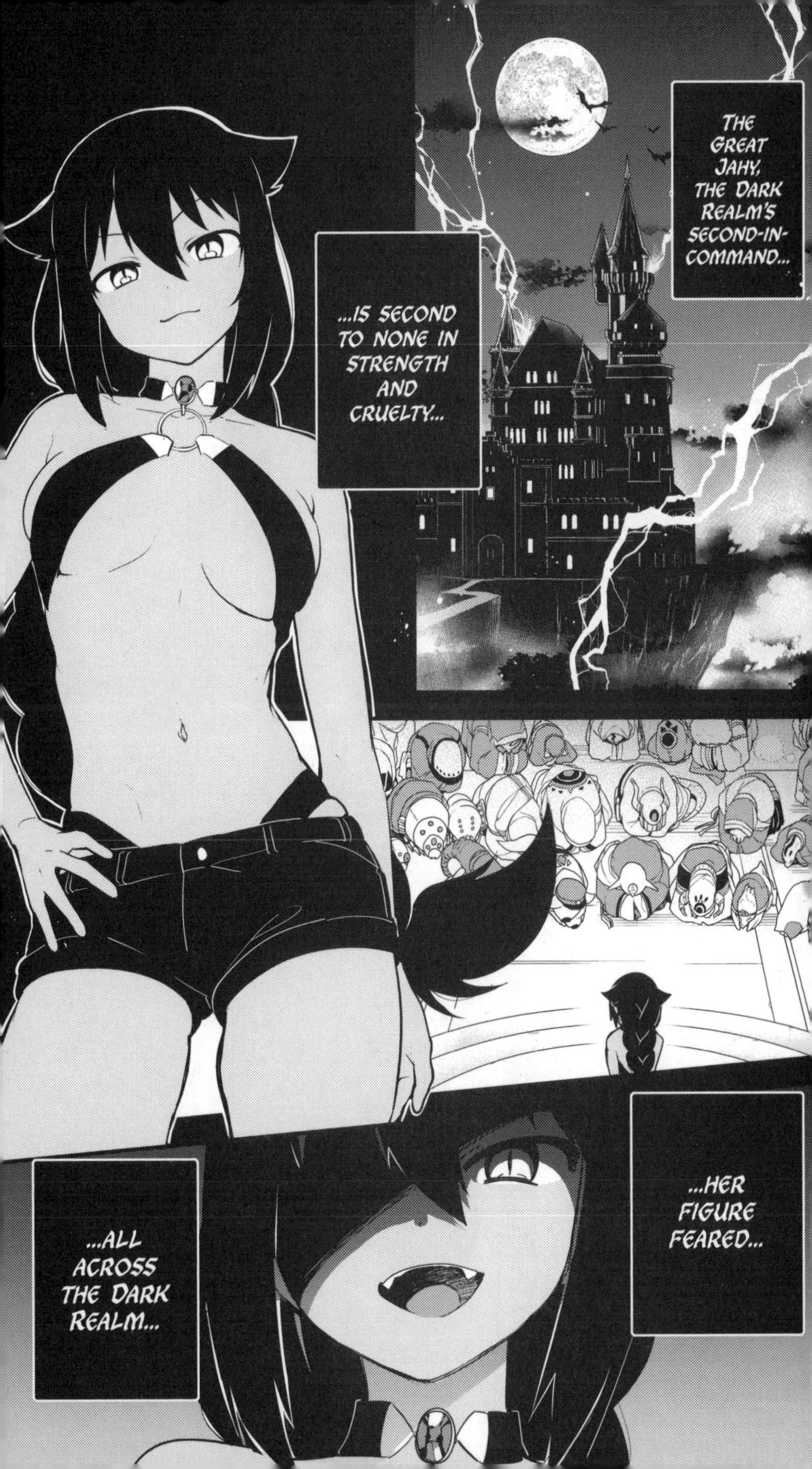
THE GREAT JAHY, THE DARK REALM'S SECOND-IN-COMMAND...
...IS SECOND TO NONE IN STRENGTH AND CRUELTY...
...HER FIGURE FEARED...
...ALL ACROSS THE DARK REALM...

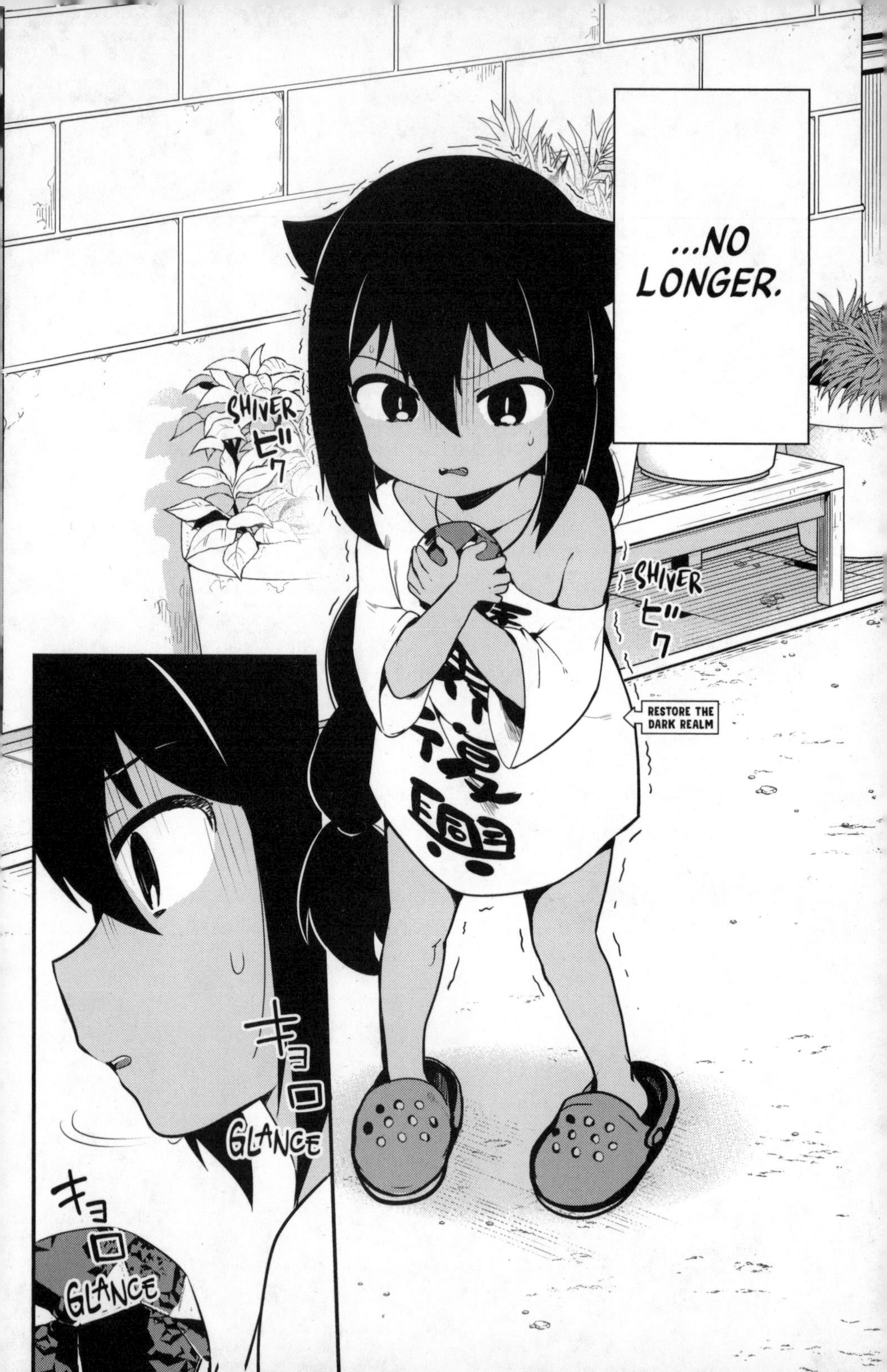
...NO LONGER.
SHIVER ビク
SHIVER ビク
RESTORE THE DARK REALM
キョロ GLANCE
キョロ GLANCE

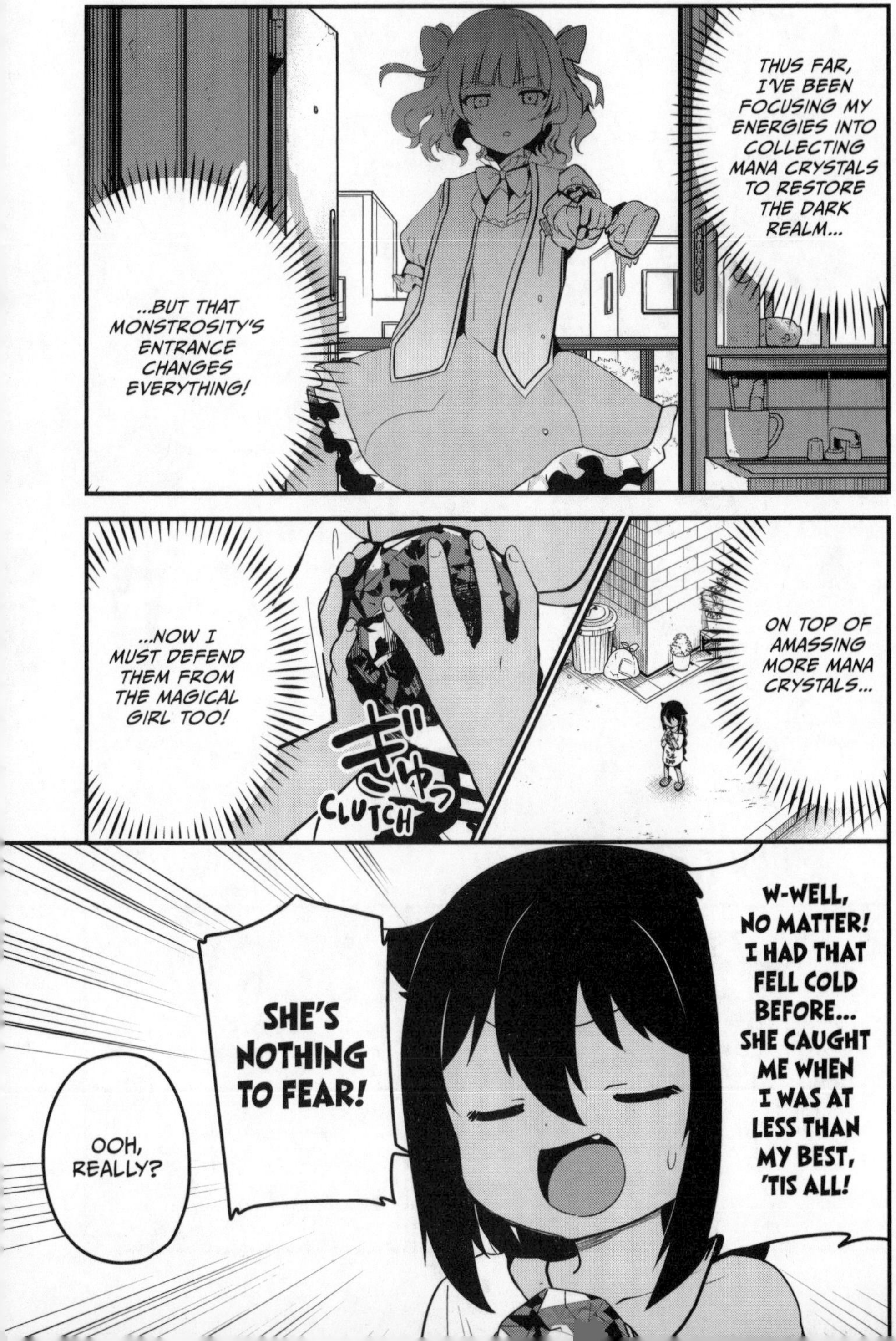
THUS FAR, I'VE BEEN FOCUSING MY ENERGIES INTO COLLECTING MANA CRYSTALS TO RESTORE THE DARK REALM...
...BUT THAT MONSTROSITY'S ENTRANCE CHANGES EVERYTHING!
ON TOP OF AMASSING MORE MANA CRYSTALS...
...NOW I MUST DEFEND THEM FROM THE MAGICAL GIRL TOO!
ぎゅっ
CLUTCH
W-WELL, NO MATTER! I HAD THAT FELL COLD BEFORE... SHE CAUGHT ME WHEN I WAS AT LESS THAN MY BEST, 'TIS ALL!
SHE'S NOTHING TO FEAR!
OOH, REALLY?

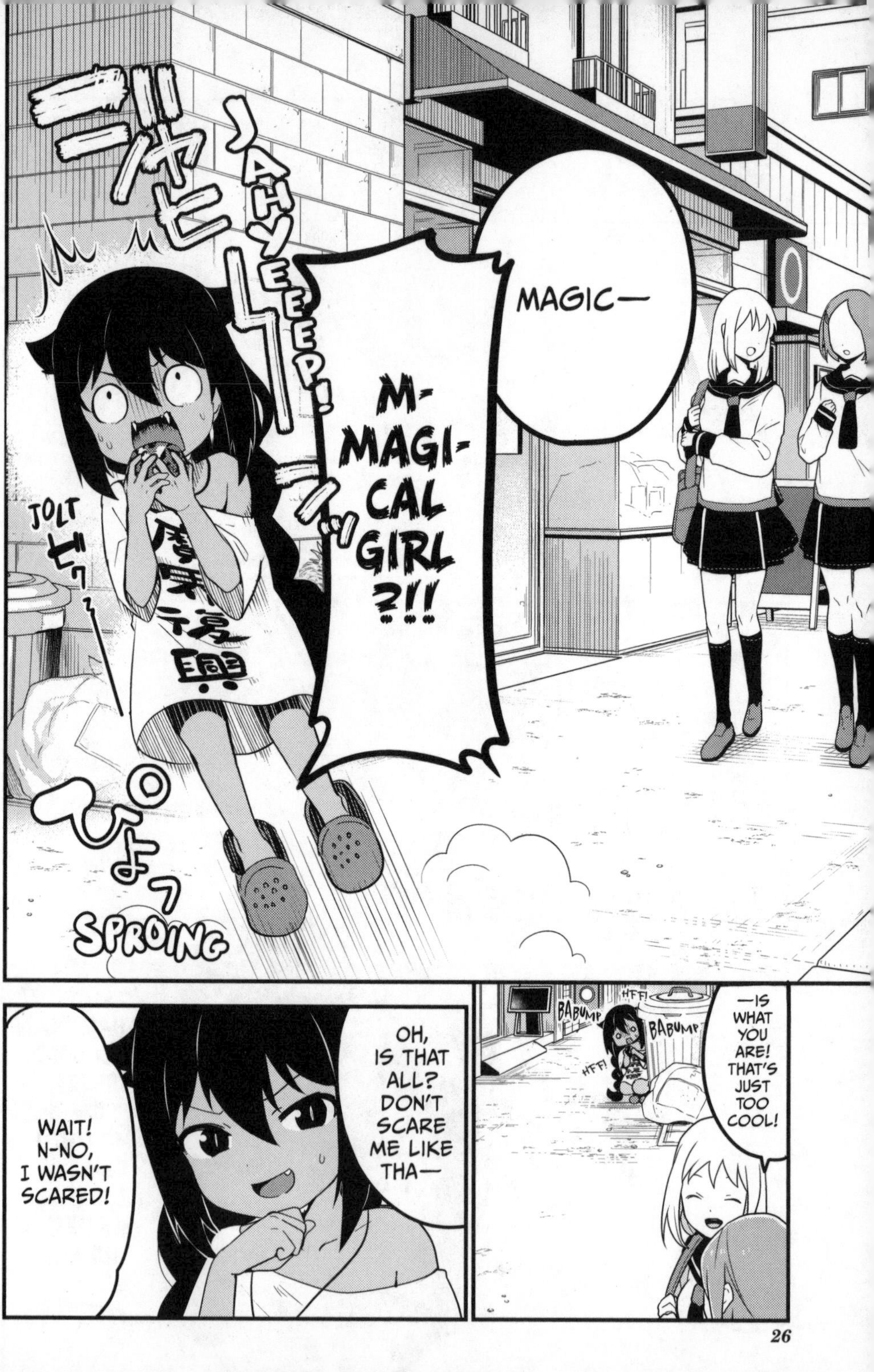

MAGIC—
M-MAGICAL GIRL?!!
AHYEEEEP!
JOLT
SPROING
—IS WHAT YOU ARE! THAT'S JUST TOO COOL!
HFF!
BABUMP
BABUMP
HFF!
OH, IS THAT ALL? DON'T SCARE ME LIKE THA—
WAIT! N-NO, I WASN'T SCARED!

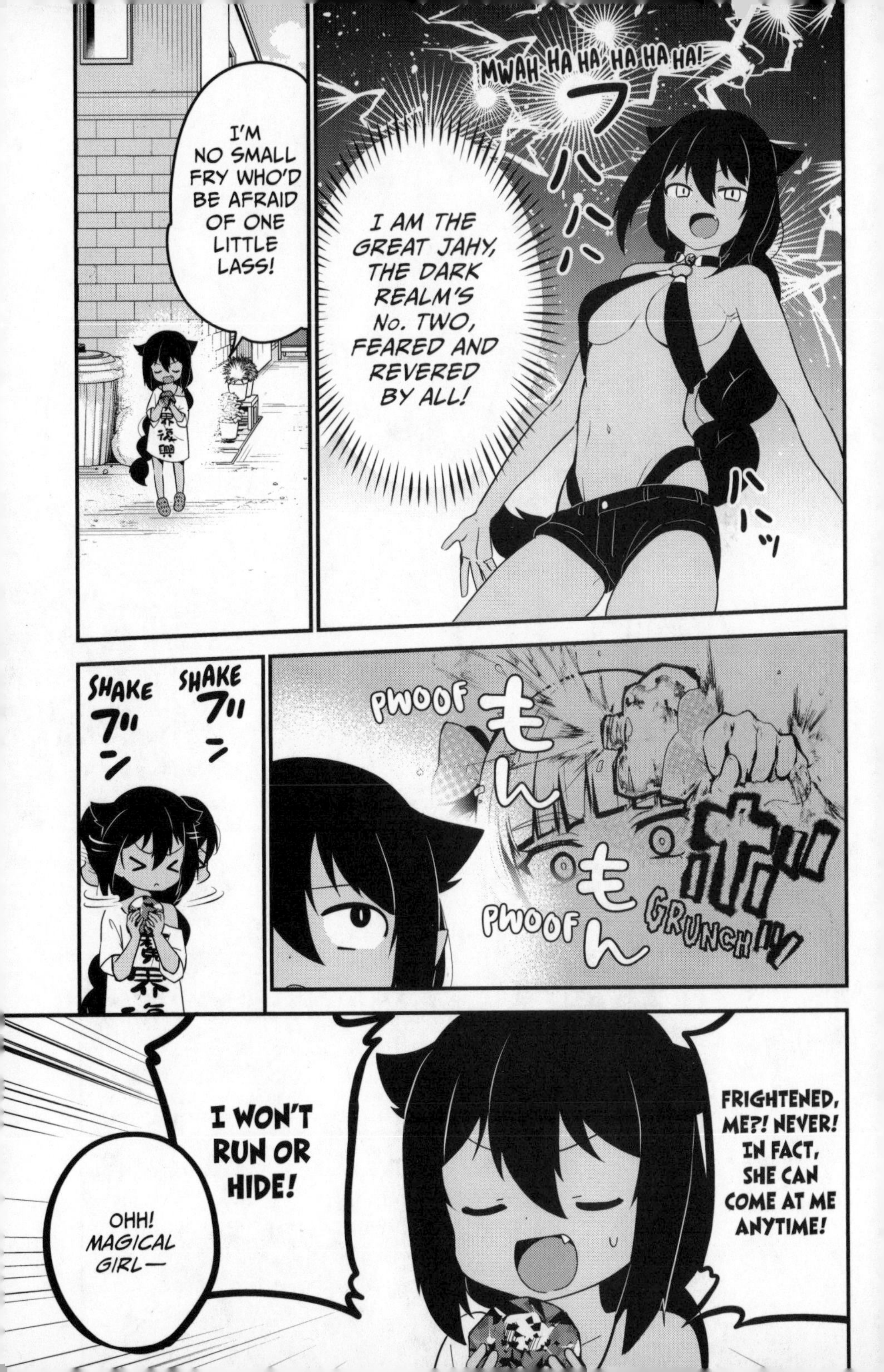
MWAH HA HA HA HA HA!
I AM THE GREAT JAHY, THE DARK REALM'S No. TWO, FEARED AND REVERED BY ALL!
I'M NO SMALL FRY WHO'D BE AFRAID OF ONE LITTLE LASS!
PWOOF
PWOOF
GRUNCH!!!
SHAKE
SHAKE
FRIGHTENED, ME?! NEVER! IN FACT, SHE CAN COME AT ME ANYTIME!
I WON'T RUN OR HIDE!
OHH! MAGICAL GIRL—

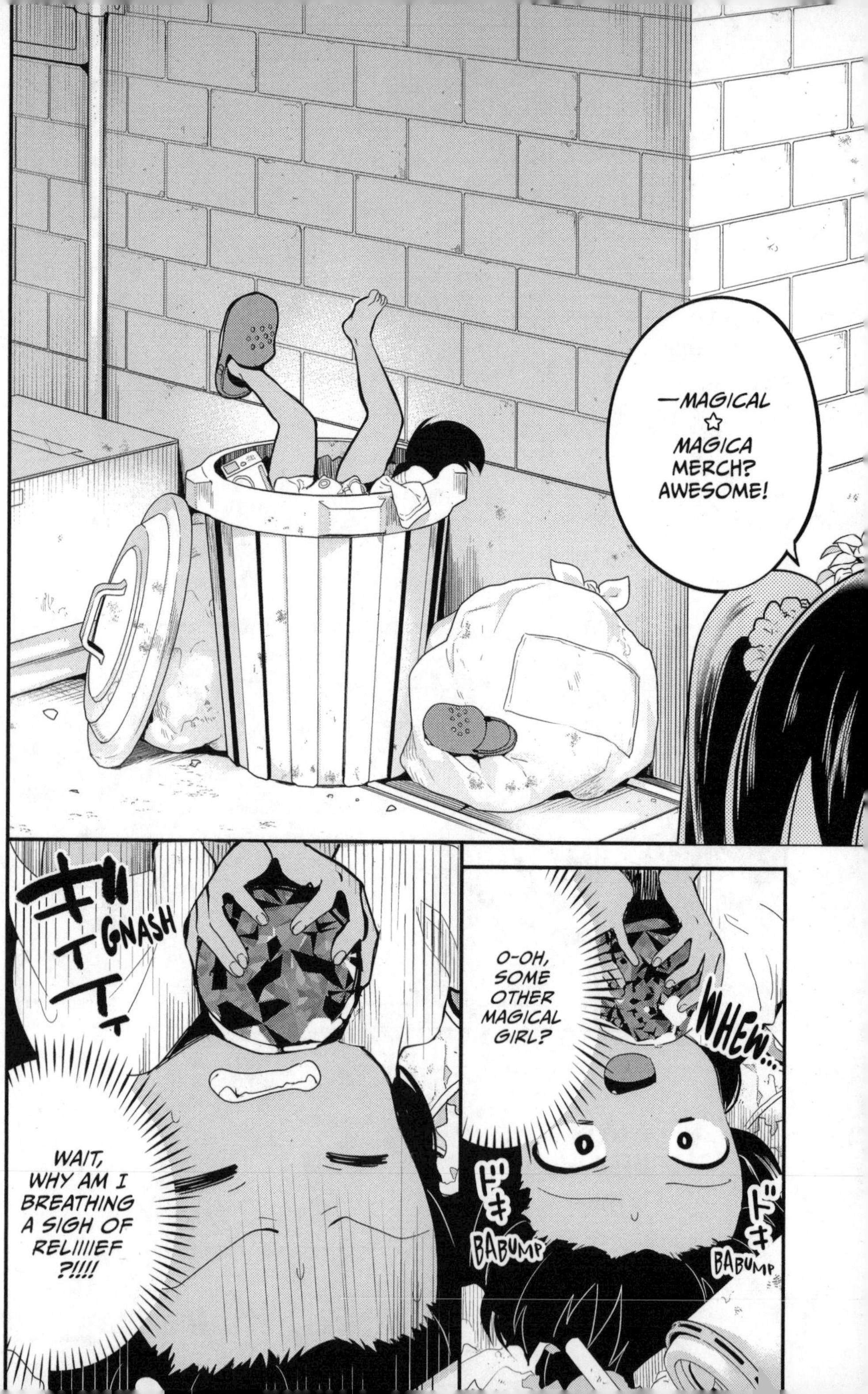
—MAGICAL ☆ MAGICA MERCH? AWESOME!
O-OH, SOME OTHER MAGICAL GIRL?
WHEW...
ドキ
BABUMP
ドキ
BABUMP
GNASH
WAIT, WHY AM I BREATHING A SIGH OF RELIIIIIEF ?!!!!

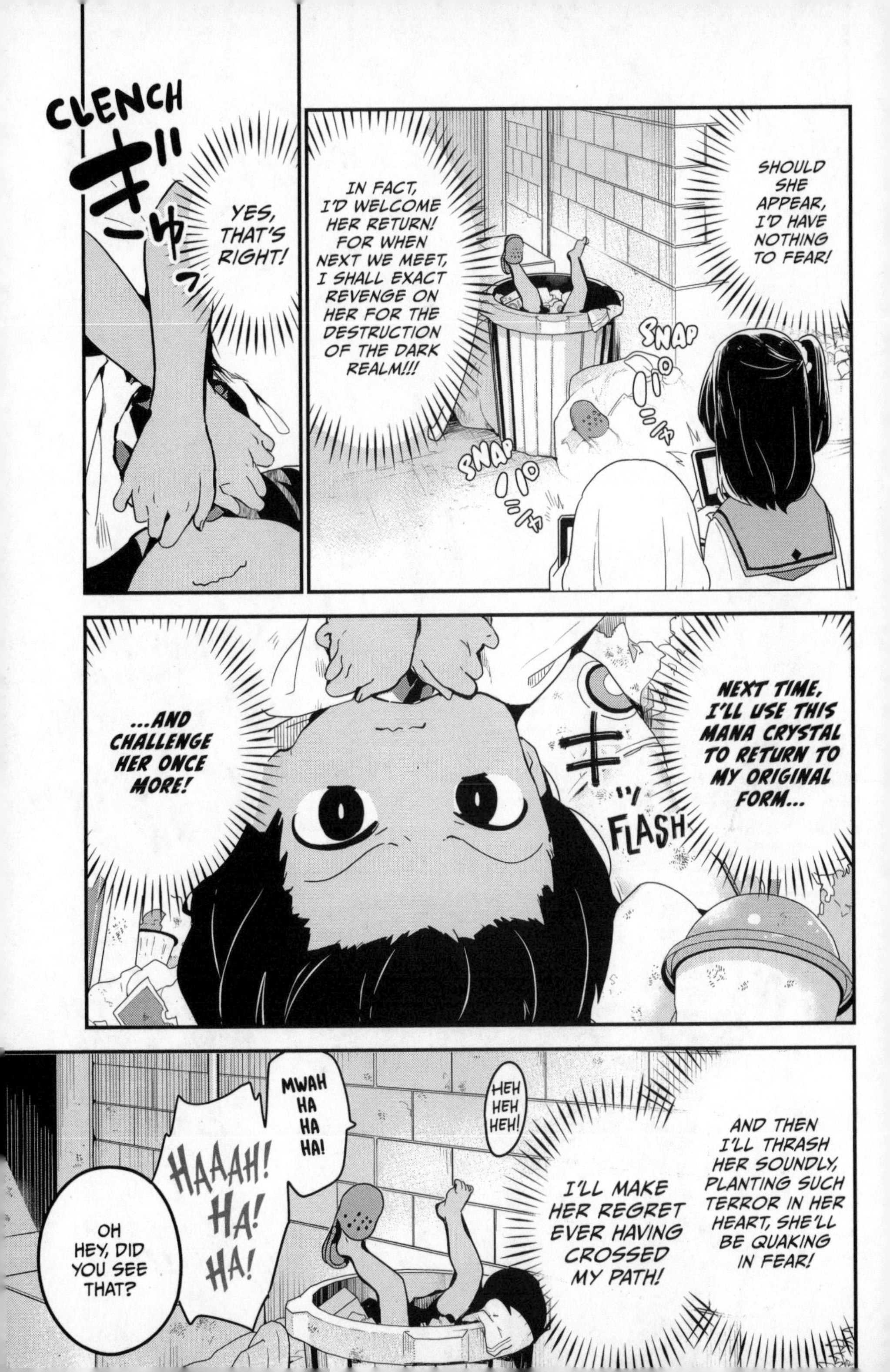
SHOULD SHE APPEAR, I'D HAVE NOTHING TO FEAR!
IN FACT, I'D WELCOME HER RETURN! FOR WHEN NEXT WE MEET, I SHALL EXACT REVENGE ON HER FOR THE DESTRUCTION OF THE DARK REALM!!!
SNAP
SNAP
YES, THAT'S RIGHT!
CLENCH
NEXT TIME, I'LL USE THIS MANA CRYSTAL TO RETURN TO MY ORIGINAL FORM...
FLASH
...AND CHALLENGE HER ONCE MORE!
AND THEN I'LL THRASH HER SOUNDLY, PLANTING SUCH TERROR IN HER HEART, SHE'LL BE QUAKING IN FEAR!
I'LL MAKE HER REGRET EVER HAVING CROSSED MY PATH!
HEH HEH HEH!
MWAH HA HA HA!
HAAAH! HA! HA!
OH HEY, DID YOU SEE THAT?

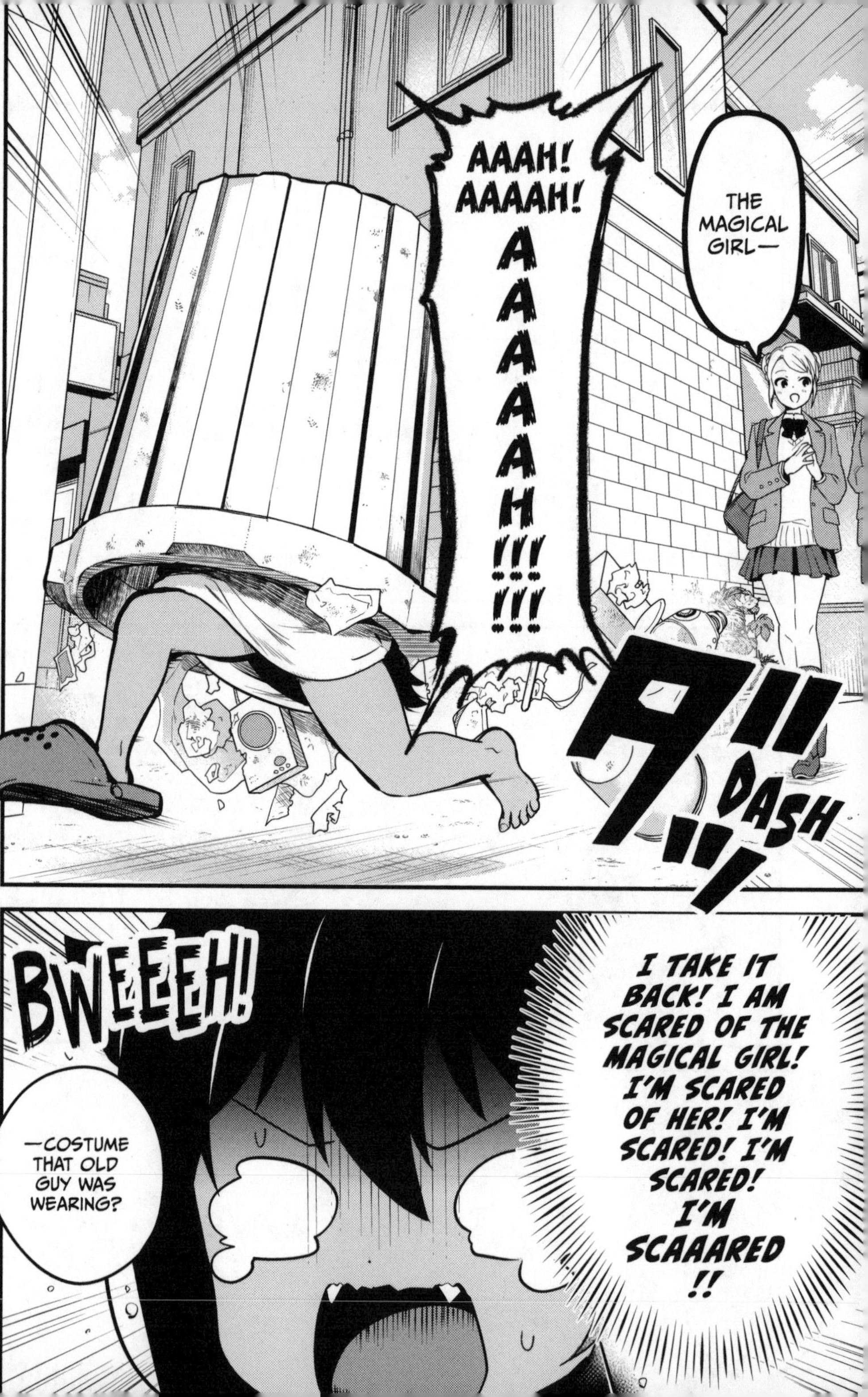
THE MAGICAL GIRL—
AAAH! AAAAH! AAAAAH!!!!!!
ダッ
DASH
I TAKE IT BACK! I AM SCARED OF THE MAGICAL GIRL! I'M SCARED OF HER! I'M SCARED! I'M SCARED! I'M SCAAARED!!
BWEEEH!
—COSTUME THAT OLD GUY WAS WEARING?

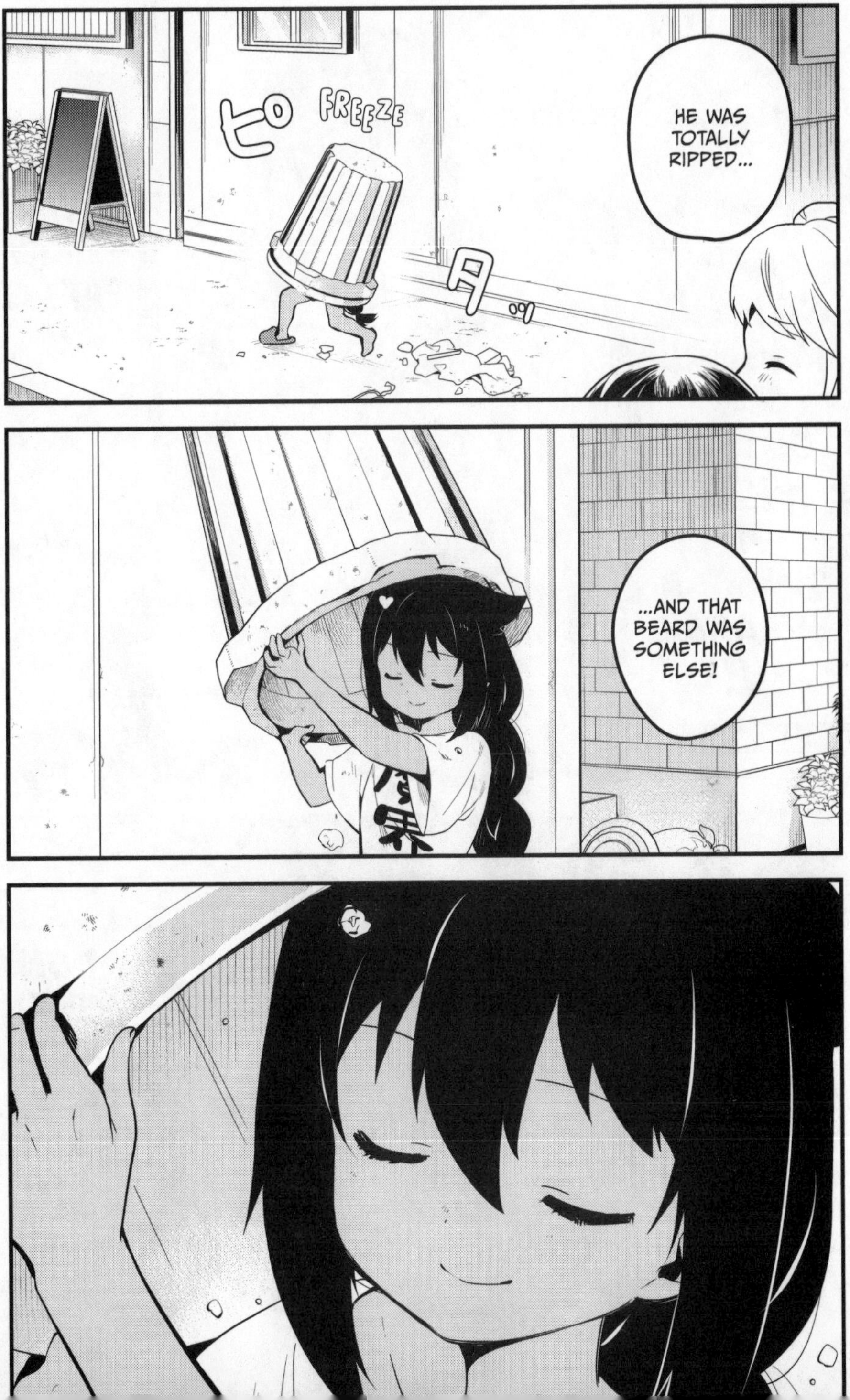
HE WAS TOTALLY RIPPED...
FREEZE
ピ
タ
...AND THAT BEARD WAS SOMETHING ELSE!

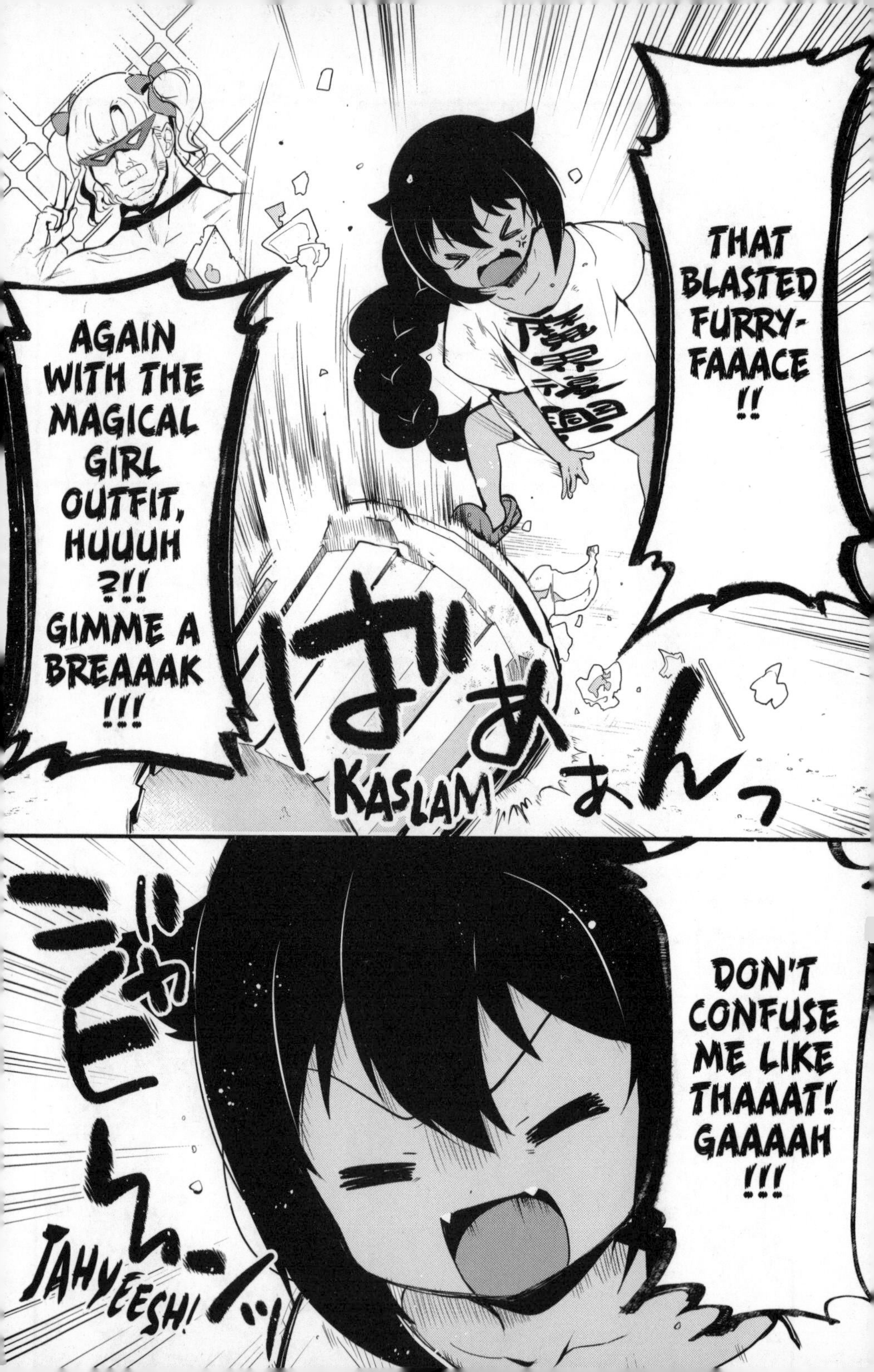
THAT BLASTED FURRY-FAAACE!!
AGAIN WITH THE MAGICAL GIRL OUTFIT, HUUUH?!! GIMME A BREAAAK!!!
KASLAM
DON'T CONFUSE ME LIKE THAAAT! GAAAAH!!!
JAHYEESH!

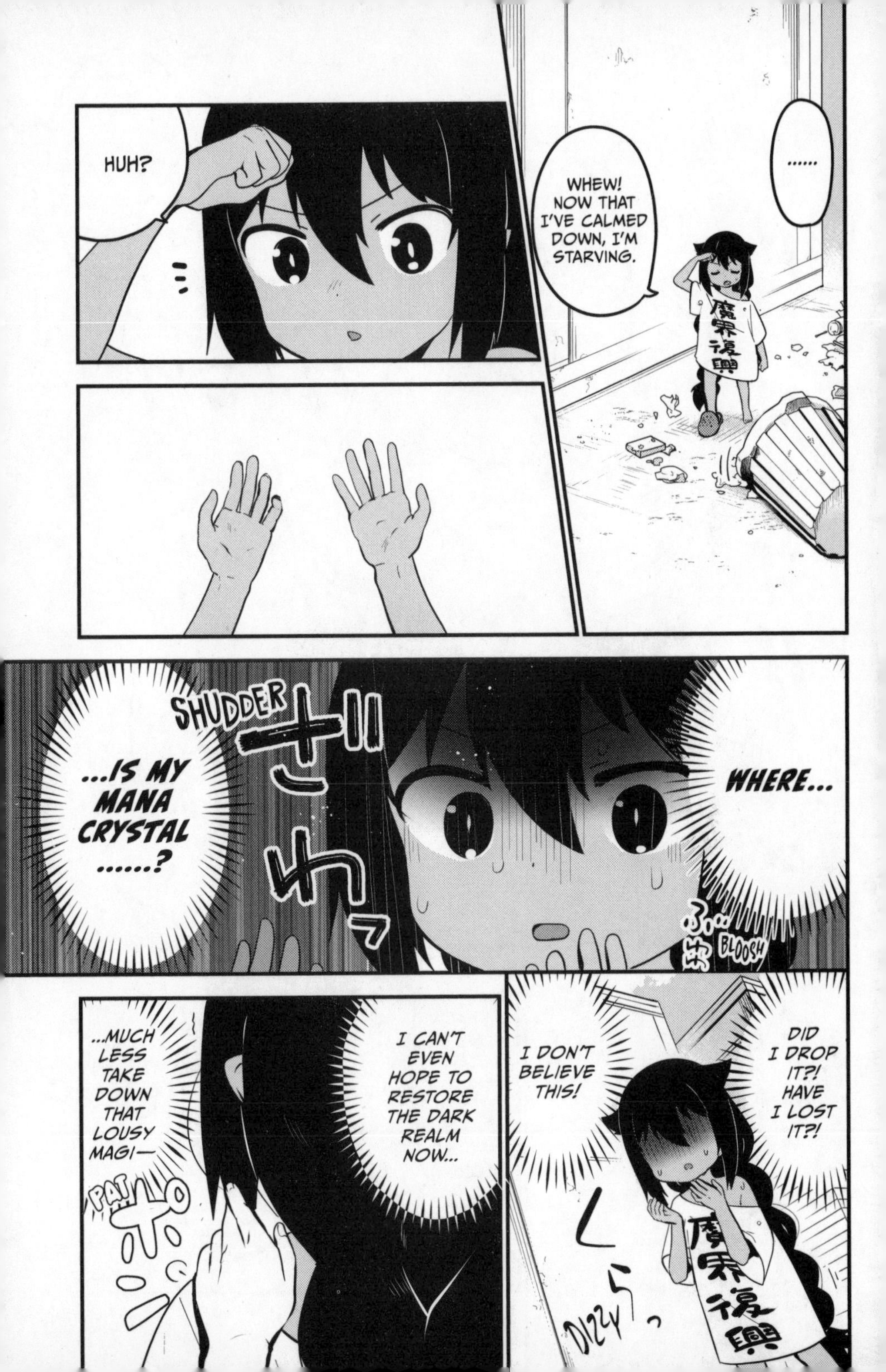
......
WHEW! NOW THAT I'VE CALMED DOWN, I'M STARVING.
HUH?
SHUDDER
WHERE...
...IS MY MANA CRYSTAL......?
BLOOSH
DID I DROP IT?! HAVE I LOST IT?!
I DON'T BELIEVE THIS!
DIZZY
I CAN'T EVEN HOPE TO RESTORE THE DARK REALM NOW...
...MUCH LESS TAKE DOWN THAT LOUSY MAGI—
PAT

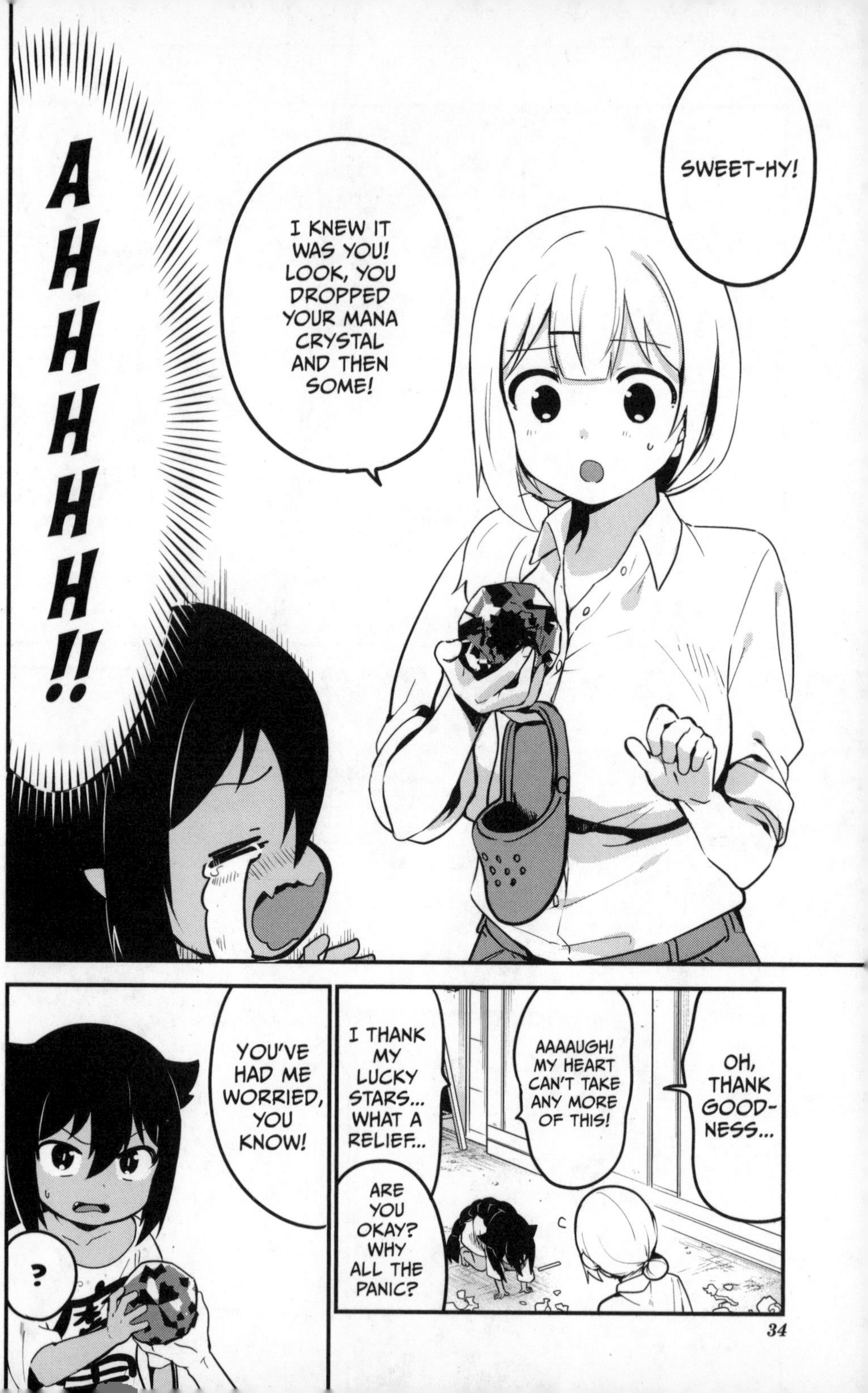
SWEET-HY!
I KNEW IT WAS YOU! LOOK, YOU DROPPED YOUR MANA CRYSTAL AND THEN SOME!
AHHHHHHH!!
OH, THANK GOOD-NESS...
AAAAUGH! MY HEART CAN'T TAKE ANY MORE OF THIS!
I THANK MY LUCKY STARS... WHAT A RELIEF...
ARE YOU OKAY? WHY ALL THE PANIC?
YOU'VE HAD ME WORRIED, YOU KNOW!
?

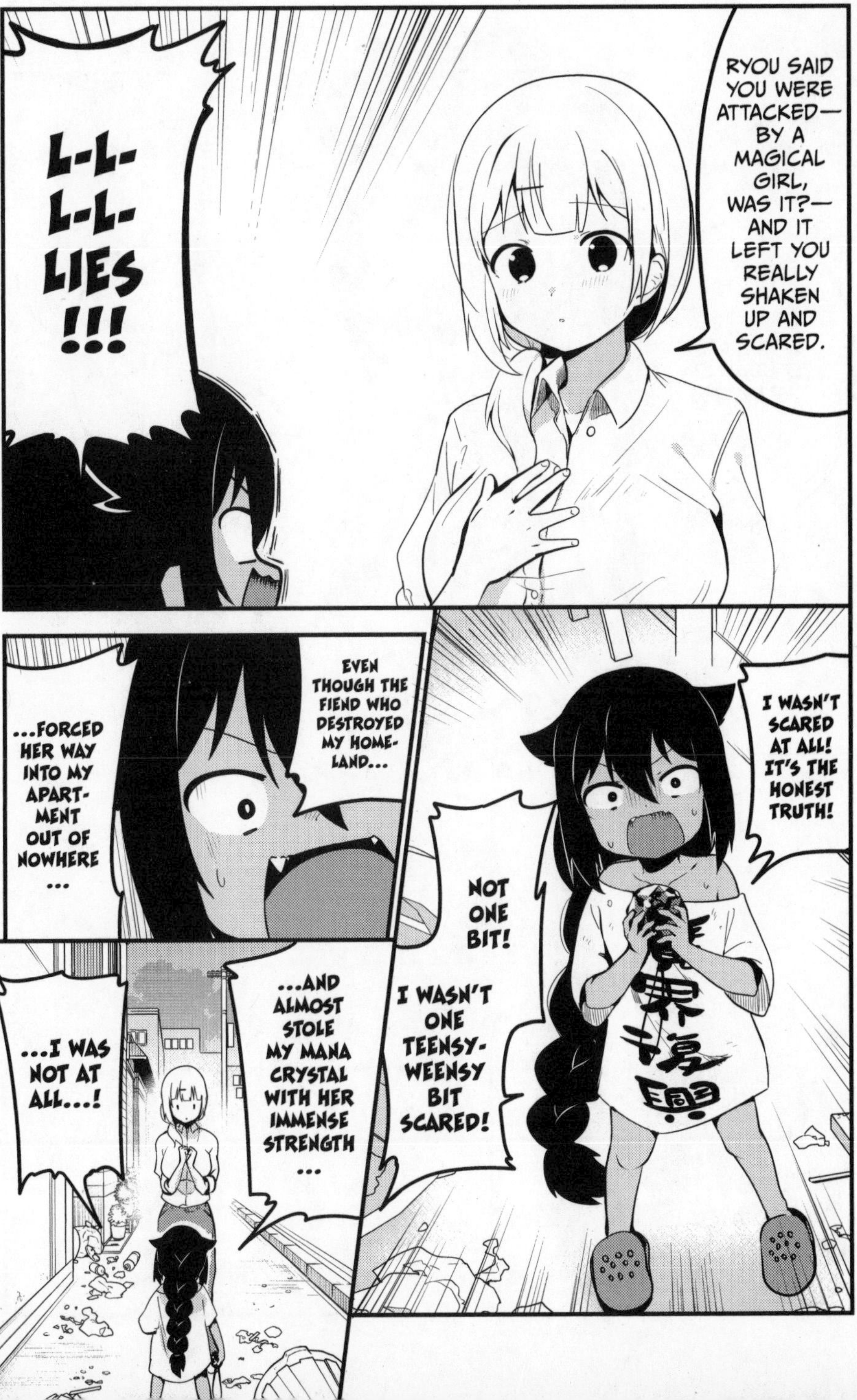
RYOU SAID YOU WERE ATTACKED—BY A MAGICAL GIRL, WAS IT?—AND IT LEFT YOU REALLY SHAKEN UP AND SCARED.
L-L-L-L-LIES!!!
I WASN'T SCARED AT ALL! IT'S THE HONEST TRUTH!
NOT ONE BIT!
I WASN'T ONE TEENSY-WEENSY BIT SCARED!
EVEN THOUGH THE FIEND WHO DESTROYED MY HOME-LAND...
...FORCED HER WAY INTO MY APART-MENT OUT OF NOWHERE...
...AND ALMOST STOLE MY MANA CRYSTAL WITH HER IMMENSE STRENGTH...
...I WAS NOT AT ALL...!

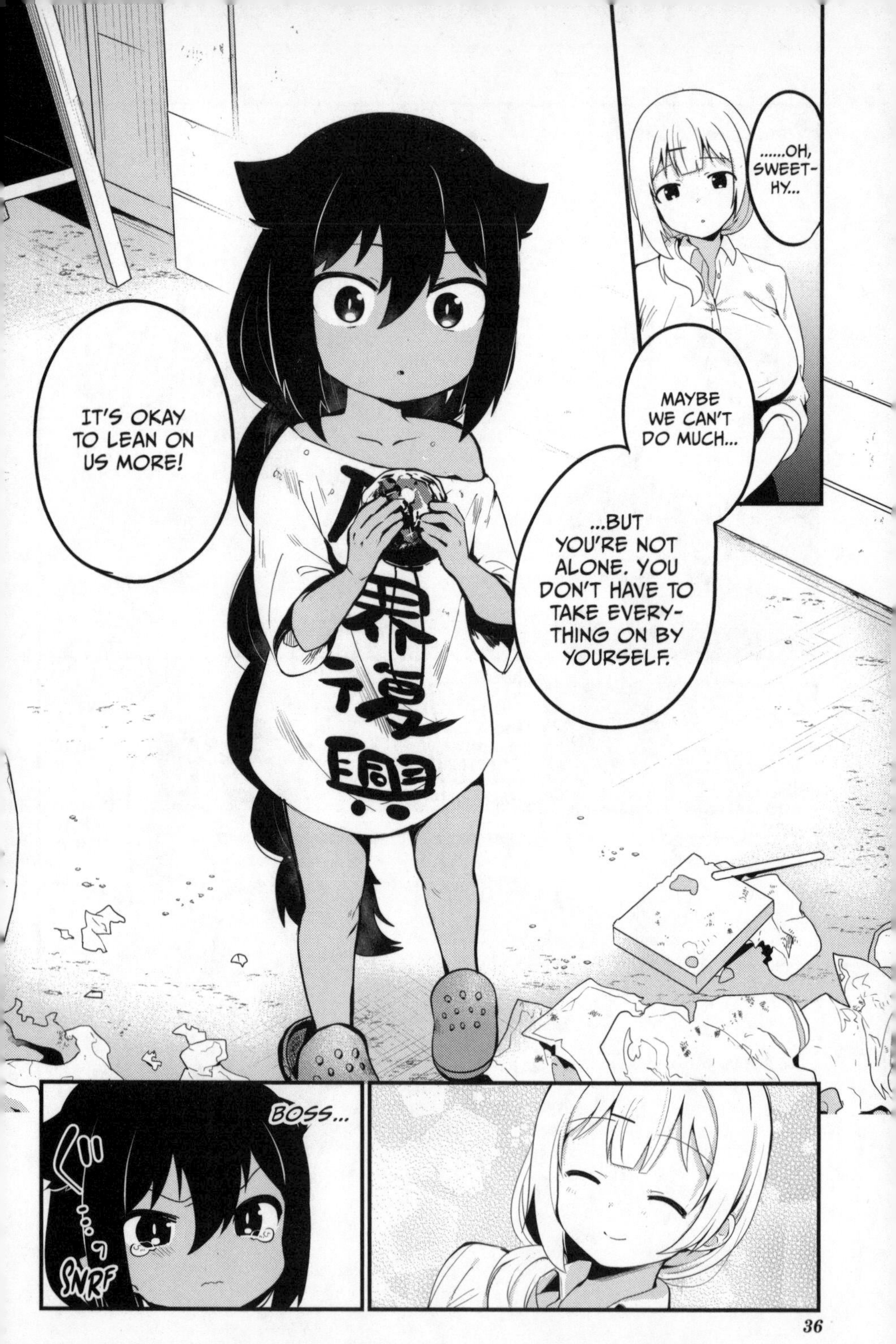
......OH, SWEET-HY...
MAYBE WE CAN'T DO MUCH...
...BUT YOU'RE NOT ALONE. YOU DON'T HAVE TO TAKE EVERY-THING ON BY YOURSELF.
IT'S OKAY TO LEAN ON US MORE!
BOSS...
SNRF

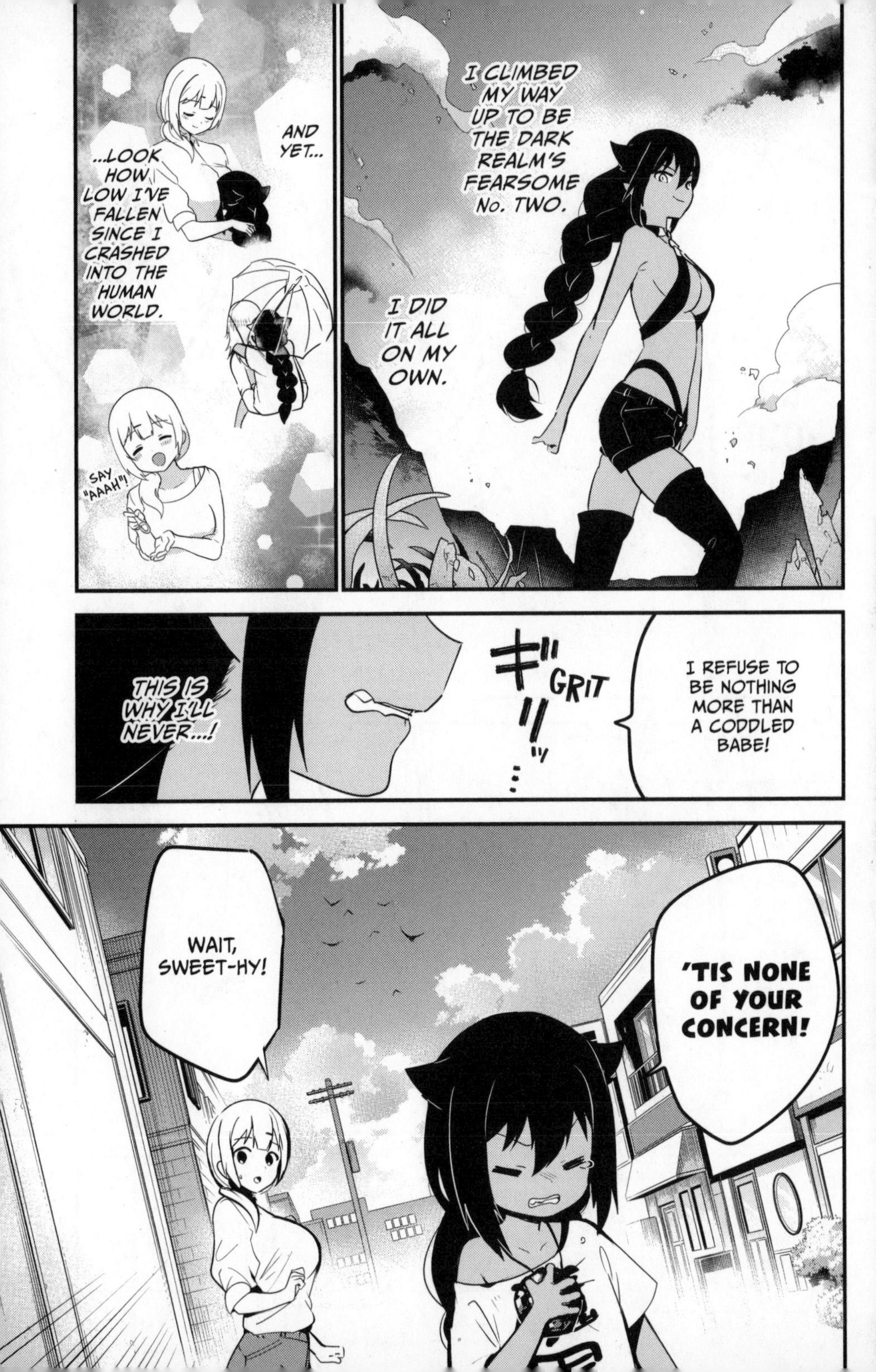
I CLIMBED MY WAY UP TO BE THE DARK REALM'S FEARSOME No. TWO.
I DID IT ALL ON MY OWN.
AND YET...
...LOOK HOW LOW I'VE FALLEN SINCE I CRASHED INTO THE HUMAN WORLD.
SAY "AAAH"!
I REFUSE TO BE NOTHING MORE THAN A CODDLED BABE!
ギリッ GRIT
THIS IS WHY I'LL NEVER...!
'TIS NONE OF YOUR CONCERN!
WAIT, SWEET-HY!

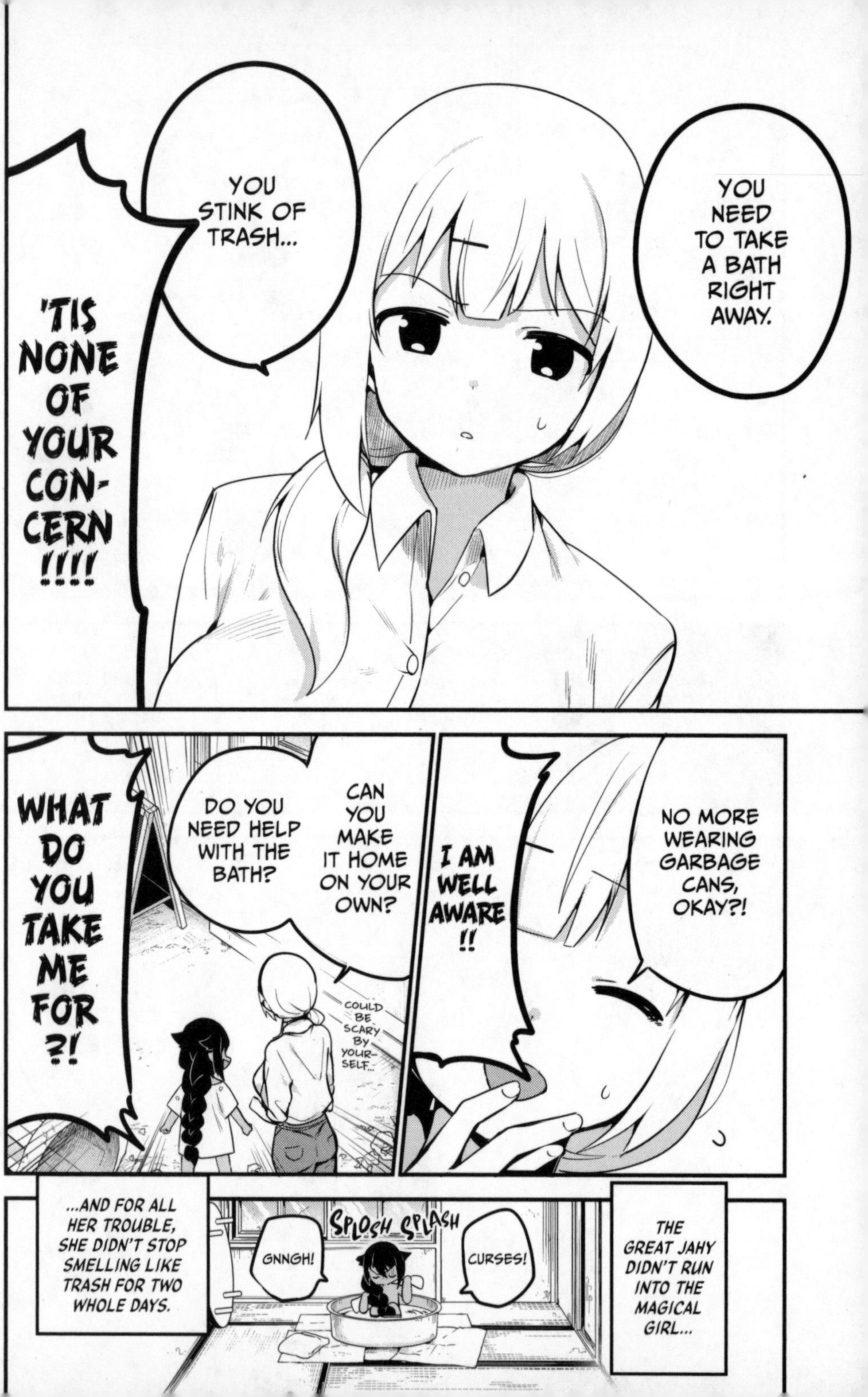
YOU NEED TO TAKE A BATH RIGHT AWAY.
YOU STINK OF TRASH...
'TIS NONE OF YOUR CON-CERN!!!!
NO MORE WEARING GARBAGE CANS, OKAY?!
I AM WELL AWARE!!
CAN YOU MAKE IT HOME ON YOUR OWN?
DO YOU NEED HELP WITH THE BATH?
COULD BE SCARY BY YOUR-SELF...
WHAT DO YOU TAKE ME FOR?!
THE GREAT JAHY DIDN'T RUN INTO THE MAGICAL GIRL...
CURSES!
SPLOSH SPLASH
GNNGH!
...AND FOR ALL HER TROUBLE, SHE DIDN'T STOP SMELLING LIKE TRASH FOR TWO WHOLE DAYS.

SPROING

CUCUMBER

The GREAT JAHY Will NOT Be DEFEATED!

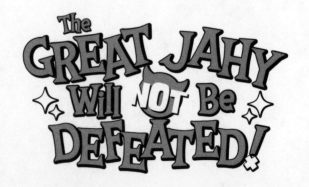

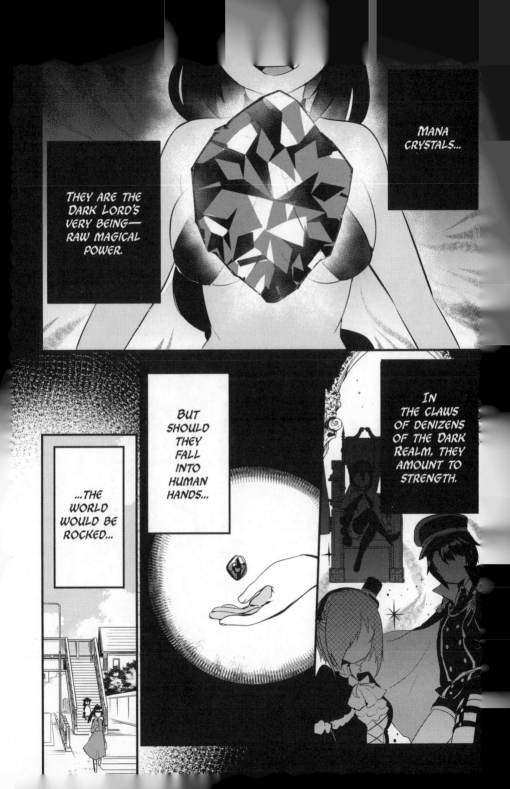

MANA CRYSTALS...

THEY ARE THE DARK LORD'S VERY BEING— RAW MAGICAL POWER.

IN THE CLAWS OF DENIZENS OF THE DARK REALM, THEY AMOUNT TO STRENGTH.

BUT SHOULD THEY FALL INTO HUMAN HANDS...

...THE WORLD WOULD BE ROCKED...

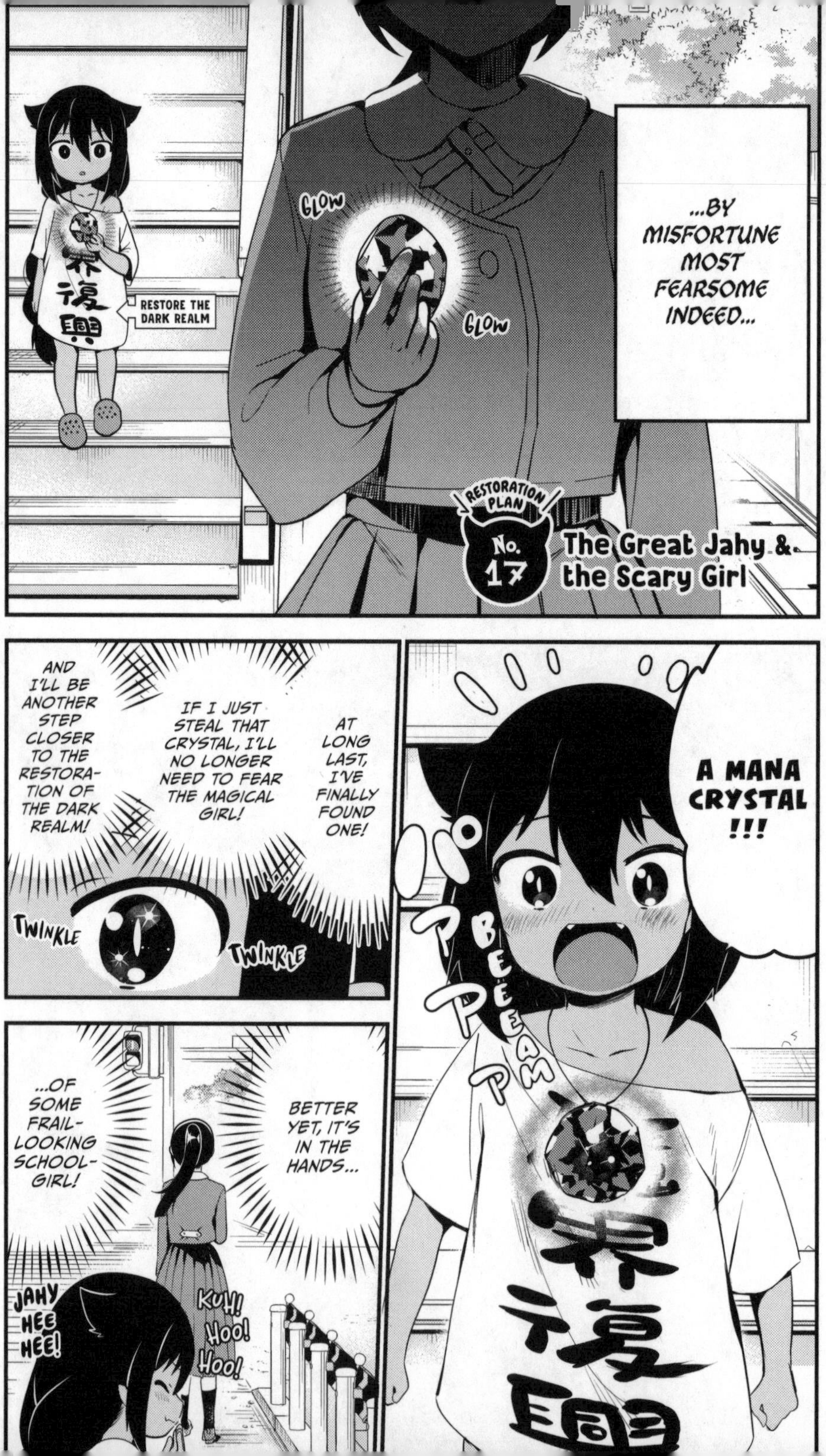
...BY MISFORTUNE MOST FEARSOME INDEED...
GLOW
GLOW
RESTORATION PLAN
No. 17
The Great Jahy & the Scary Girl
RESTORE THE DARK REALM
A MANA CRYSTAL!!!
BEEEEAM
AT LONG LAST, I'VE FINALLY FOUND ONE!
IF I JUST STEAL THAT CRYSTAL, I'LL NO LONGER NEED TO FEAR THE MAGICAL GIRL!
AND I'LL BE ANOTHER STEP CLOSER TO THE RESTORATION OF THE DARK REALM!
TWINKLE
TWINKLE
BETTER YET, IT'S IN THE HANDS...
...OF SOME FRAIL-LOOKING SCHOOLGIRL!
KUH! HOO! HOO!
JAHY HEE HEE!

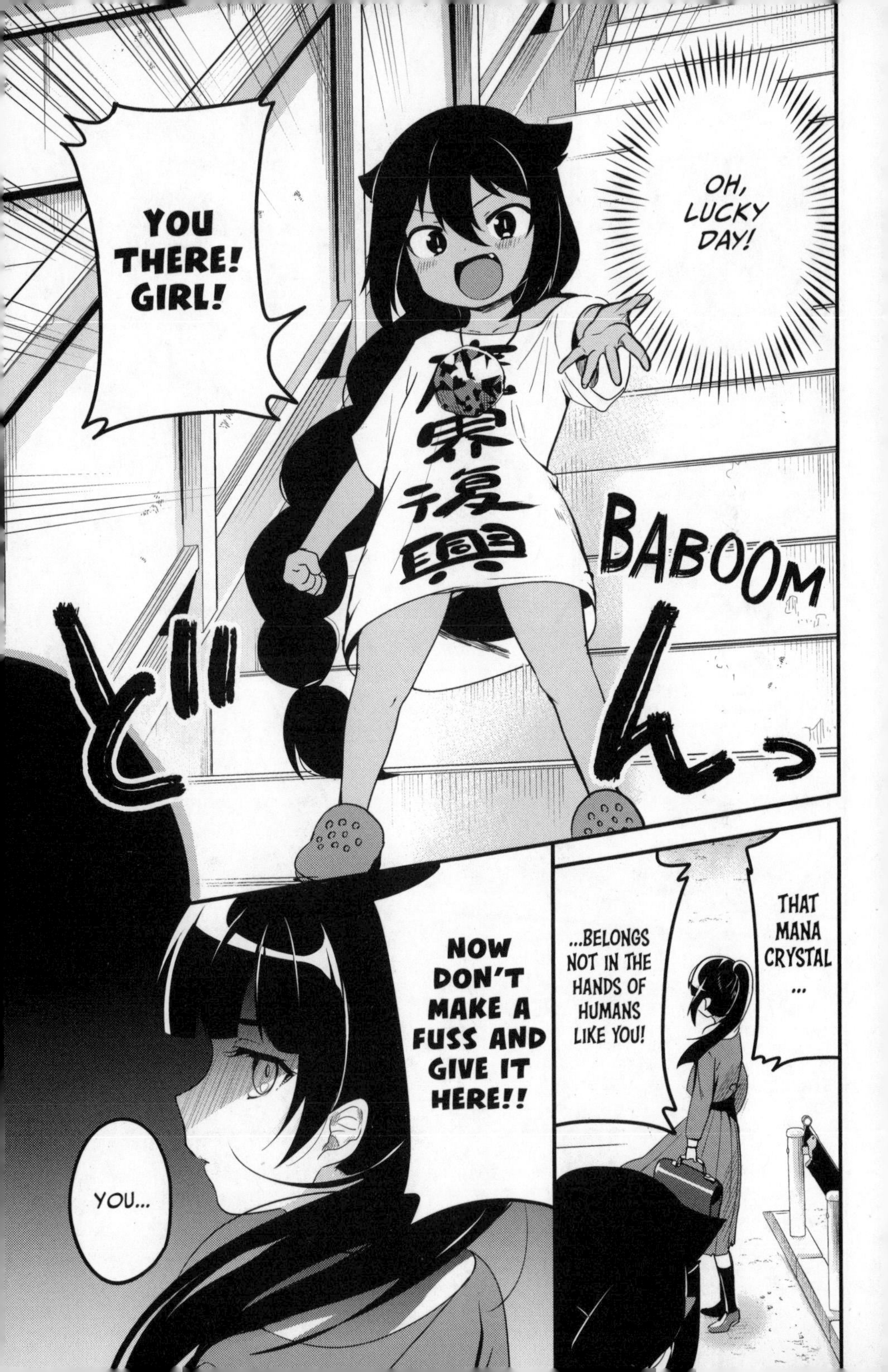
OH, LUCKY DAY!
YOU THERE! GIRL!
BABOOM
どんっ
THAT MANA CRYSTAL ...
...BELONGS NOT IN THE HANDS OF HUMANS LIKE YOU!
NOW DON'T MAKE A FUSS AND GIVE IT HERE!!
YOU...

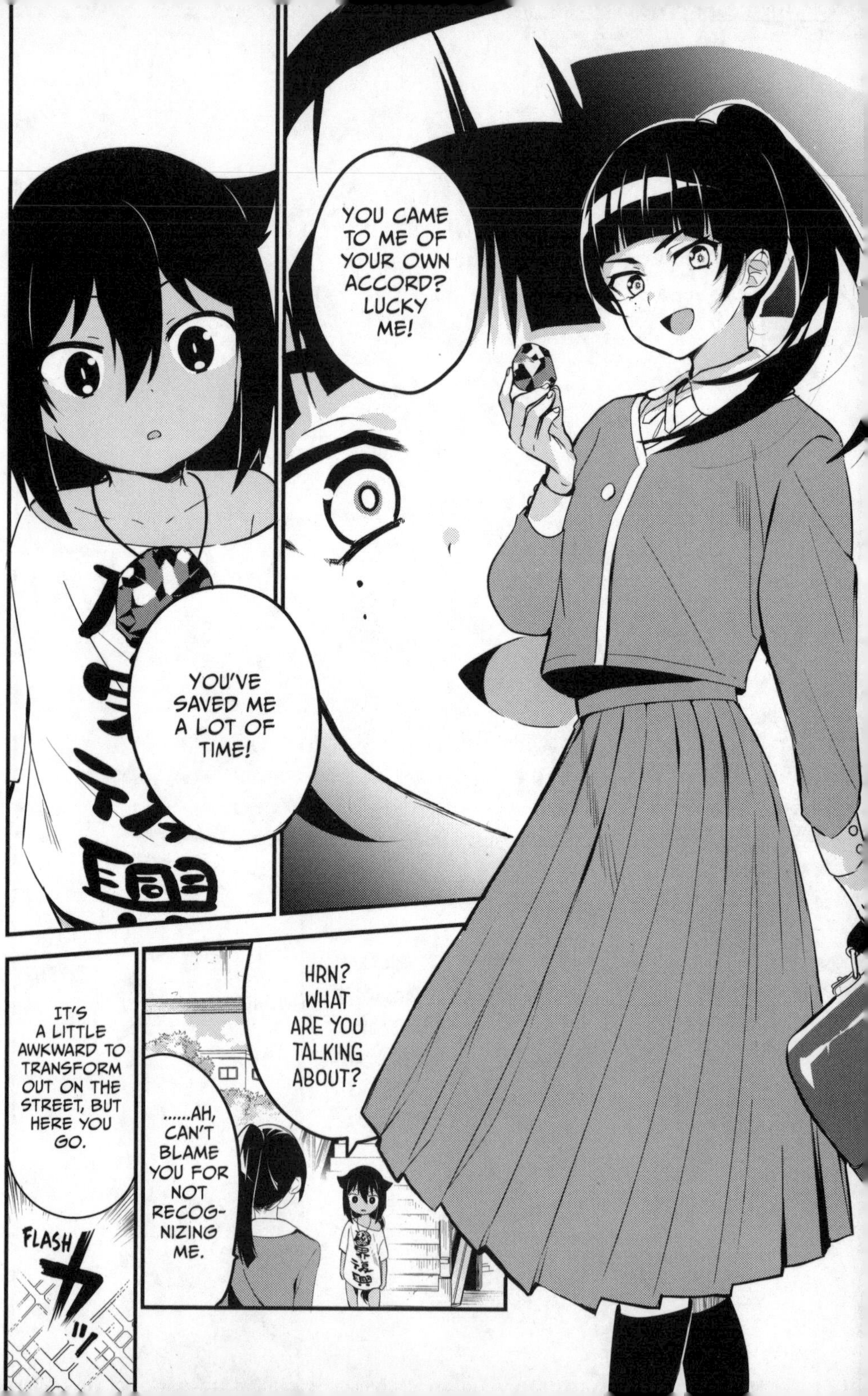
YOU CAME TO ME OF YOUR OWN ACCORD? LUCKY ME!
YOU'VE SAVED ME A LOT OF TIME!
HRN? WHAT ARE YOU TALKING ABOUT?
......AH, CAN'T BLAME YOU FOR NOT RECOGNIZING ME.
IT'S A LITTLE AWKWARD TO TRANSFORM OUT ON THE STREET, BUT HERE YOU GO.
FLASH

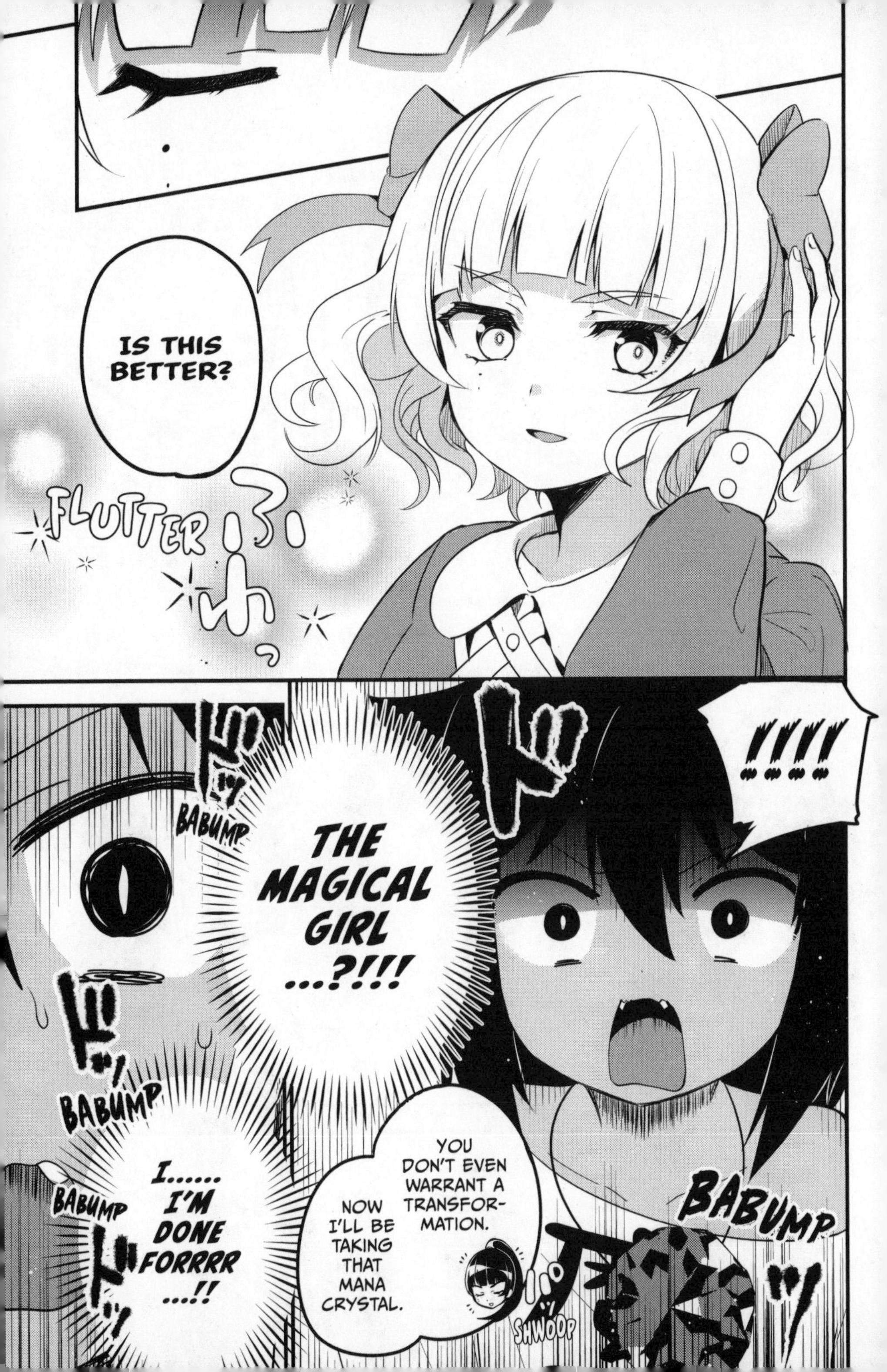
IS THIS BETTER?
FLUTTER
!!!!
BABUMP
SHWOOP
YOU DON'T EVEN WARRANT A TRANSFORMATION.
NOW I'LL BE TAKING THAT MANA CRYSTAL.
THE MAGICAL GIRL ...?!!!
BABUMP
BABUMP
BABUMP
I...... I'M DONE FORRRR ...!!

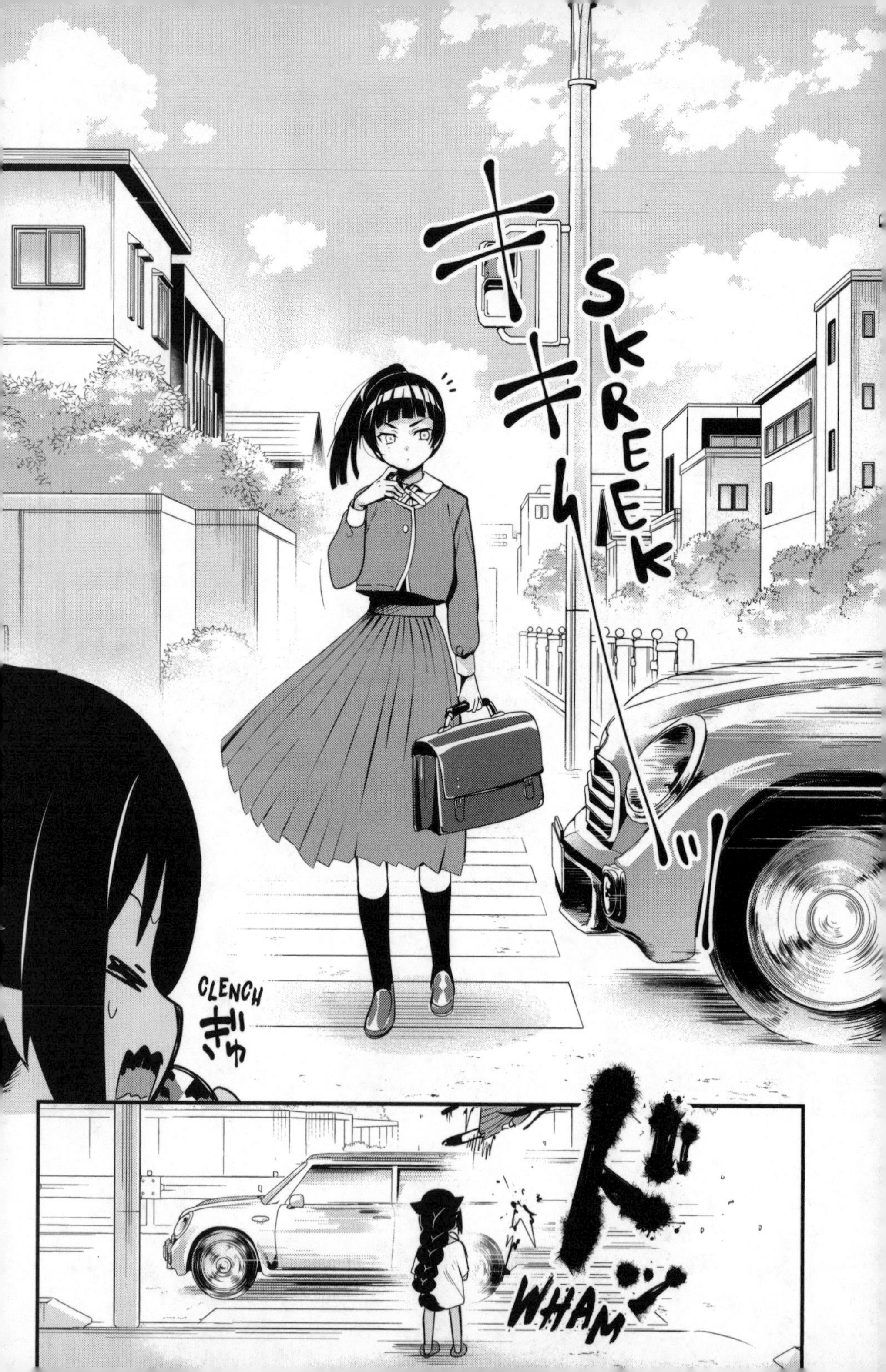
SKREEK
CLENCH
ぎゅ
WHAM

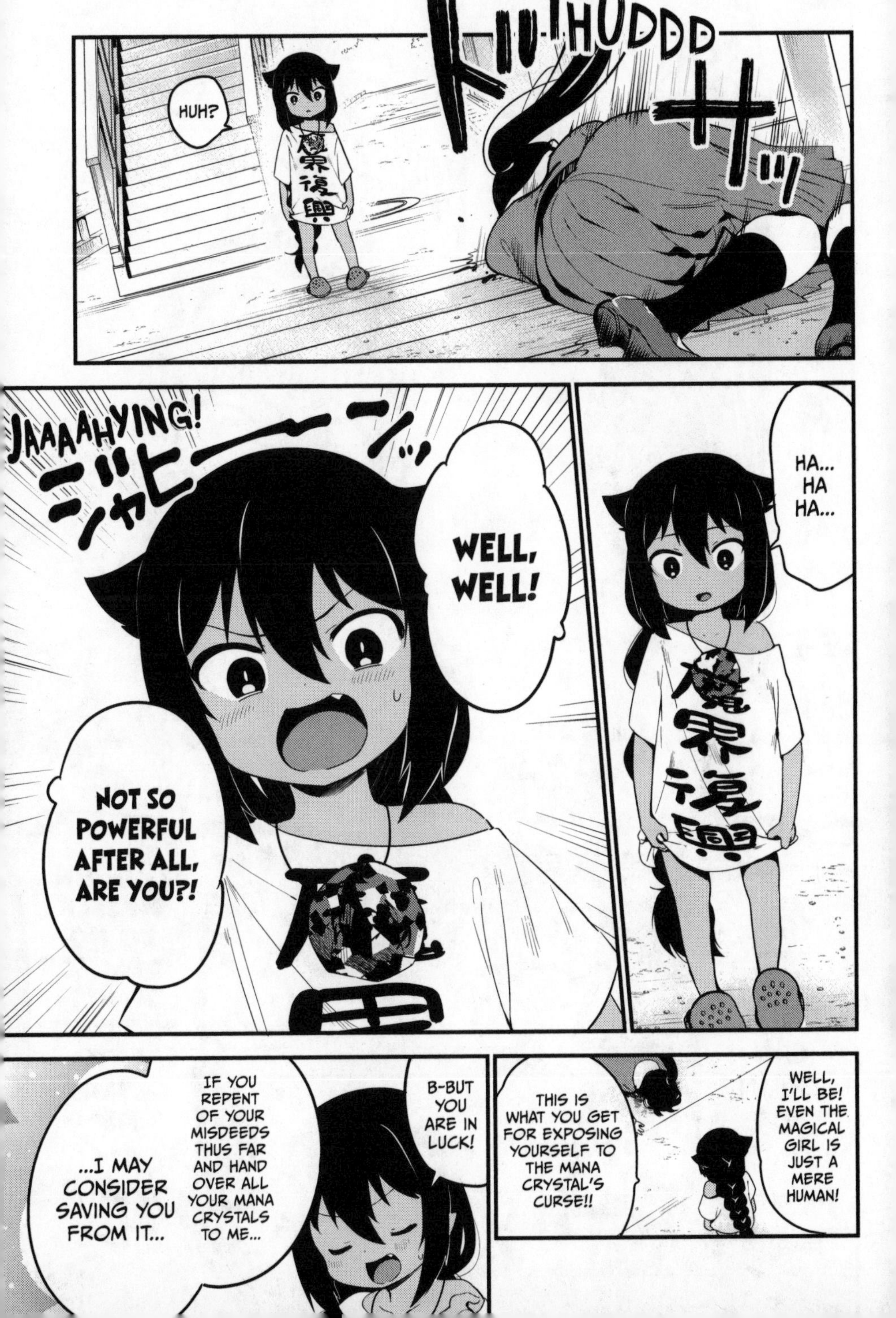
THUDDD
HUH?
HA... HA HA...
JAAAAHYING!
WELL, WELL!
NOT SO POWERFUL AFTER ALL, ARE YOU?!
WELL, I'LL BE! EVEN THE MAGICAL GIRL IS JUST A MERE HUMAN!
THIS IS WHAT YOU GET FOR EXPOSING YOURSELF TO THE MANA CRYSTAL'S CURSE!!
B-BUT YOU ARE IN LUCK!
IF YOU REPENT OF YOUR MISDEEDS THUS FAR AND HAND OVER ALL YOUR MANA CRYSTALS TO ME...
...I MAY CONSIDER SAVING YOU FROM IT...

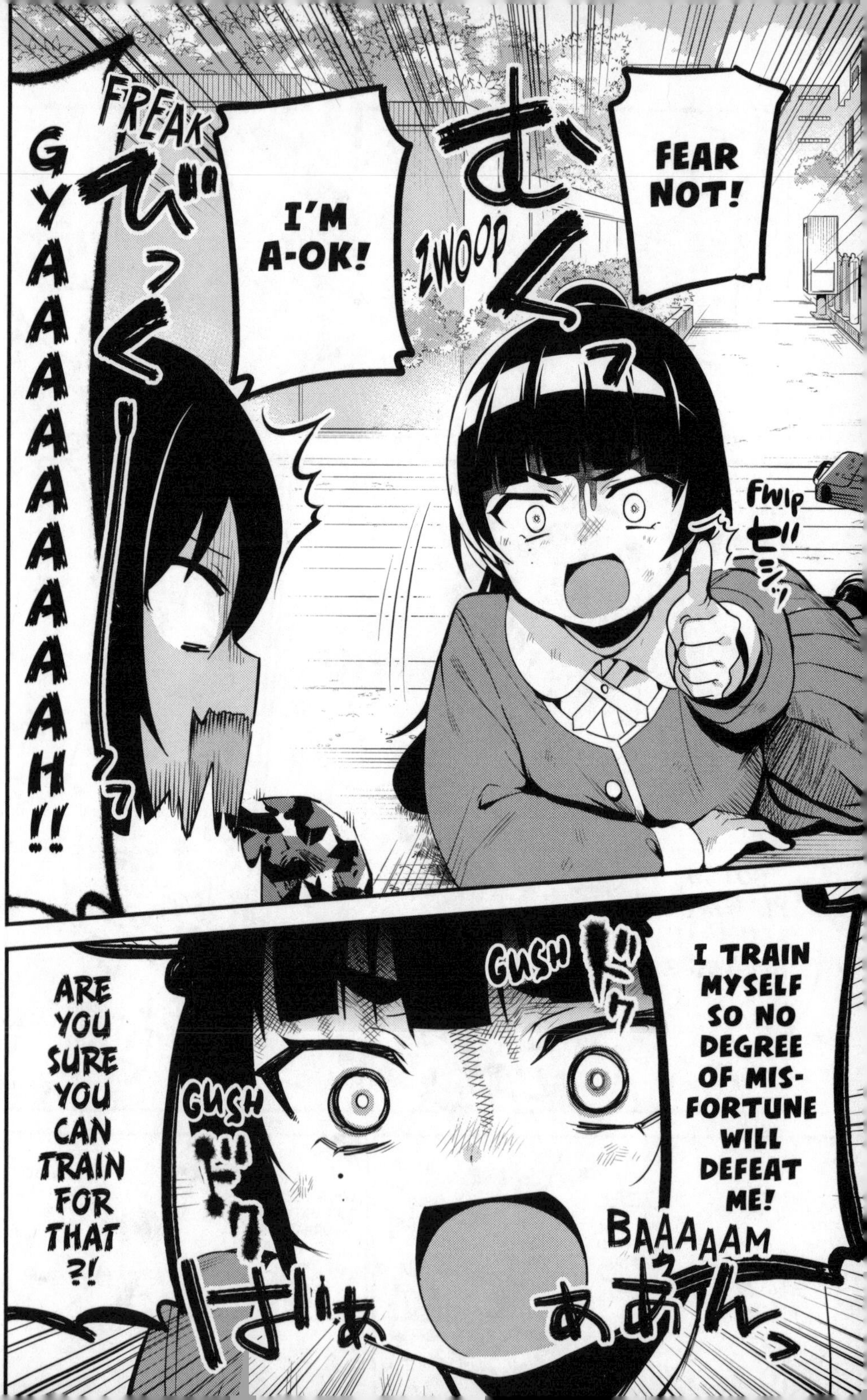
FEAR NOT!
ZWOOP
I'M A-OK!
FREAK
GYAAAAAAAAAAAAAAH!!
FWIP
I TRAIN MYSELF SO NO DEGREE OF MIS-FORTUNE WILL DEFEAT ME!
GUSH
BAAAAAM
GUSH
ARE YOU SURE YOU CAN TRAIN FOR THAT?!

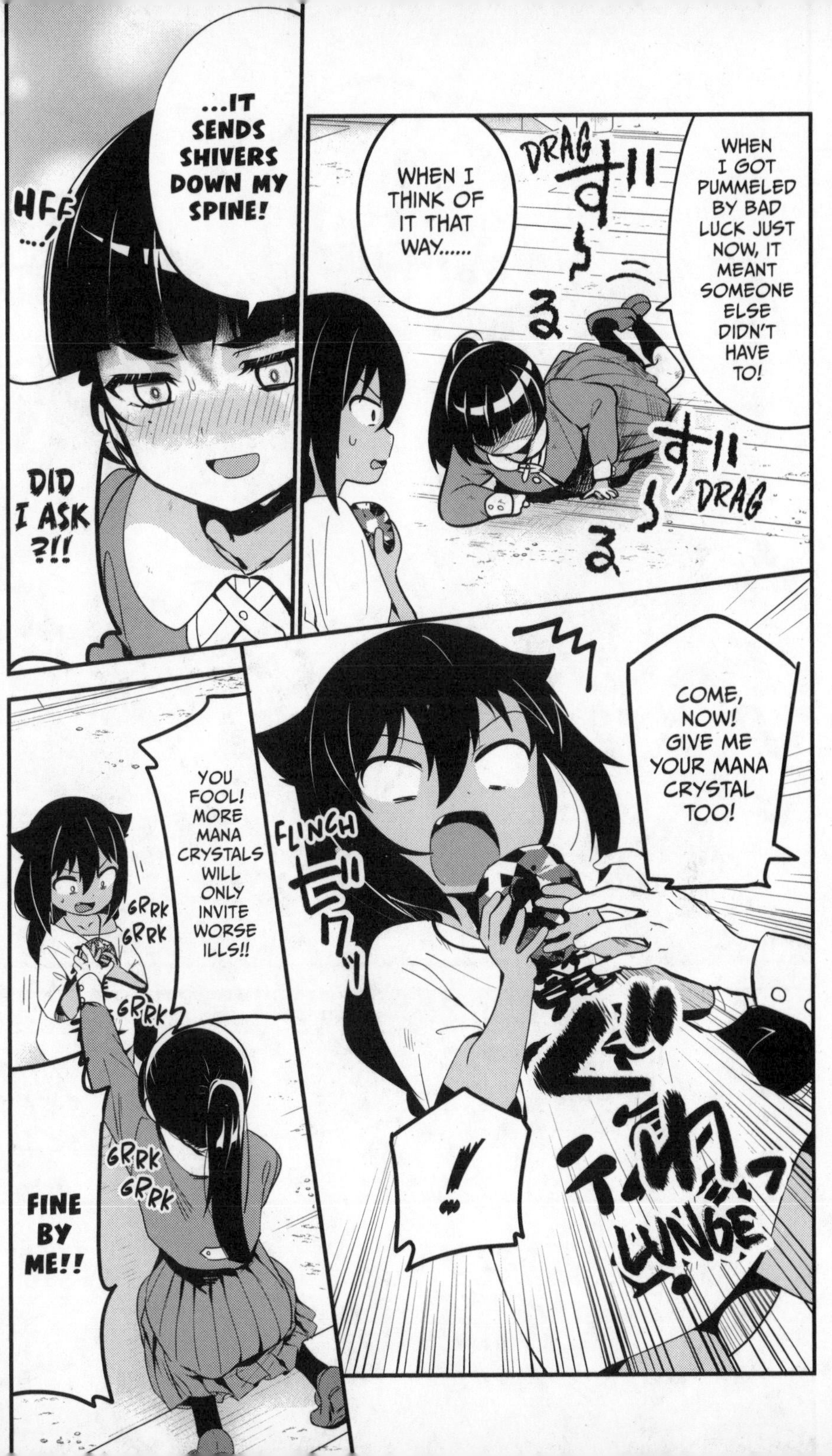
WHEN I GOT PUMMELED BY BAD LUCK JUST NOW, IT MEANT SOMEONE ELSE DIDN'T HAVE TO!
DRAG
WHEN I THINK OF IT THAT WAY......
DRAG
...IT SENDS SHIVERS DOWN MY SPINE!
HFF....!
DID I ASK ?!!
COME, NOW! GIVE ME YOUR MANA CRYSTAL TOO!
LUNGE
FLINCH
!
YOU FOOL! MORE MANA CRYSTALS WILL ONLY INVITE WORSE ILLS!!
GRRK GRRK
GRRK
GRRK GRRK
FINE BY ME!!

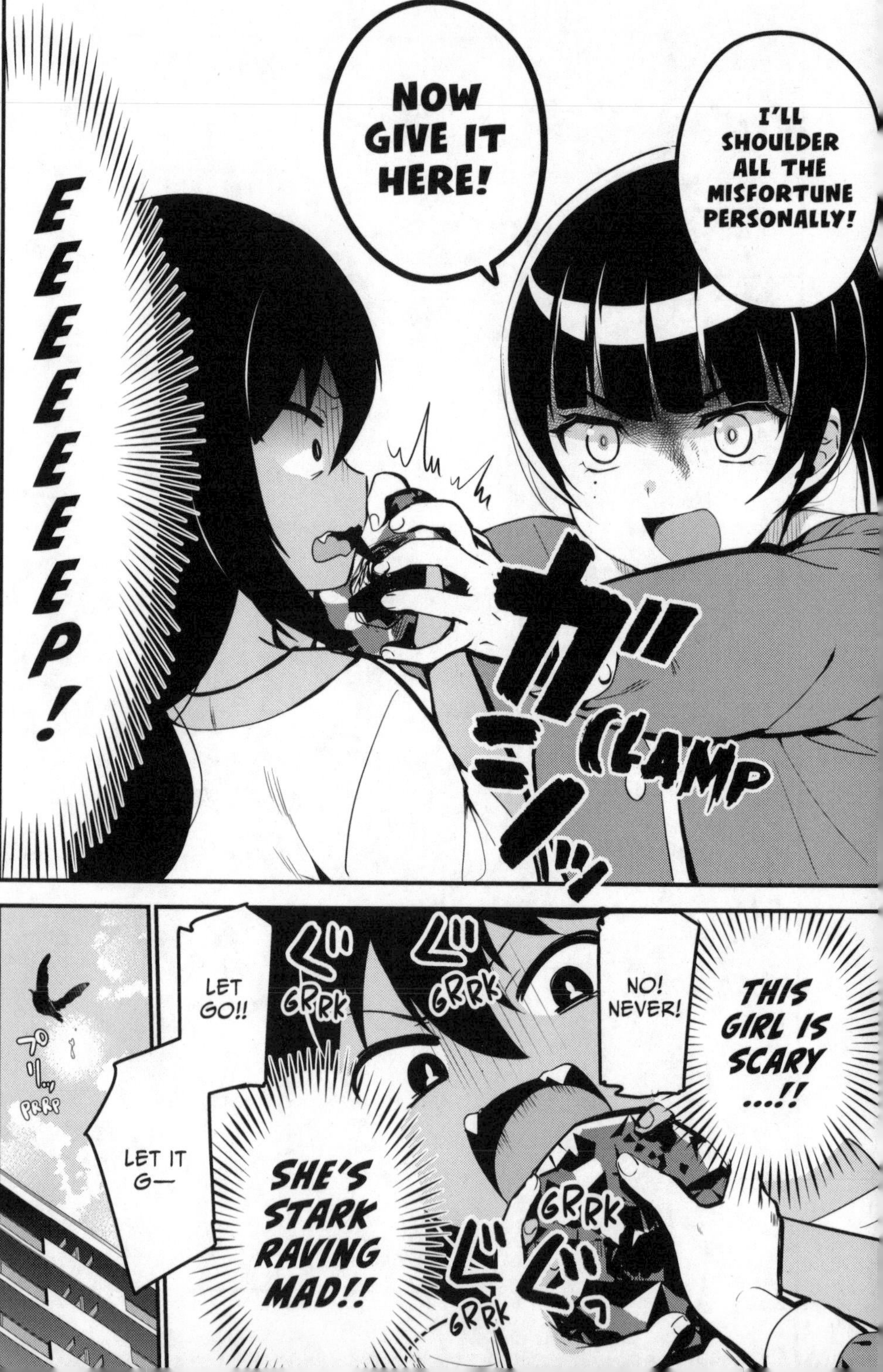
I'LL SHOULDER ALL THE MISFORTUNE PERSONALLY!
NOW GIVE IT HERE!
CLAMP
EEEEEEEP!
THIS GIRL IS SCARY ...!!
NO! NEVER!
GRRK
GRRK
LET GO!!
GRRK
GRRK
SHE'S STARK RAVING MAD!!
LET IT G—
PRRP

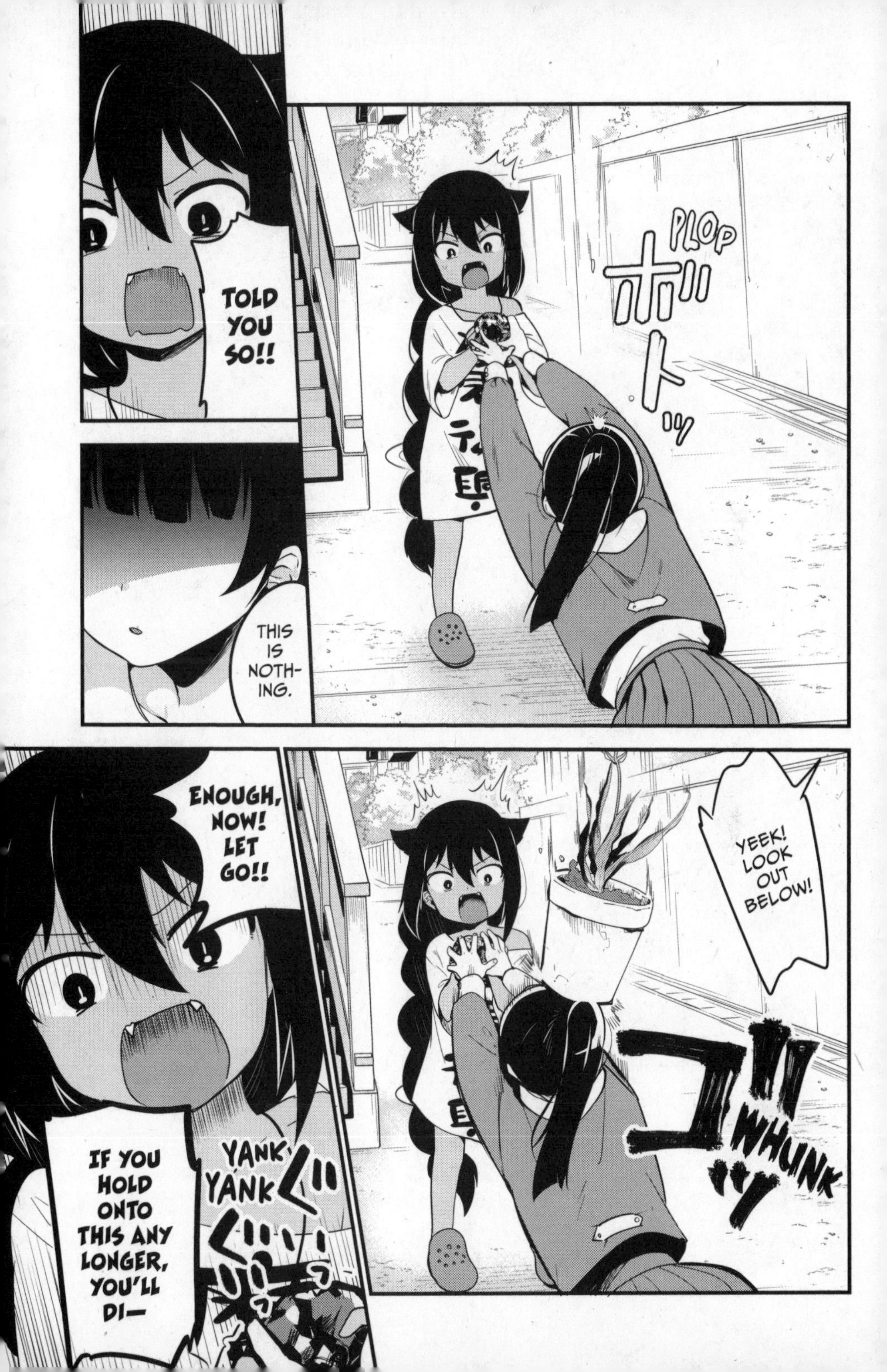
PLOP
TOLD YOU SO!!
THIS IS NOTHING.
YEEK! LOOK OUT BELOW!
WHUNK
ENOUGH, NOW! LET GO!!
YANK YANK
IF YOU HOLD ONTO THIS ANY LONGER, YOU'LL DI—

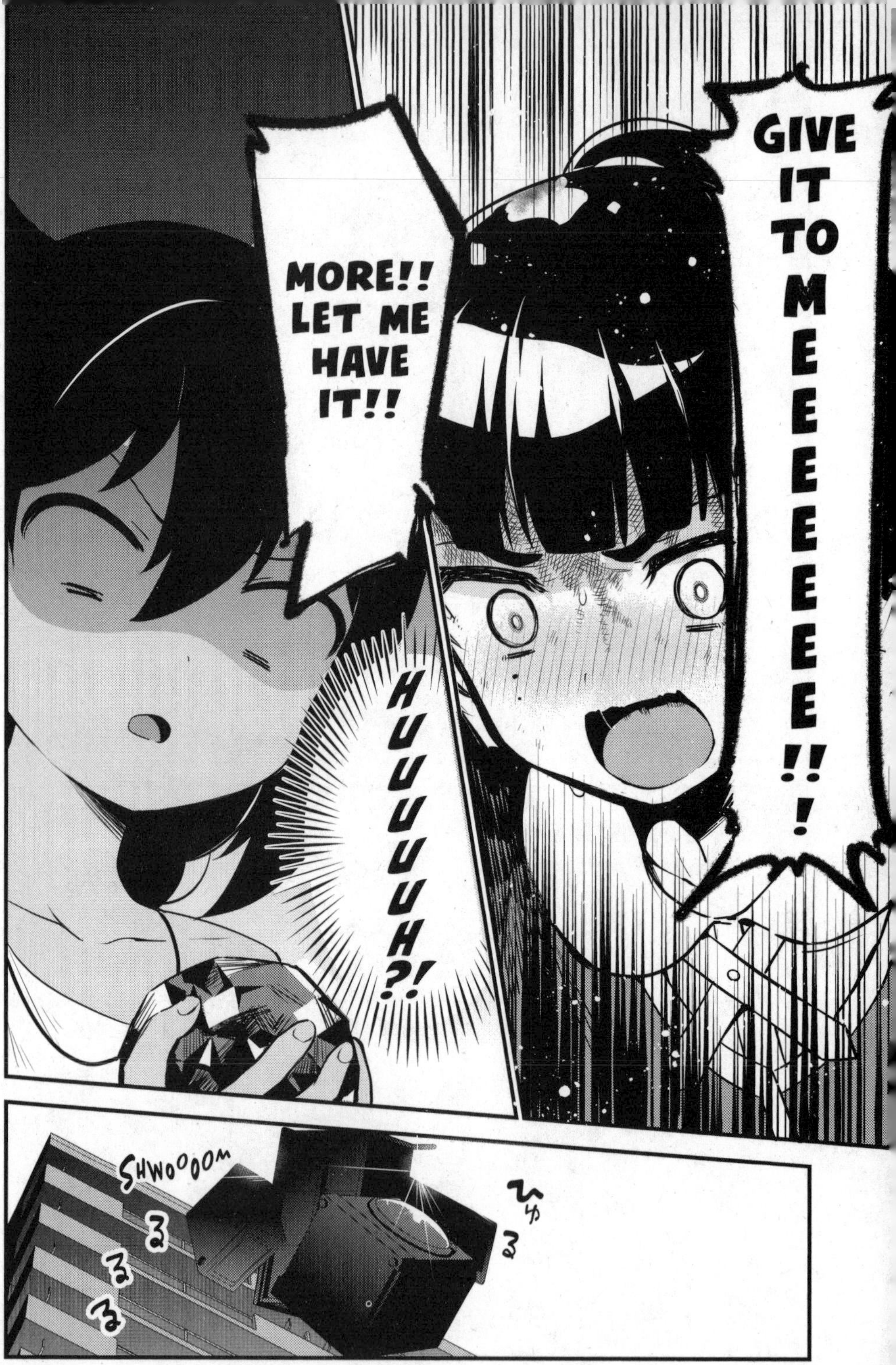
GIVE IT TO MEEEEEEEEE!!!
MORE!! LET ME HAVE IT!!
HUUUUUH?!
ひゅるるるる
SHWOOOOM

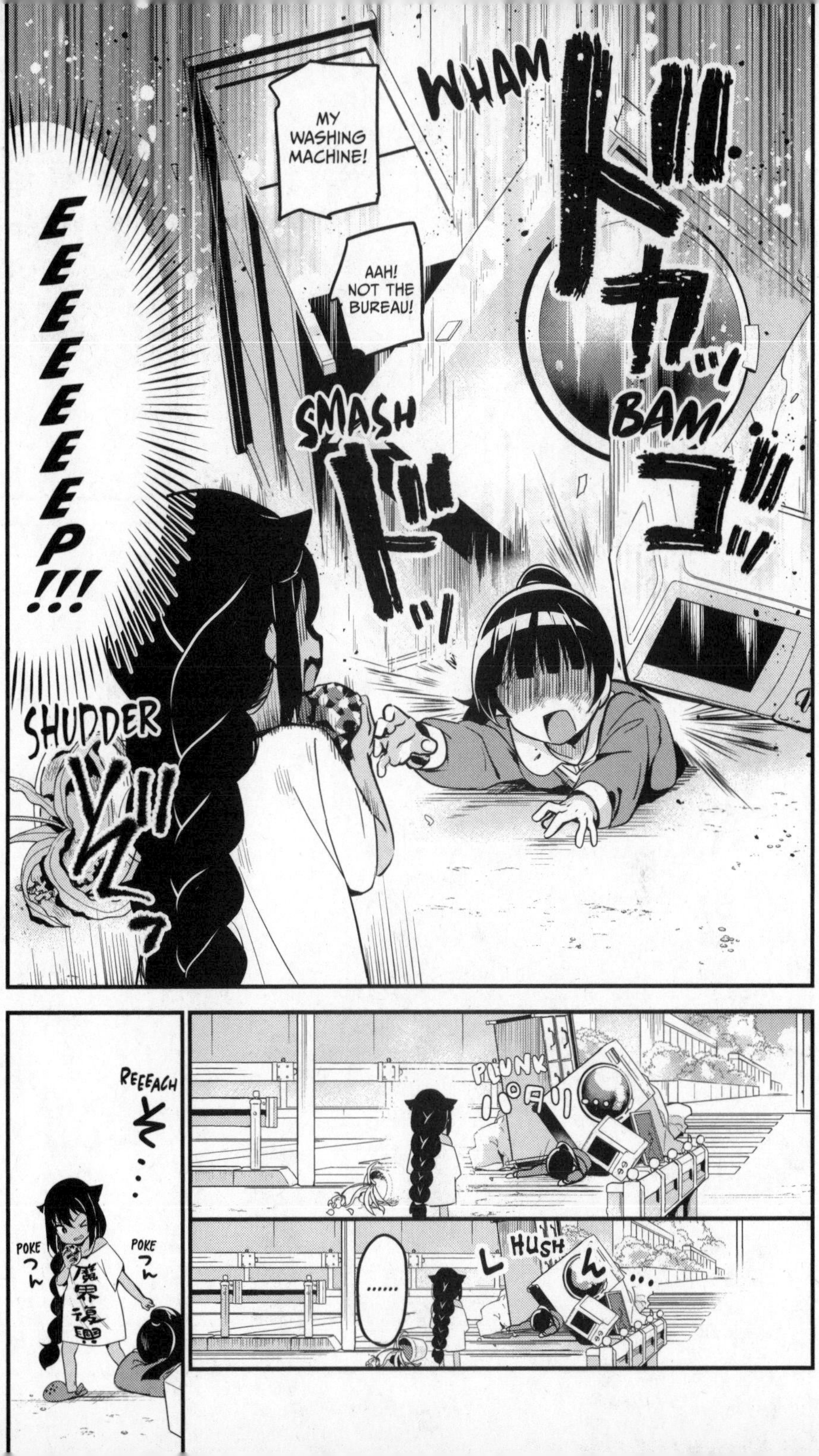
WHAM
BAM
MY WASHING MACHINE!
AAH! NOT THE BUREAU!
SMASH
EEEEEEEEEEEP!!!
SHUDDER
PLUNK
HUSH
......
REEEACH
POKE
POKE

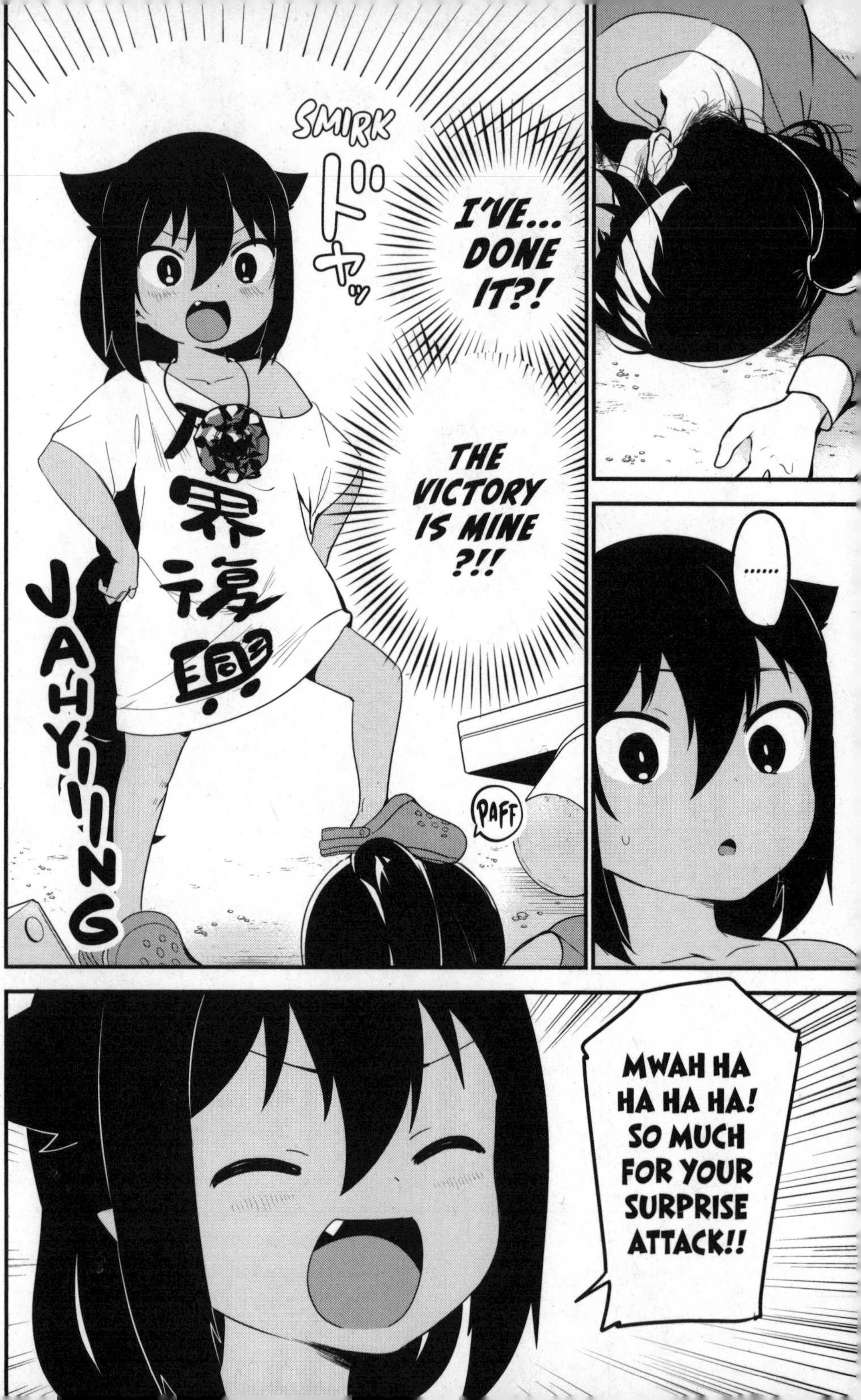
......
SMIRK
ドヤッ
I'VE... DONE IT?!
THE VICTORY IS MINE ?!!
界復興
JAHYIIING
PAFF
MWAH HA HA HA HA! SO MUCH FOR YOUR SURPRISE ATTACK!!

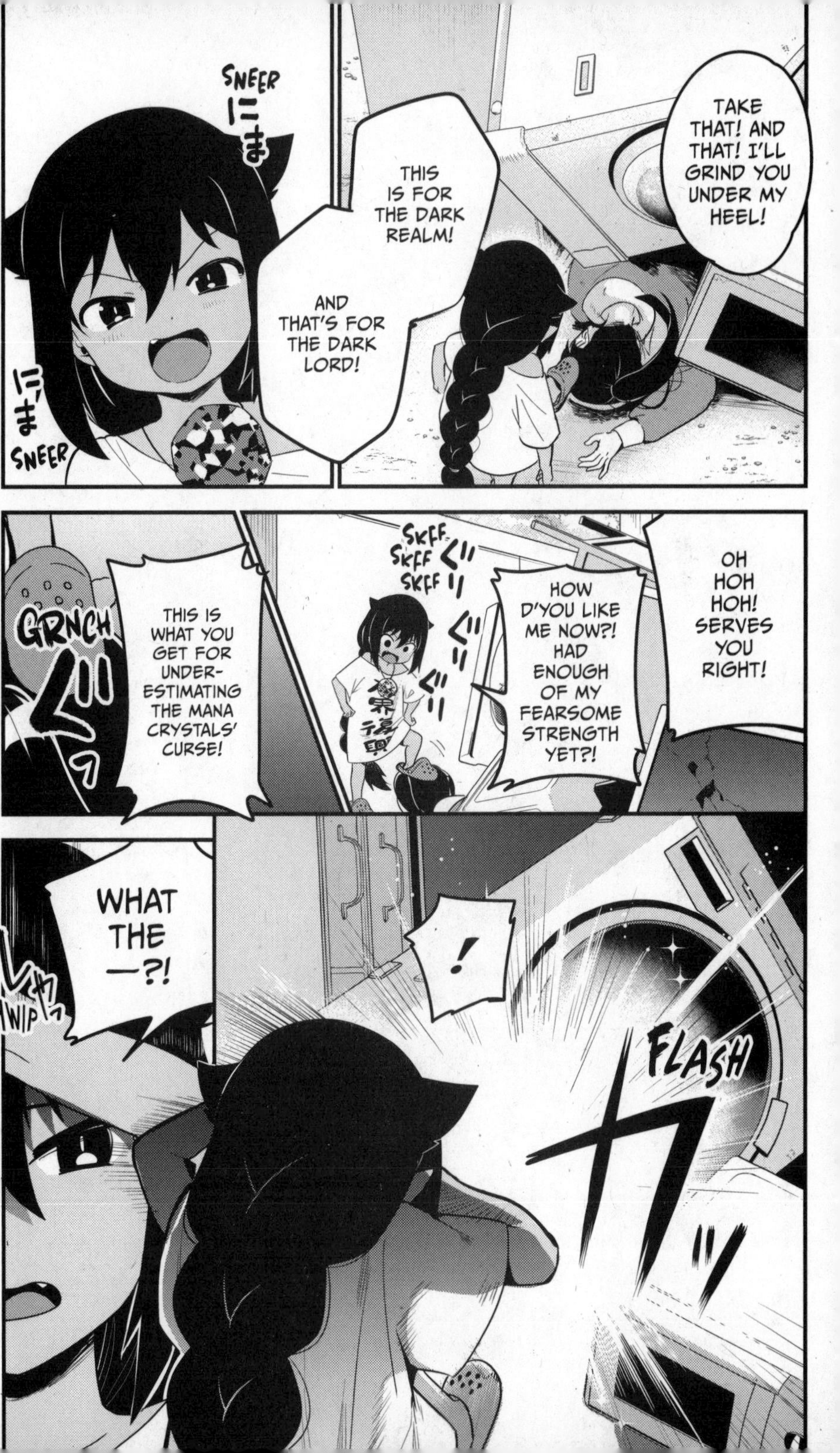
TAKE THAT! AND THAT! I'LL GRIND YOU UNDER MY HEEL!
THIS IS FOR THE DARK REALM!
AND THAT'S FOR THE DARK LORD!
SNEER にま
にま SNEER
OH HOH HOH! SERVES YOU RIGHT!
HOW D'YOU LIKE ME NOW?! HAD ENOUGH OF MY FEARSOME STRENGTH YET?!
SKFF SKFF SKFF
THIS IS WHAT YOU GET FOR UNDER-ESTIMATING THE MANA CRYSTALS' CURSE!
GRNCH
!
FLASH
カッ
WHAT THE—?!
SHWIP

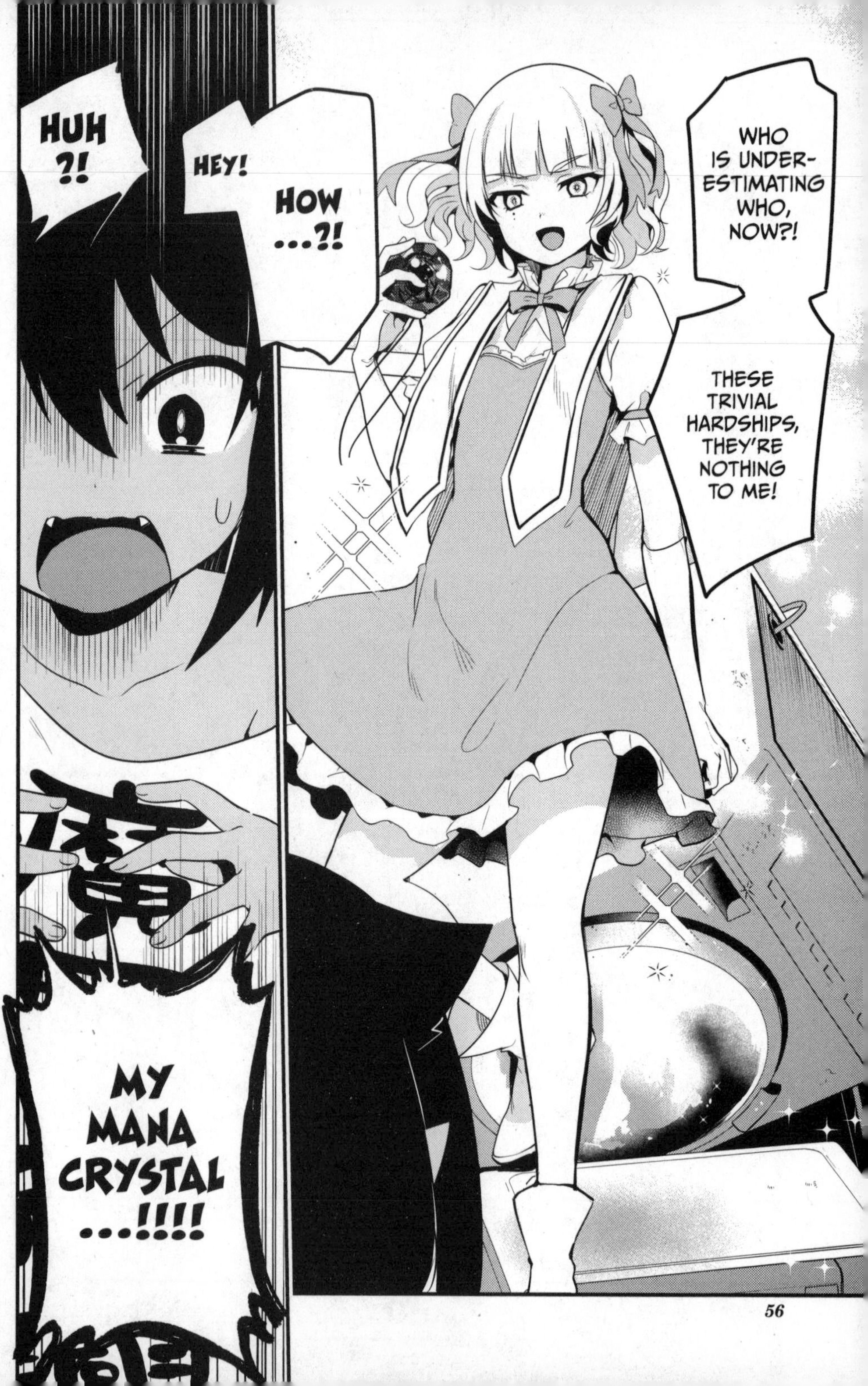
WHO IS UNDER-ESTIMATING WHO, NOW?!
THESE TRIVIAL HARDSHIPS, THEY'RE NOTHING TO ME!
HEY!
HOW ...?!
HUH ?!
MY MANA CRYSTAL ...!!!!

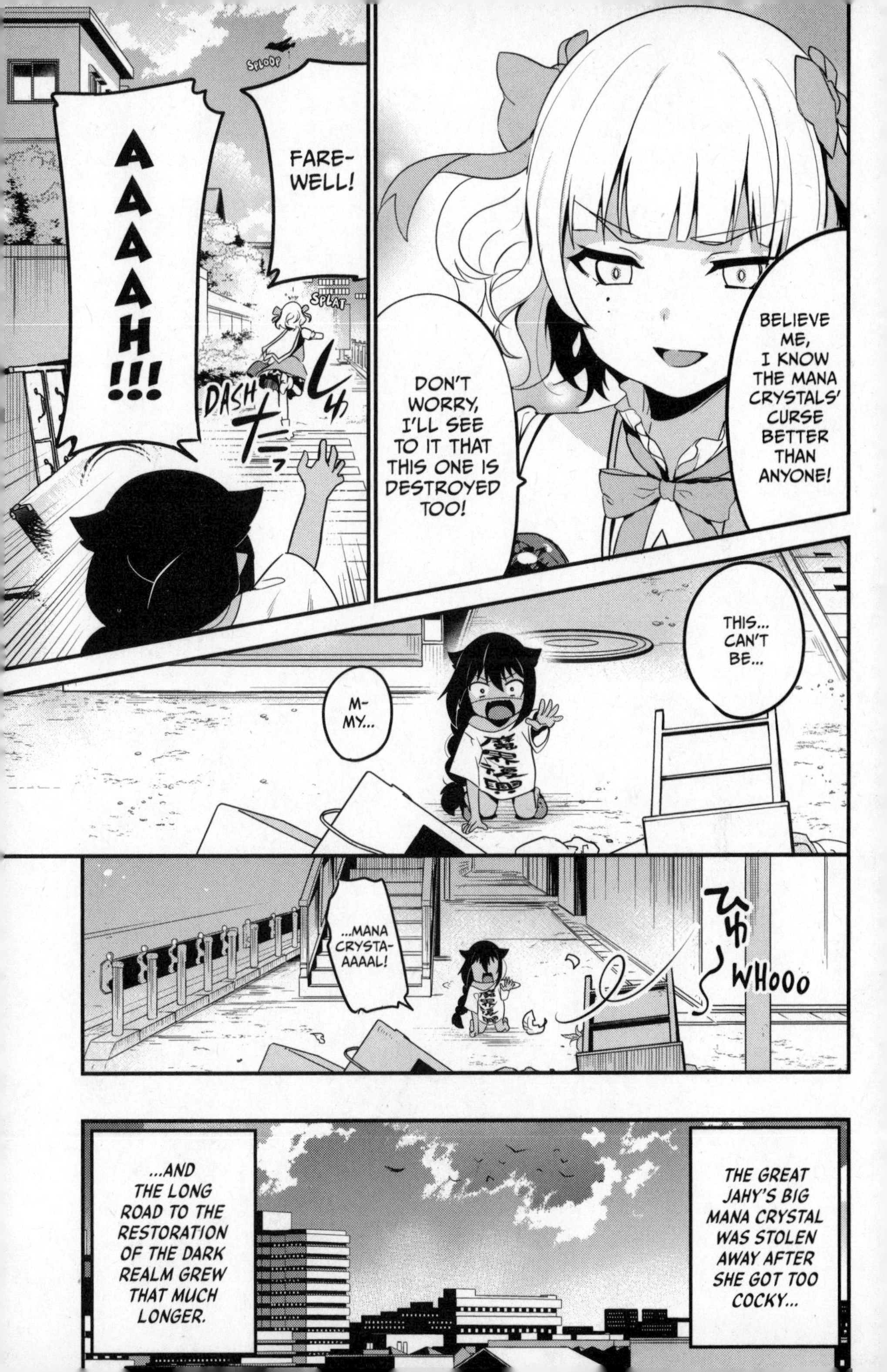
BELIEVE ME, I KNOW THE MANA CRYSTALS' CURSE BETTER THAN ANYONE!
DON'T WORRY, I'LL SEE TO IT THAT THIS ONE IS DESTROYED TOO!
SPLOOP
FARE-WELL!
SPLAT
DASH
AAAAH!!!
THIS... CAN'T BE...
M-MY...
WHOOO
...MANA CRYSTA-AAAAL!
THE GREAT JAHY'S BIG MANA CRYSTAL WAS STOLEN AWAY AFTER SHE GOT TOO COCKY...
...AND THE LONG ROAD TO THE RESTORATION OF THE DARK REALM GREW THAT MUCH LONGER.

The GREAT JAHY Will NOT Be DEFEATED!

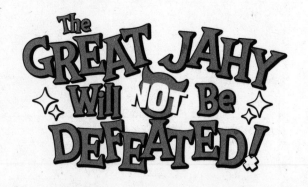

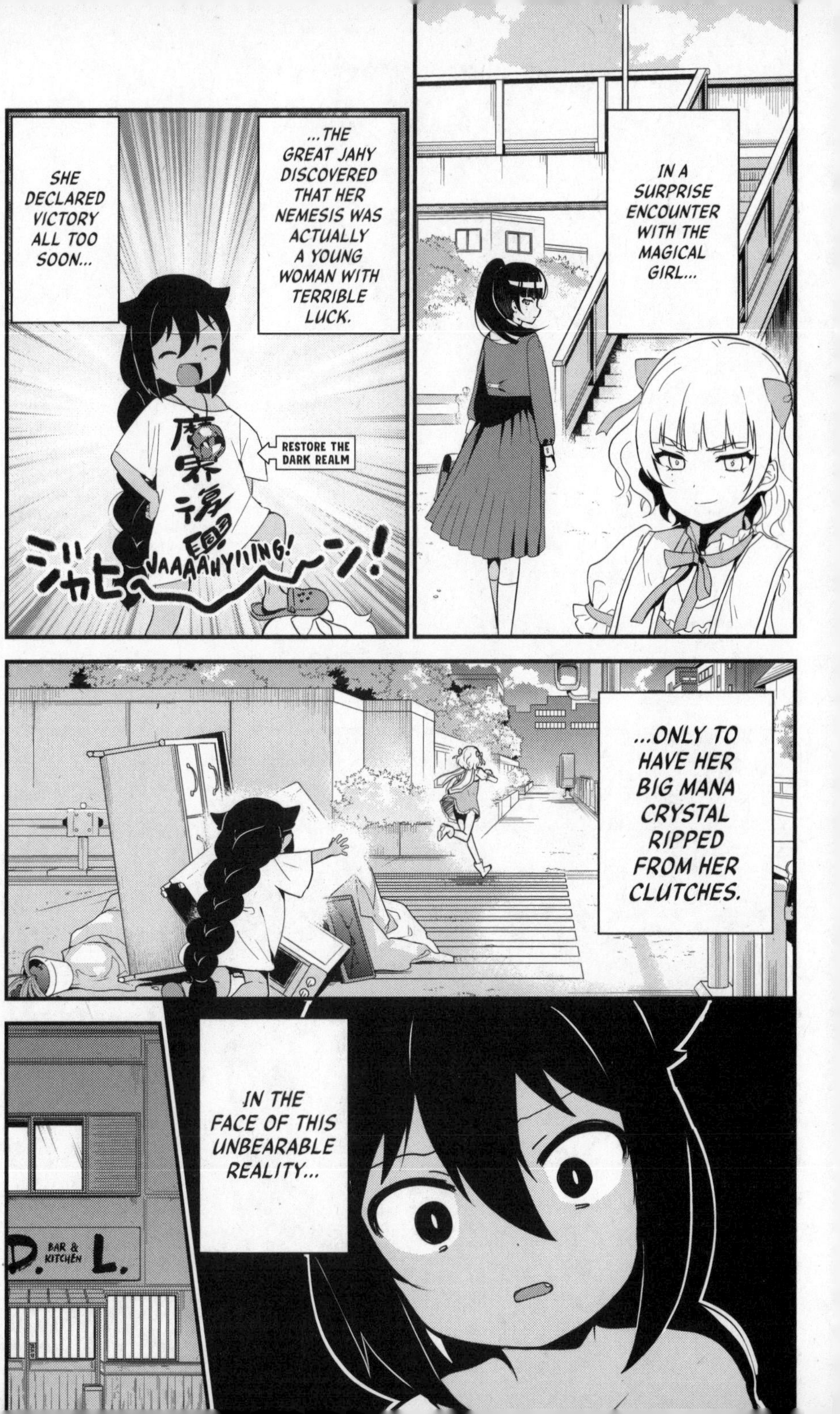
IN A SURPRISE ENCOUNTER WITH THE MAGICAL GIRL...
...THE GREAT JAHY DISCOVERED THAT HER NEMESIS WAS ACTUALLY A YOUNG WOMAN WITH TERRIBLE LUCK.
SHE DECLARED VICTORY ALL TOO SOON...
RESTORE THE DARK REALM
JAAAAHYIIING!
...ONLY TO HAVE HER BIG MANA CRYSTAL RIPPED FROM HER CLUTCHES.
IN THE FACE OF THIS UNBEARABLE REALITY...
D. BAR & KITCHEN L.

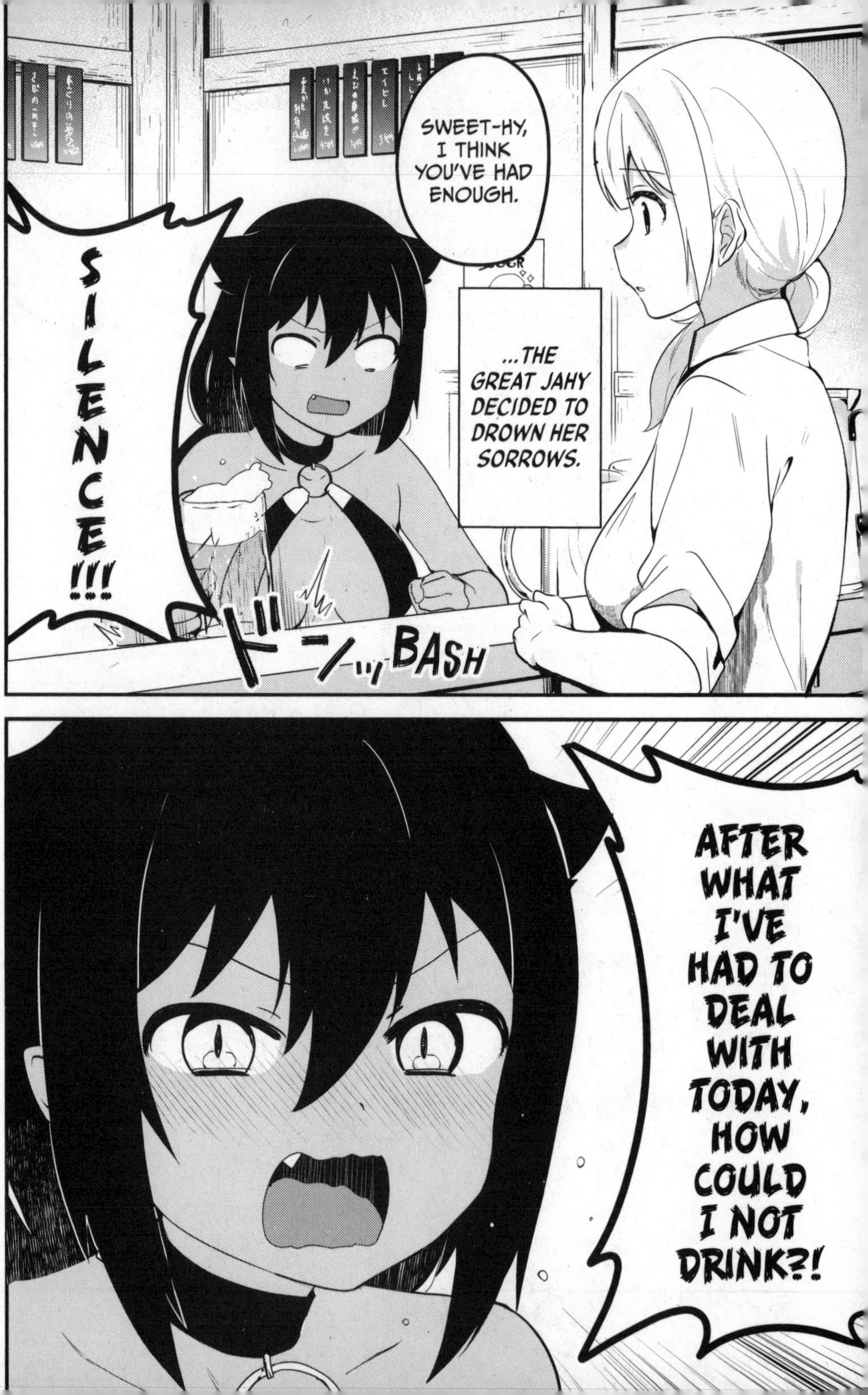
SWEET-HY, I THINK YOU'VE HAD ENOUGH.
...THE GREAT JAHY DECIDED TO DROWN HER SORROWS.
SILENCE!!!
BASH
AFTER WHAT I'VE HAD TO DEAL WITH TODAY, HOW COULD I NOT DRINK?!

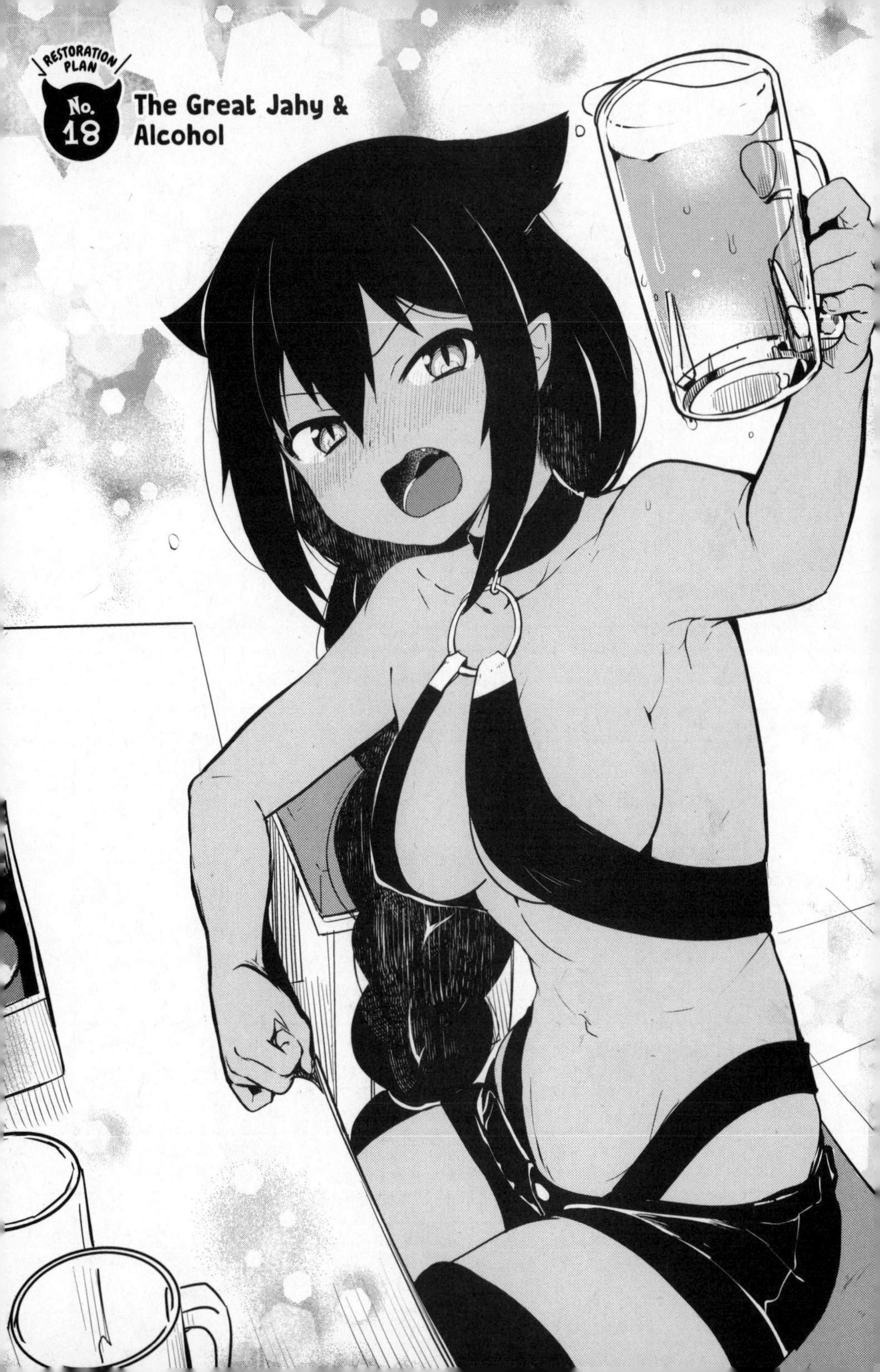
RESTORATION PLAN
No. 18
The Great Jahy & Alcohol

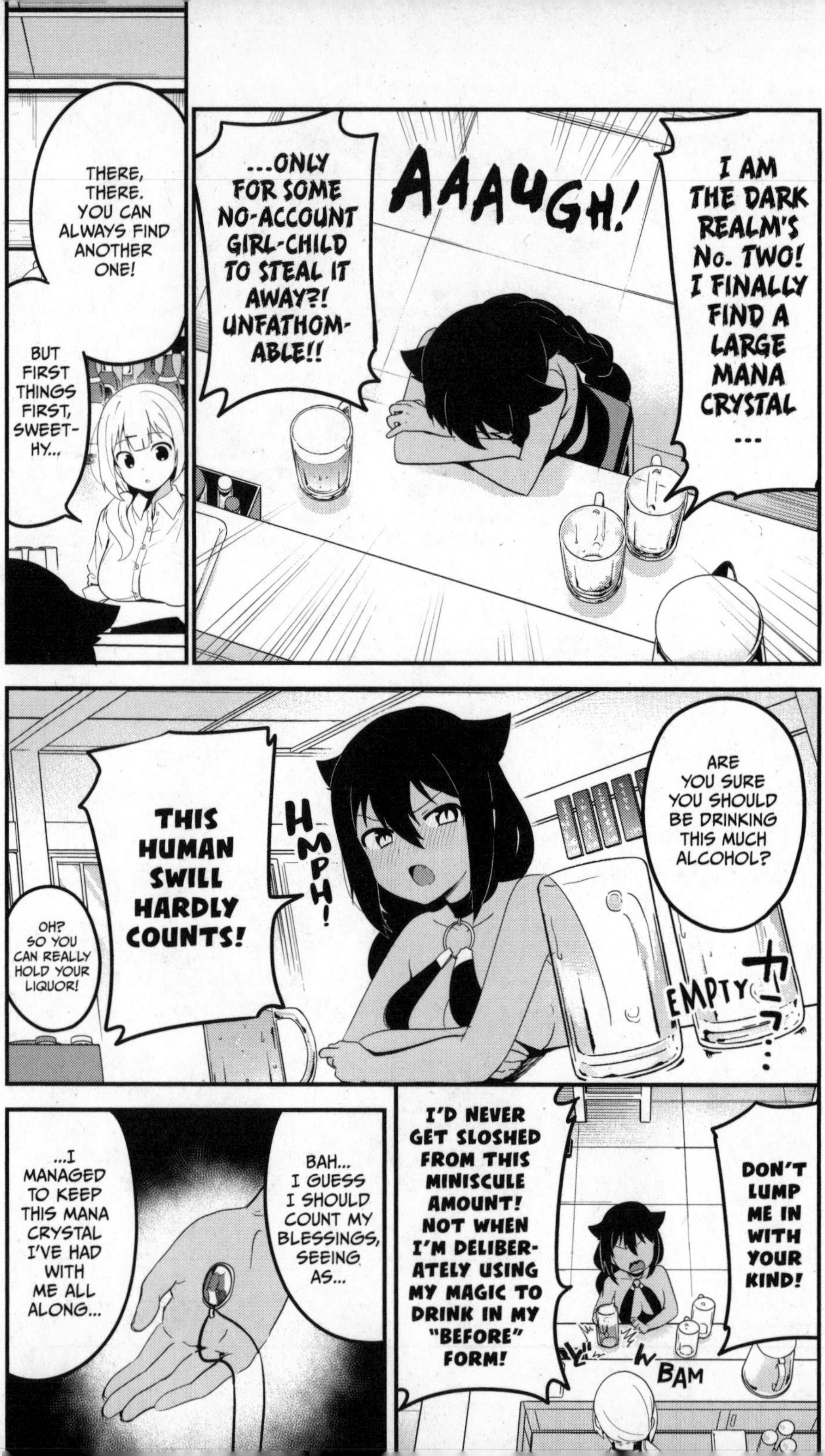
I AM THE DARK REALM'S No. TWO! I FINALLY FIND A LARGE MANA CRYSTAL ...
AAAUGH!
...ONLY FOR SOME NO-ACCOUNT GIRL-CHILD TO STEAL IT AWAY?! UNFATHOMABLE!!
THERE, THERE. YOU CAN ALWAYS FIND ANOTHER ONE!
BUT FIRST THINGS FIRST, SWEETHY...
ARE YOU SURE YOU SHOULD BE DRINKING THIS MUCH ALCOHOL?
EMPTY
HMPH!
THIS HUMAN SWILL HARDLY COUNTS!
OH? SO YOU CAN REALLY HOLD YOUR LIQUOR!
DON'T LUMP ME IN WITH YOUR KIND!
I'D NEVER GET SLOSHED FROM THIS MINISCULE AMOUNT! NOT WHEN I'M DELIBERATELY USING MY MAGIC TO DRINK IN MY "BEFORE" FORM!
BAM
BAH... I GUESS I SHOULD COUNT MY BLESSINGS, SEEING AS...
...I MANAGED TO KEEP THIS MANA CRYSTAL I'VE HAD WITH ME ALL ALONG...

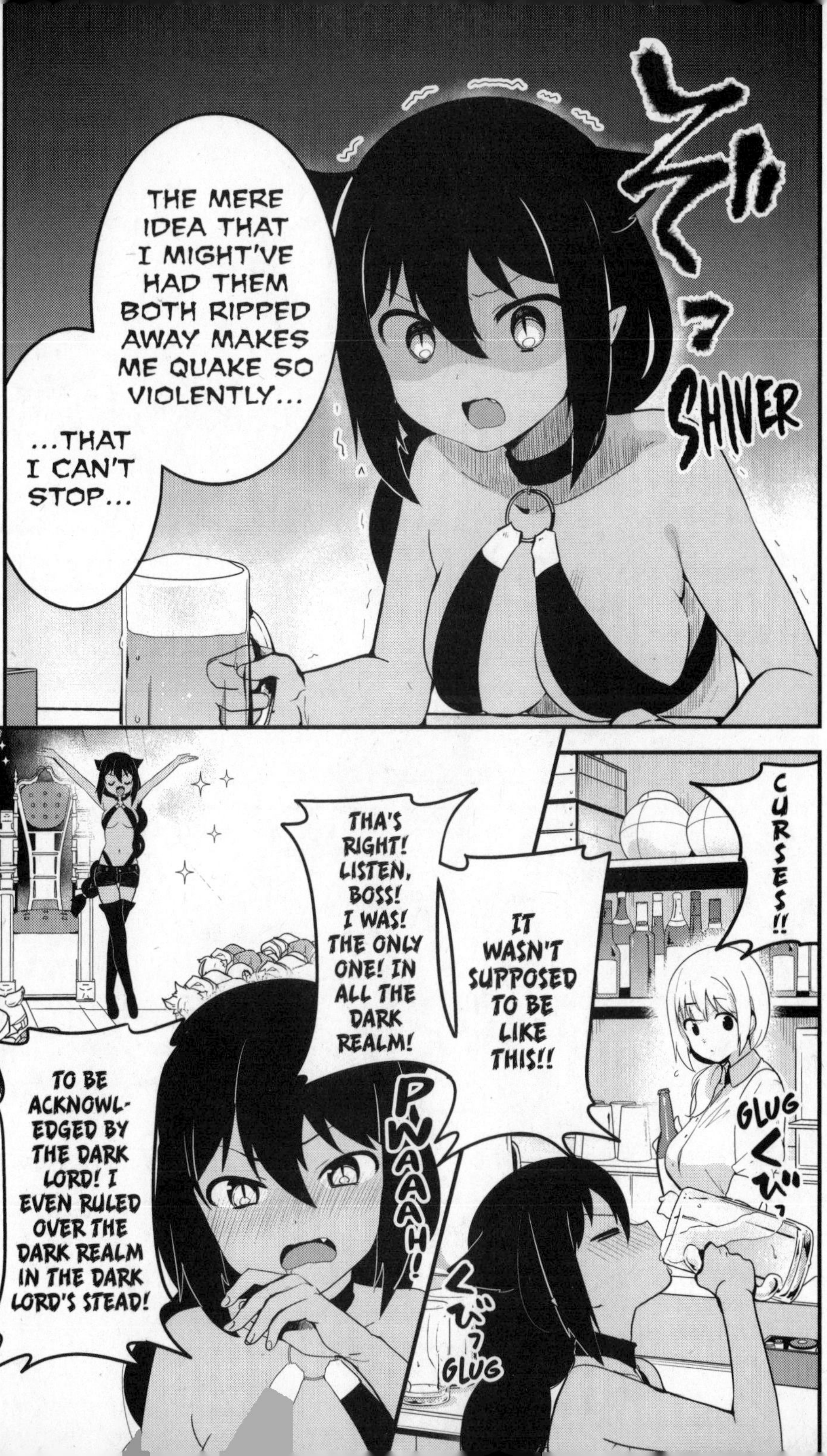
SHIVER
THE MERE IDEA THAT I MIGHT'VE HAD THEM BOTH RIPPED AWAY MAKES ME QUAKE SO VIOLENTLY...
...THAT I CAN'T STOP...
CURSES!!
IT WASN'T SUPPOSED TO BE LIKE THIS!!
THA'S RIGHT! LISTEN, BOSS! I WAS! THE ONLY ONE! IN ALL THE DARK REALM!
GLUG
PWAAAAH!
TO BE ACKNOWL-EDGED BY THE DARK LORD! I EVEN RULED OVER THE DARK REALM IN THE DARK LORD'S STEAD!
GLUG

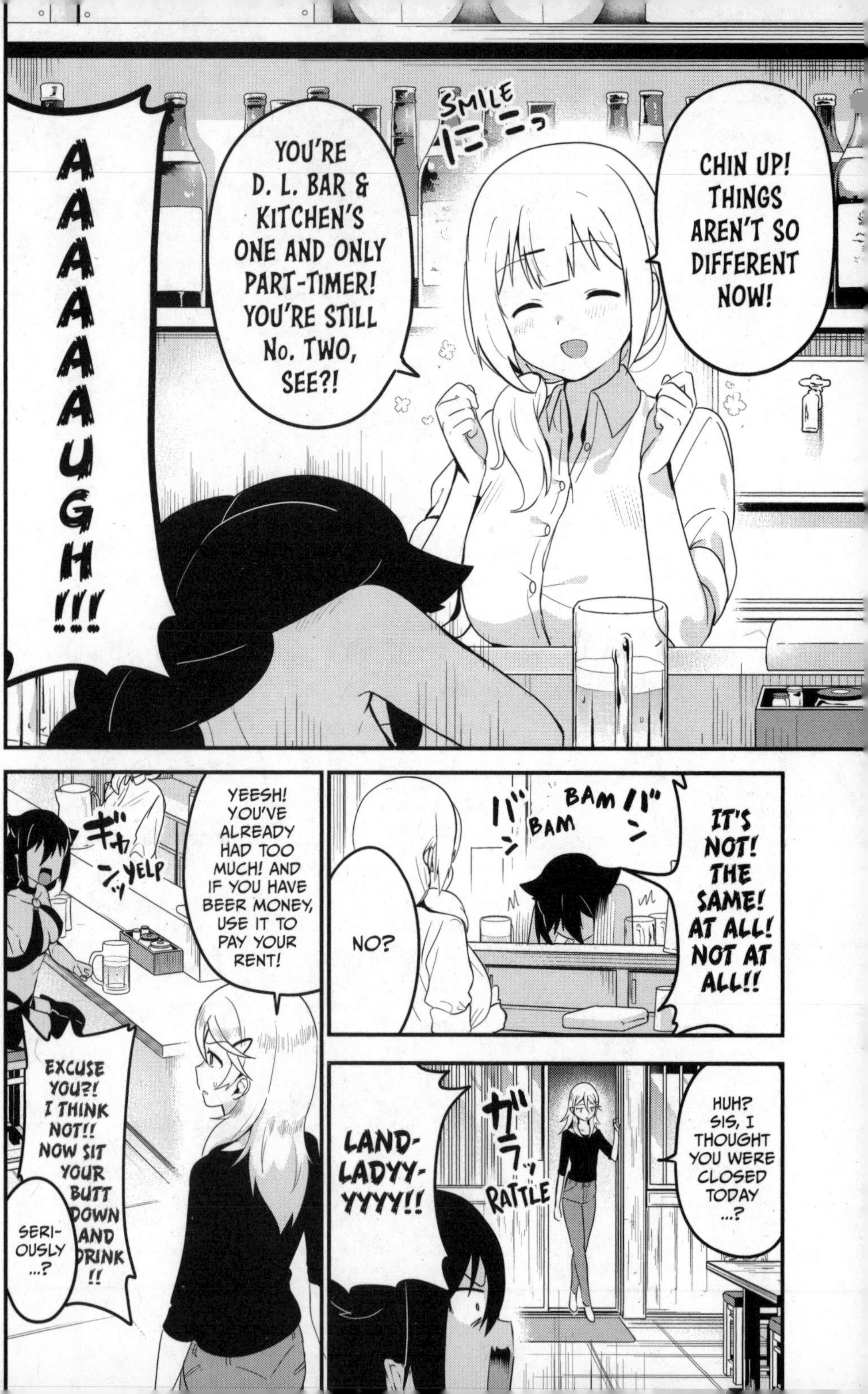
CHIN UP! THINGS AREN'T SO DIFFERENT NOW!
SMILE にこっ
YOU'RE D. L. BAR & KITCHEN'S ONE AND ONLY PART-TIMER! YOU'RE STILL No. TWO, SEE?!
AAAAAAAAUGH!!!
IT'S NOT! THE SAME! AT ALL! NOT AT ALL!!
バン BAM バン BAM
NO?
HUH? SIS, I THOUGHT YOU WERE CLOSED TODAY ...?
ガラッ RATTLE
LAND-LADYY-YYYY!!
YEESH! YOU'VE ALREADY HAD TOO MUCH! AND IF YOU HAVE BEER MONEY, USE IT TO PAY YOUR RENT!
ギャンッ YELP
EXCUSE YOU?! I THINK NOT!! NOW SIT YOUR BUTT DOWN AND DRINK!!
SERI-OUSLY ...?

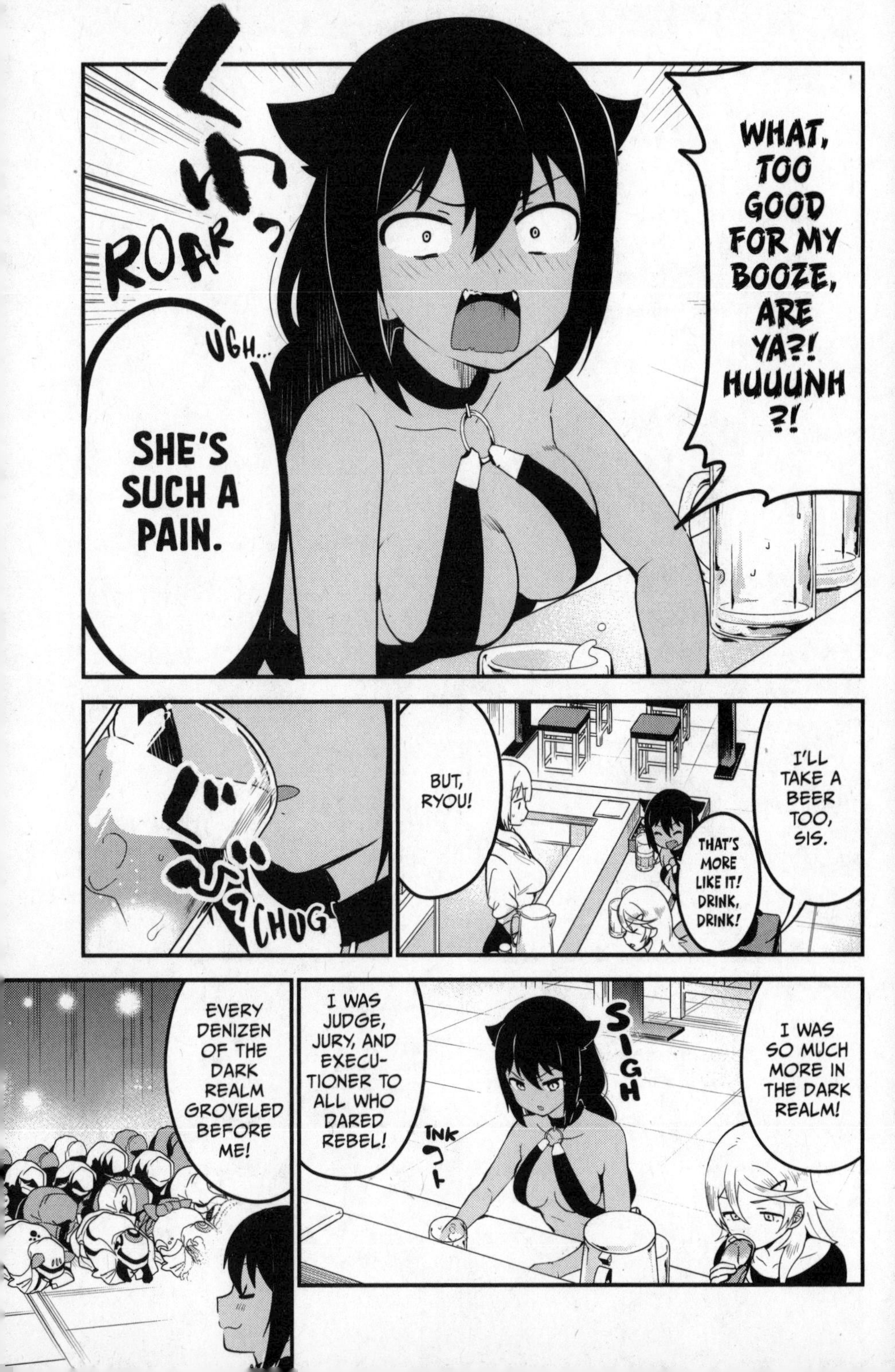
WHAT, TOO GOOD FOR MY BOOZE, ARE YA?! HUUUNH?!
ROAR
UGH... SHE'S SUCH A PAIN.
I'LL TAKE A BEER TOO, SIS.
THAT'S MORE LIKE IT! DRINK, DRINK!
BUT, RYOU!
CHUG
I WAS SO MUCH MORE IN THE DARK REALM!
SIGH
I WAS JUDGE, JURY, AND EXECUTIONER TO ALL WHO DARED REBEL!
TNK
EVERY DENIZEN OF THE DARK REALM GROVELED BEFORE ME!

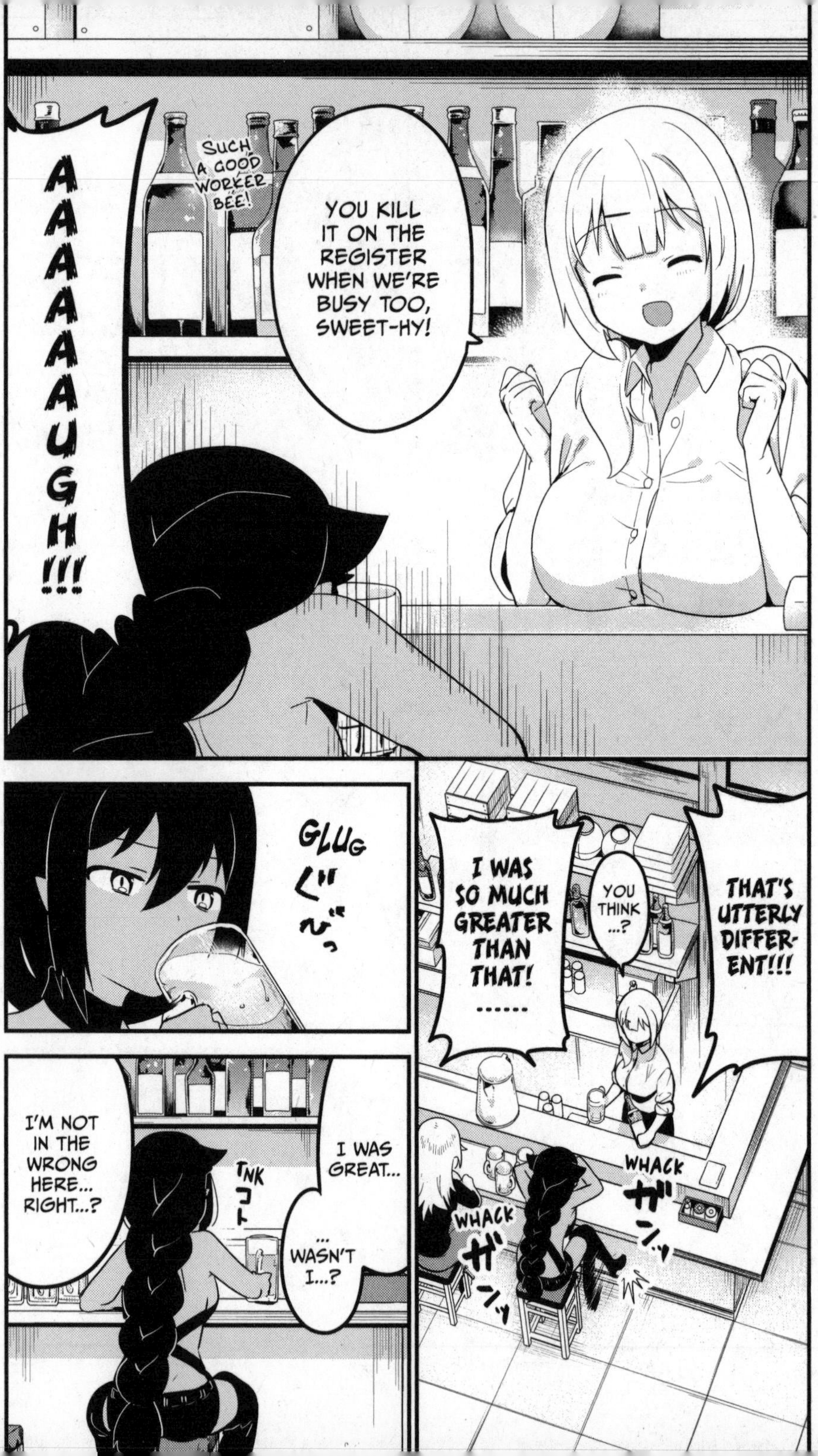

YOU KILL IT ON THE REGISTER WHEN WE'RE BUSY TOO, SWEET-HY!
SUCH A GOOD WORKER BEE!
AAAAAAUGH!!!
THAT'S UTTERLY DIFFER-ENT!!!
YOU THINK ...?
I WAS SO MUCH GREATER THAN THAT! ......
WHACK ガンッ
WHACK ガンッ
GLUG ぐびっ
I WAS GREAT...
... WASN'T I...?
TNK コト
I'M NOT IN THE WRONG HERE... RIGHT...?

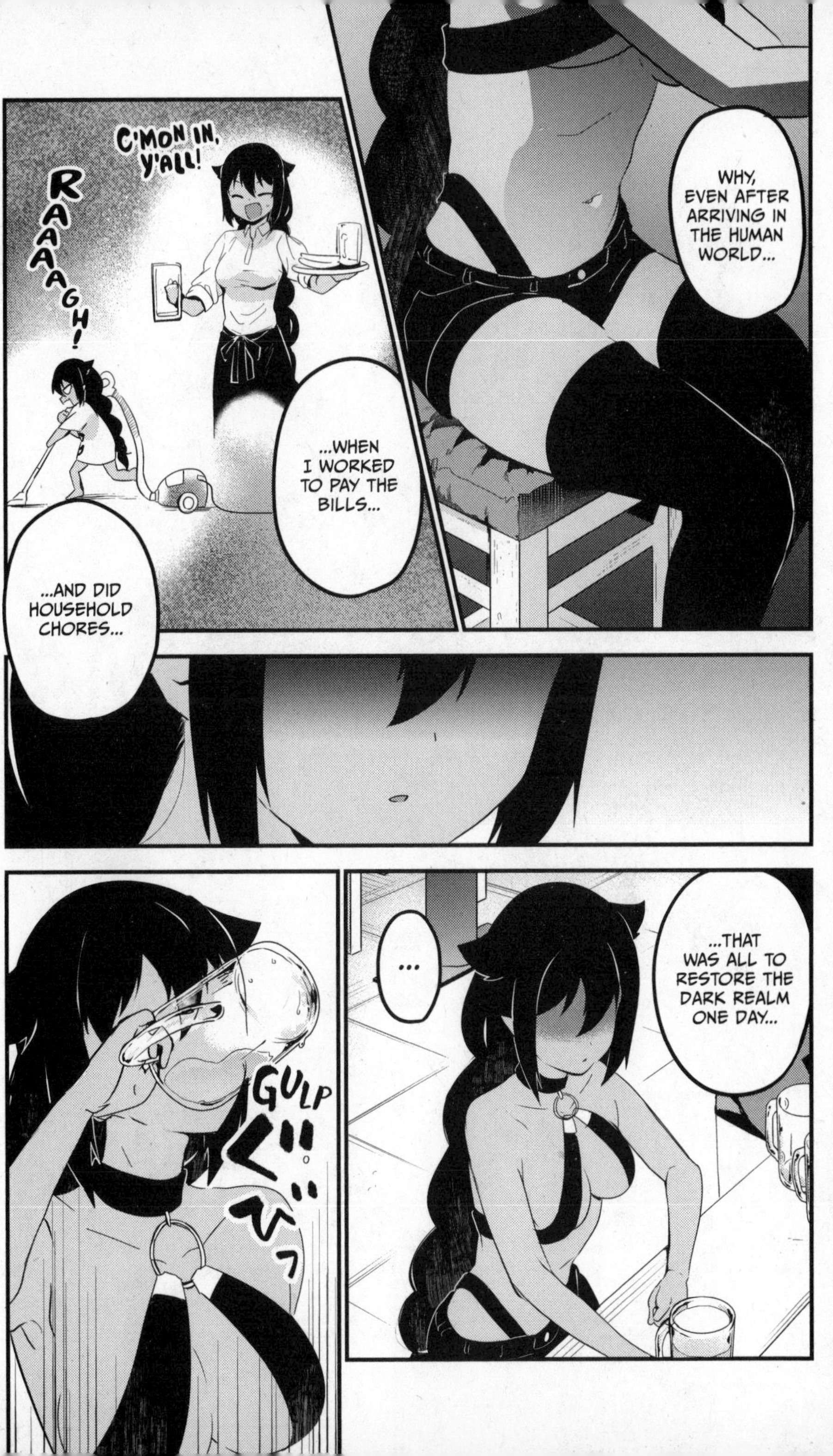
WHY, EVEN AFTER ARRIVING IN THE HUMAN WORLD...
C'MON IN, Y'ALL!
RAAAAAGH!
...WHEN I WORKED TO PAY THE BILLS...
...AND DID HOUSEHOLD CHORES...
...THAT WAS ALL TO RESTORE THE DARK REALM ONE DAY...
...
GULP

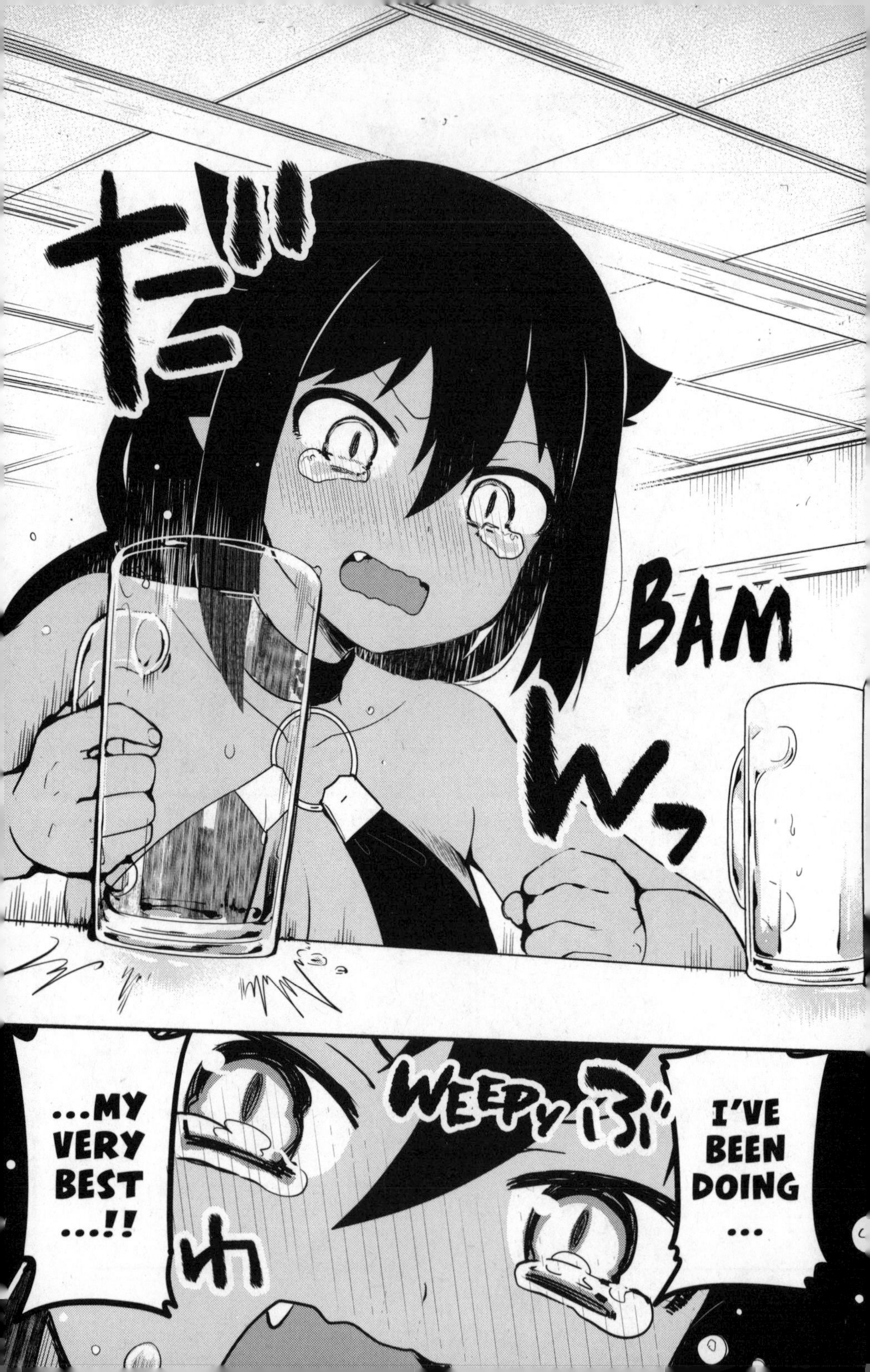
BAM
Wッ
だ
I'VE BEEN DOING ...
WEEPY ぶ
...MY VERY BEST ...!!

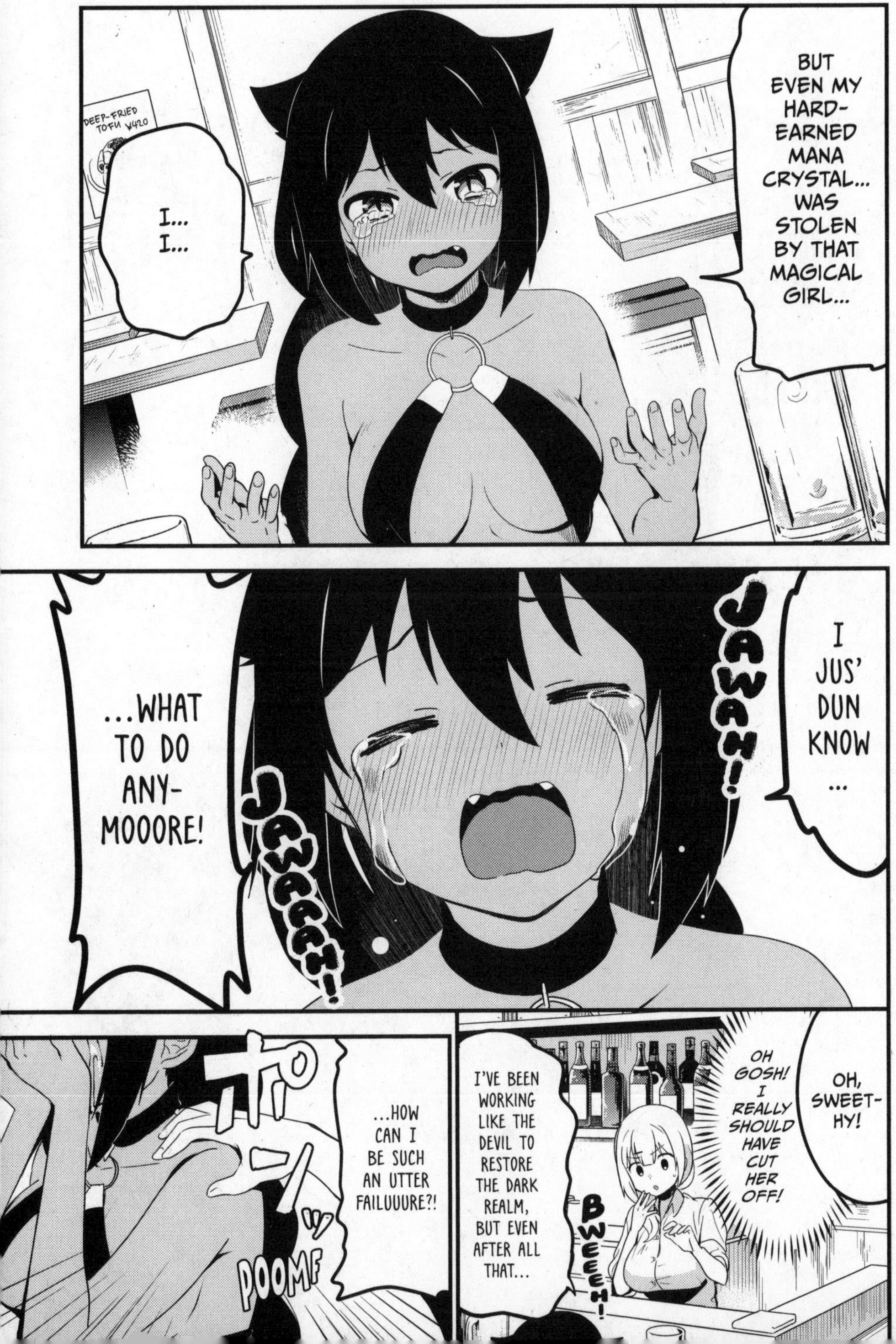
BUT EVEN MY HARD-EARNED MANA CRYSTAL... WAS STOLEN BY THAT MAGICAL GIRL...
DEEP-FRIED TOFU ¥420
I... I...
I JUS' DUN KNOW ...
JAWAH!
JAWAAAH!
...WHAT TO DO ANY-MOOORE!
OH, SWEET-HY!
OH GOSH! I REALLY SHOULD HAVE CUT HER OFF!
BWEEEH!
I'VE BEEN WORKING LIKE THE DEVIL TO RESTORE THE DARK REALM, BUT EVEN AFTER ALL THAT...
...HOW CAN I BE SUCH AN UTTER FAILUUURE?!
POOMF

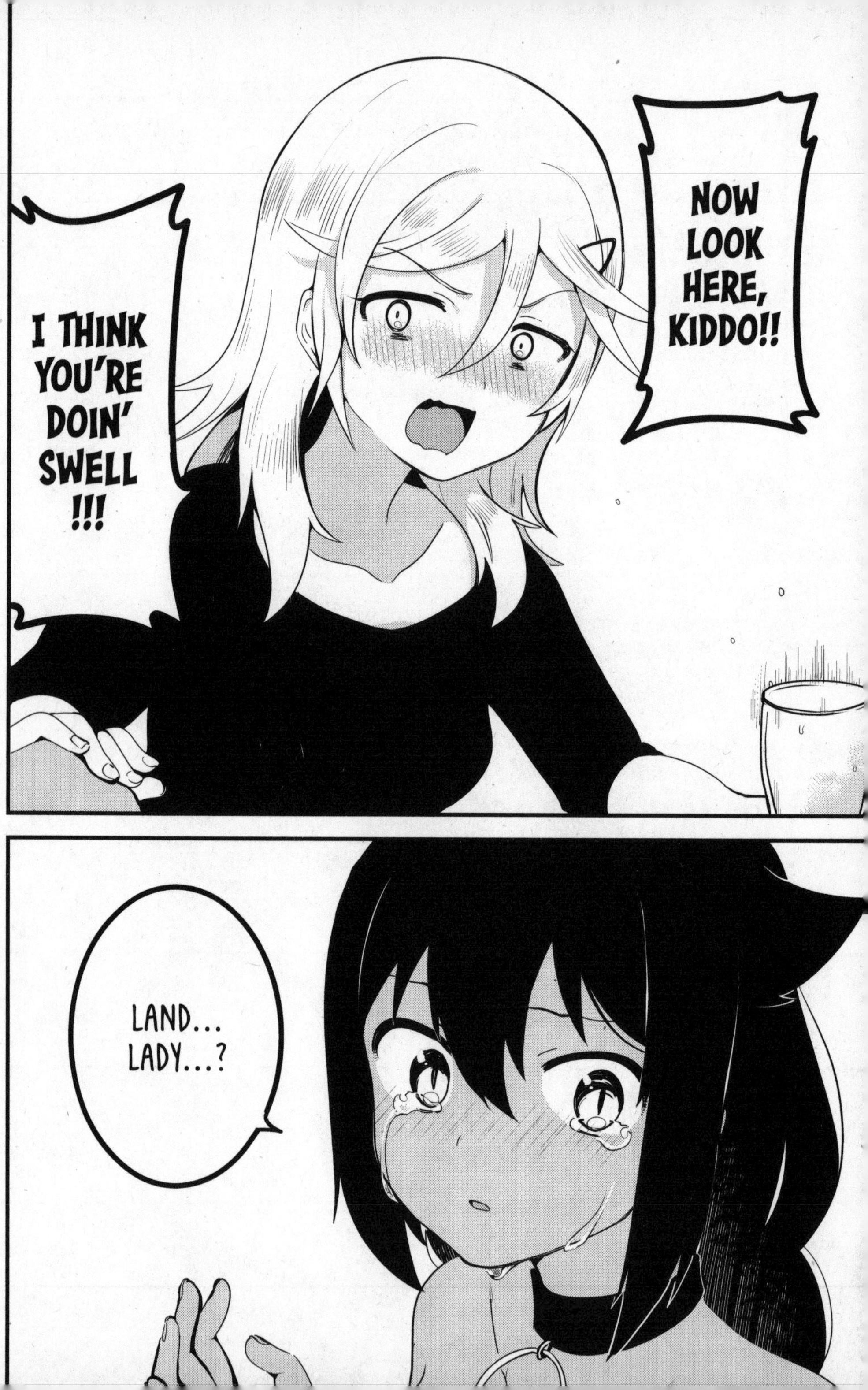
NOW LOOK HERE, KIDDO!!
I THINK YOU'RE DOIN' SWELL!!!
LAND... LADY...?

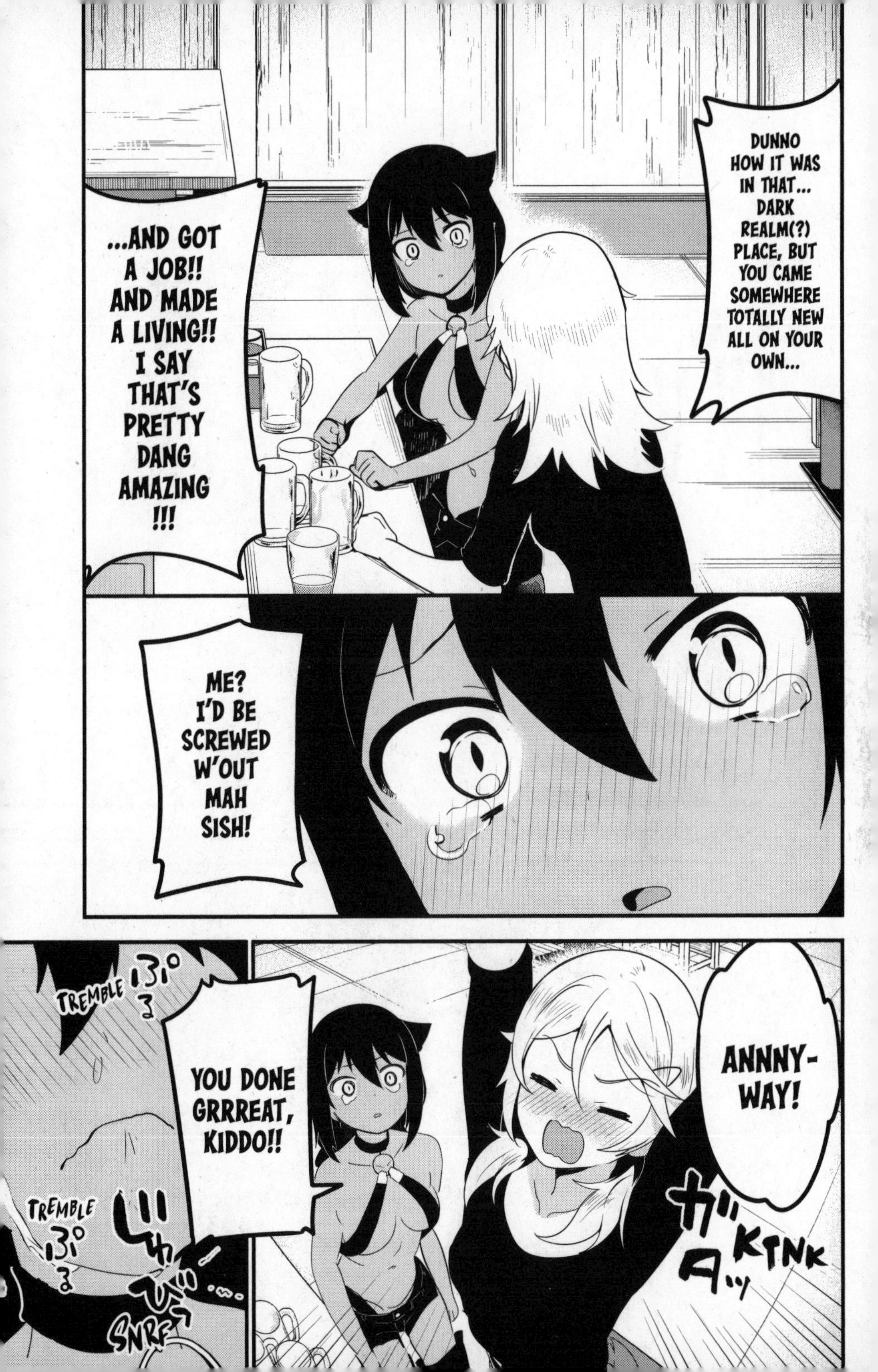
DUNNO HOW IT WAS IN THAT... DARK REALM(?) PLACE, BUT YOU CAME SOMEWHERE TOTALLY NEW ALL ON YOUR OWN...
...AND GOT A JOB!! AND MADE A LIVING!! I SAY THAT'S PRETTY DANG AMAZING !!!
ME? I'D BE SCREWED W'OUT MAH SISH!
ANNNY-WAY!
KTNK
YOU DONE GRRREAT, KIDDO!!
TREMBLE
TREMBLE
SNRF

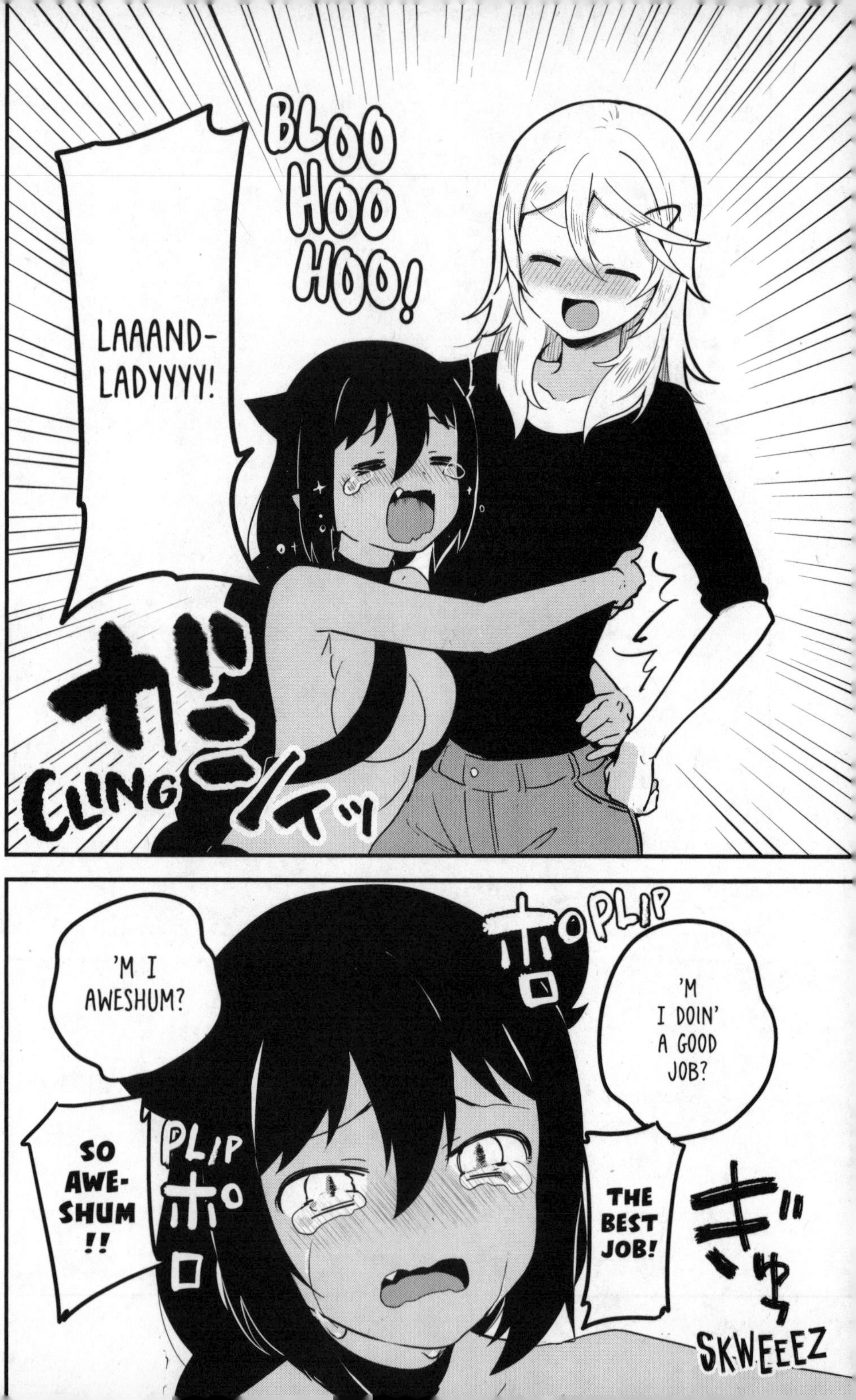
BLOO HOO HOO!
LAAAND-LADYYYY!
CLING
PLIP
'M I DOIN' A GOOD JOB?
'M I AWESHUM?
THE BEST JOB!
SKWEEEZ
PLIP
SO AWE-SHUM!!

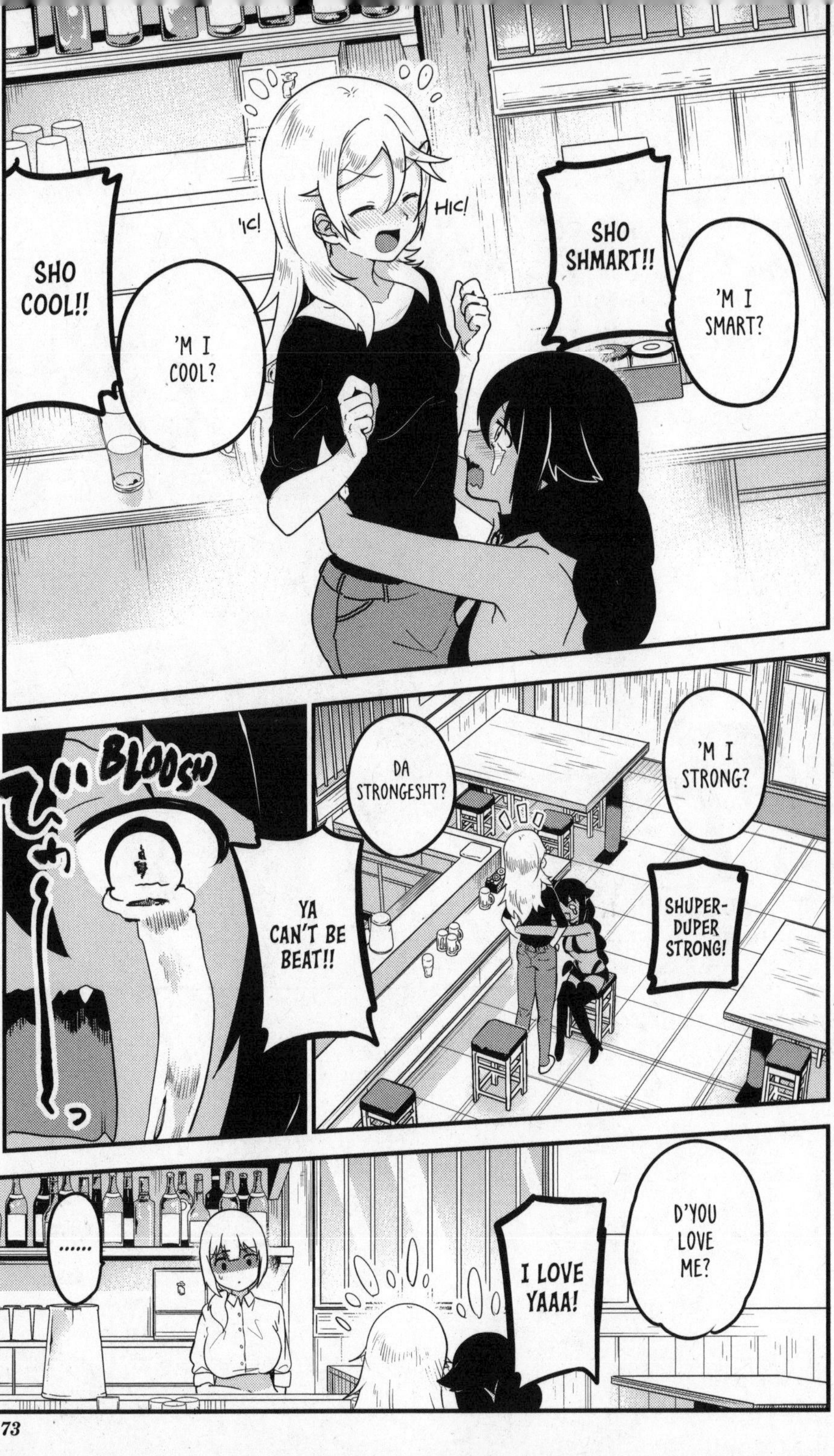
'M I SMART?
SHO SHMART!!
HIC!
'IC!
'M I COOL?
SHO COOL!!
'M I STRONG?
SHUPER-DUPER STRONG!
DA STRONGESHT?
YA CAN'T BE BEAT!!
BLOOSH
D'YOU LOVE ME?
I LOVE YAAA!
......

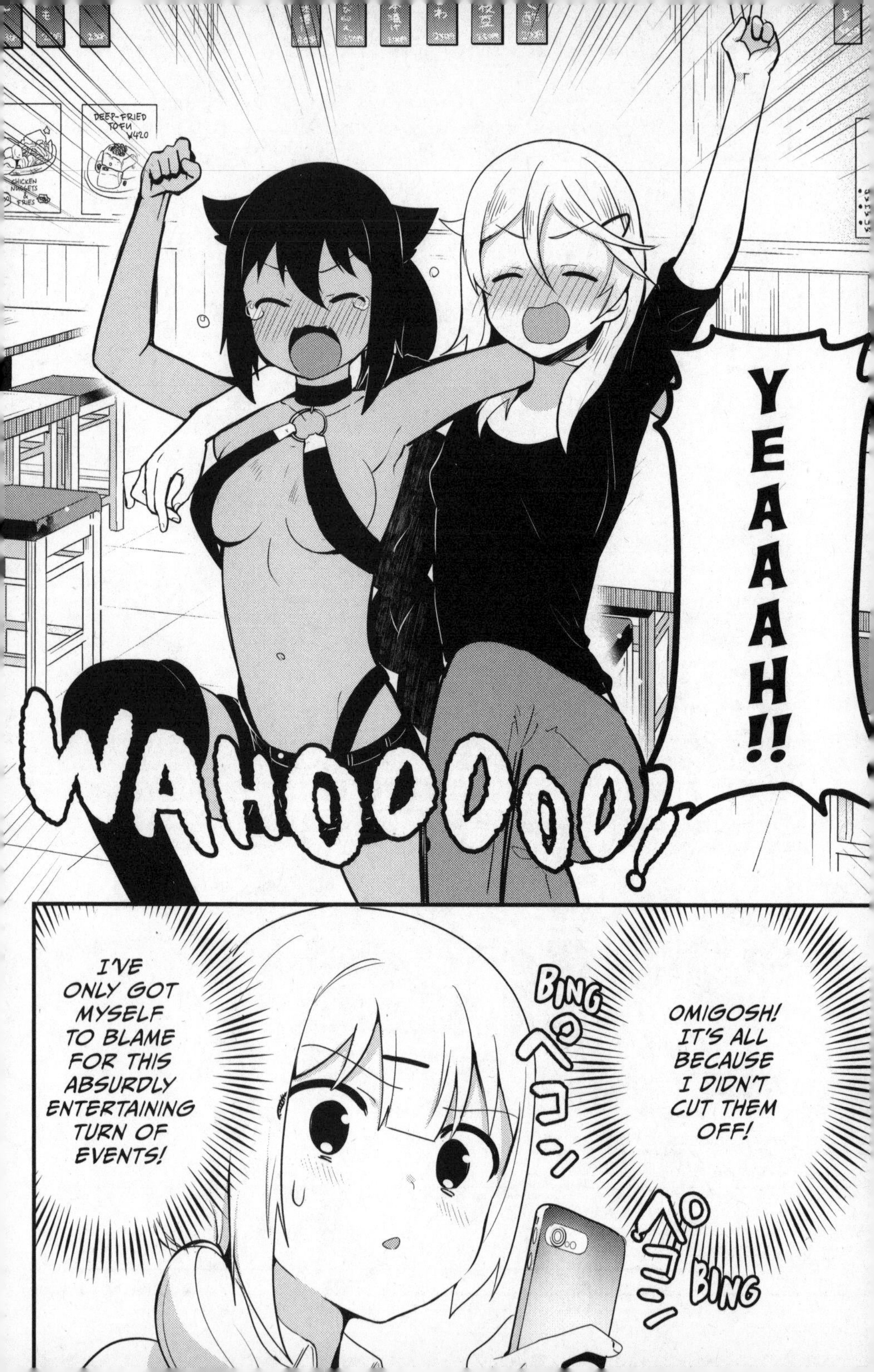
DEEP-FRIED TOFU ¥420
CHICKEN NUGGETS & FRIES
YEAAAAH!!
WAHOOOOOO!
OMIGOSH! IT'S ALL BECAUSE I DIDN'T CUT THEM OFF!
BING
BING
I'VE ONLY GOT MYSELF TO BLAME FOR THIS ABSURDLY ENTERTAINING TURN OF EVENTS!

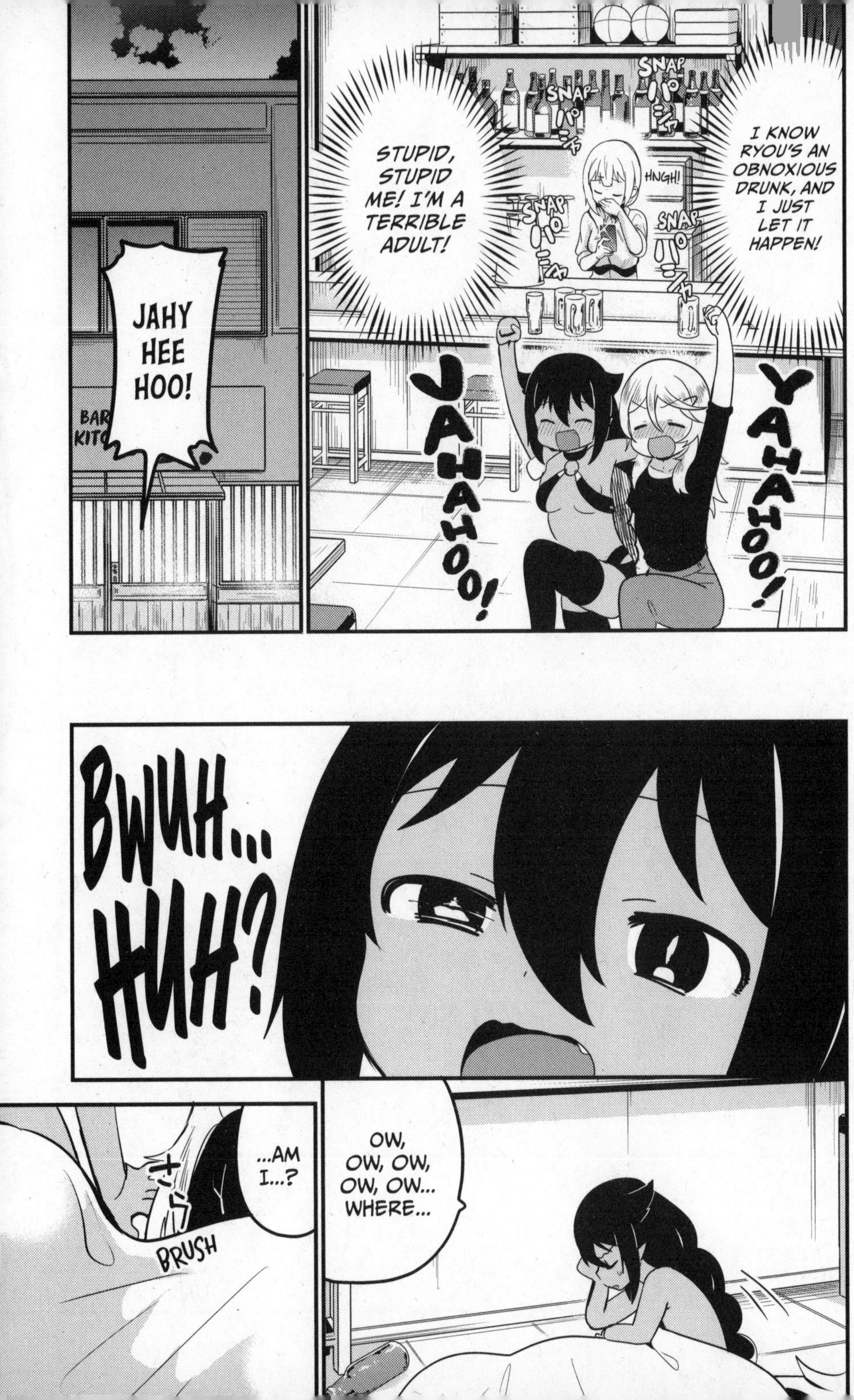

I KNOW RYOU'S AN OBNOXIOUS DRUNK, AND I JUST LET IT HAPPEN!
SNAP
SNAP
HNGH!
SNAP
SNAP
STUPID, STUPID ME! I'M A TERRIBLE ADULT!
YAHAHOO!
JAHAHOO!
JAHY HEE HOO!
BWUH... HUH?
OW, OW, OW, OW, OW... WHERE...
...AM I...?
BRUSH

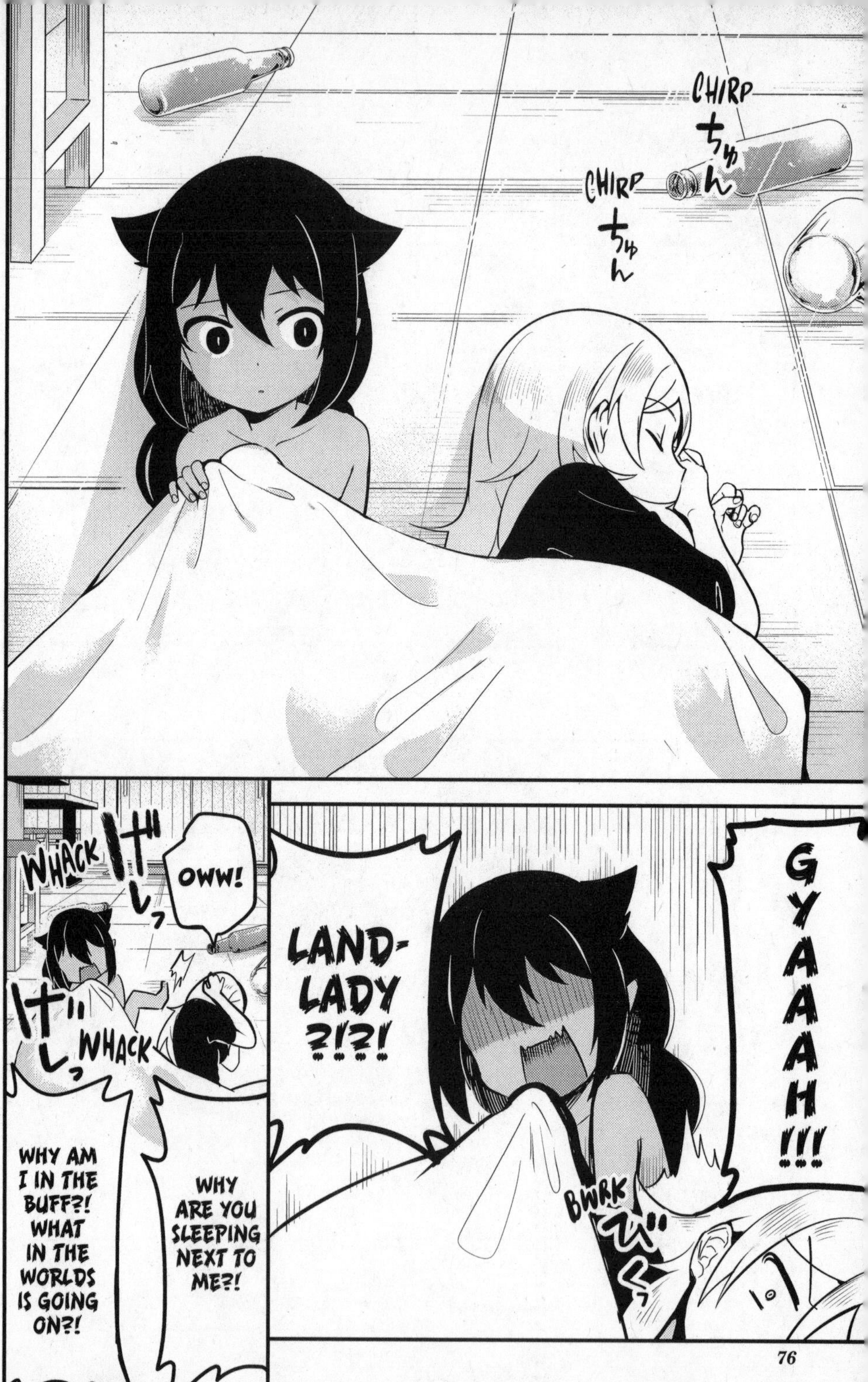
CHIRP
ちゅん
CHIRP
ちゅん
GYAAAAH!!!
BWRK
びくっ
LAND-LADY?!?!
WHACK
げしっ
OWW!
げしっ
WHACK
WHY ARE YOU SLEEPING NEXT TO ME?!
WHY AM I IN THE BUFF?! WHAT IN THE WORLDS IS GOING ON?!

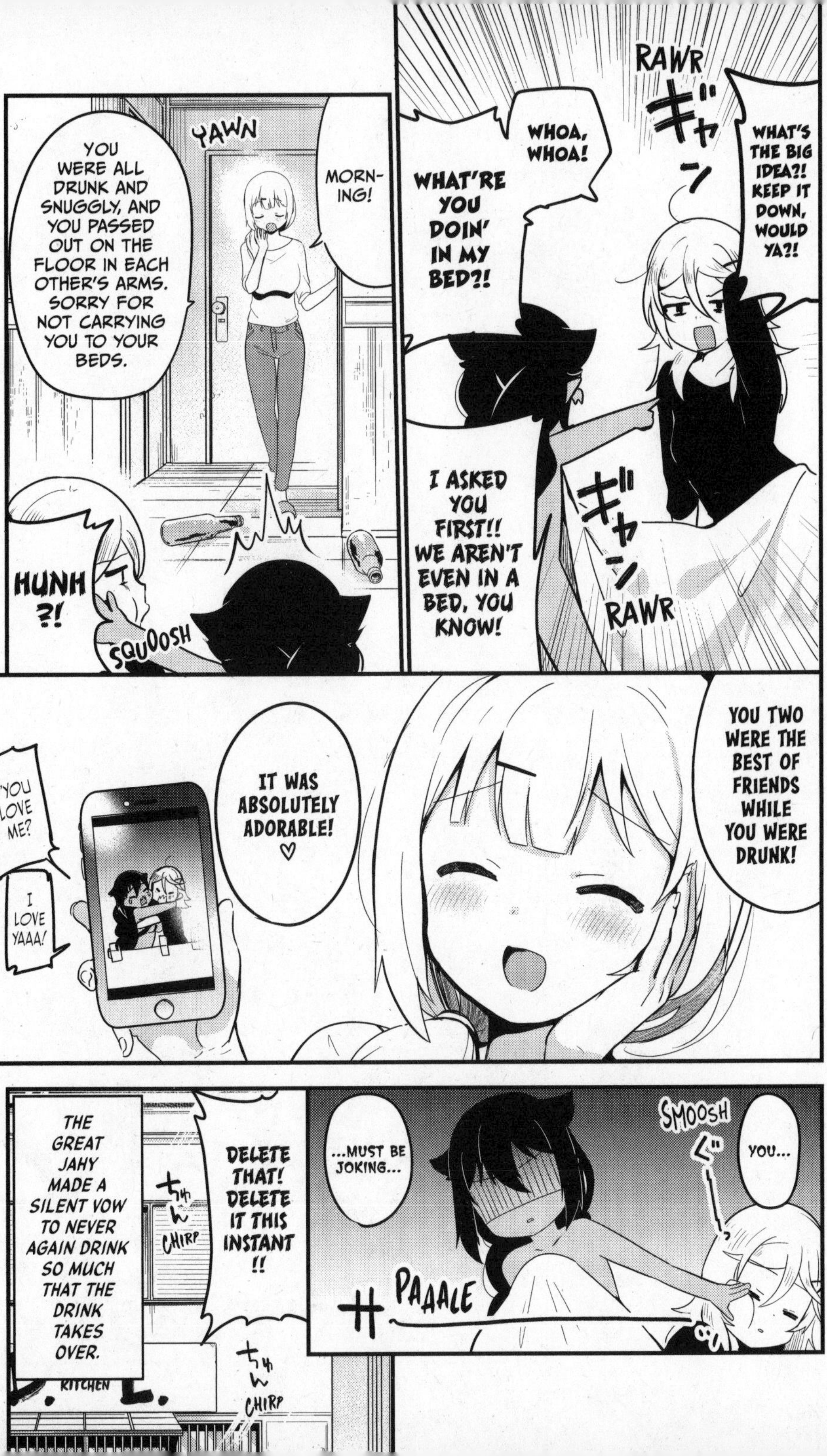
RAWR
ギャン
WHAT'S THE BIG IDEA?! KEEP IT DOWN, WOULD YA?!
WHOA, WHOA!
WHAT'RE YOU DOIN' IN MY BED?!
ギャン
RAWR
I ASKED YOU FIRST!! WE AREN'T EVEN IN A BED, YOU KNOW!
MORN-ING!
YAWN
YOU WERE ALL DRUNK AND SNUGGLY, AND YOU PASSED OUT ON THE FLOOR IN EACH OTHER'S ARMS. SORRY FOR NOT CARRYING YOU TO YOUR BEDS.
HUNH ?!
SQUOOSH
YOU TWO WERE THE BEST OF FRIENDS WHILE YOU WERE DRUNK!
IT WAS ABSOLUTELY ADORABLE! ♡
D'YOU LOVE ME?
I LOVE YAAA!
YOU...
SMOOSH
ぐー
...MUST BE JOKING...
PAAALE
DELETE THAT! DELETE IT THIS INSTANT !!
ちゅん
CHIRP
THE GREAT JAHY MADE A SILENT VOW TO NEVER AGAIN DRINK SO MUCH THAT THE DRINK TAKES OVER.
KITCHEN
ちゅん
CHIRP

The GREAT JAHY Will NOT Be DEFEATED!

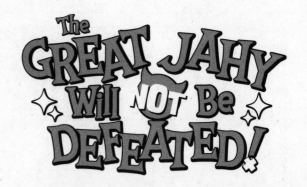

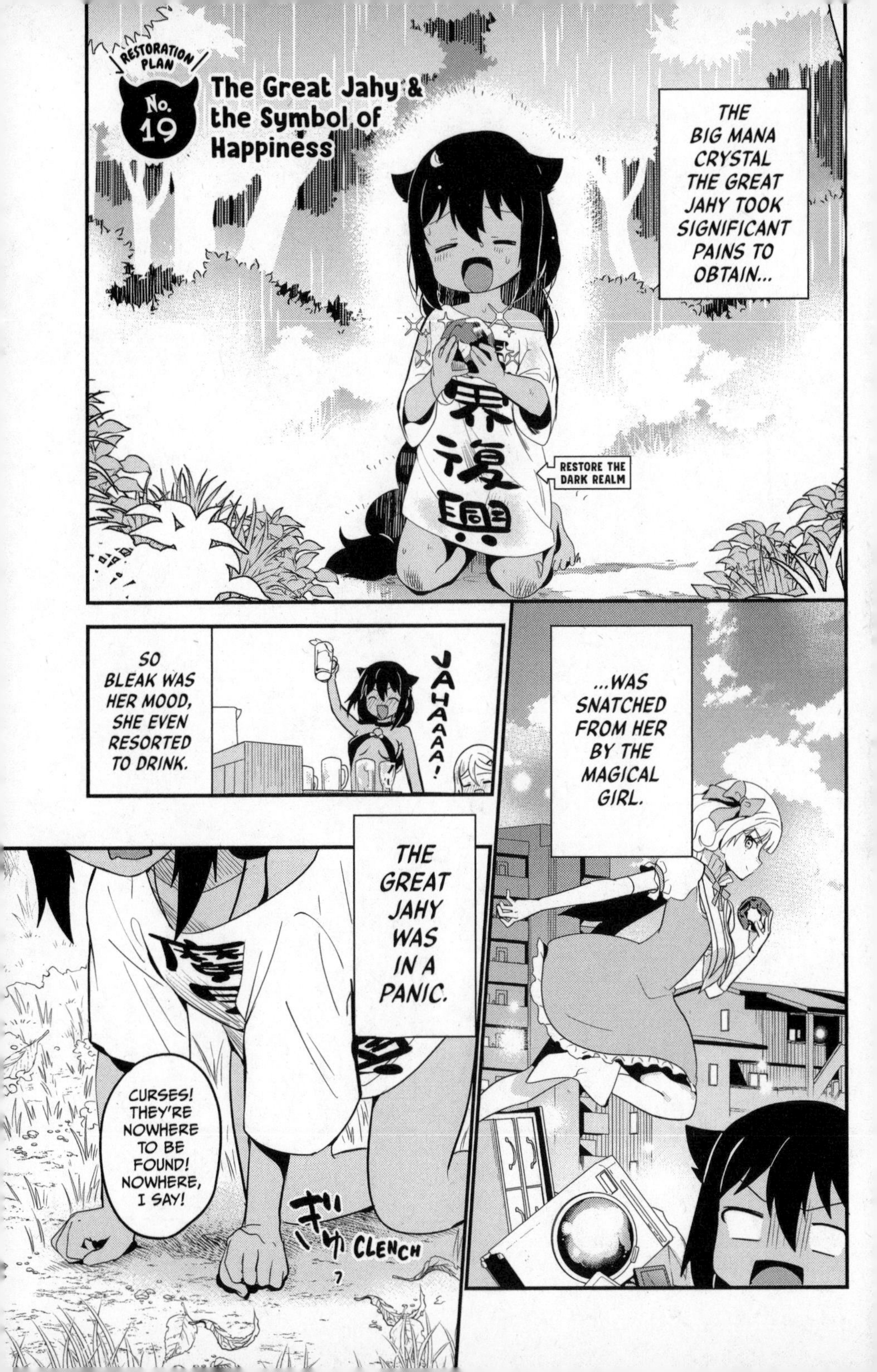
RESTORATION PLAN
No. 19
The Great Jahy & the Symbol of Happiness
THE BIG MANA CRYSTAL THE GREAT JAHY TOOK SIGNIFICANT PAINS TO OBTAIN...
RESTORE THE DARK REALM
...WAS SNATCHED FROM HER BY THE MAGICAL GIRL.
SO BLEAK WAS HER MOOD, SHE EVEN RESORTED TO DRINK.
JAHAAAAA!
THE GREAT JAHY WAS IN A PANIC.
CURSES! THEY'RE NOWHERE TO BE FOUND! NOWHERE, I SAY!
ぎゅ CLENCH

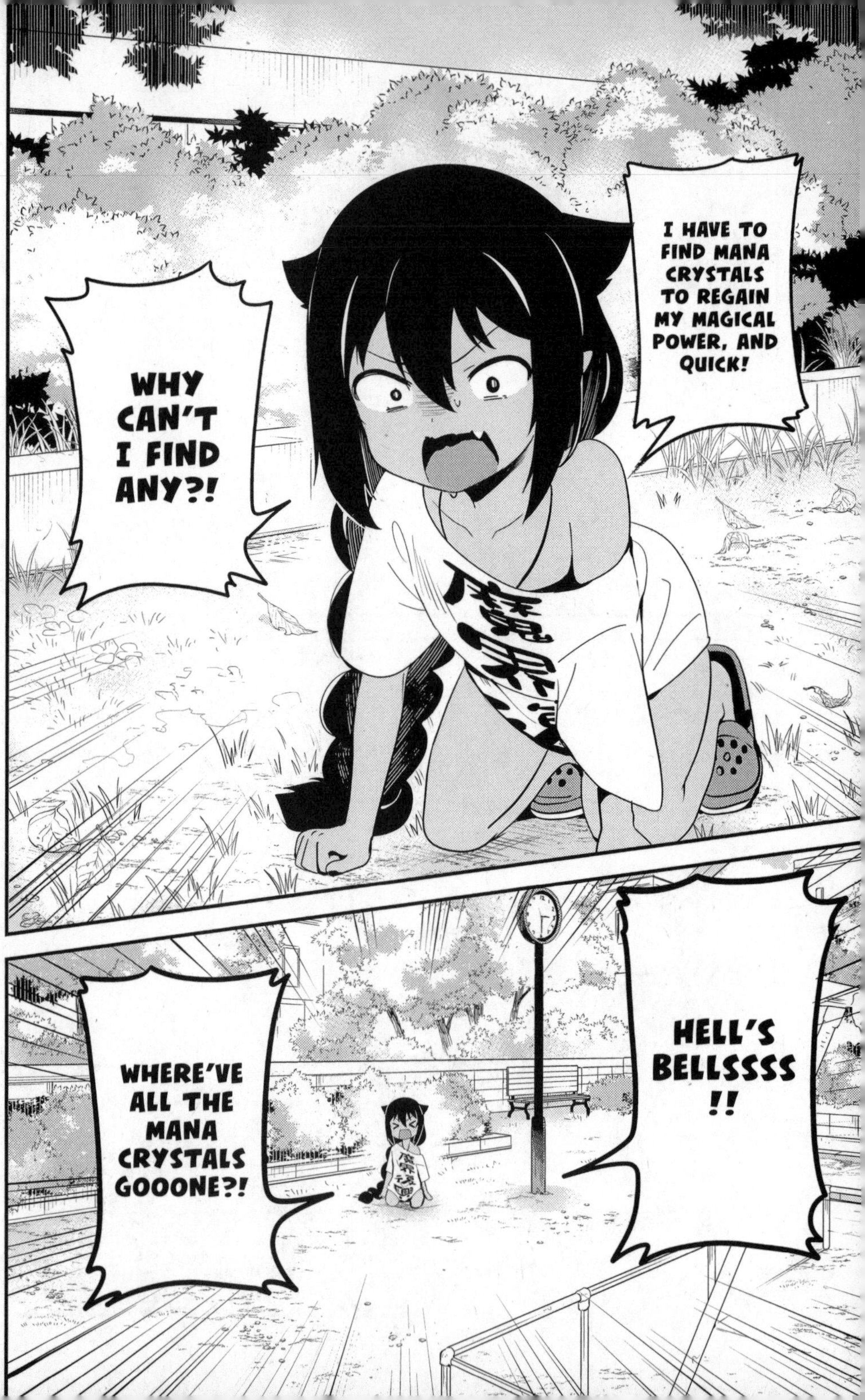
I HAVE TO FIND MANA CRYSTALS TO REGAIN MY MAGICAL POWER, AND QUICK!
WHY CAN'T I FIND ANY?!
HELL'S BELLSSSS !!
WHERE'VE ALL THE MANA CRYSTALS GOOONE?!

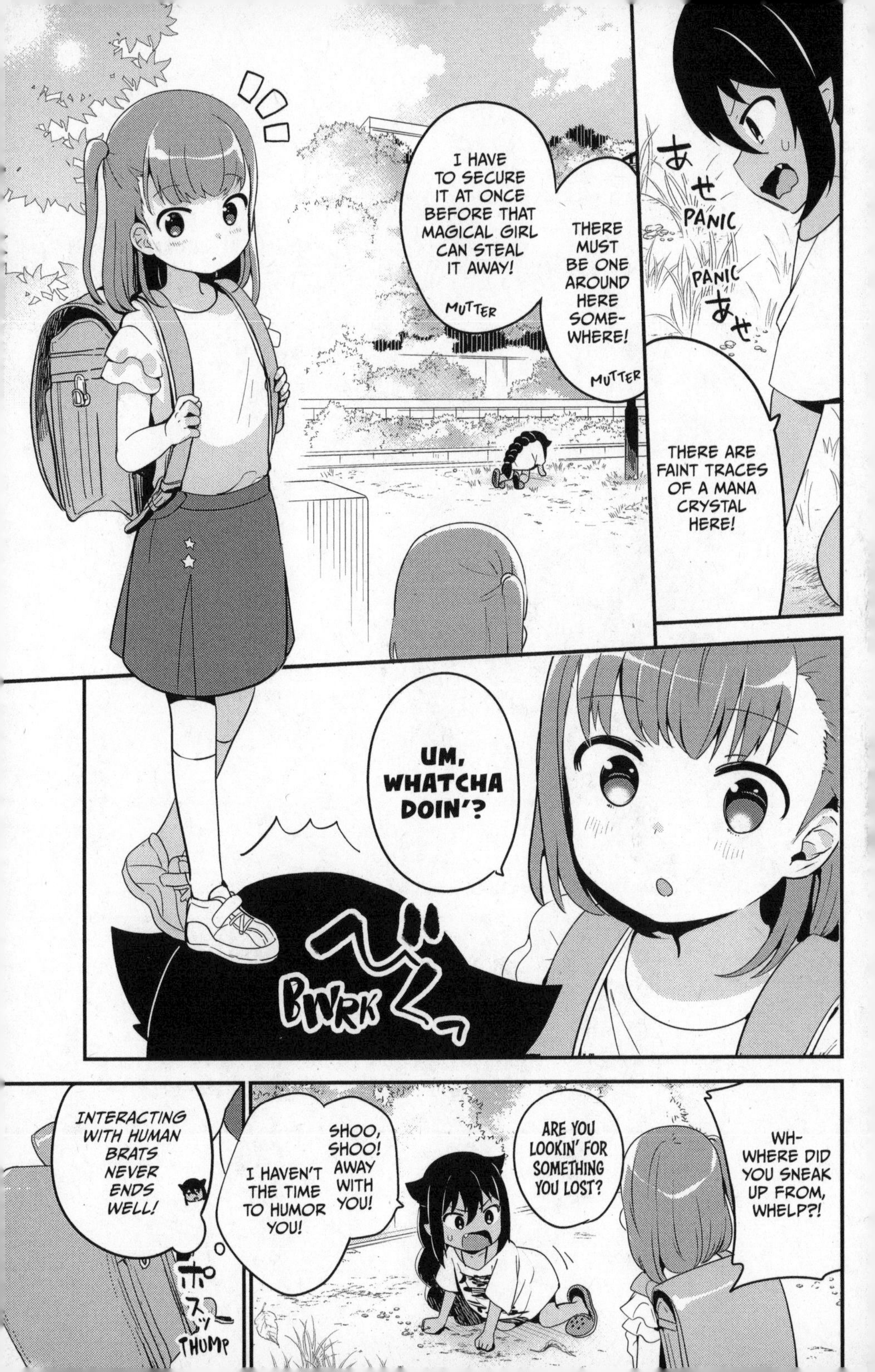
あせ
PANIC
PANIC
あせ
THERE ARE FAINT TRACES OF A MANA CRYSTAL HERE!
THERE MUST BE ONE AROUND HERE SOME-WHERE!
MUTTER
I HAVE TO SECURE IT AT ONCE BEFORE THAT MAGICAL GIRL CAN STEAL IT AWAY!
MUTTER
UM, WHATCHA DOIN'?
へぐっ
BWRK
WH- WHERE DID YOU SNEAK UP FROM, WHELP?!
ARE YOU LOOKIN' FOR SOMETHING YOU LOST?
SHOO, SHOO! AWAY WITH YOU!
I HAVEN'T THE TIME TO HUMOR YOU!
INTERACTING WITH HUMAN BRATS NEVER ENDS WELL!
ポスッ
THUMP

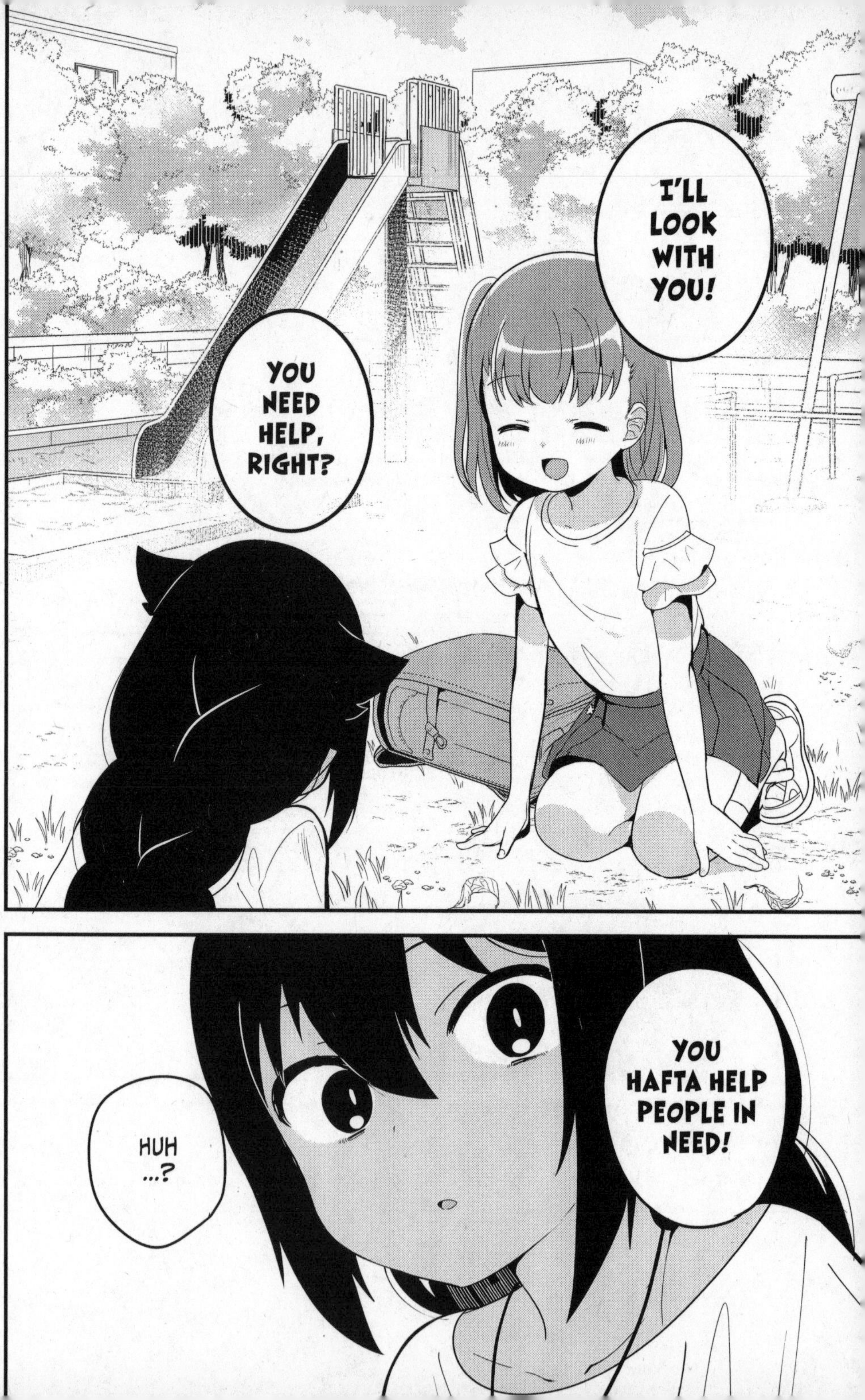
I'LL LOOK WITH YOU!
YOU NEED HELP, RIGHT?
YOU HAFTA HELP PEOPLE IN NEED!
HUH ...?

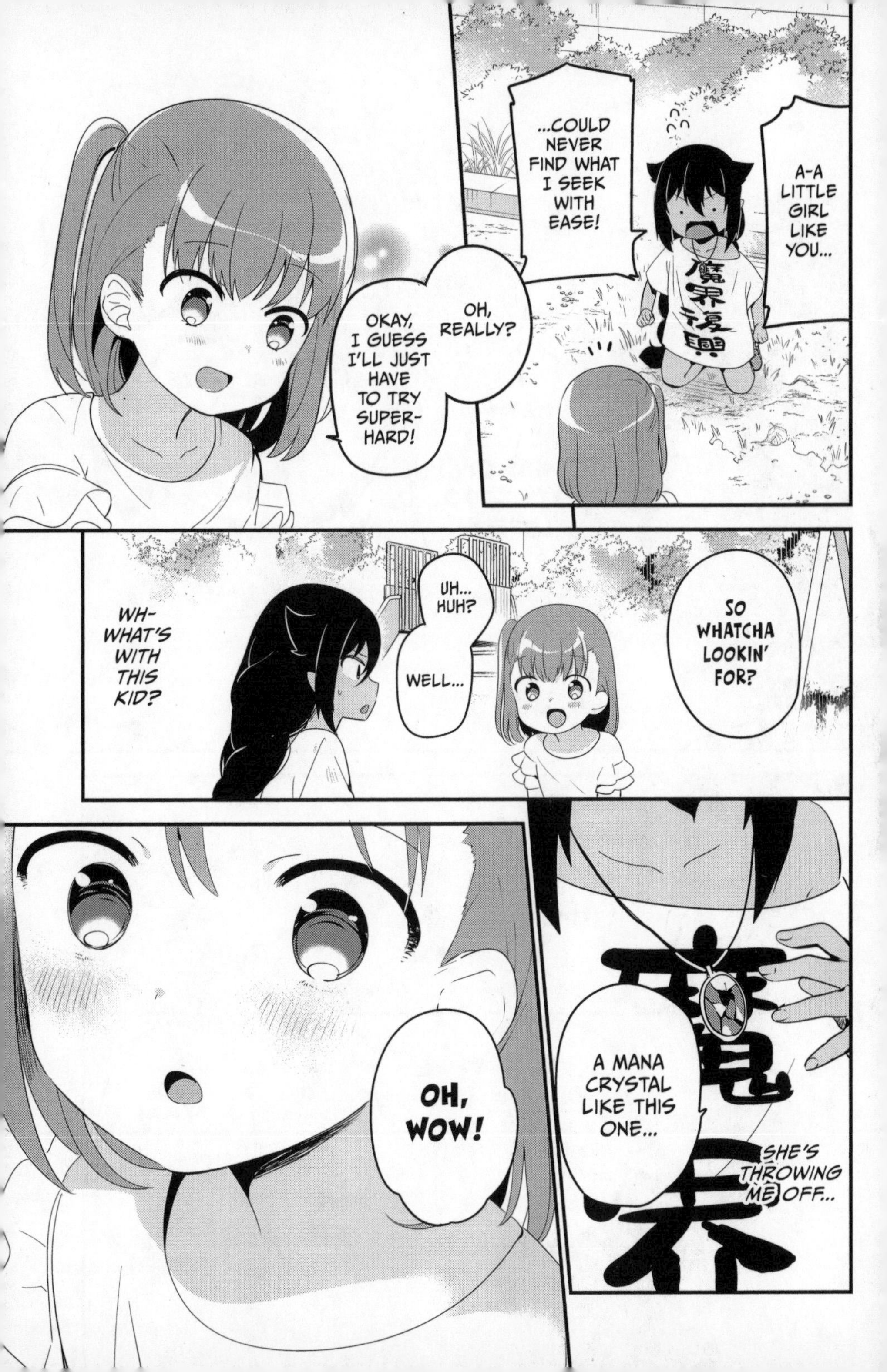
A-A LITTLE GIRL LIKE YOU...
...COULD NEVER FIND WHAT I SEEK WITH EASE!
魔界復興
OH, REALLY?
OKAY, I GUESS I'LL JUST HAVE TO TRY SUPER-HARD!
SO WHATCHA LOOKIN' FOR?
UH... HUH?
WELL...
WH-WHAT'S WITH THIS KID?
A MANA CRYSTAL LIKE THIS ONE...
SHE'S THROWING ME OFF...
OH, WOW!

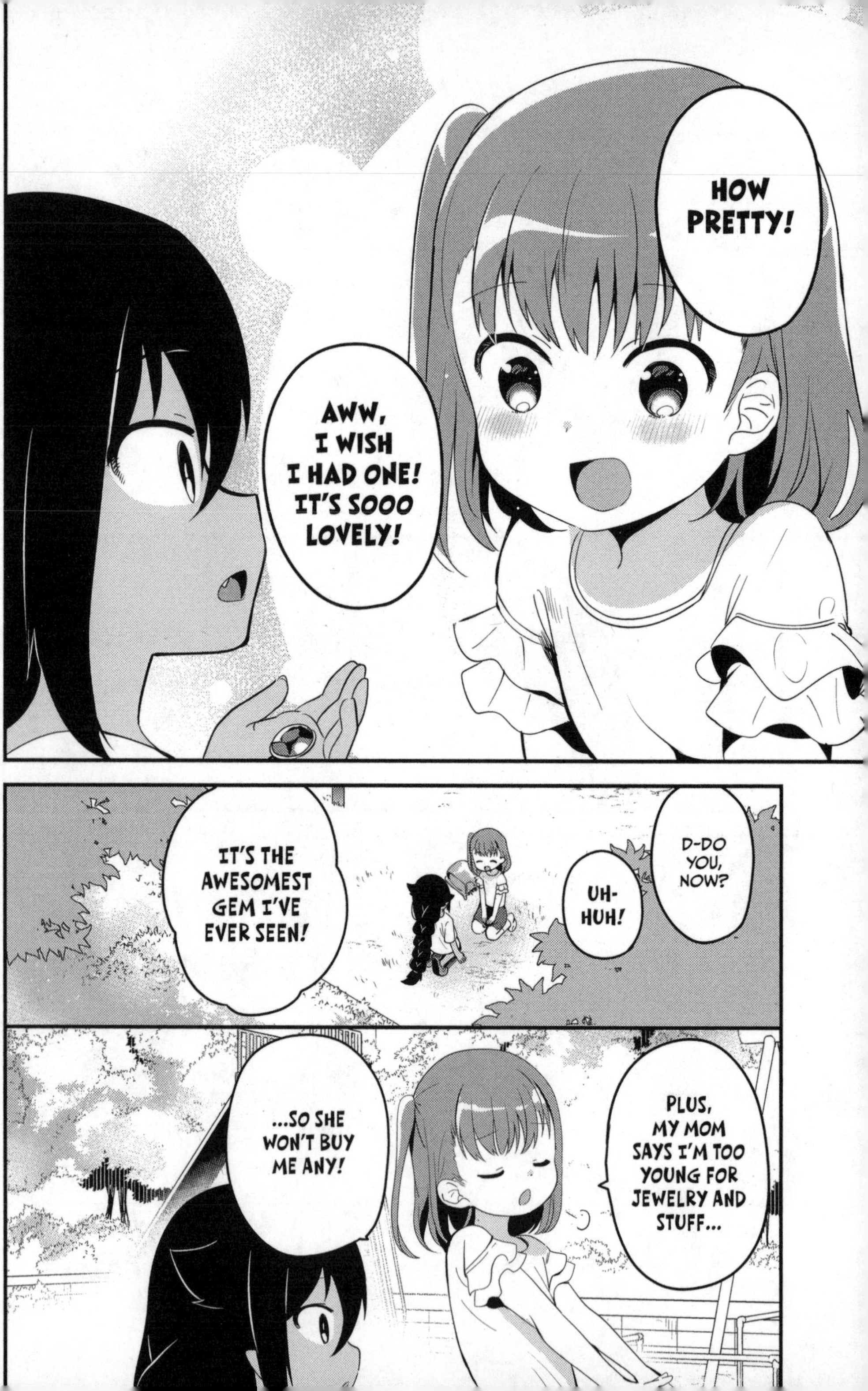
HOW PRETTY!
AWW, I WISH I HAD ONE! IT'S SOOO LOVELY!
D-DO YOU, NOW?
UH-HUH!
IT'S THE AWESOMEST GEM I'VE EVER SEEN!
PLUS, MY MOM SAYS I'M TOO YOUNG FOR JEWELRY AND STUFF...
...SO SHE WON'T BUY ME ANY!

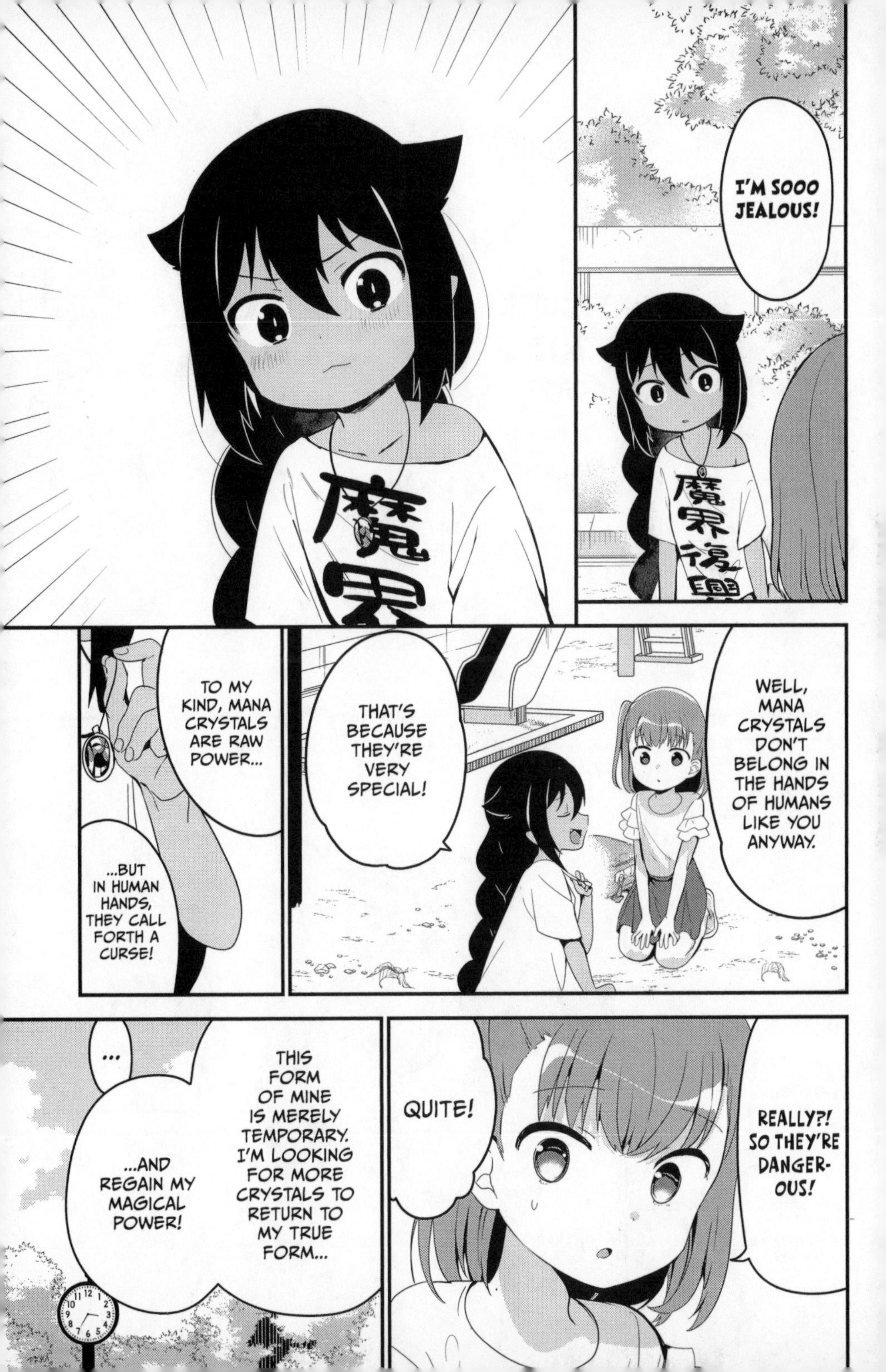
I'M SOOO JEALOUS!
WELL, MANA CRYSTALS DON'T BELONG IN THE HANDS OF HUMANS LIKE YOU ANYWAY.
THAT'S BECAUSE THEY'RE VERY SPECIAL!
TO MY KIND, MANA CRYSTALS ARE RAW POWER...
...BUT IN HUMAN HANDS, THEY CALL FORTH A CURSE!
REALLY?! SO THEY'RE DANGER-OUS!
QUITE!
THIS FORM OF MINE IS MERELY TEMPORARY. I'M LOOKING FOR MORE CRYSTALS TO RETURN TO MY TRUE FORM...
...AND REGAIN MY MAGICAL POWER!
...

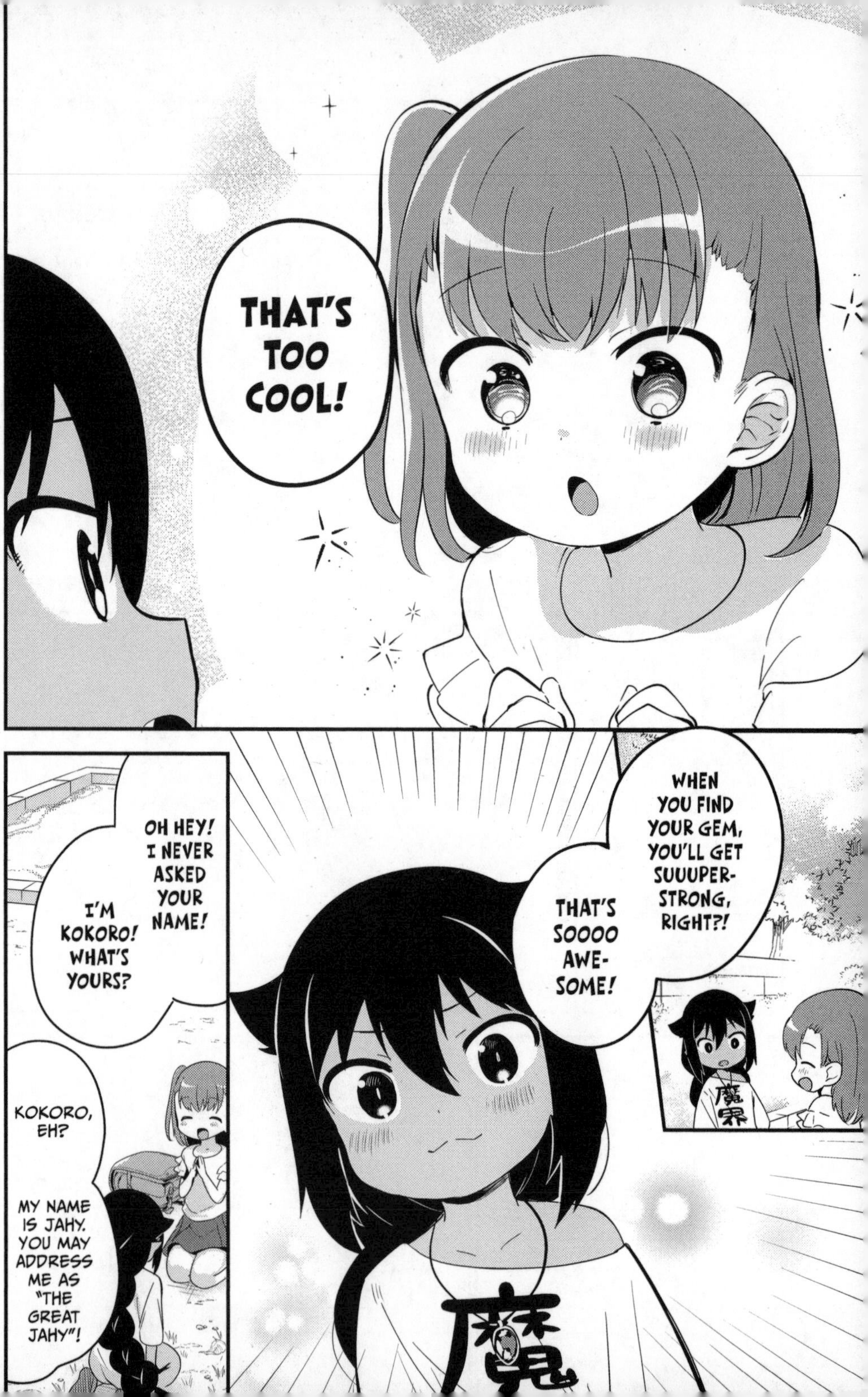
THAT'S TOO COOL!
WHEN YOU FIND YOUR GEM, YOU'LL GET SUUUPER-STRONG, RIGHT?!
THAT'S SOOOO AWE-SOME!
OH HEY! I NEVER ASKED YOUR NAME!
I'M KOKORO! WHAT'S YOURS?
KOKORO, EH?
MY NAME IS JAHY. YOU MAY ADDRESS ME AS "THE GREAT JAHY"!

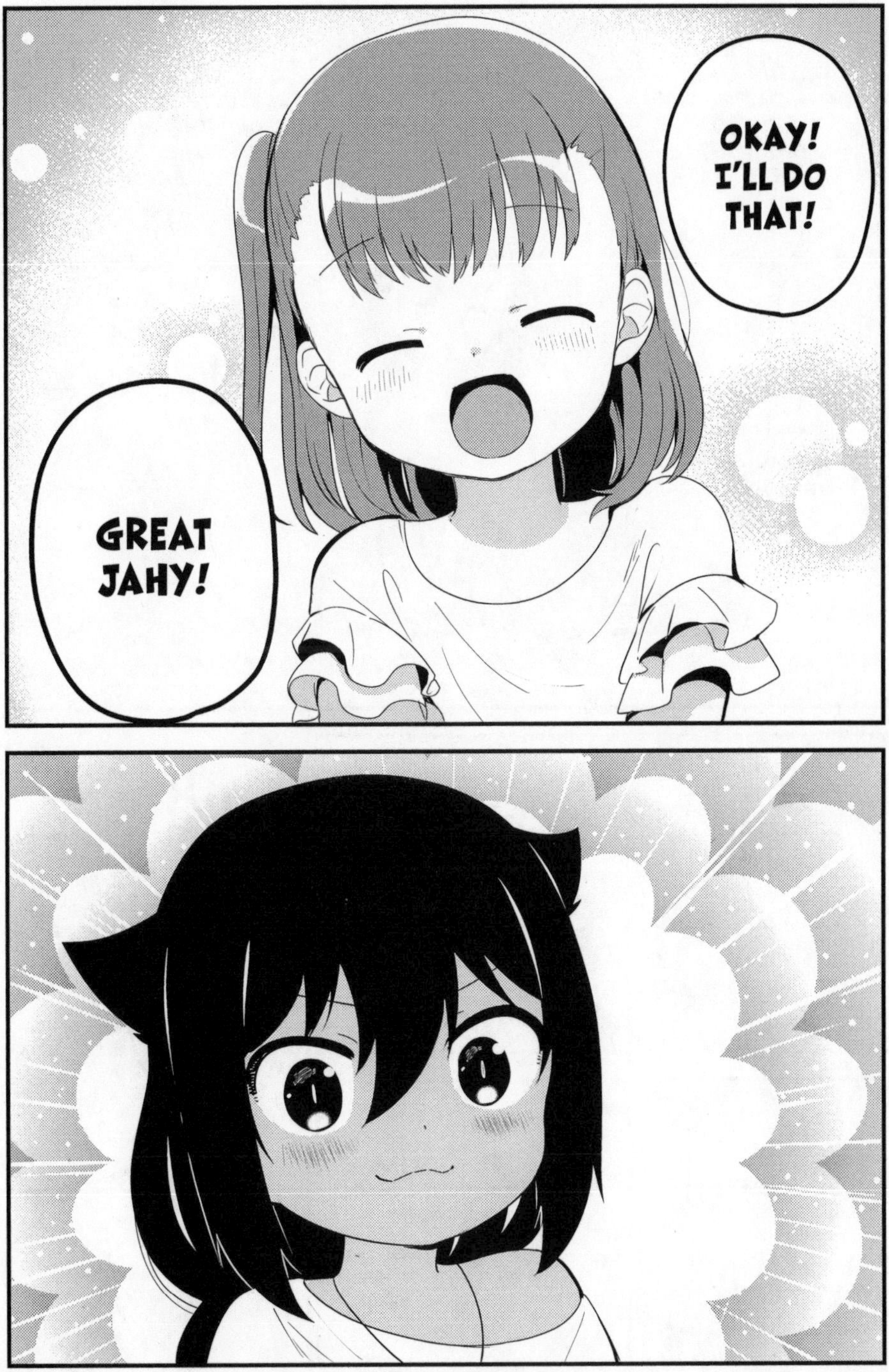
OKAY! I'LL DO THAT!
GREAT JAHY!

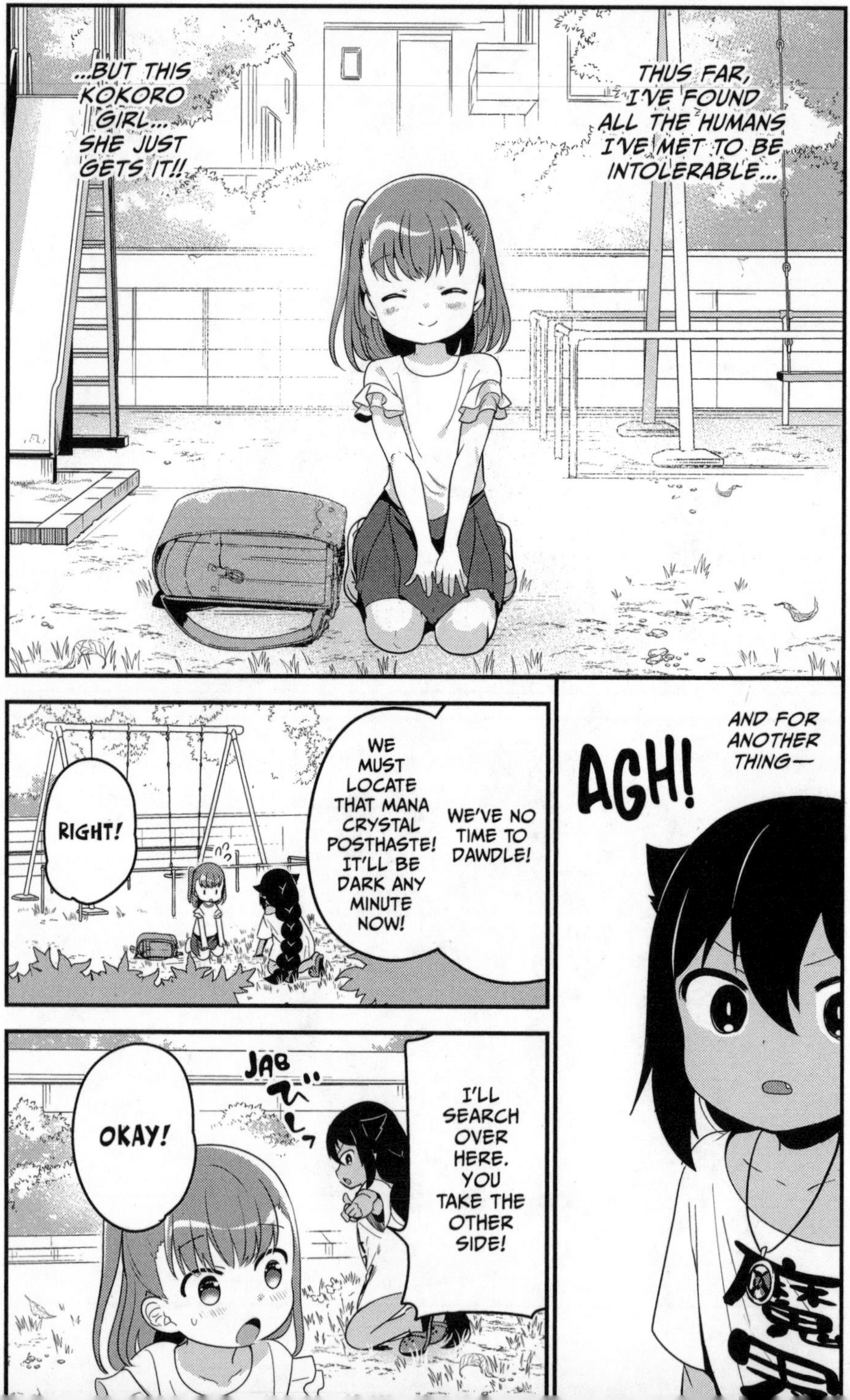
THUS FAR, I'VE FOUND ALL THE HUMANS I'VE MET TO BE INTOLERABLE...
...BUT THIS KOKORO GIRL... SHE JUST GETS IT!!
AND FOR ANOTHER THING—
AGH!
WE'VE NO TIME TO DAWDLE!
WE MUST LOCATE THAT MANA CRYSTAL POSTHASTE! IT'LL BE DARK ANY MINUTE NOW!
RIGHT!
I'LL SEARCH OVER HERE. YOU TAKE THE OTHER SIDE!
JAB
OKAY!

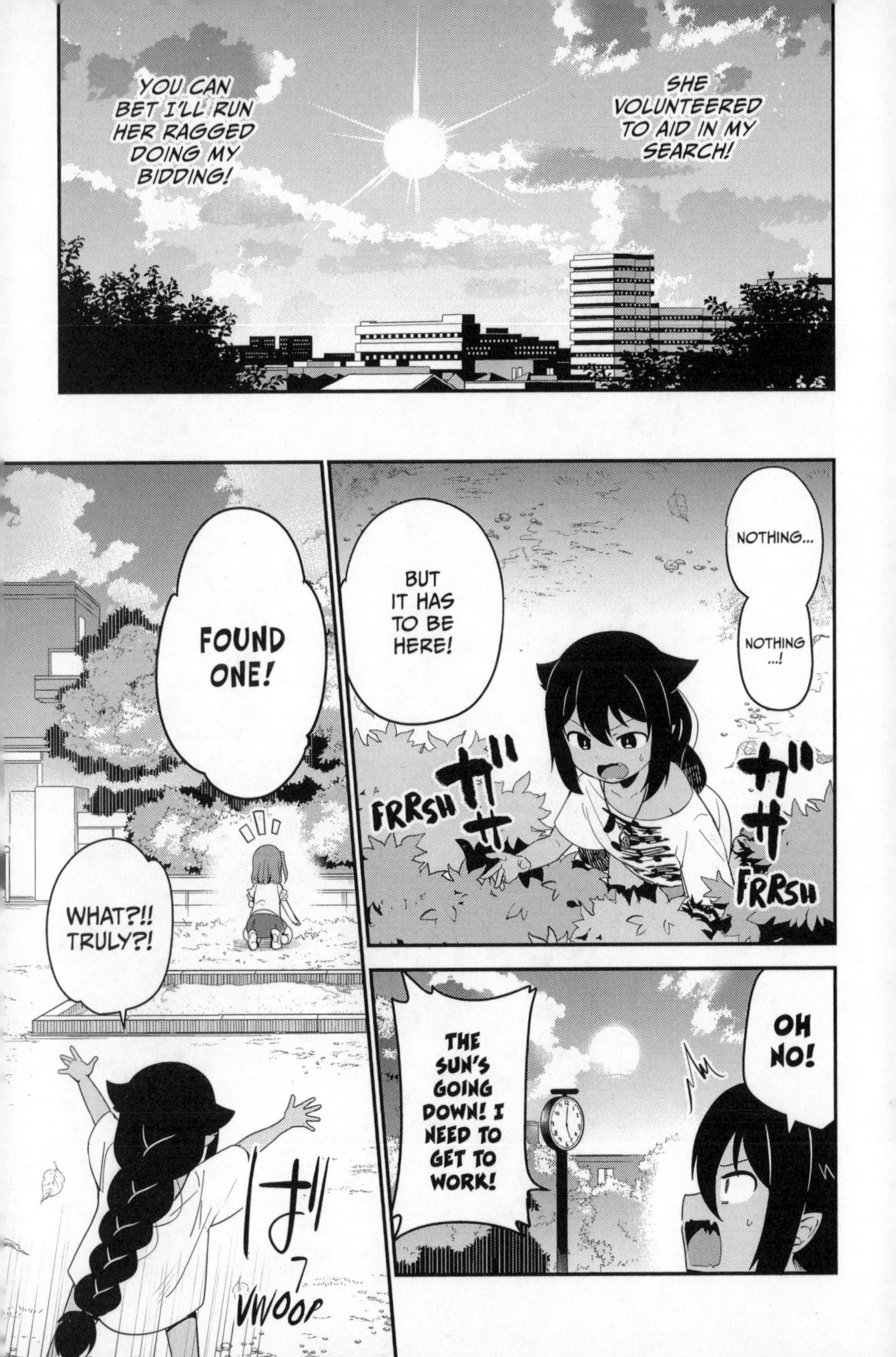
SHE VOLUNTEERED TO AID IN MY SEARCH!
YOU CAN BET I'LL RUN HER RAGGED DOING MY BIDDING!
NOTHING...
NOTHING ...!
ガサ
FRRSH
BUT IT HAS TO BE HERE!
ガサ
FRRSH
OH NO!
THE SUN'S GOING DOWN! I NEED TO GET TO WORK!
FOUND ONE!
WHAT?!! TRULY?!
ばっ
VWOOP

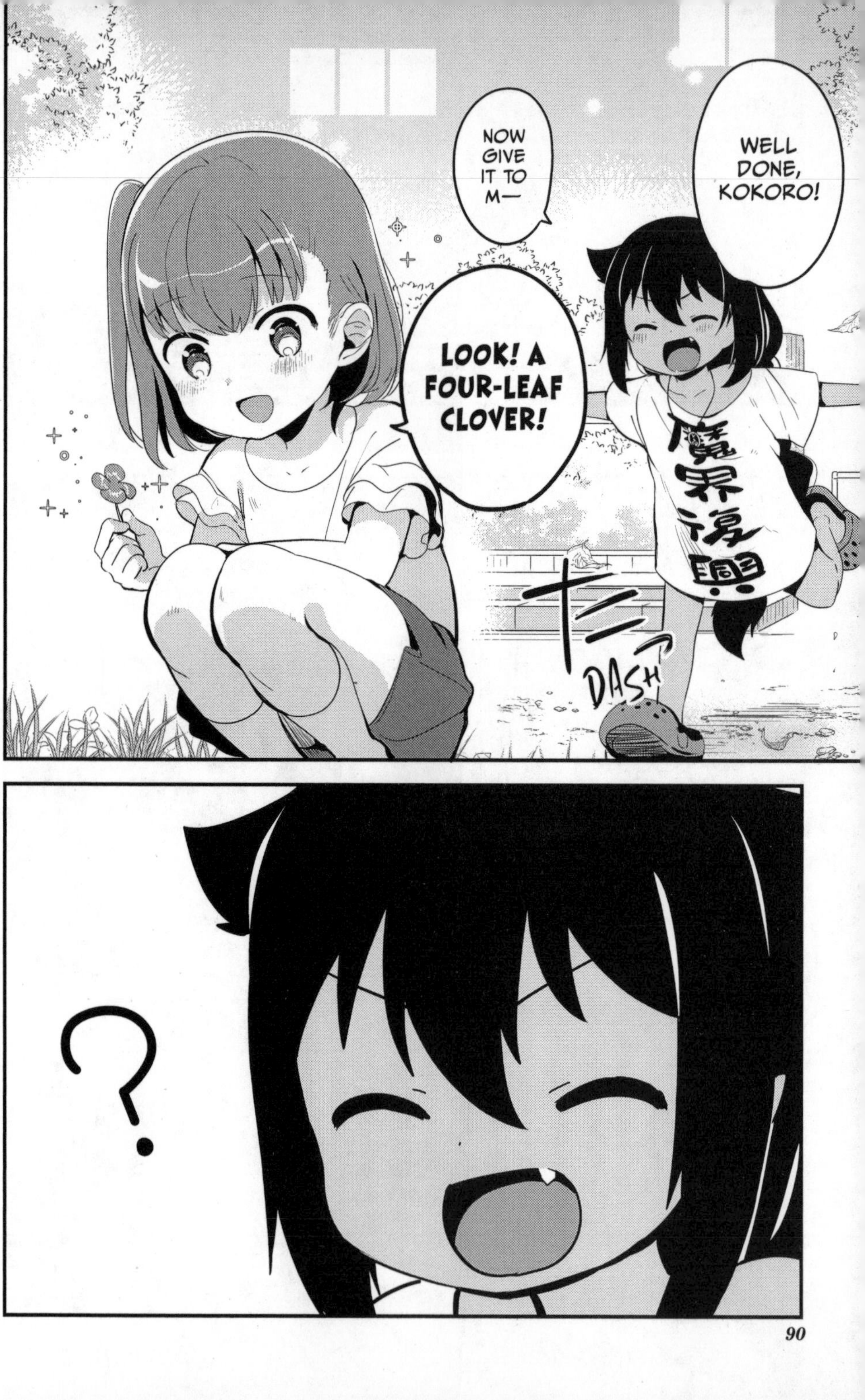
WELL DONE, KOKORO!
NOW GIVE IT TO M—
LOOK! A FOUR-LEAF CLOVER!
魔界復興
DASH
?

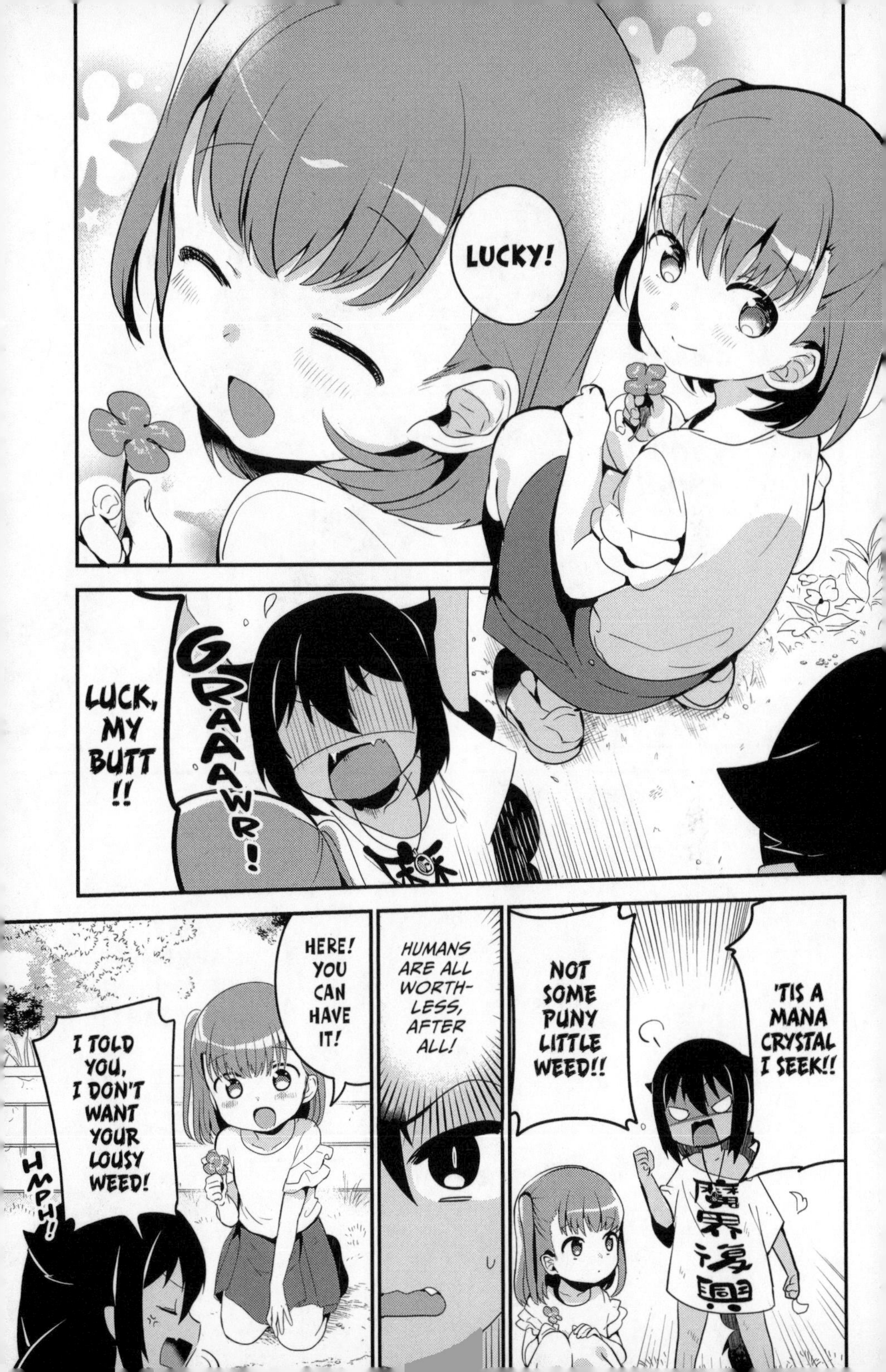
LUCKY!
GRAAAAWR!
LUCK, MY BUTT!!
'TIS A MANA CRYSTAL I SEEK!!
NOT SOME PUNY LITTLE WEED!!
魔界復興
HUMANS ARE ALL WORTH-LESS, AFTER ALL!
HERE! YOU CAN HAVE IT!
I TOLD YOU, I DON'T WANT YOUR LOUSY WEED!
HMPH!!

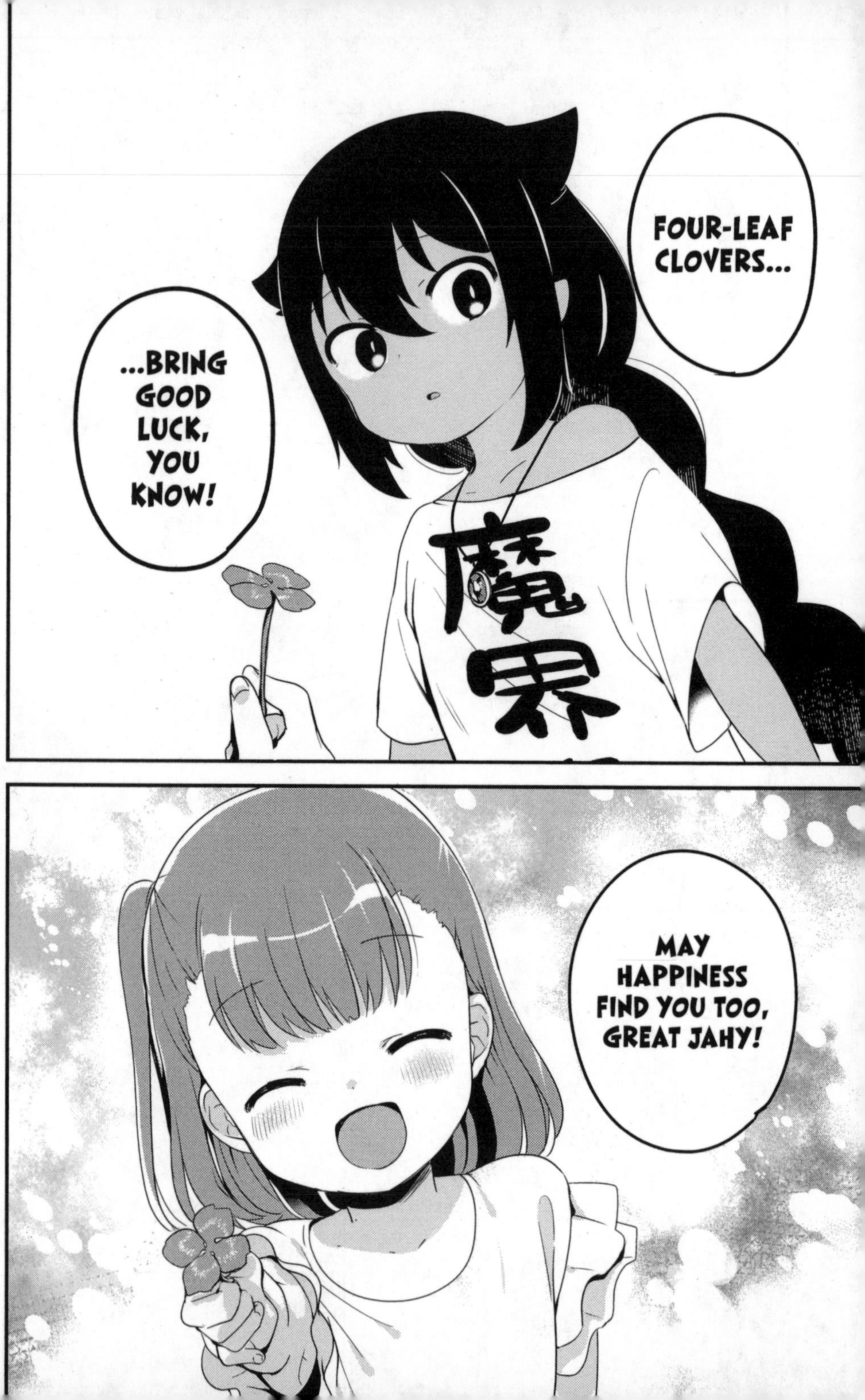
FOUR-LEAF CLOVERS...
...BRING GOOD LUCK, YOU KNOW!
魔界
MAY HAPPINESS FIND YOU TOO, GREAT JAHY!

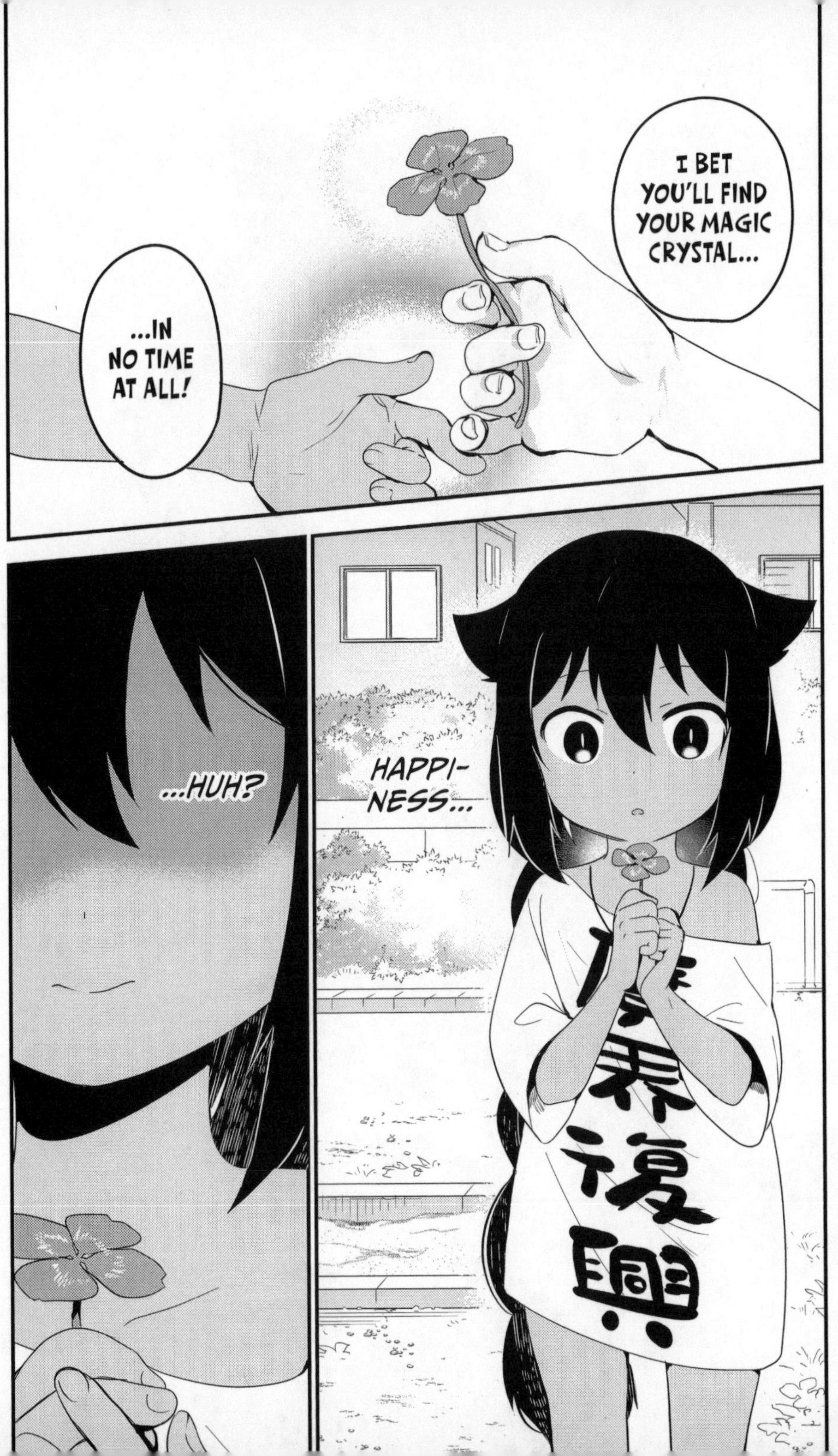
I BET YOU'LL FIND YOUR MAGIC CRYSTAL...
...IN NO TIME AT ALL!
HAPPI-NESS...
...HUH?

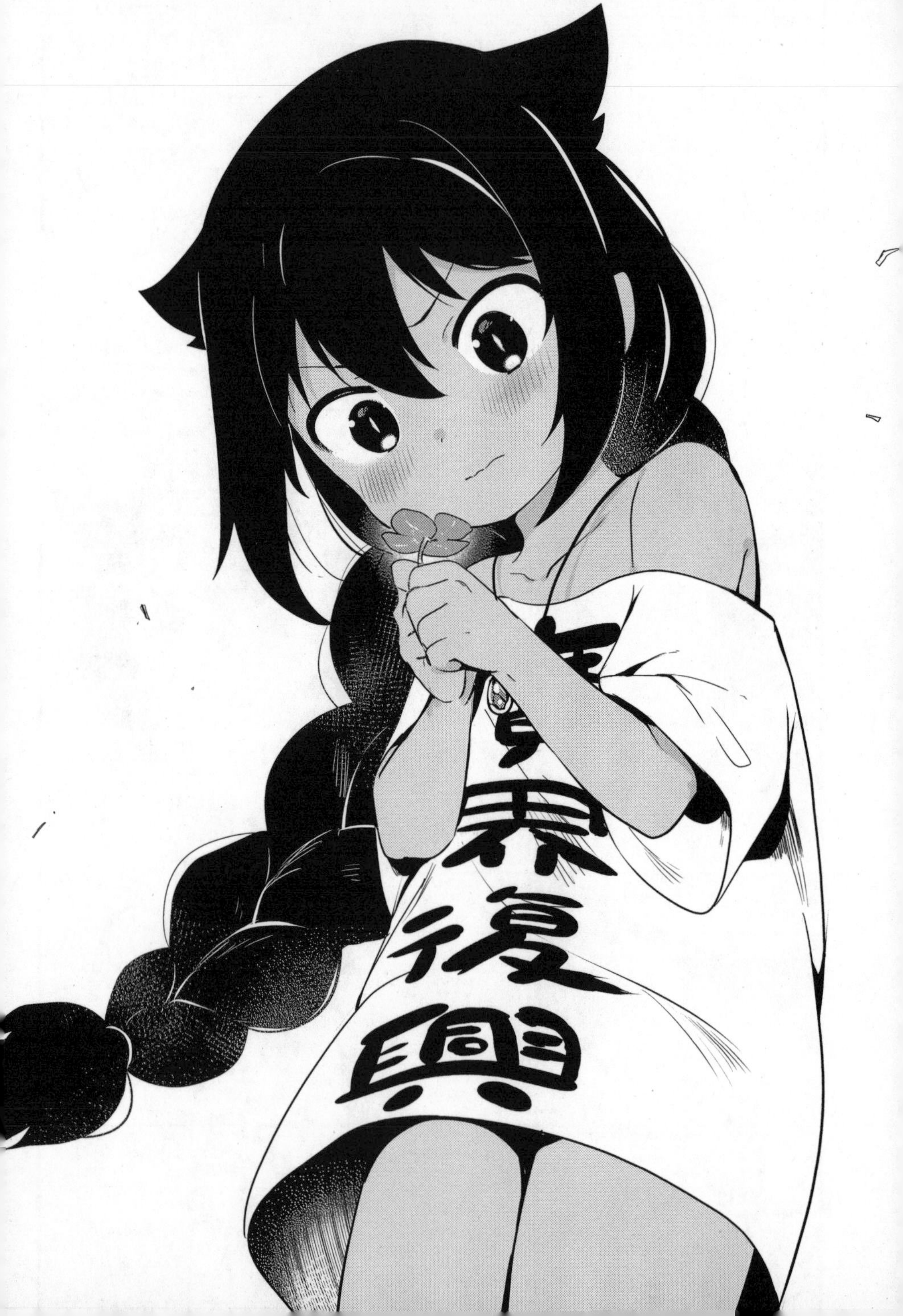
復興

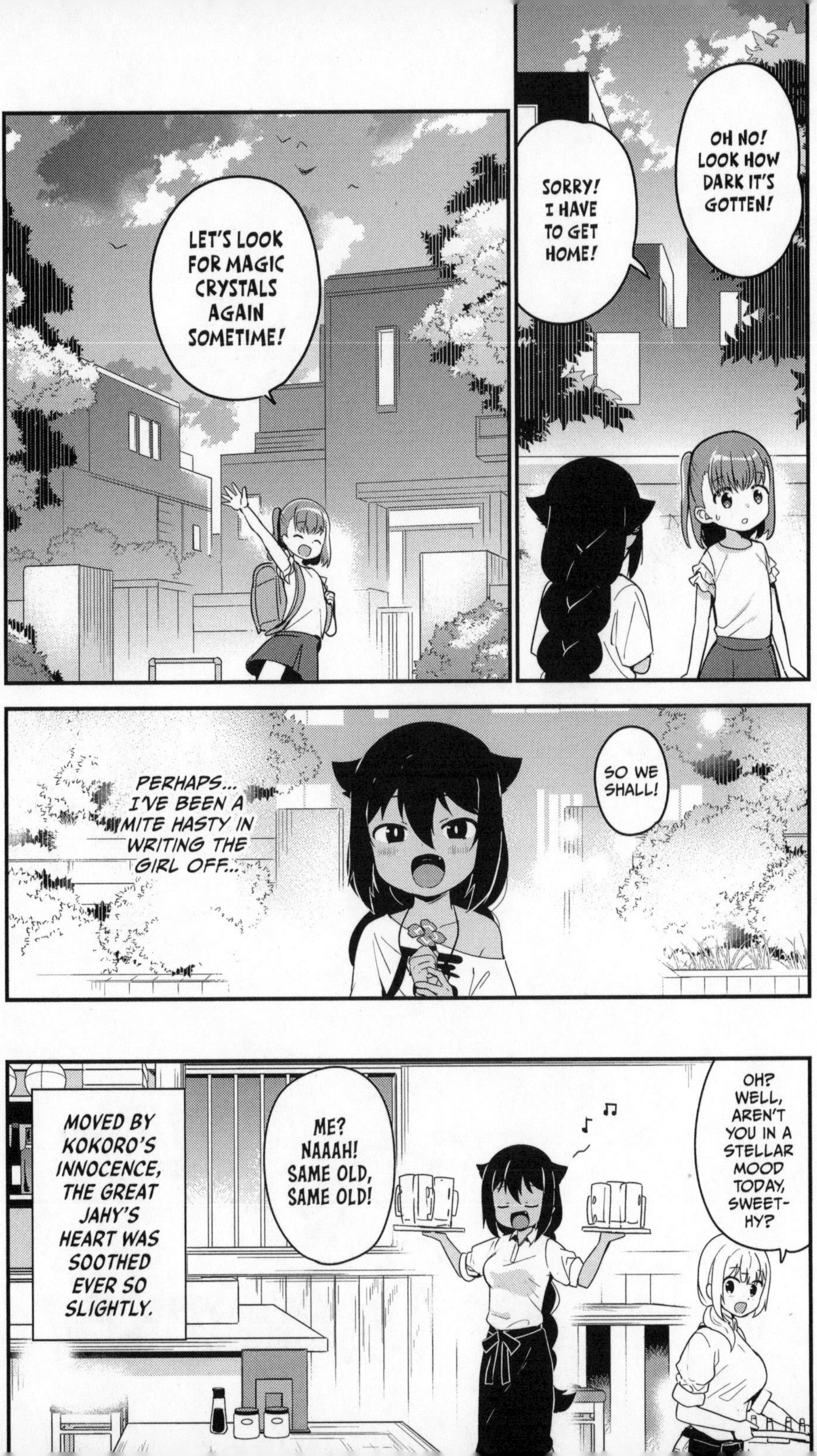

OH NO! LOOK HOW DARK IT'S GOTTEN!
SORRY! I HAVE TO GET HOME!
LET'S LOOK FOR MAGIC CRYSTALS AGAIN SOMETIME!
SO WE SHALL!
PERHAPS... I'VE BEEN A MITE HASTY IN WRITING THE GIRL OFF...
OH? WELL, AREN'T YOU IN A STELLAR MOOD TODAY, SWEET-HY?
ME? NAAAH! SAME OLD, SAME OLD!
MOVED BY KOKORO'S INNOCENCE, THE GREAT JAHY'S HEART WAS SOOTHED EVER SO SLIGHTLY.

The GREAT JAHY Will NOT Be DEFEATED!

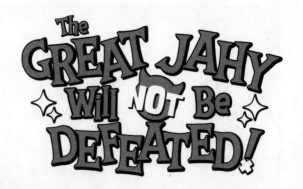

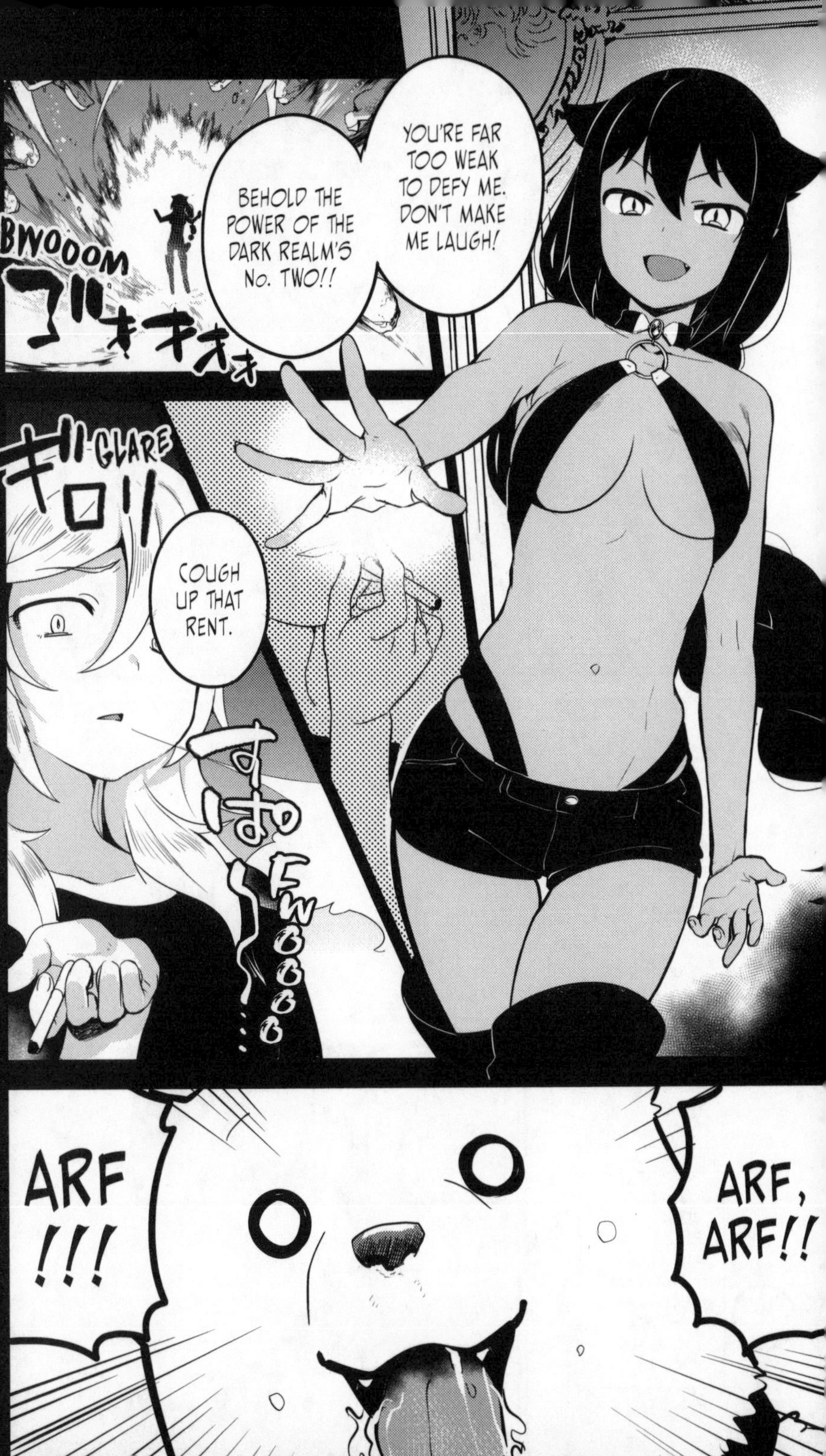
YOU'RE FAR TOO WEAK TO DEFY ME. DON'T MAKE ME LAUGH!
BEHOLD THE POWER OF THE DARK REALM'S No. TWO!!
BWOOOM
ギロリ GLARE
COUGH UP THAT RENT.
FWOOOO
ARF, ARF!!
ARF !!!

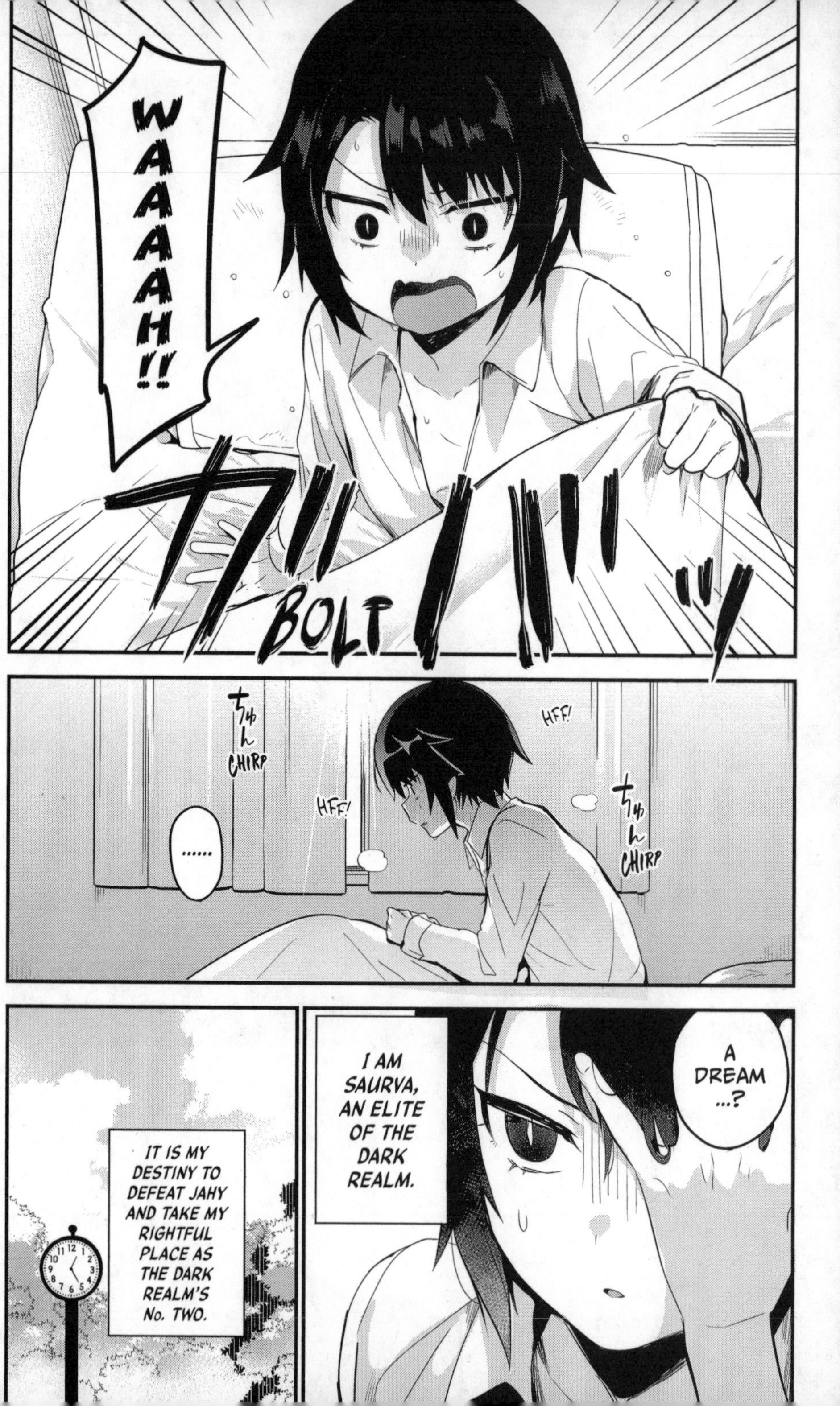
WAAAAAH!!
カッ
BOLT
HFF!
ちゅん
CHIRP
ちゅん
CHIRP
HFF!
......
A DREAM ...?
I AM SAURVA, AN ELITE OF THE DARK REALM.
IT IS MY DESTINY TO DEFEAT JAHY AND TAKE MY RIGHTFUL PLACE AS THE DARK REALM'S No. TWO.

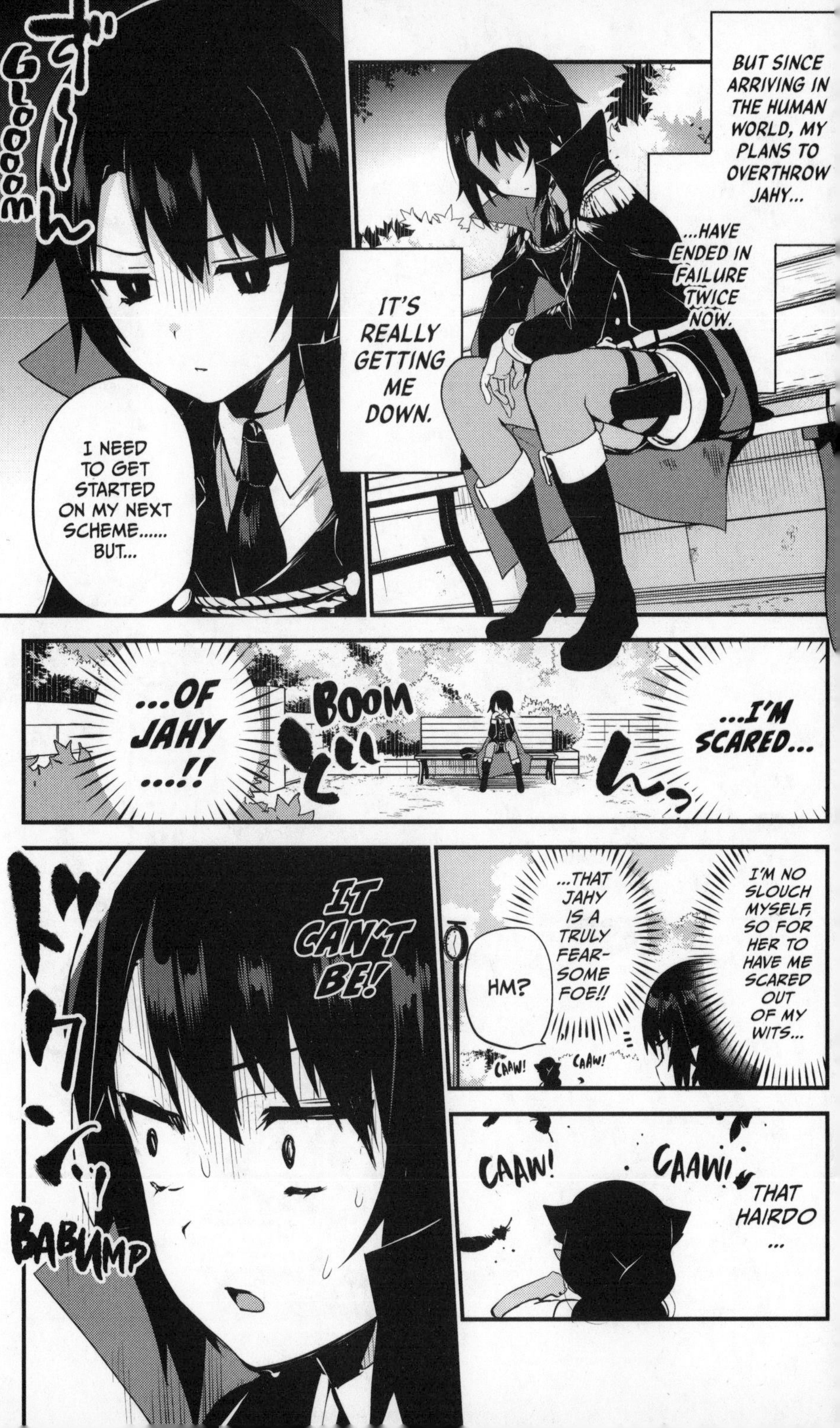
BUT SINCE ARRIVING IN THE HUMAN WORLD, MY PLANS TO OVERTHROW JAHY...
...HAVE ENDED IN FAILURE TWICE NOW.
IT'S REALLY GETTING ME DOWN.
GLOOOOOM
I NEED TO GET STARTED ON MY NEXT SCHEME...... BUT...
...I'M SCARED...
BOOM
...OF JAHY ...!!
I'M NO SLOUCH MYSELF, SO FOR HER TO HAVE ME SCARED OUT OF MY WITS...
...THAT JAHY IS A TRULY FEAR-SOME FOE!!
HM?
CAAW!
CAAW!
THAT HAIRDO ...
CAAW!
CAAW!
IT CAN'T BE!
BABUMP

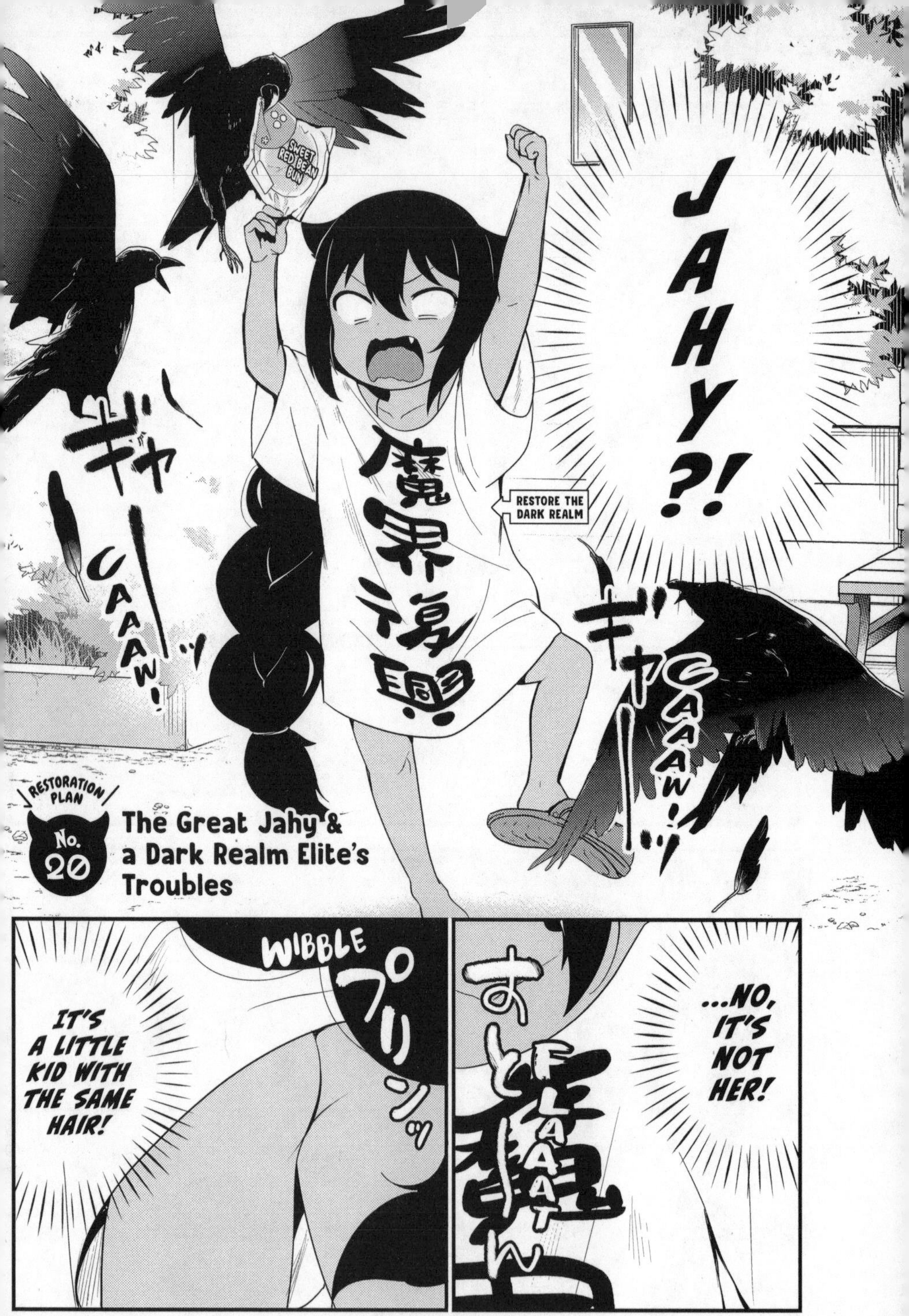
JAHY?!
RESTORE THE DARK REALM
魔界復興
SWEET RED BEAN BUN
CAAAAW!!
CAAAW!
RESTORATION PLAN
No. 20
The Great Jahy & a Dark Realm Elite's Troubles
...NO, IT'S NOT HER!
FLAAAT
WIBBLE
IT'S A LITTLE KID WITH THE SAME HAIR!

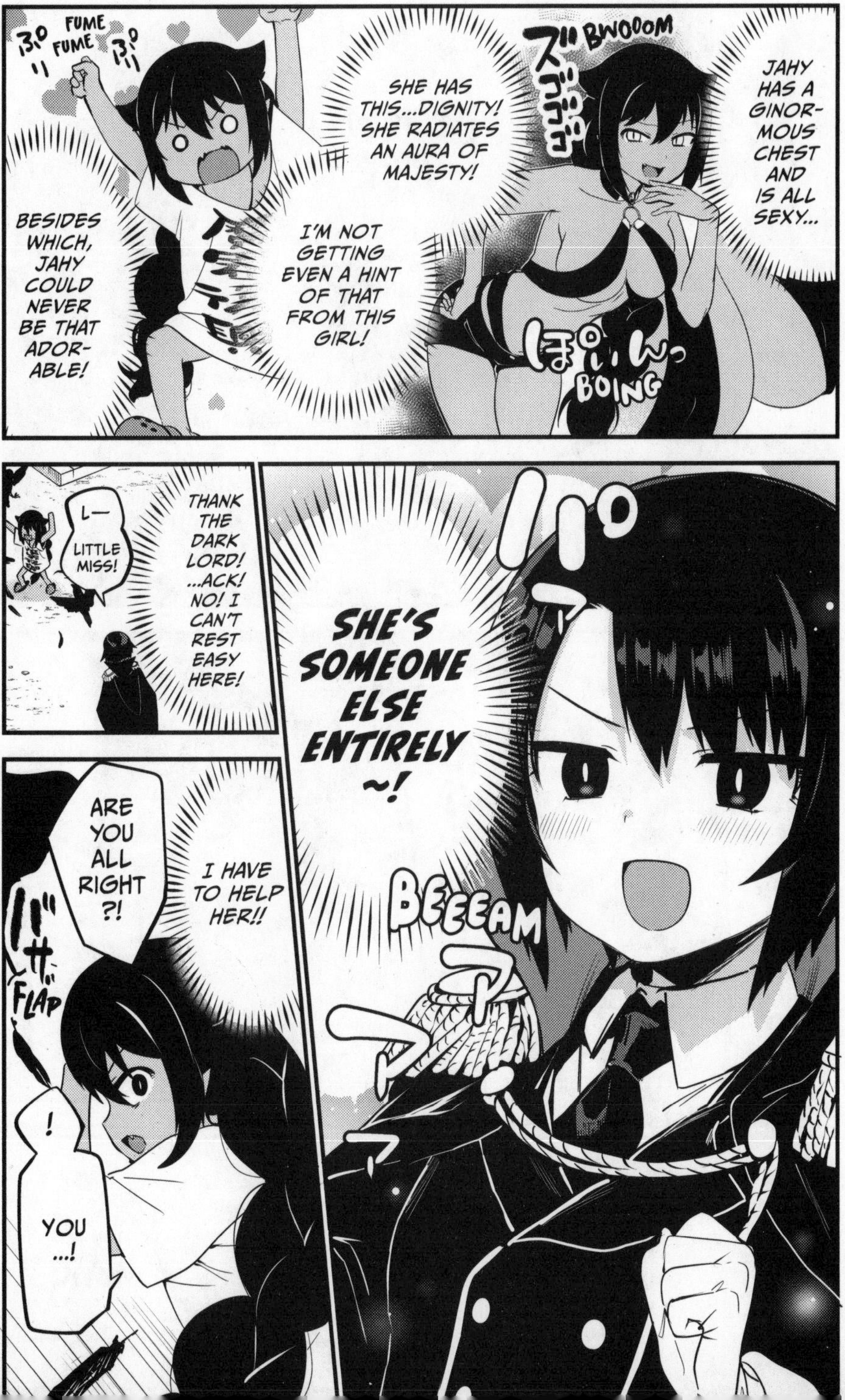
BWOOOM
JAHY HAS A GINORMOUS CHEST AND IS ALL SEXY...
SHE HAS THIS...DIGNITY! SHE RADIATES AN AURA OF MAJESTY!
BOING
I'M NOT GETTING EVEN A HINT OF THAT FROM THIS GIRL!
BESIDES WHICH, JAHY COULD NEVER BE THAT ADORABLE!
FUME FUME
SHE'S SOMEONE ELSE ENTIRELY ~!
BEEEAM
THANK THE DARK LORD! ...ACK! NO! I CAN'T REST EASY HERE!
L— LITTLE MISS!
I HAVE TO HELP HER!!
ARE YOU ALL RIGHT?!
FLAP
!
YOU ...!

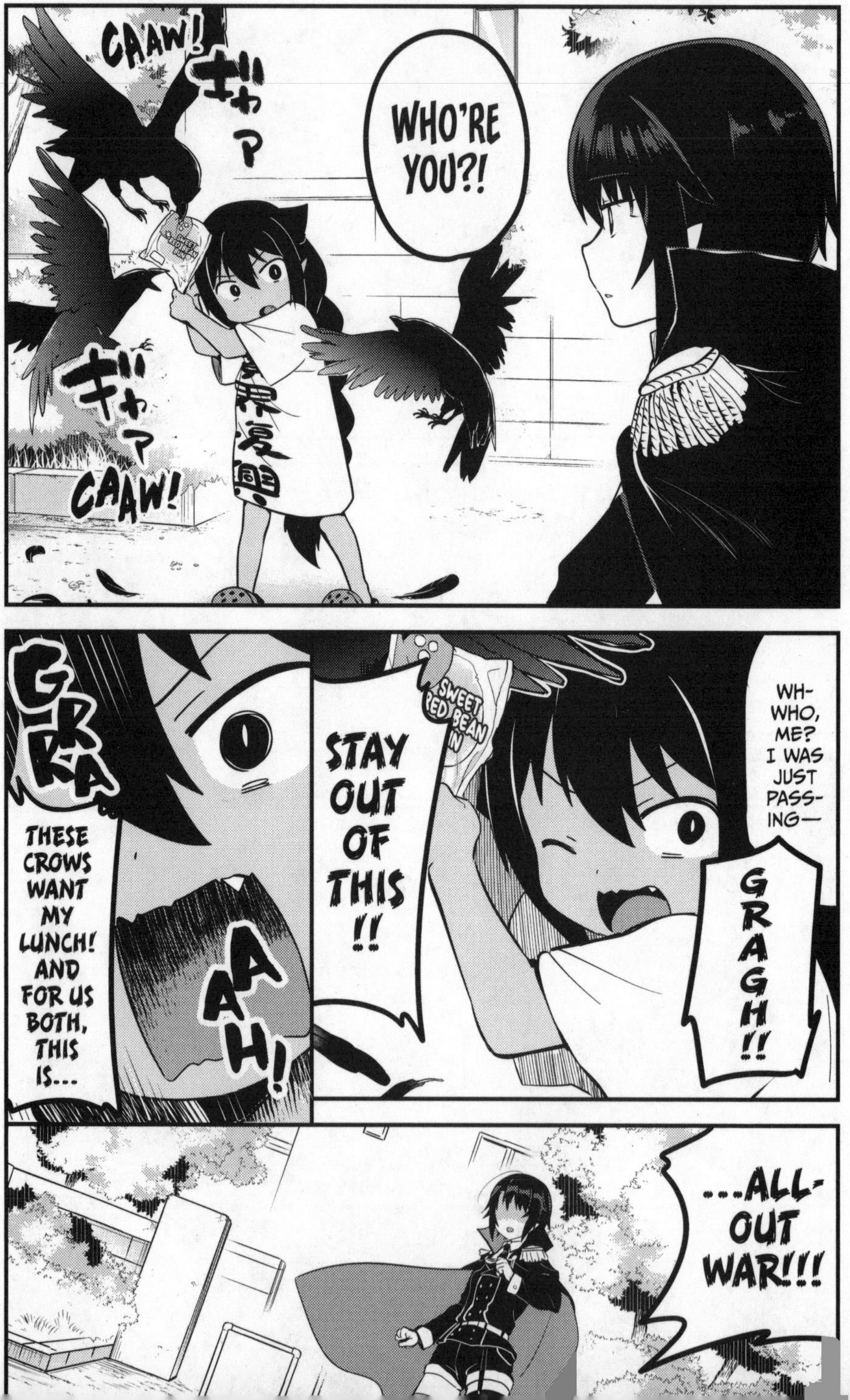
WHO'RE YOU?!
CAAW!
ギャア
ギャア
CAAW!
WH-WHO, ME? I WAS JUST PASSING—
GRAGH!!
SWEET RED BEAN
STAY OUT OF THIS!!
GRRA
THESE CROWS WANT MY LUNCH! AND FOR US BOTH, THIS IS...
AAAH!
...ALL-OUT WAR!!!

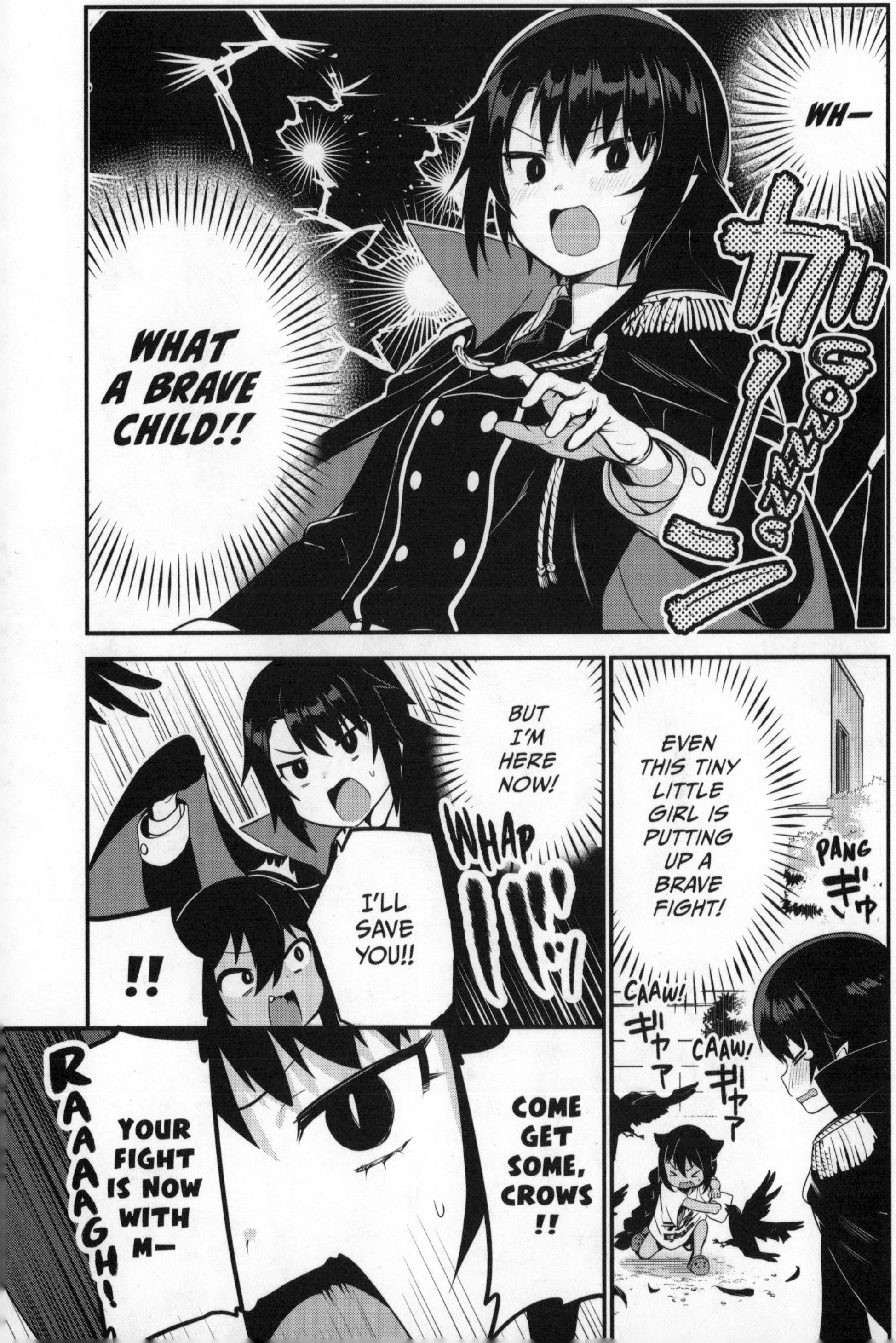
WH—
GONNNG!
ガーン
WHAT A BRAVE CHILD!!
EVEN THIS TINY LITTLE GIRL IS PUTTING UP A BRAVE FIGHT!
PANG
ぎゅ
CAAW!
ギャア
CAAW!
ギャア
BUT I'M HERE NOW!
WHAP
バッ
I'LL SAVE YOU!!
!!
COME GET SOME, CROWS!!
YOUR FIGHT IS NOW WITH M—
RAAAAGH!

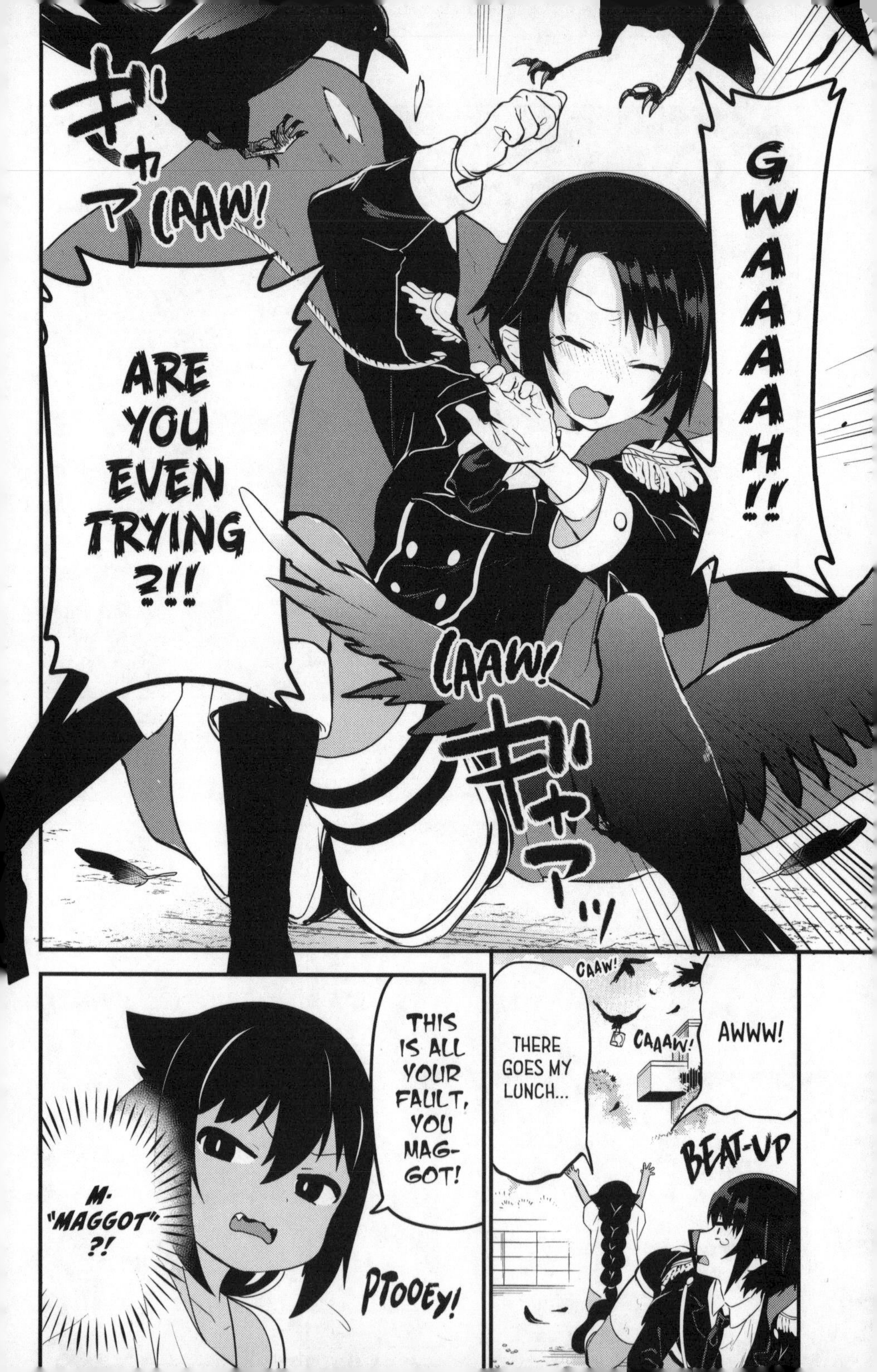
GWAAAAAAH!!
ギャアー
CAAW!
ARE YOU EVEN TRYING?!!
CAAW!
ギャアッ
AWWW!
CAAW!
CAAAW!
THERE GOES MY LUNCH...
BEAT-UP
THIS IS ALL YOUR FAULT, YOU MAG-GOT!
M-"MAGGOT"?!
PTOOEY!

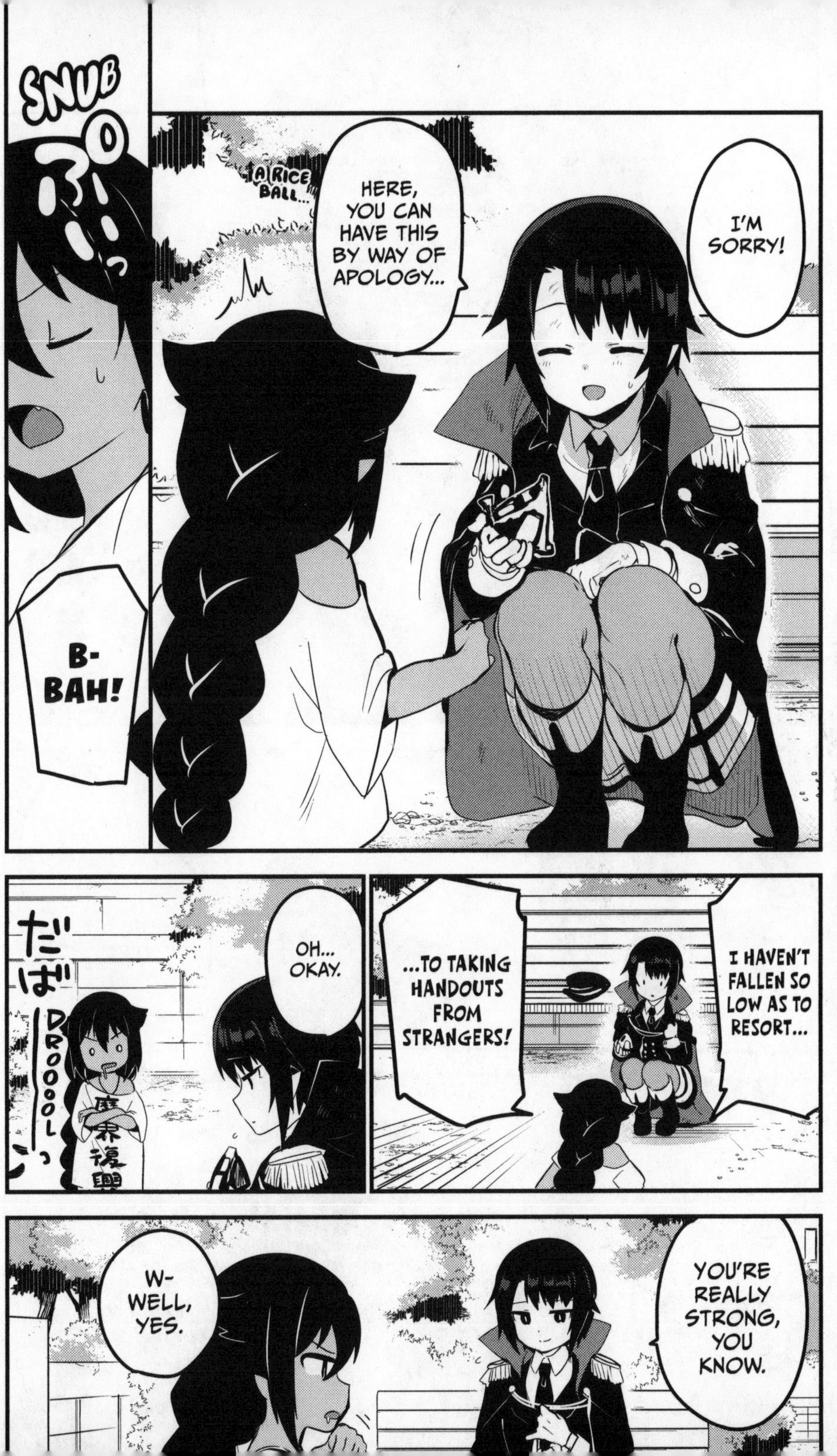
I'M SORRY!
HERE, YOU CAN HAVE THIS BY WAY OF APOLOGY...
A RICE BALL...
SNUB
ぷいっ
B-BAH!
I HAVEN'T FALLEN SO LOW AS TO RESORT...
...TO TAKING HANDOUTS FROM STRANGERS!
OH... OKAY.
だばー
DROOOOOL
YOU'RE REALLY STRONG, YOU KNOW.
W-WELL, YES.

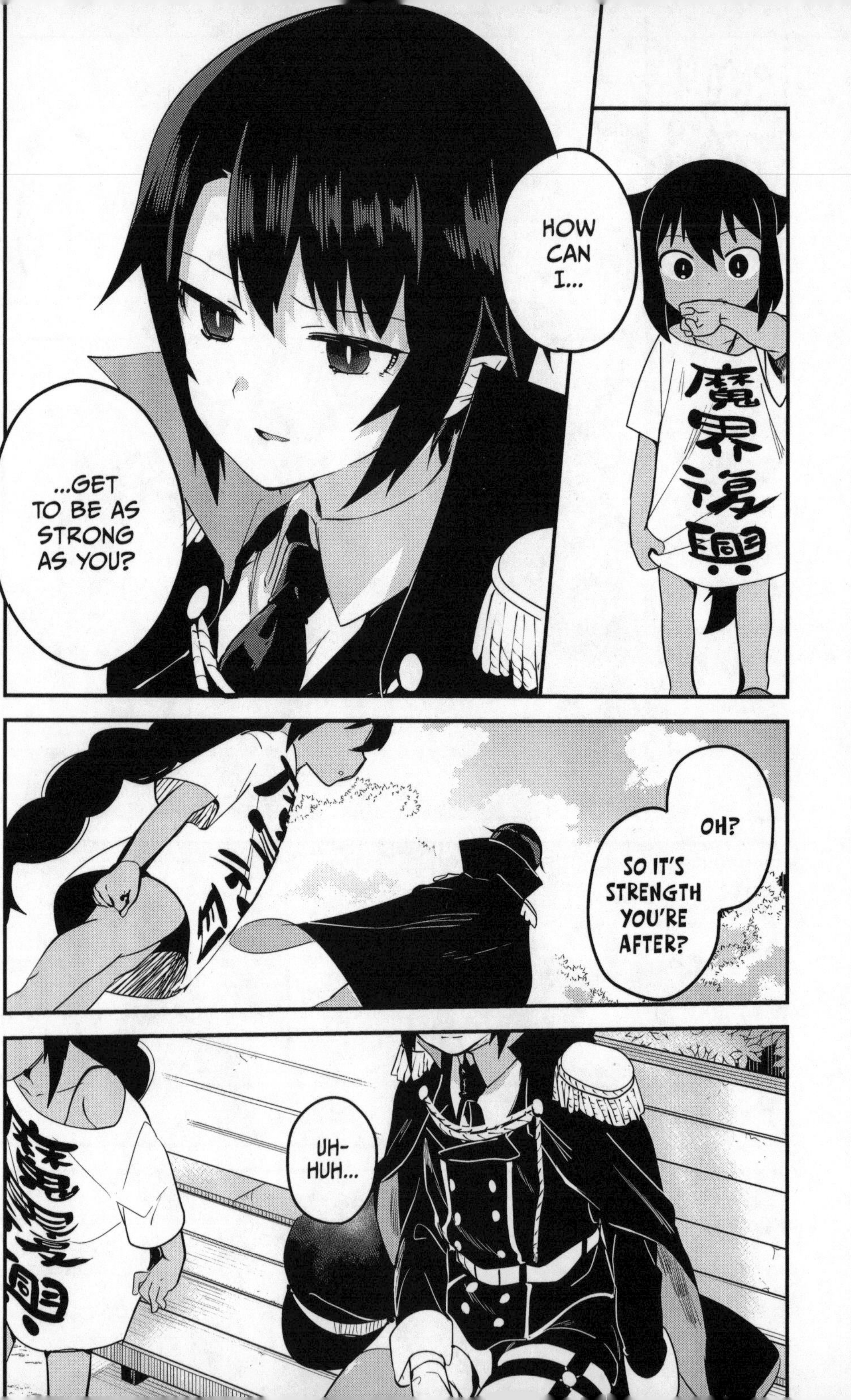
HOW CAN I...
魔界復興
...GET TO BE AS STRONG AS YOU?
OH?
SO IT'S STRENGTH YOU'RE AFTER?
UH-HUH...

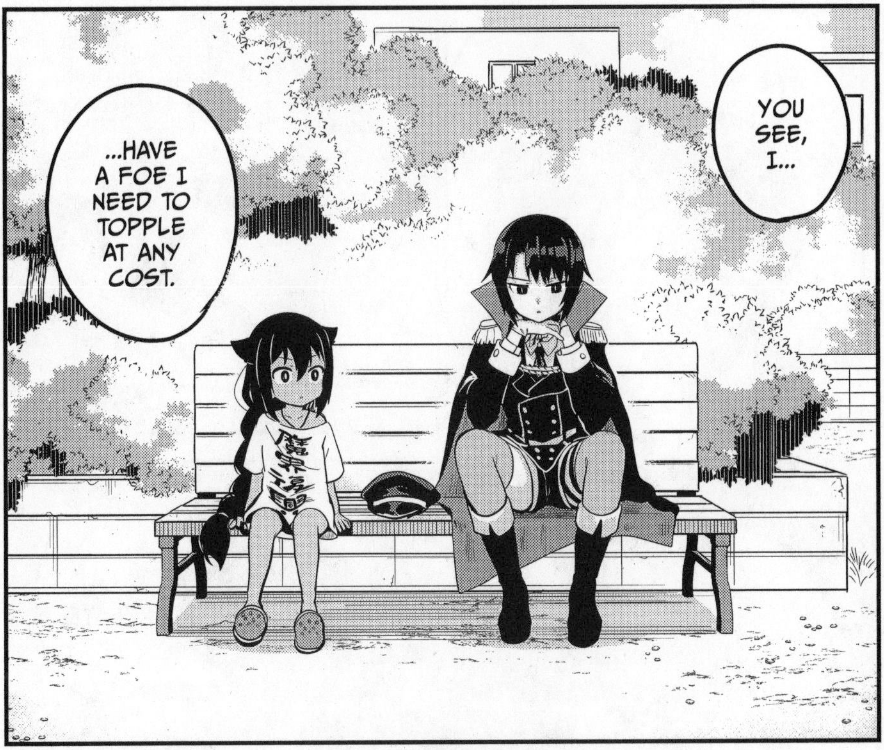
YOU SEE, I...
...HAVE A FOE I NEED TO TOPPLE AT ANY COST.
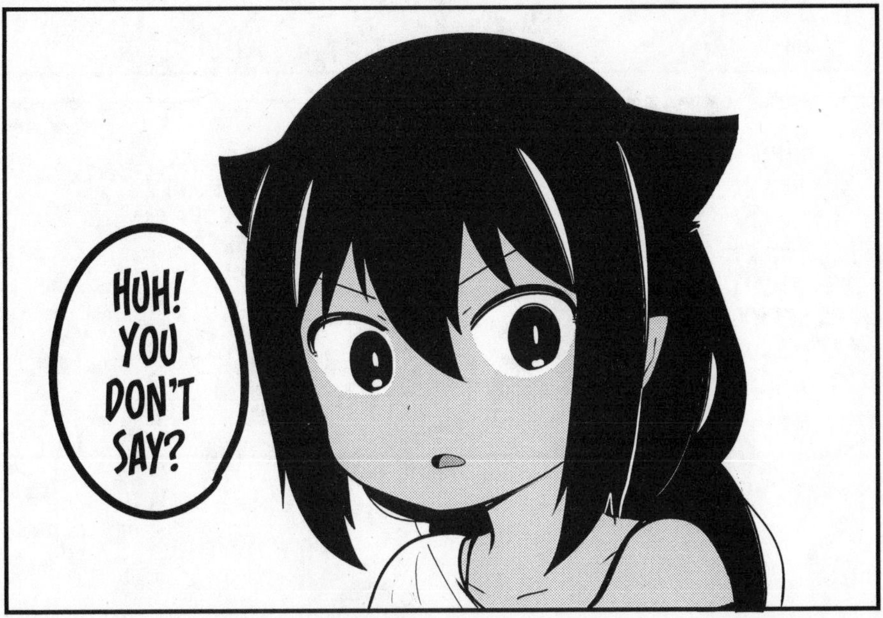
HUH! YOU DON'T SAY?

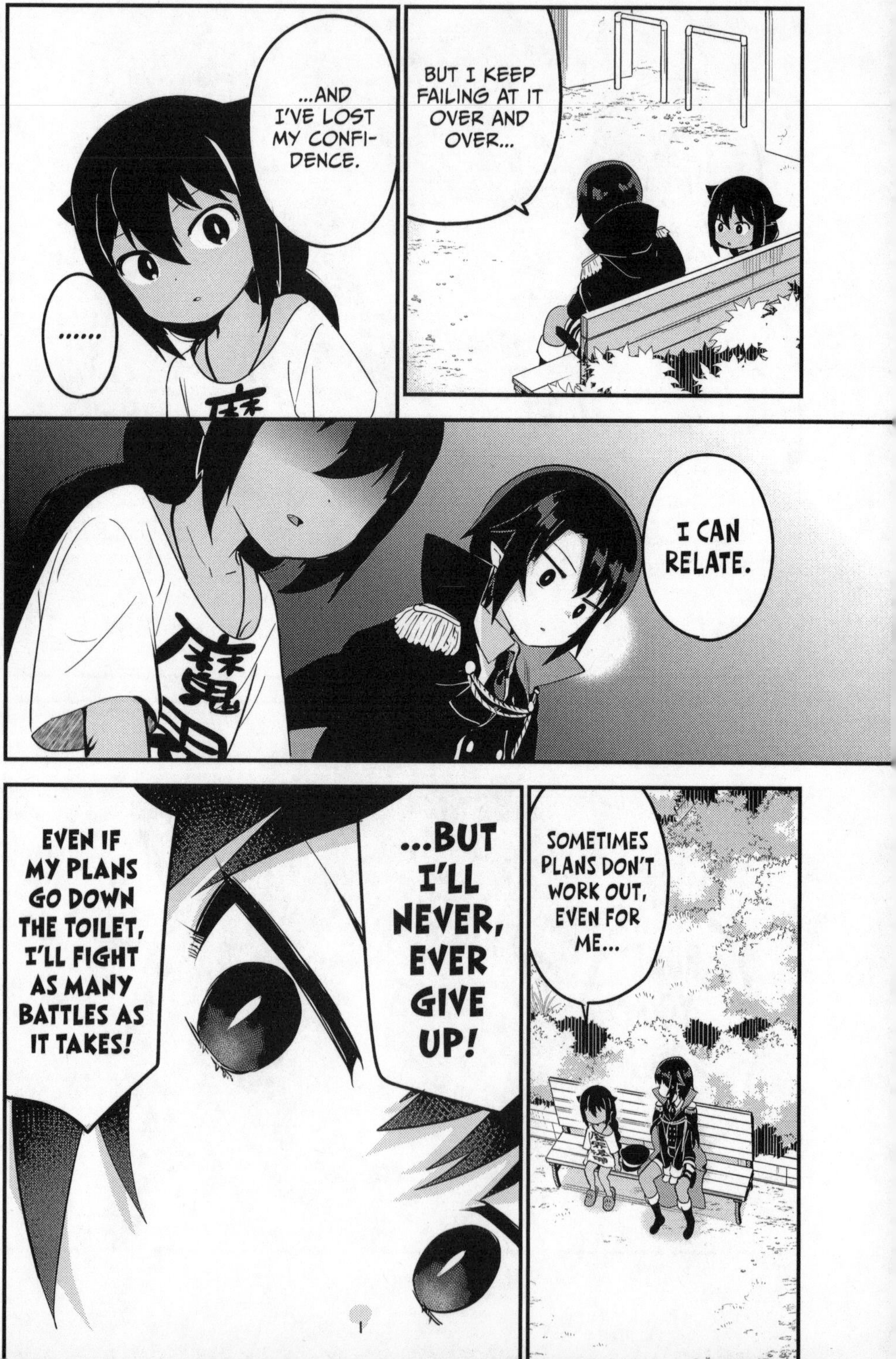
BUT I KEEP FAILING AT IT OVER AND OVER...
...AND I'VE LOST MY CONFI-DENCE.
......
I CAN RELATE.
SOMETIMES PLANS DON'T WORK OUT, EVEN FOR ME...
...BUT I'LL NEVER, EVER GIVE UP!
EVEN IF MY PLANS GO DOWN THE TOILET, I'LL FIGHT AS MANY BATTLES AS IT TAKES!

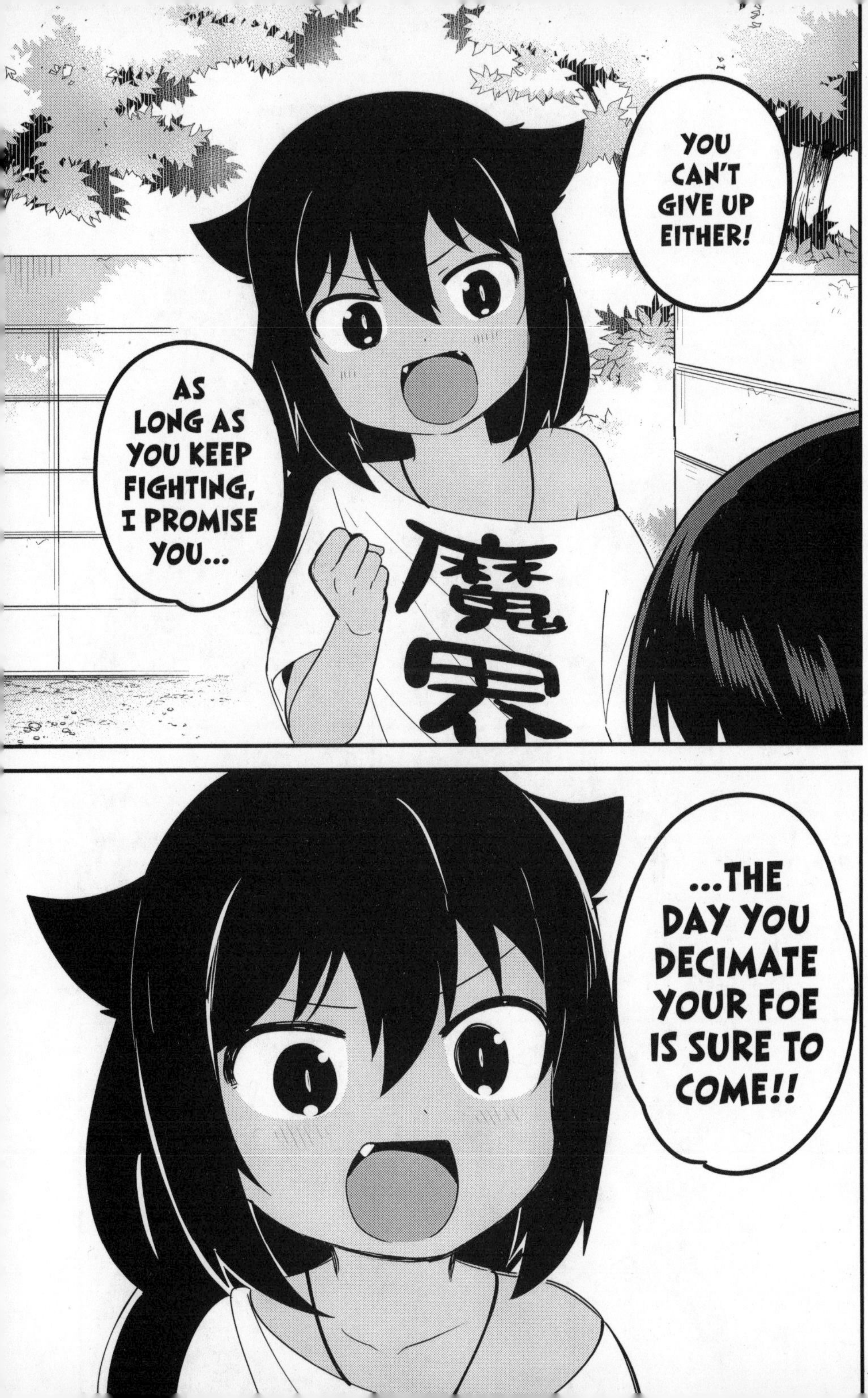
YOU CAN'T GIVE UP EITHER!
AS LONG AS YOU KEEP FIGHTING, I PROMISE YOU...
...THE DAY YOU DECIMATE YOUR FOE IS SURE TO COME!!

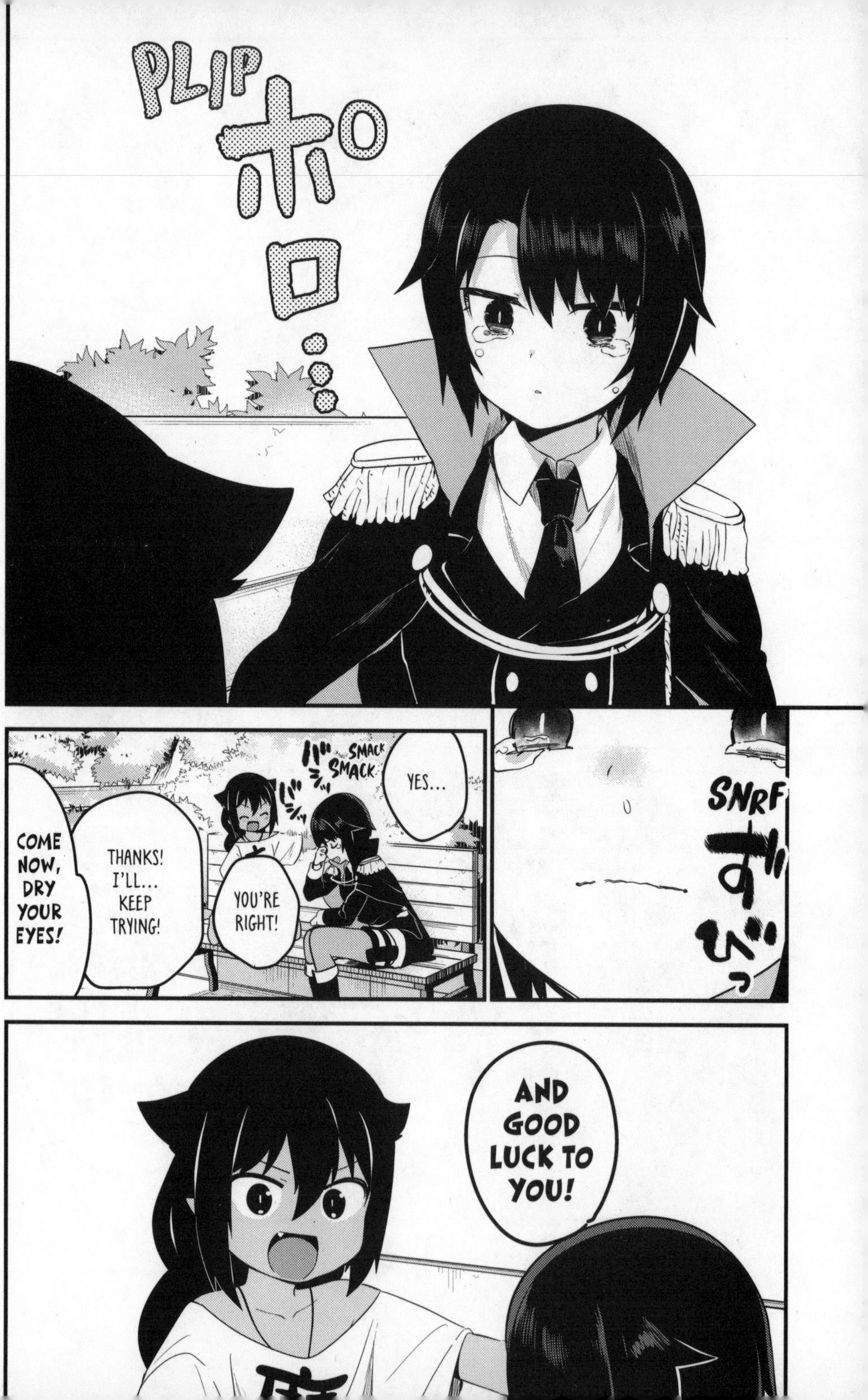
PLIP
ポロ…
SNRF
ずびっ
YES…
SMACK SMACK
YOU'RE RIGHT!
THANKS! I'LL… KEEP TRYING!
COME NOW, DRY YOUR EYES!
AND GOOD LUCK TO YOU!

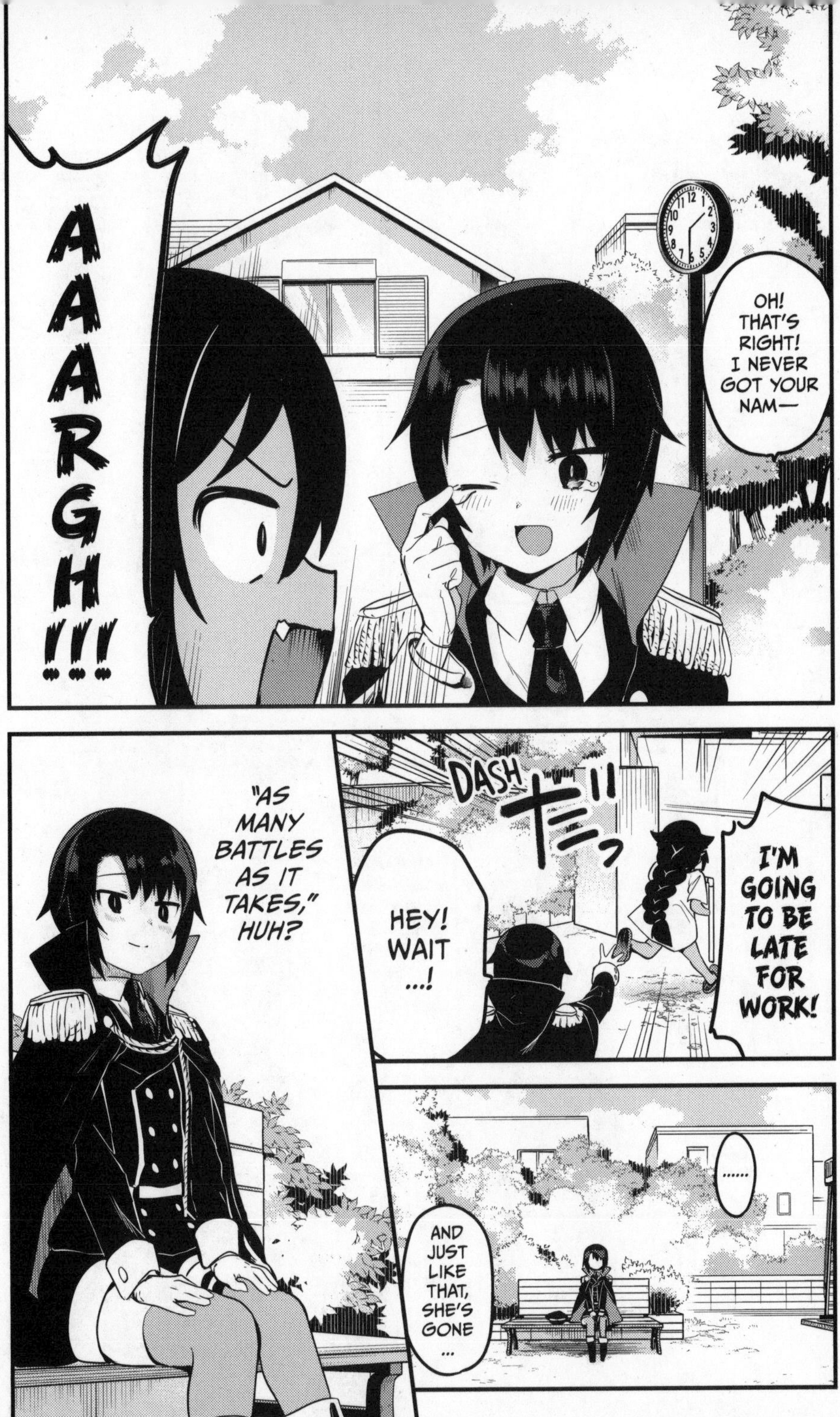
OH! THAT'S RIGHT! I NEVER GOT YOUR NAM—
AAARGH!!!
DASH
I'M GOING TO BE LATE FOR WORK!
HEY! WAIT ...!
......
AND JUST LIKE THAT, SHE'S GONE ...
"AS MANY BATTLES AS IT TAKES," HUH?

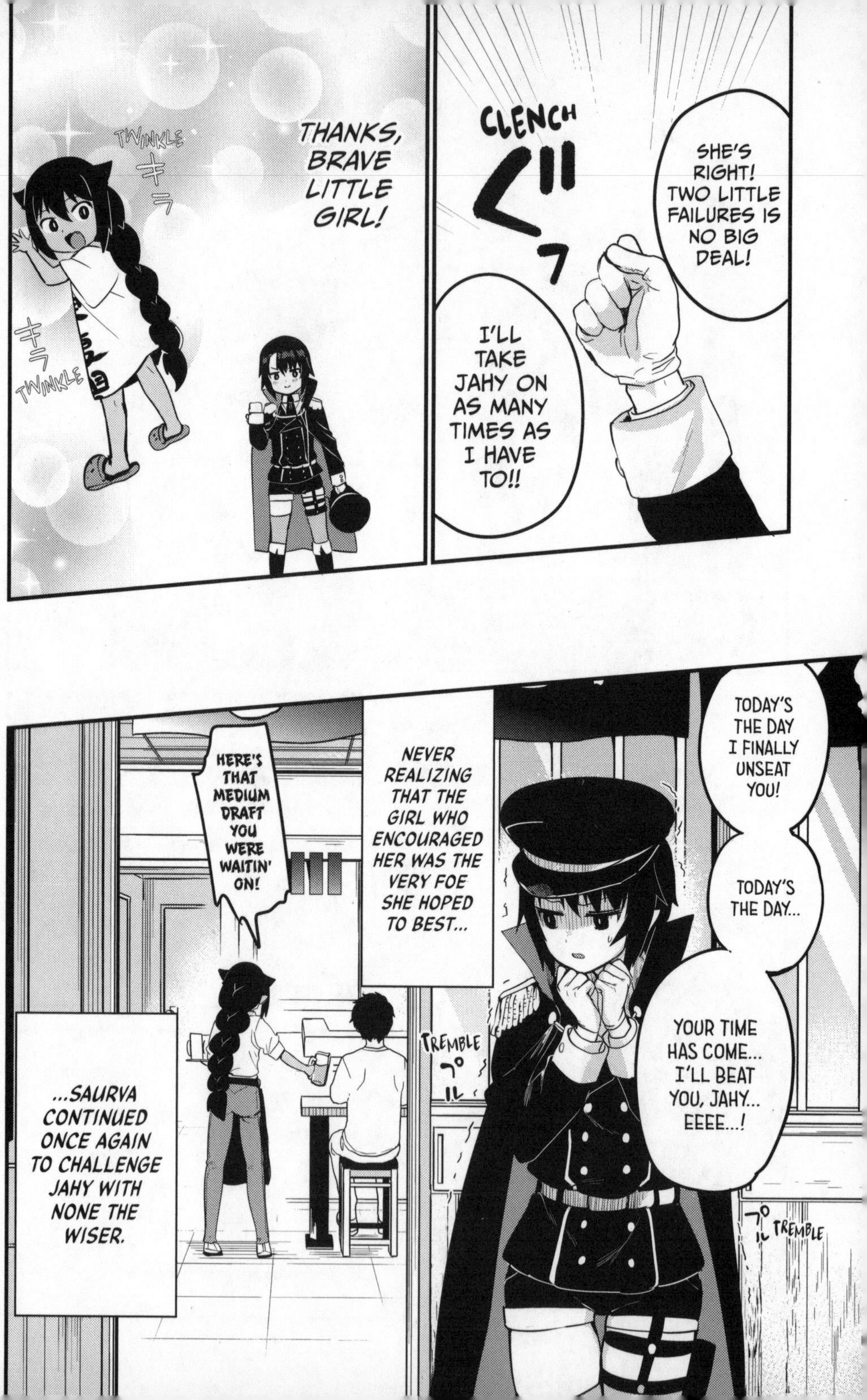
CLENCH
SHE'S RIGHT! TWO LITTLE FAILURES IS NO BIG DEAL!
I'LL TAKE JAHY ON AS MANY TIMES AS I HAVE TO!!
THANKS, BRAVE LITTLE GIRL!
TWINKLE
キラ
TWINKLE
キラ
TODAY'S THE DAY I FINALLY UNSEAT YOU!
TODAY'S THE DAY...
YOUR TIME HAS COME... I'LL BEAT YOU, JAHY... EEEE...!
TREMBLE
TREMBLE
NEVER REALIZING THAT THE GIRL WHO ENCOURAGED HER WAS THE VERY FOE SHE HOPED TO BEST...
HERE'S THAT MEDIUM DRAFT YOU WERE WAITIN' ON!
...SAURVA CONTINUED ONCE AGAIN TO CHALLENGE JAHY WITH NONE THE WISER.

The GREAT JAHY Will NOT Be DEFEATED!

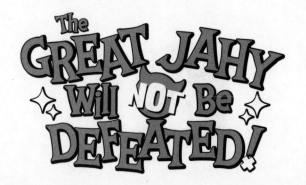

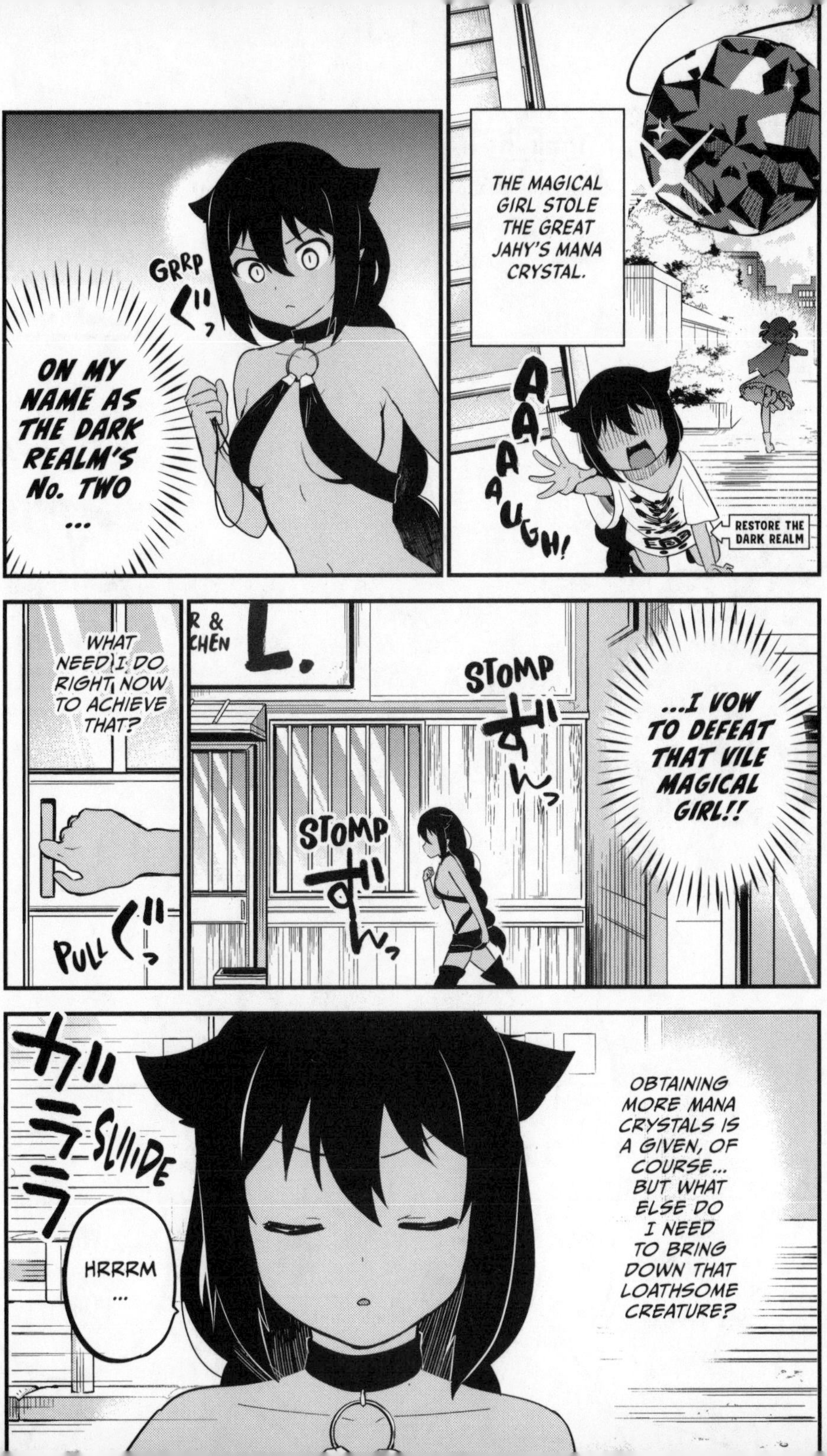
THE MAGICAL GIRL STOLE THE GREAT JAHY'S MANA CRYSTAL.
AAAAAUGH!
RESTORE THE DARK REALM
GRRP ぐっ
ON MY NAME AS THE DARK REALM'S No. TWO ...
STOMP ずんっ
...I VOW TO DEFEAT THAT VILE MAGICAL GIRL!!
STOMP ずんっ
WHAT NEED I DO RIGHT NOW TO ACHIEVE THAT?
PULL ぐっ
OBTAINING MORE MANA CRYSTALS IS A GIVEN, OF COURSE... BUT WHAT ELSE DO I NEED TO BRING DOWN THAT LOATHSOME CREATURE?
ガララ SLIIIDE
HRRRM ...

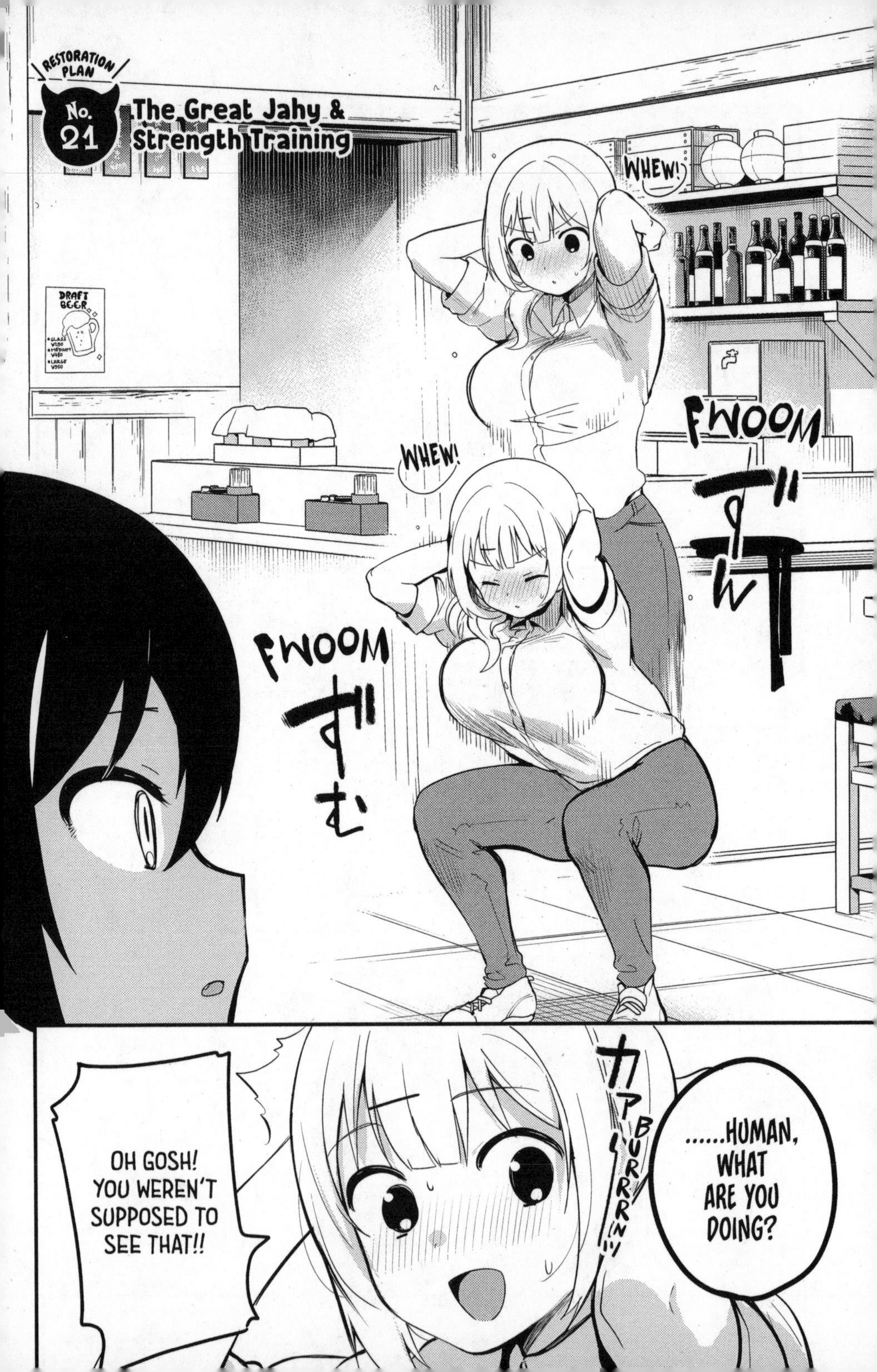
RESTORATION PLAN
No. 21
The Great Jahy & Strength Training
WHEW!
FWOOM
DRAFT BEER
WHEW!
FWOOM
......HUMAN, WHAT ARE YOU DOING?
BURRRN!!
OH GOSH! YOU WEREN'T SUPPOSED TO SEE THAT!!

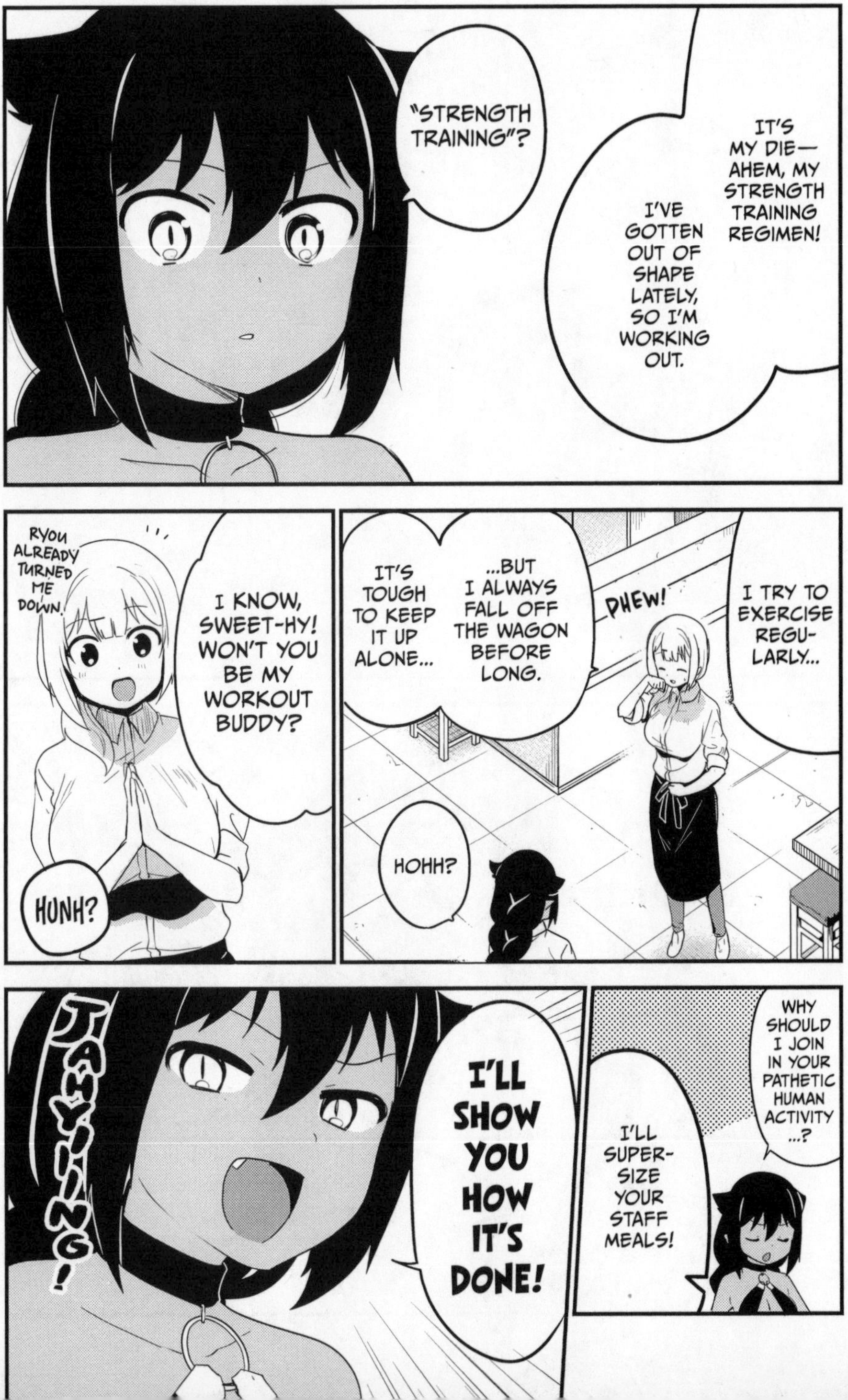
IT'S MY DIE— AHEM, MY STRENGTH TRAINING REGIMEN!
I'VE GOTTEN OUT OF SHAPE LATELY, SO I'M WORKING OUT.
"STRENGTH TRAINING"?
I TRY TO EXERCISE REGU-LARLY...
PHEW!
...BUT I ALWAYS FALL OFF THE WAGON BEFORE LONG.
IT'S TOUGH TO KEEP IT UP ALONE...
HOHH?
I KNOW, SWEET-HY! WON'T YOU BE MY WORKOUT BUDDY?
RYOU ALREADY TURNED ME DOWN.
HUNH?
WHY SHOULD I JOIN IN YOUR PATHETIC HUMAN ACTIVITY ...?
I'LL SUPER-SIZE YOUR STAFF MEALS!
I'LL SHOW YOU HOW IT'S DONE!
JAHYIIING!

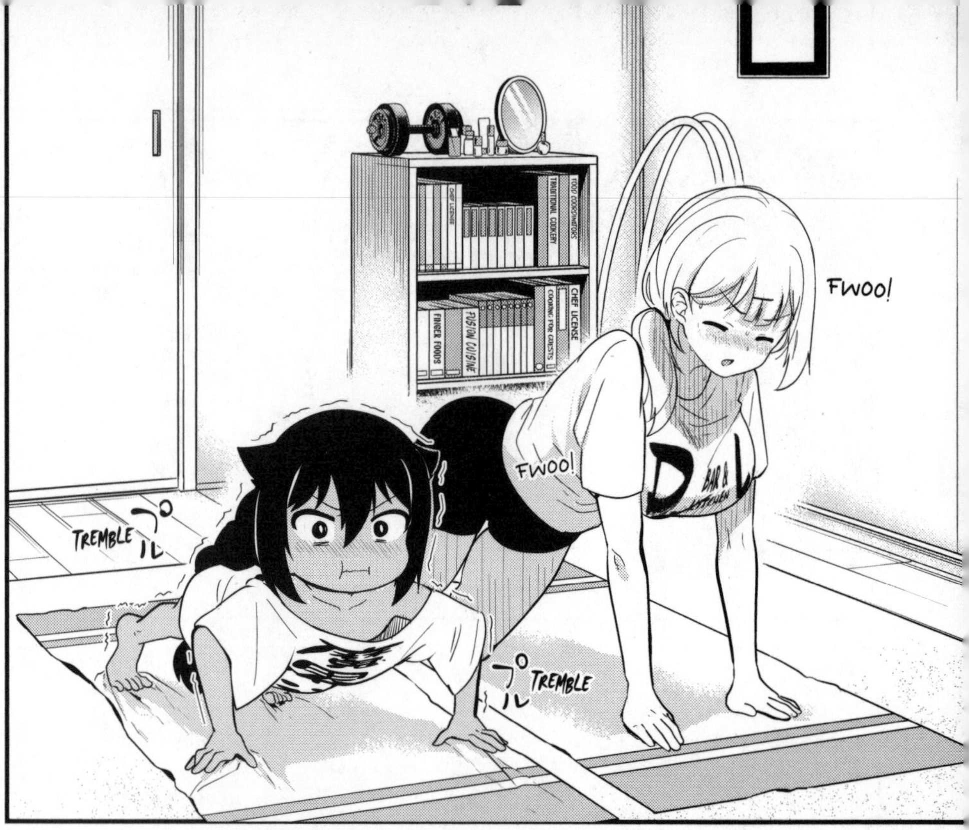
FWOO!
FWOO!
TRADITIONAL COOKERY
CHEF LICENSE
COOKING FOR GUESTS
FUSION CUISINE
FINGER FOODS
プル
TREMBLE
プル
TREMBLE

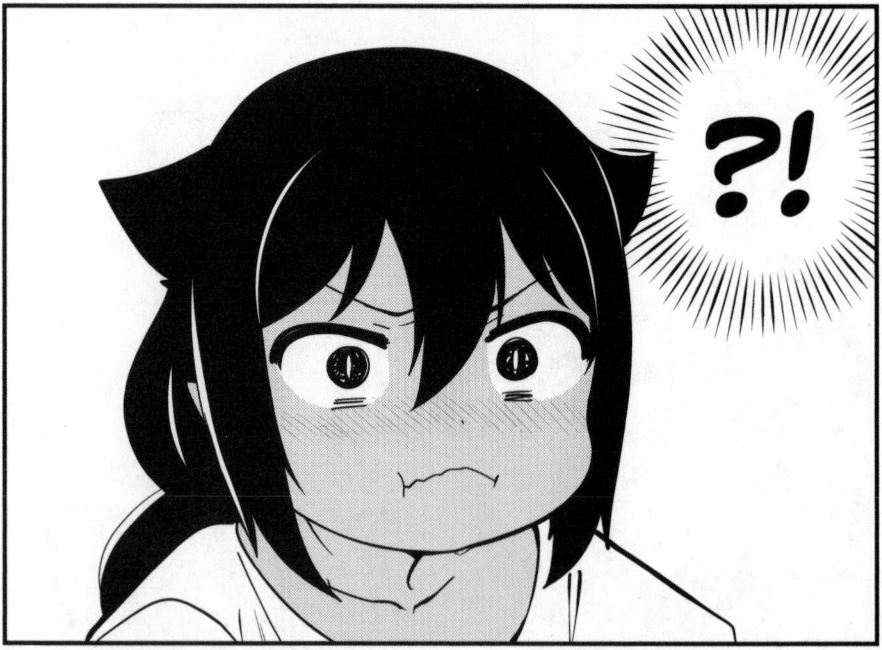
?!

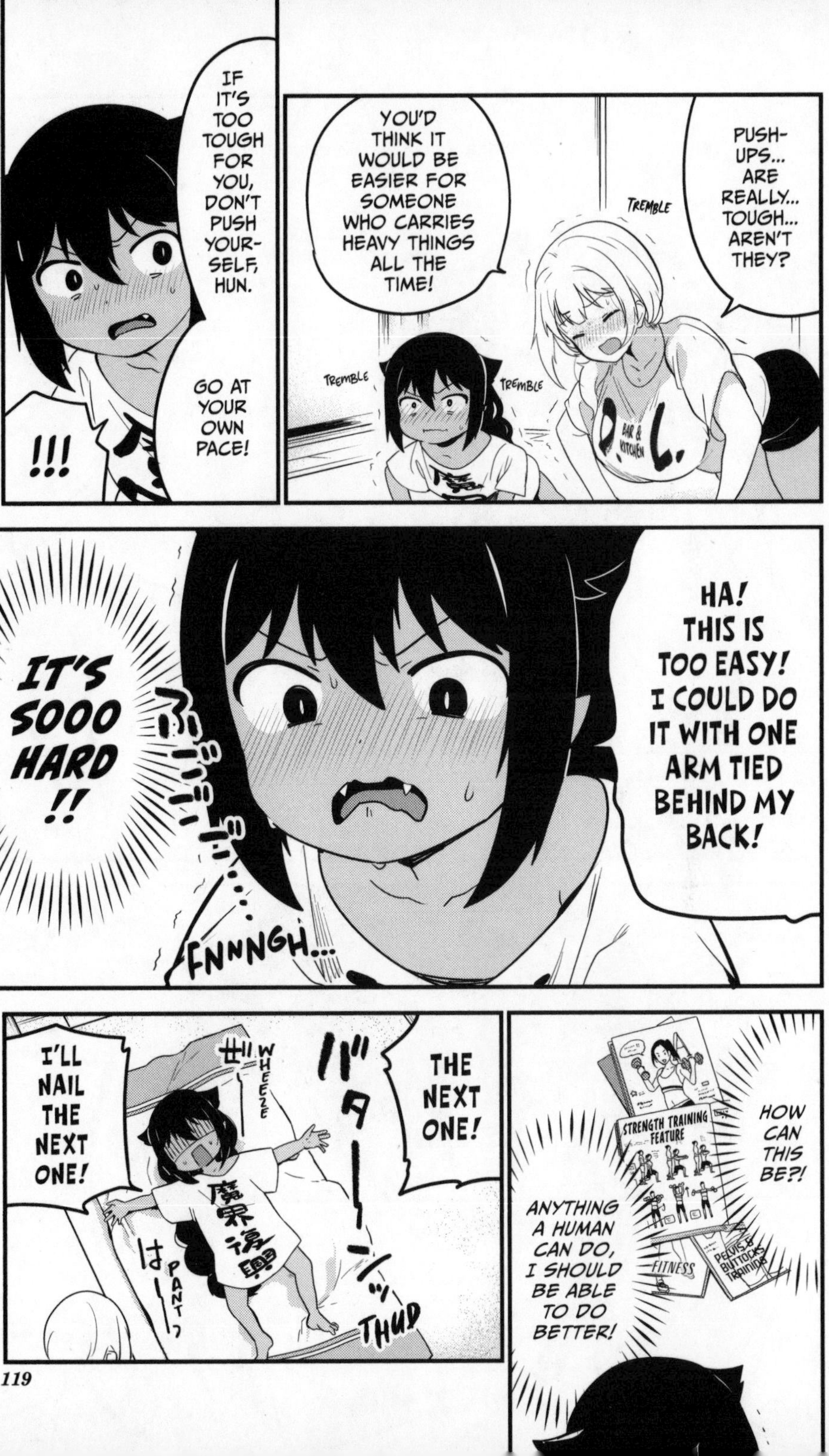
PUSH-UPS... ARE REALLY... TOUGH... AREN'T THEY?
TREMBLE
YOU'D THINK IT WOULD BE EASIER FOR SOMEONE WHO CARRIES HEAVY THINGS ALL THE TIME!
TREMBLE
TREMBLE
D.L.
BAR & KITCHEN
IF IT'S TOO TOUGH FOR YOU, DON'T PUSH YOURSELF, HUN.
GO AT YOUR OWN PACE!
!!!
HA! THIS IS TOO EASY! I COULD DO IT WITH ONE ARM TIED BEHIND MY BACK!
IT'S SOOO HARD!!
FNNNGH...
HOW CAN THIS BE?!
STRENGTH TRAINING FEATURE
FITNESS
PELVIS & BUTTOCKS TRAINING
ANYTHING A HUMAN CAN DO, I SHOULD BE ABLE TO DO BETTER!
THE NEXT ONE!
バタ
THUD
I'LL NAIL THE NEXT ONE!
WHEEZE
魔界復興
PANT

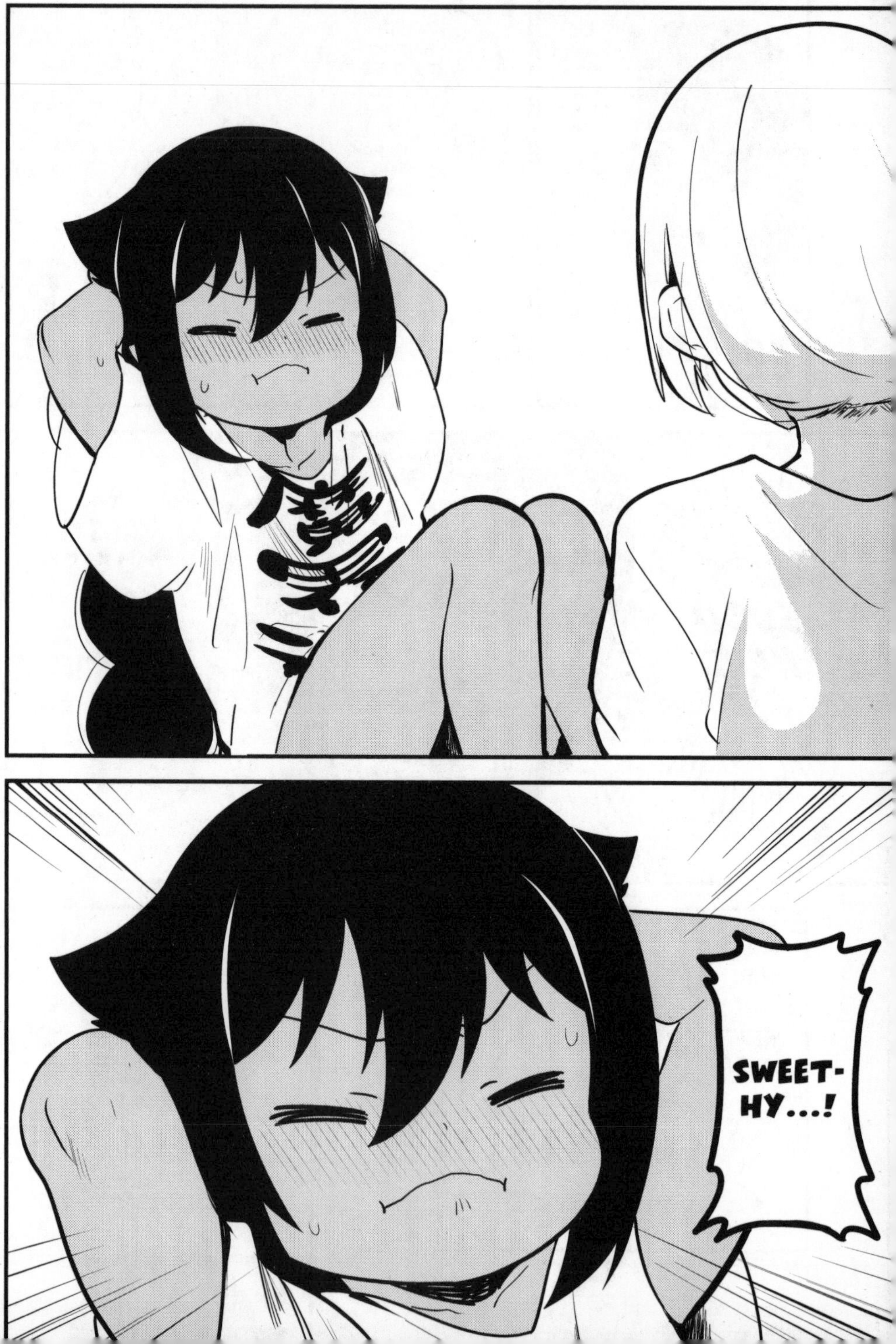
SWEET-HY...!

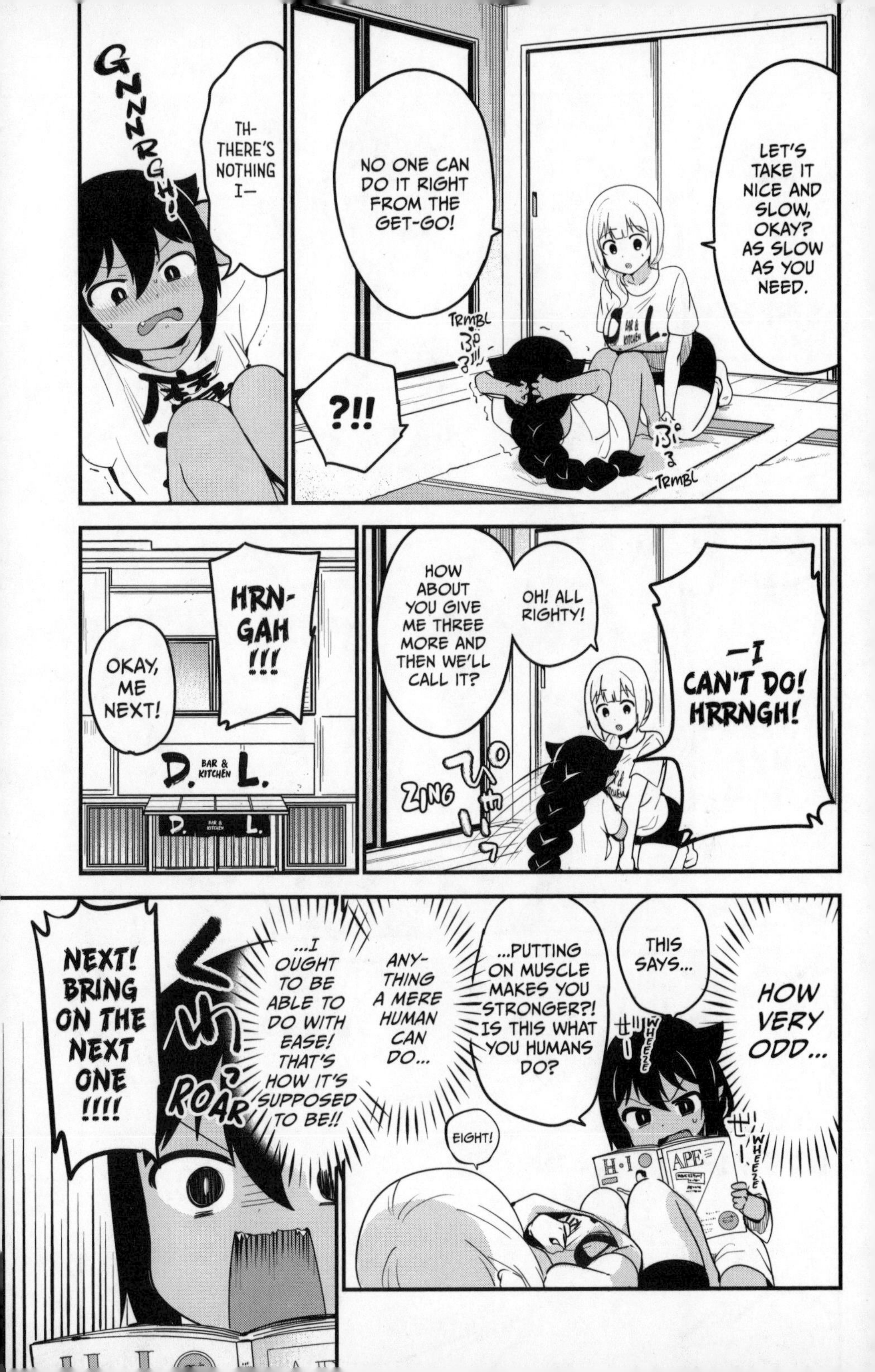
LET'S TAKE IT NICE AND SLOW, OKAY? AS SLOW AS YOU NEED.
NO ONE CAN DO IT RIGHT FROM THE GET-GO!
TRMBL
?!!
TRMBL
TH- THERE'S NOTHING I—
GNNNRGH!
—I CAN'T DO! HRRNGH!
OH! ALL RIGHTY!
HOW ABOUT YOU GIVE ME THREE MORE AND THEN WE'LL CALL IT?
ZING
HRN-GAH!!!
OKAY, ME NEXT!
D. BAR & KITCHEN L.
HOW VERY ODD...
THIS SAYS...
...PUTTING ON MUSCLE MAKES YOU STRONGER?! IS THIS WHAT YOU HUMANS DO?
WHEEZE
WHEEZE
EIGHT!
ANY-THING A MERE HUMAN CAN DO...
...I OUGHT TO BE ABLE TO DO WITH EASE! THAT'S HOW IT'S SUPPOSED TO BE!!
ROAR
NEXT! BRING ON THE NEXT ONE!!!!

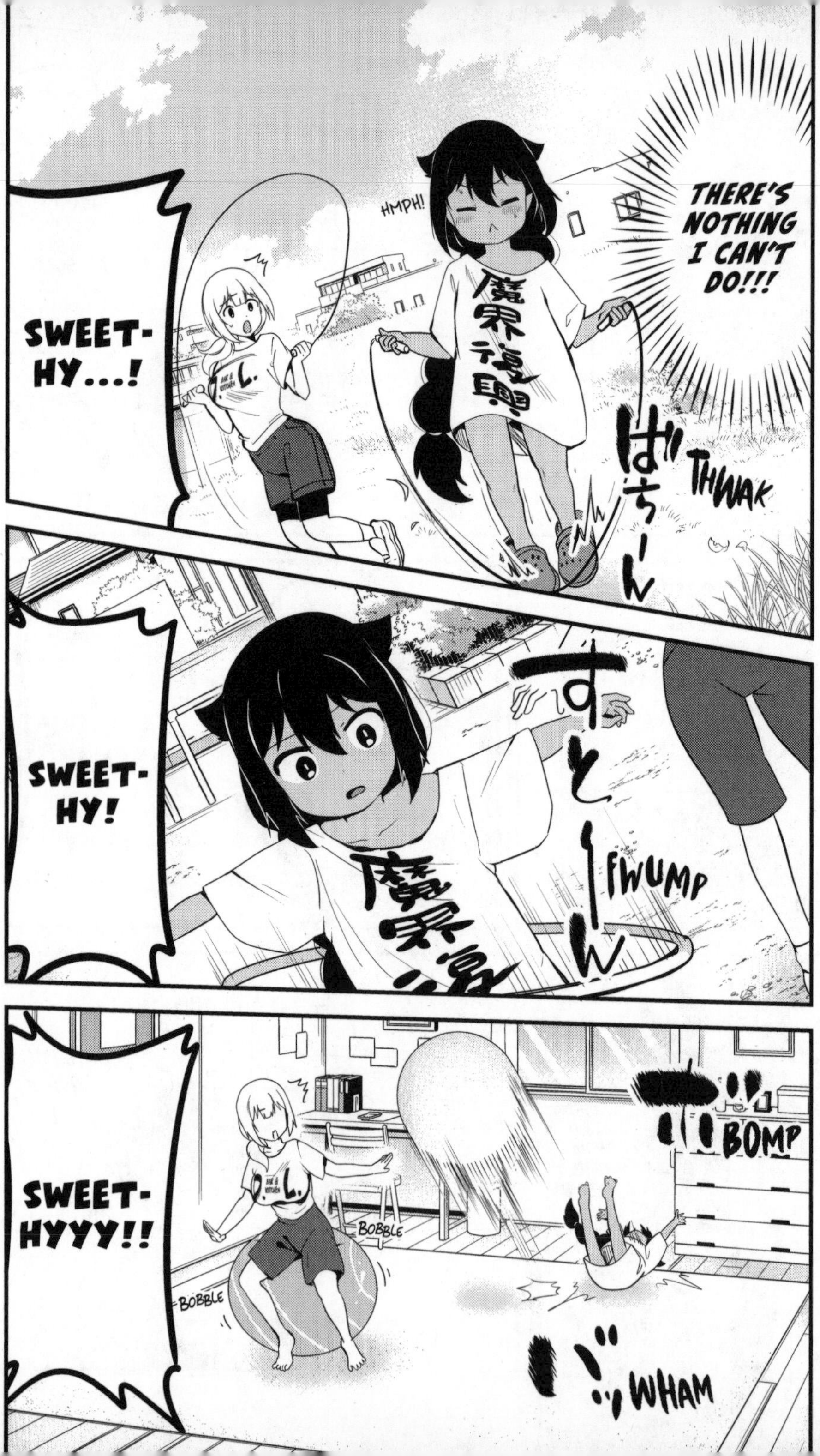
THERE'S NOTHING I CAN'T DO!!!
HMPH!
魔界復興
ばちーん
THWAK
SWEET-HY...!
すとーん
FWUMP
SWEET-HY!
BOMP
WHAM
BOBBLE
BOBBLE
SWEET-HYYY!!

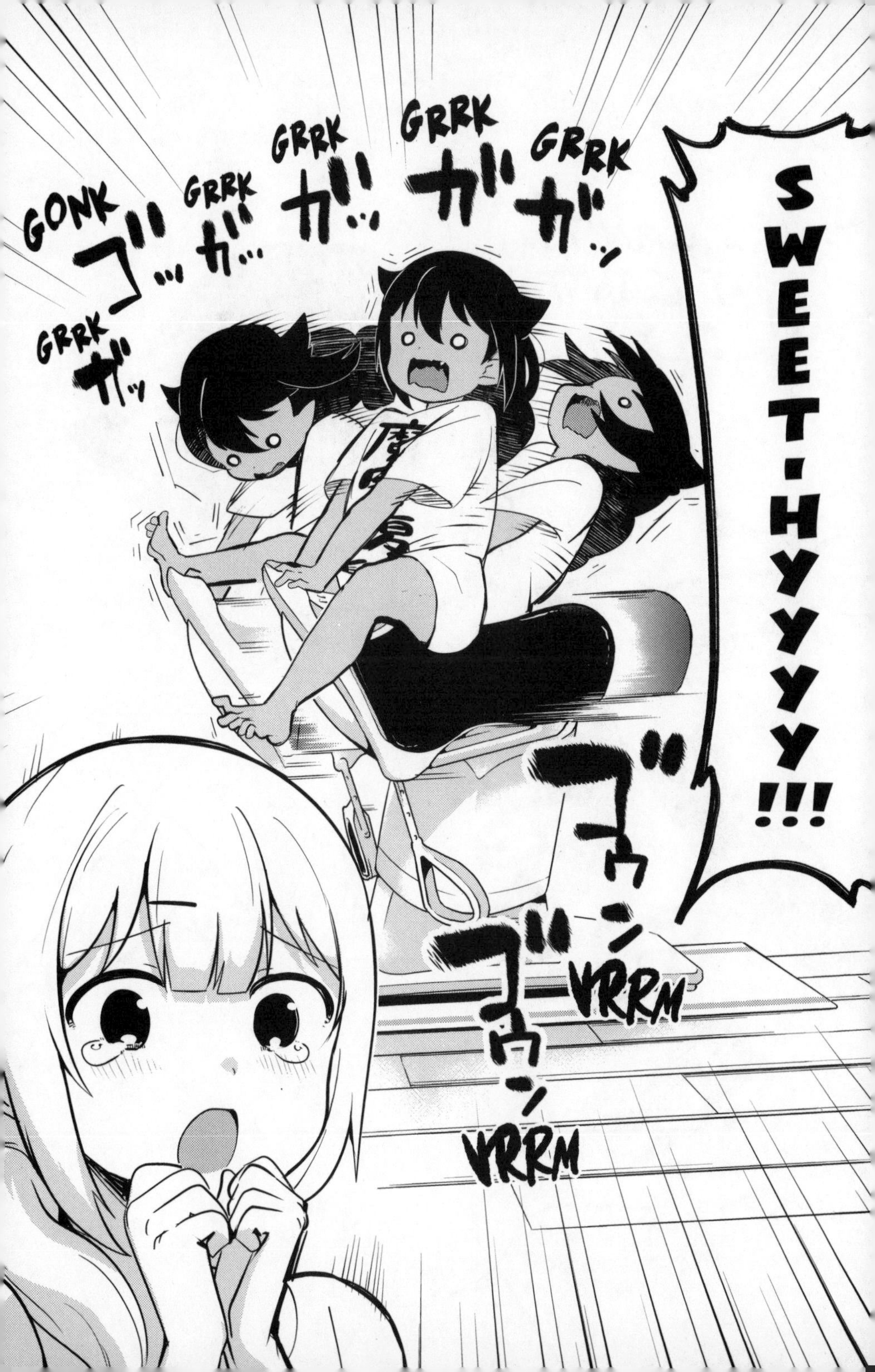
SWEET-HYYYYY!!!
GRRK ガッ
GRRK ガッ
GRRK ガッ
GRRK ガッ
GONK ゴッ
GRRK ガッ
ゴウン VRRM
ゴウン VRRM

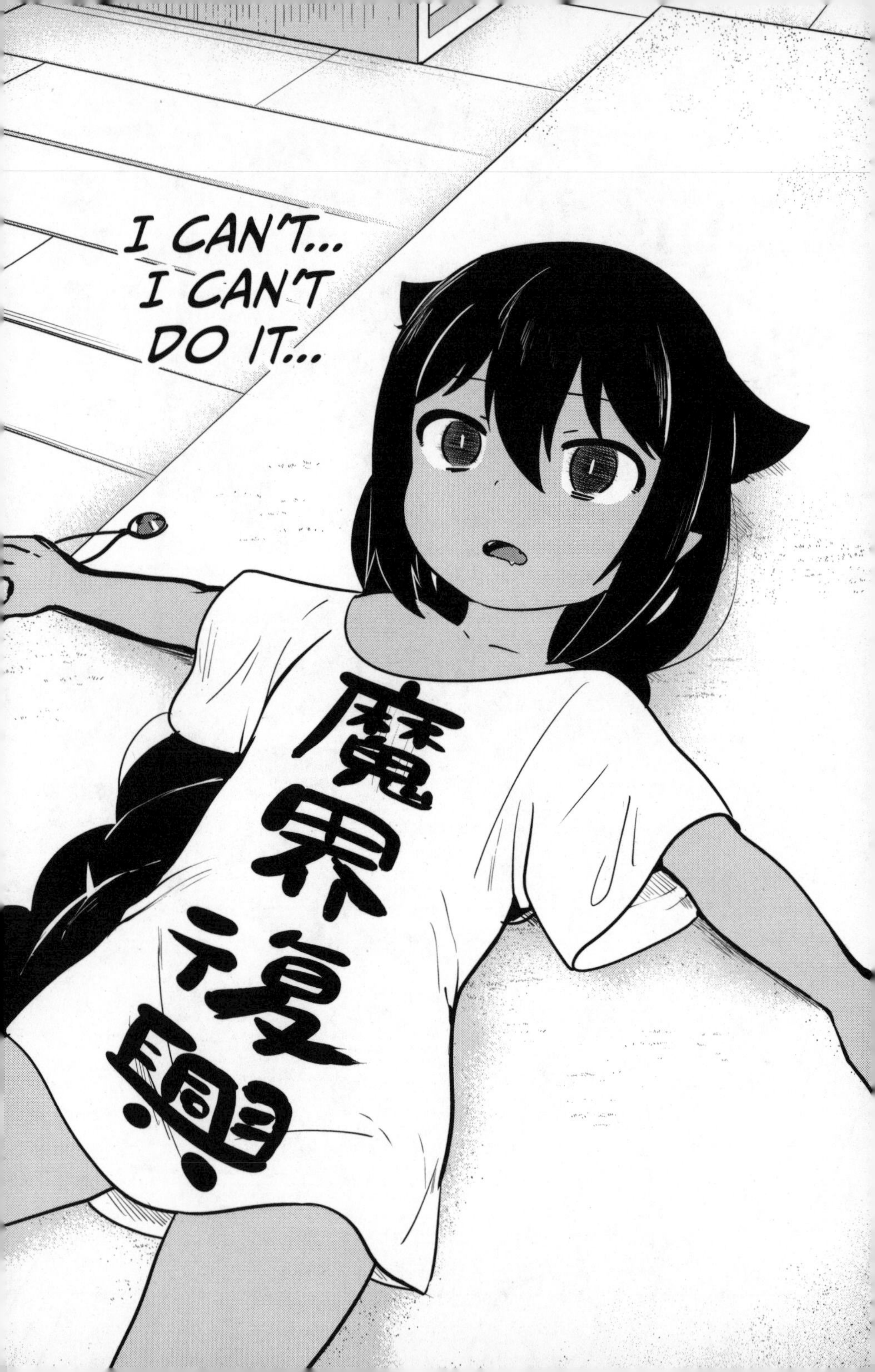
I CAN'T... I CAN'T DO IT...
魔界復興

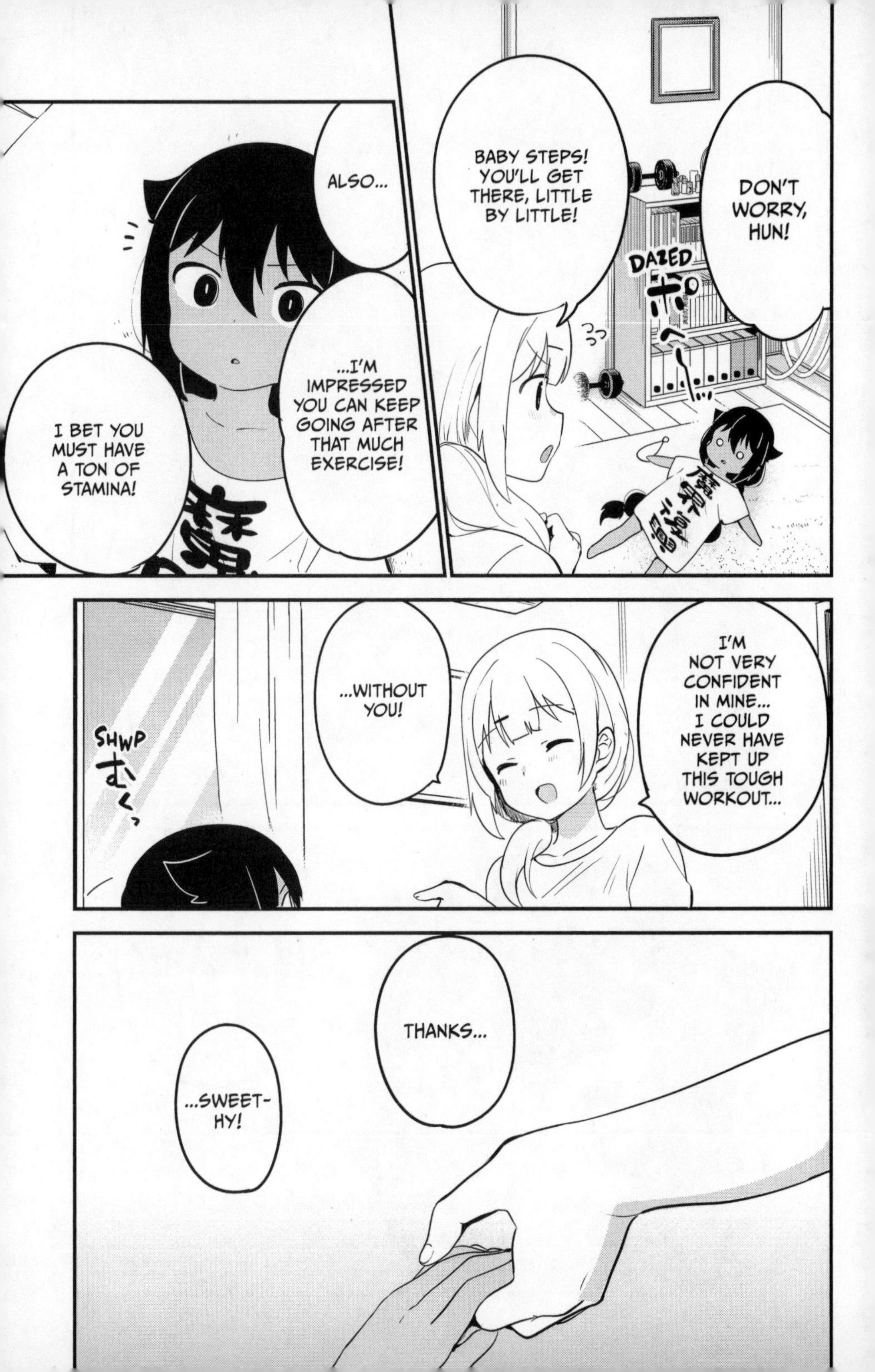
DON'T WORRY, HUN!
BABY STEPS! YOU'LL GET THERE, LITTLE BY LITTLE!
DAZED
ALSO...
...I'M IMPRESSED YOU CAN KEEP GOING AFTER THAT MUCH EXERCISE!
I BET YOU MUST HAVE A TON OF STAMINA!
I'M NOT VERY CONFIDENT IN MINE... I COULD NEVER HAVE KEPT UP THIS TOUGH WORKOUT...
...WITHOUT YOU!
SHWP
むくっ
THANKS...
...SWEET-HY!

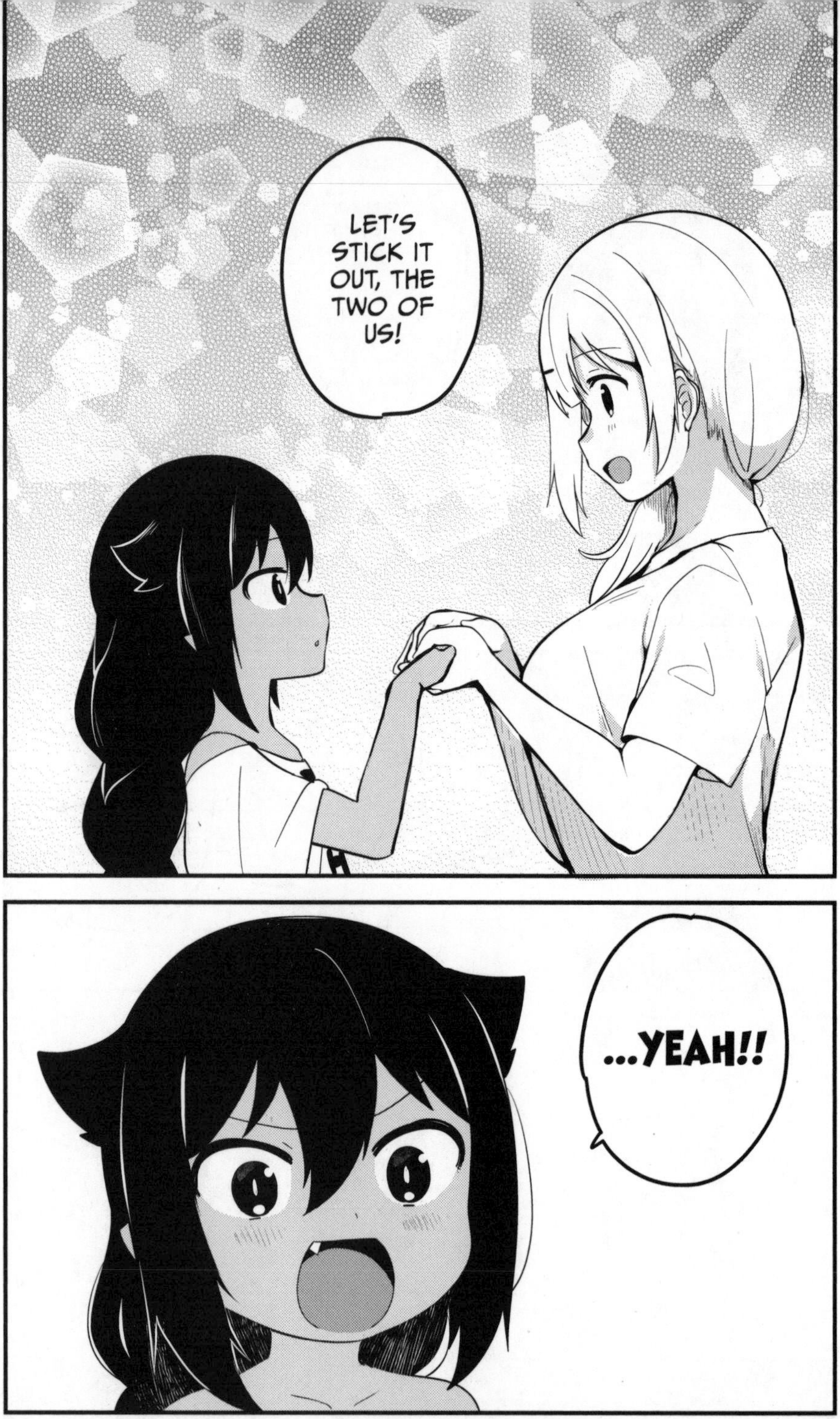
LET'S STICK IT OUT, THE TWO OF US!
...YEAH!!

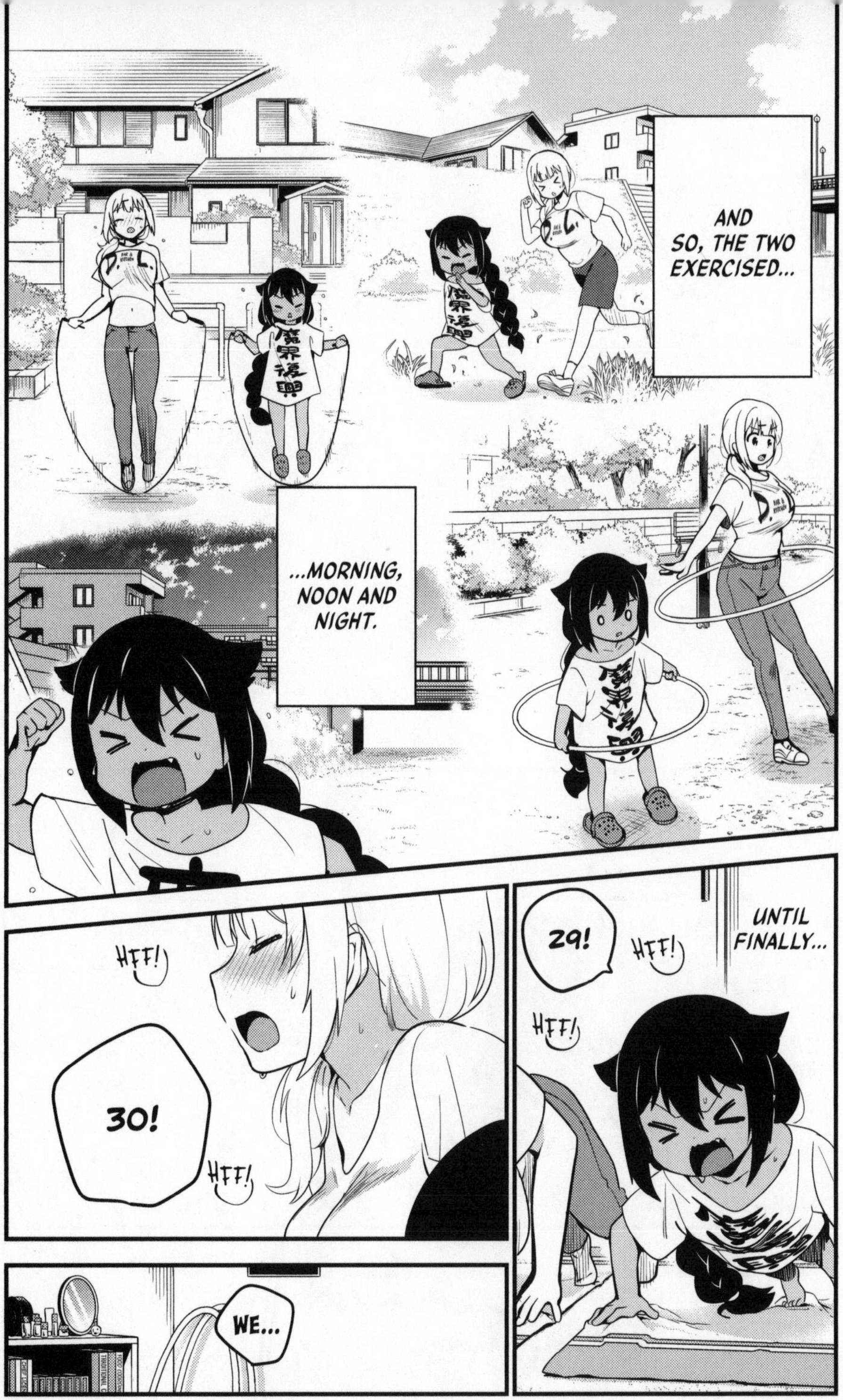
AND SO, THE TWO EXERCISED...
...MORNING, NOON AND NIGHT.
UNTIL FINALLY...
29!
HFF!
HFF!
HFF!
30!
HFF!
WE...

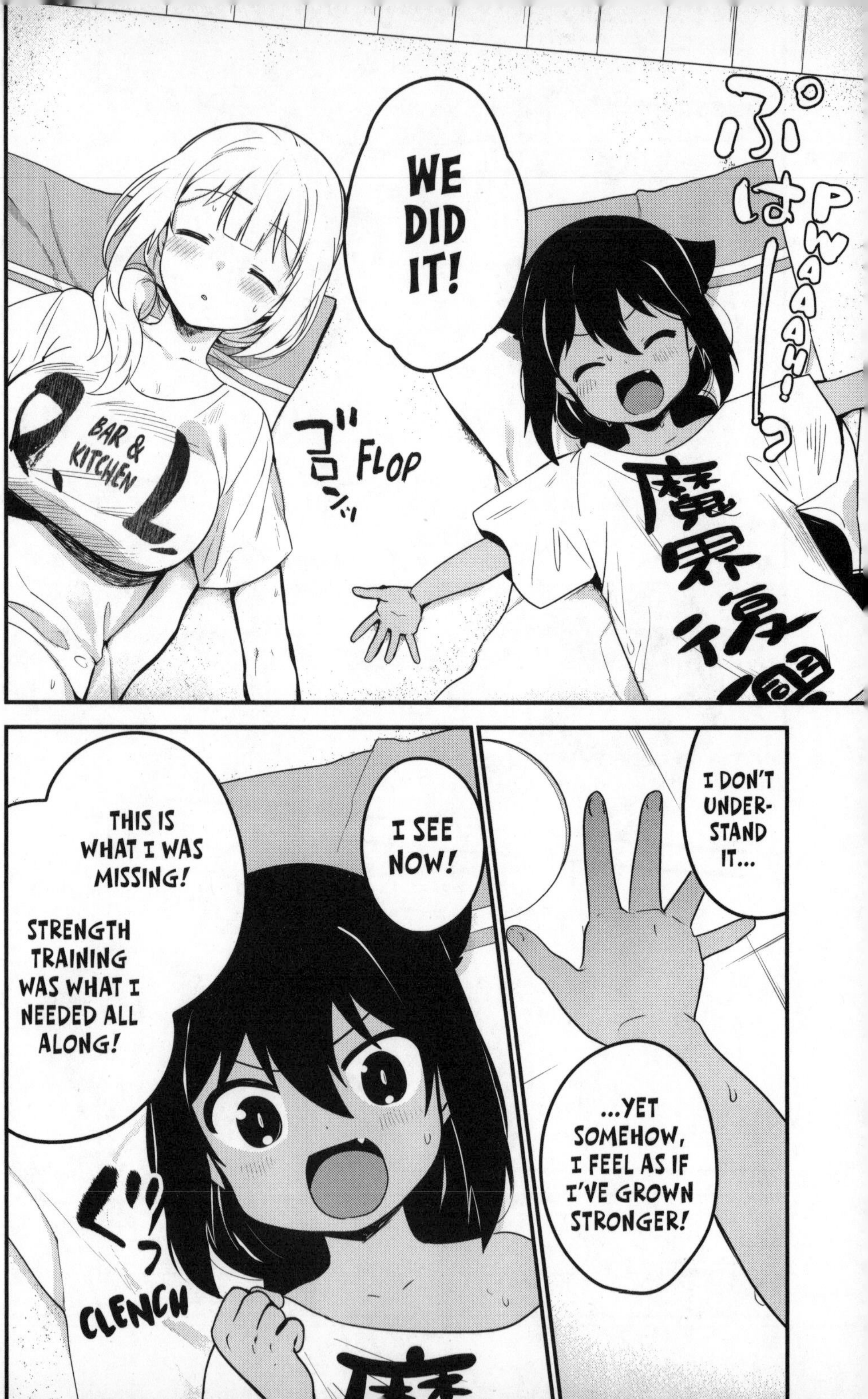
ぷは
PWAAAAH!
WE DID IT!
ゴロンっ
FLOP
BAR & KITCHEN
I DON'T UNDER-STAND IT...
...YET SOMEHOW, I FEEL AS IF I'VE GROWN STRONGER!
I SEE NOW!
THIS IS WHAT I WAS MISSING!
STRENGTH TRAINING WAS WHAT I NEEDED ALL ALONG!
ぐっ
CLENCH

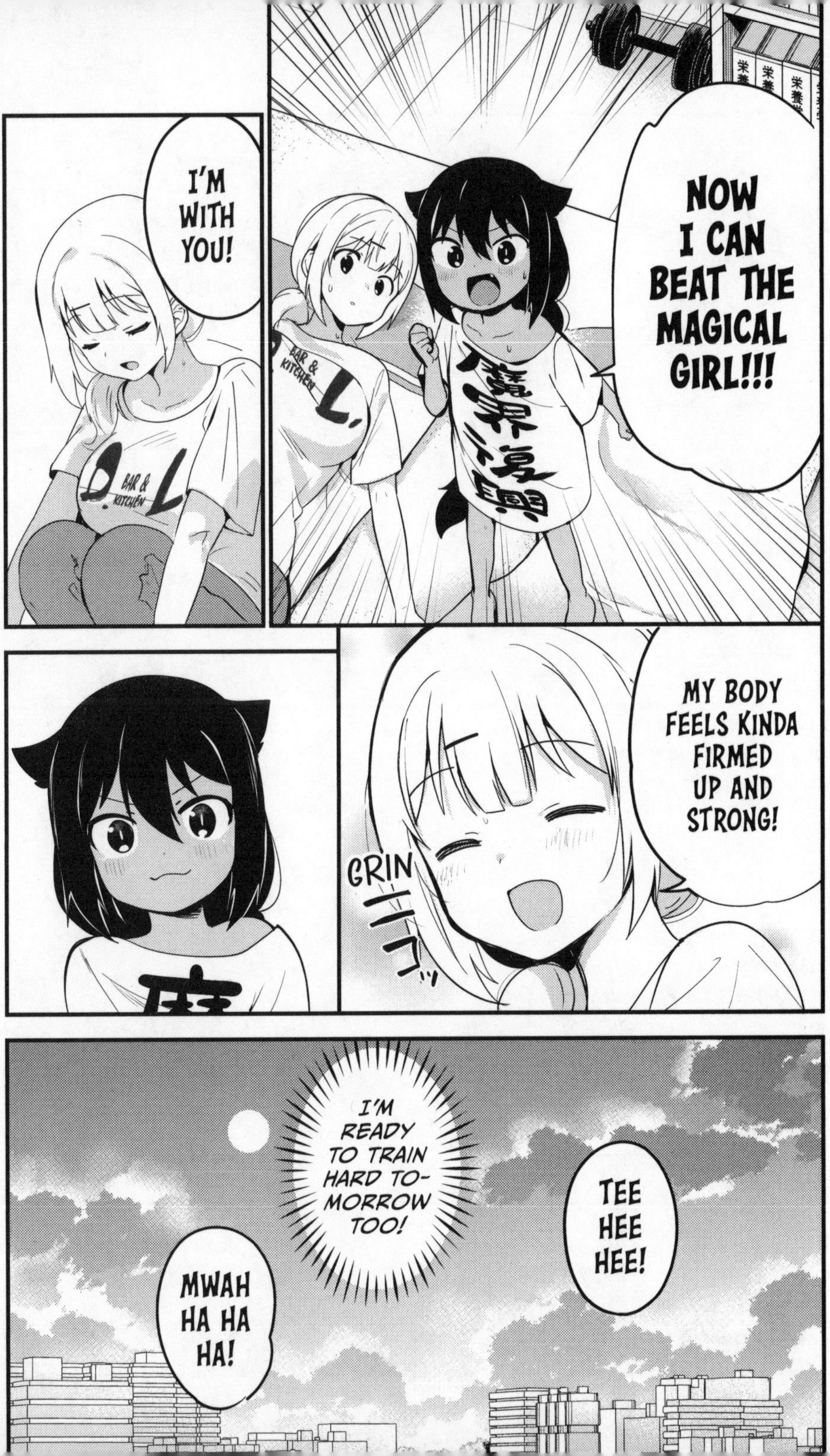
NOW I CAN BEAT THE MAGICAL GIRL!!!
I'M WITH YOU!
MY BODY FEELS KINDA FIRMED UP AND STRONG!
GRIN
I'M READY TO TRAIN HARD TO-MORROW TOO!
TEE HEE HEE!
MWAH HA HA HA!

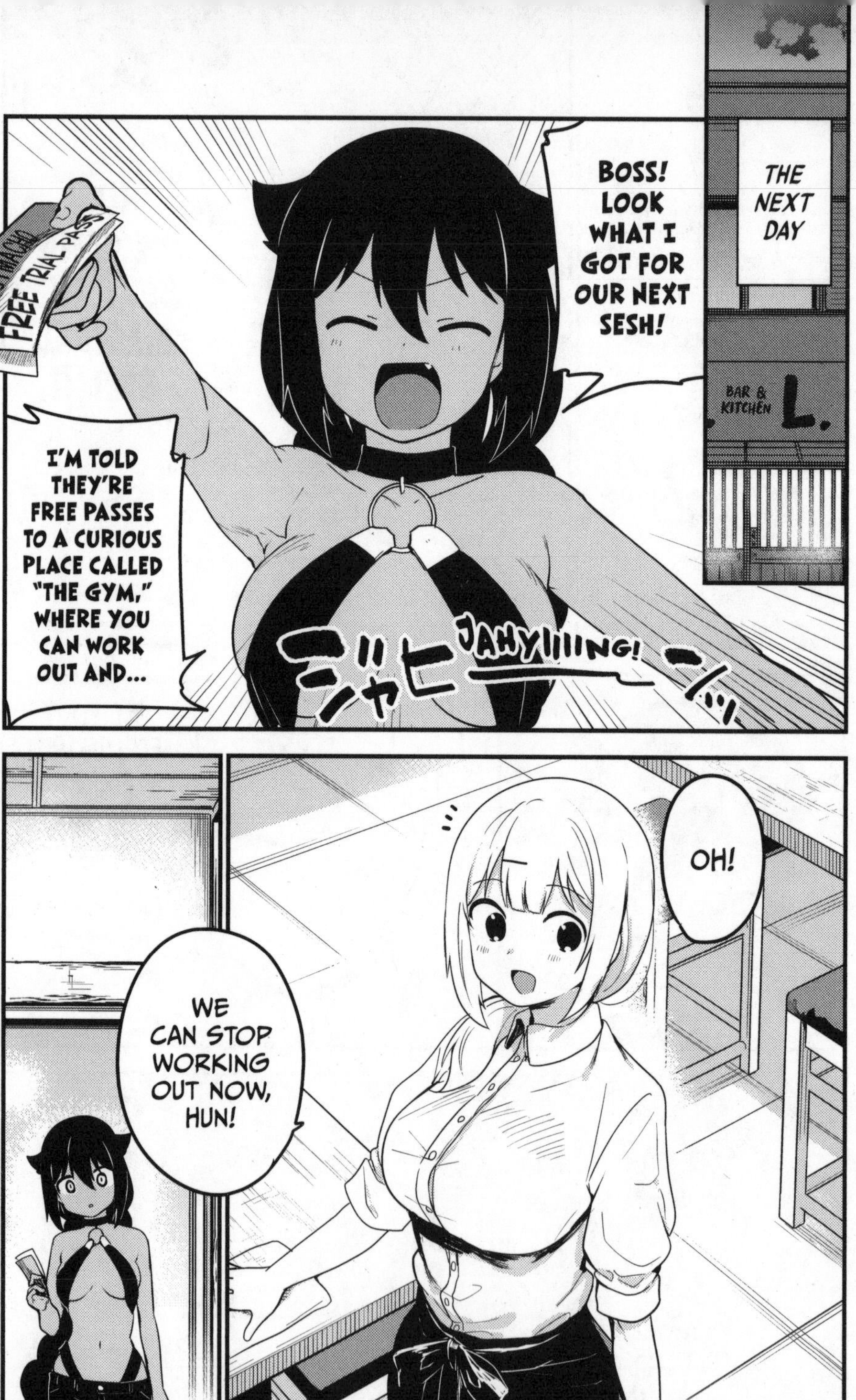
THE NEXT DAY
BAR & KITCHEN L.
BOSS! LOOK WHAT I GOT FOR OUR NEXT SESH!
JOYMACHO
FREE TRIAL PASS
I'M TOLD THEY'RE FREE PASSES TO A CURIOUS PLACE CALLED "THE GYM," WHERE YOU CAN WORK OUT AND...
ジャヒーーーっ
JAHYIIIIING!
OH!
WE CAN STOP WORKING OUT NOW, HUN!

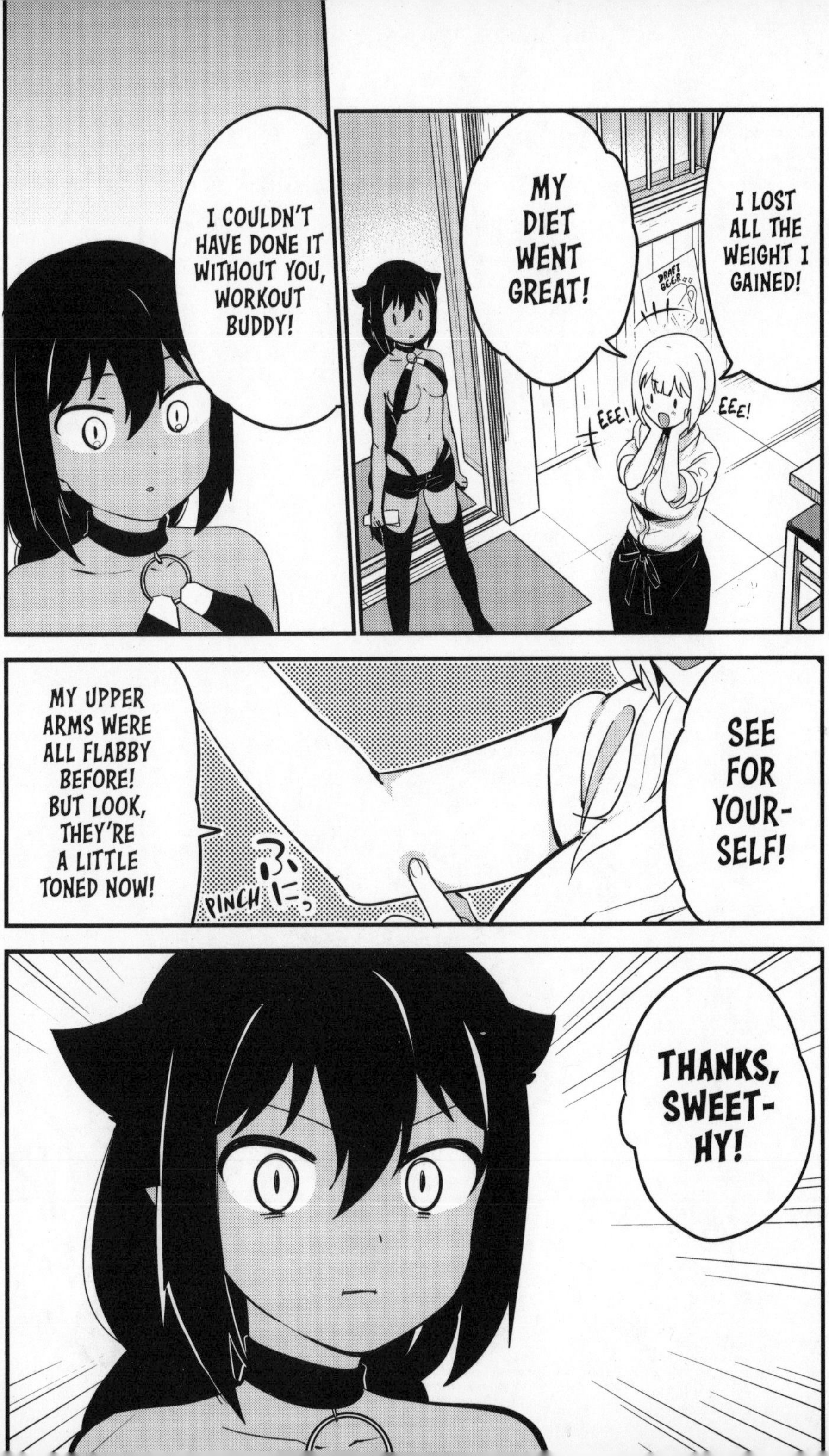
I LOST ALL THE WEIGHT I GAINED!
MY DIET WENT GREAT!
DRAFT BEER
EEE!
EEE!
I COULDN'T HAVE DONE IT WITHOUT YOU, WORKOUT BUDDY!
SEE FOR YOUR-SELF!
MY UPPER ARMS WERE ALL FLABBY BEFORE! BUT LOOK, THEY'RE A LITTLE TONED NOW!
PINCH
ぷにっ
THANKS, SWEET-HY!

The GREAT JAHY Will NOT Be DEFEATED!

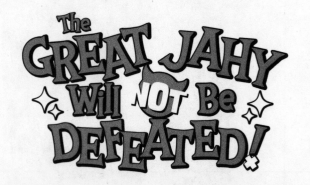

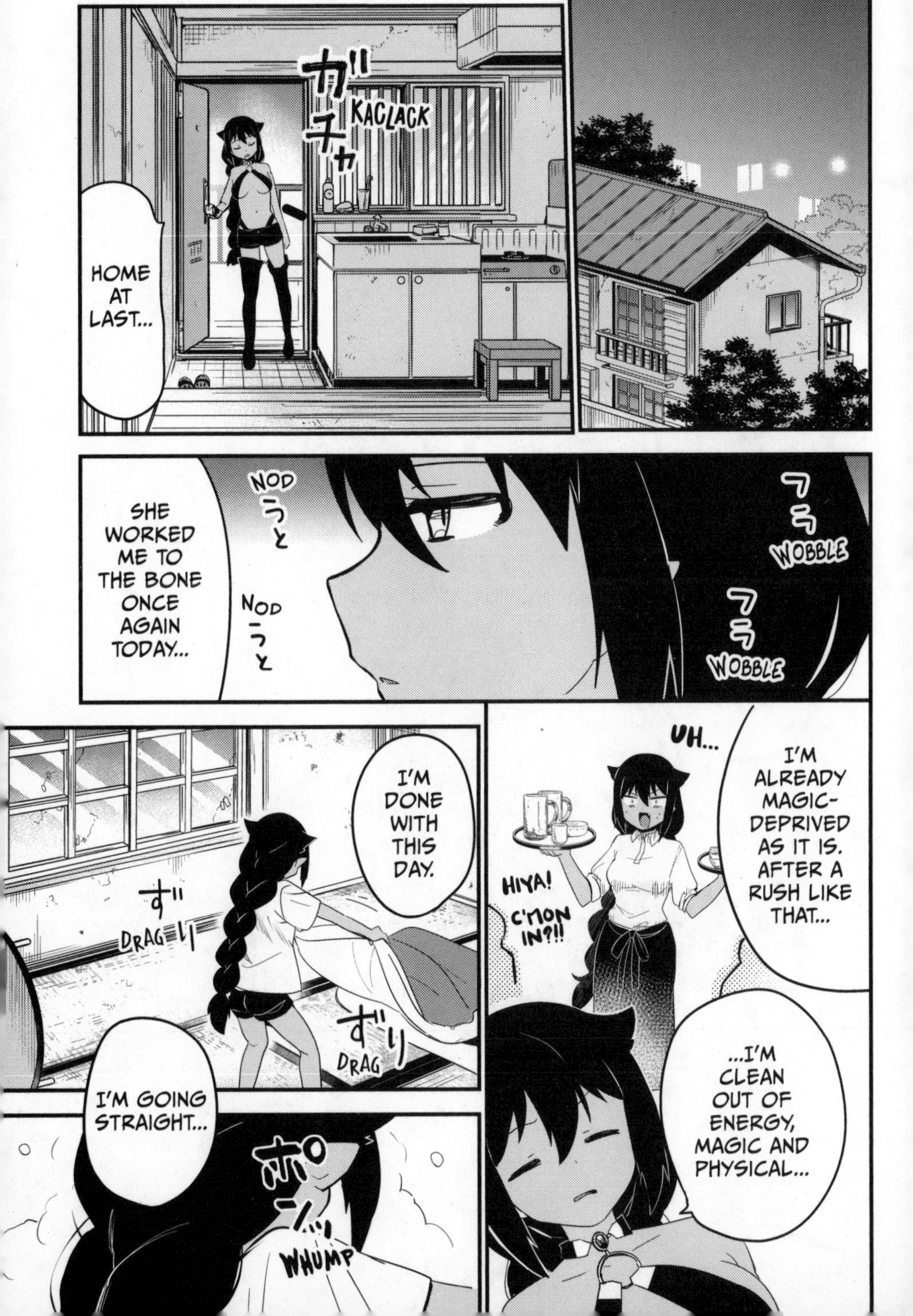

カチャ
KACLACK
HOME AT LAST...
フラ
WOBBLE
フラ
WOBBLE
うと
NOD
うと
NOD
SHE WORKED ME TO THE BONE ONCE AGAIN TODAY...
UH...
I'M ALREADY MAGIC-DEPRIVED AS IT IS. AFTER A RUSH LIKE THAT...
HIYA!
C'MON IN?!!
...I'M CLEAN OUT OF ENERGY, MAGIC AND PHYSICAL...
I'M DONE WITH THIS DAY.
ずり
DRAG
ずり
DRAG
I'M GOING STRAIGHT...
WHUMP

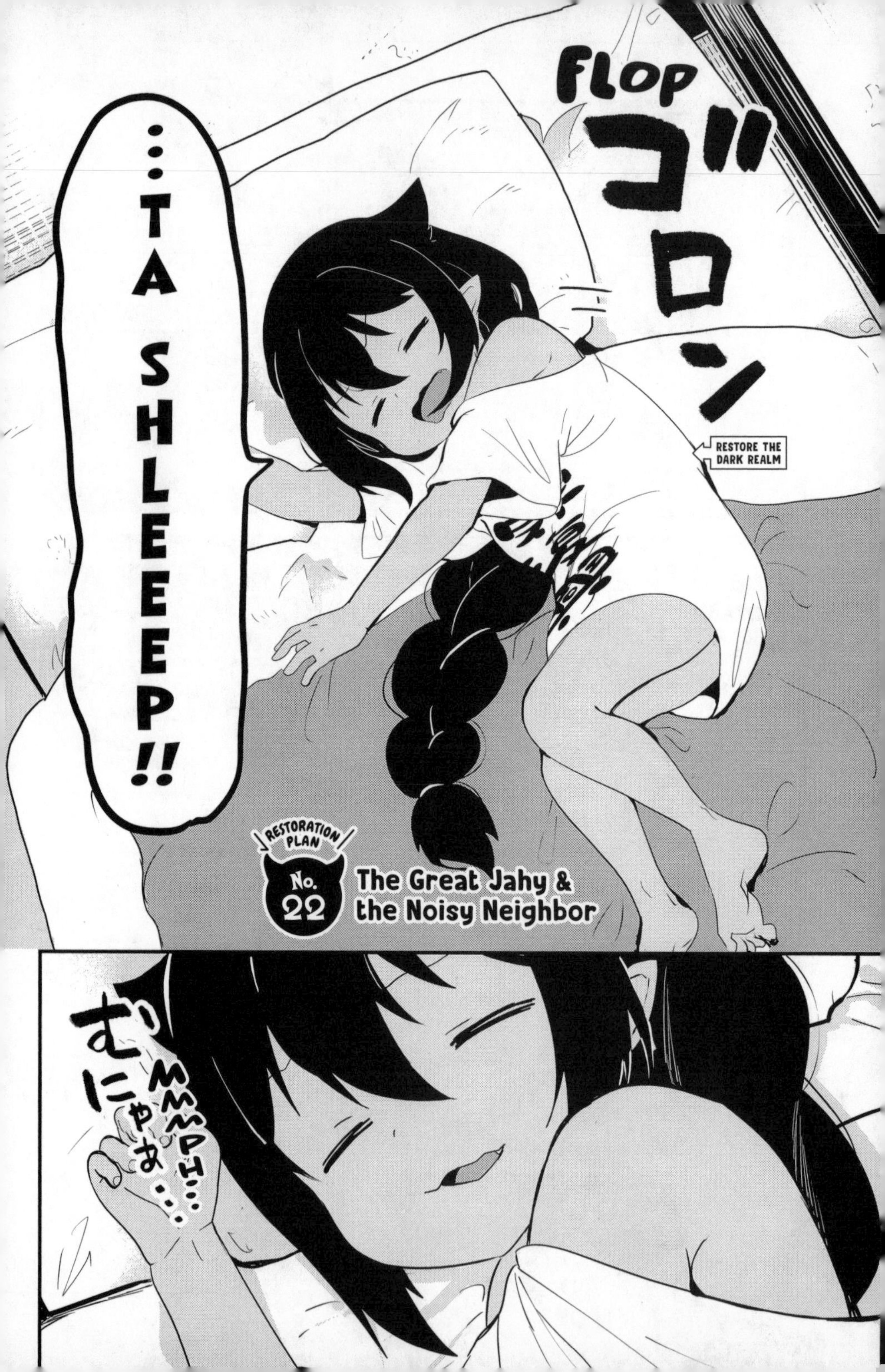
FLOP
ゴロン
RESTORE THE DARK REALM
...TA SHLEEEEP!!
RESTORATION PLAN No. 22
The Great Jahy & the Noisy Neighbor
むにゃぁ...
MMMPH...

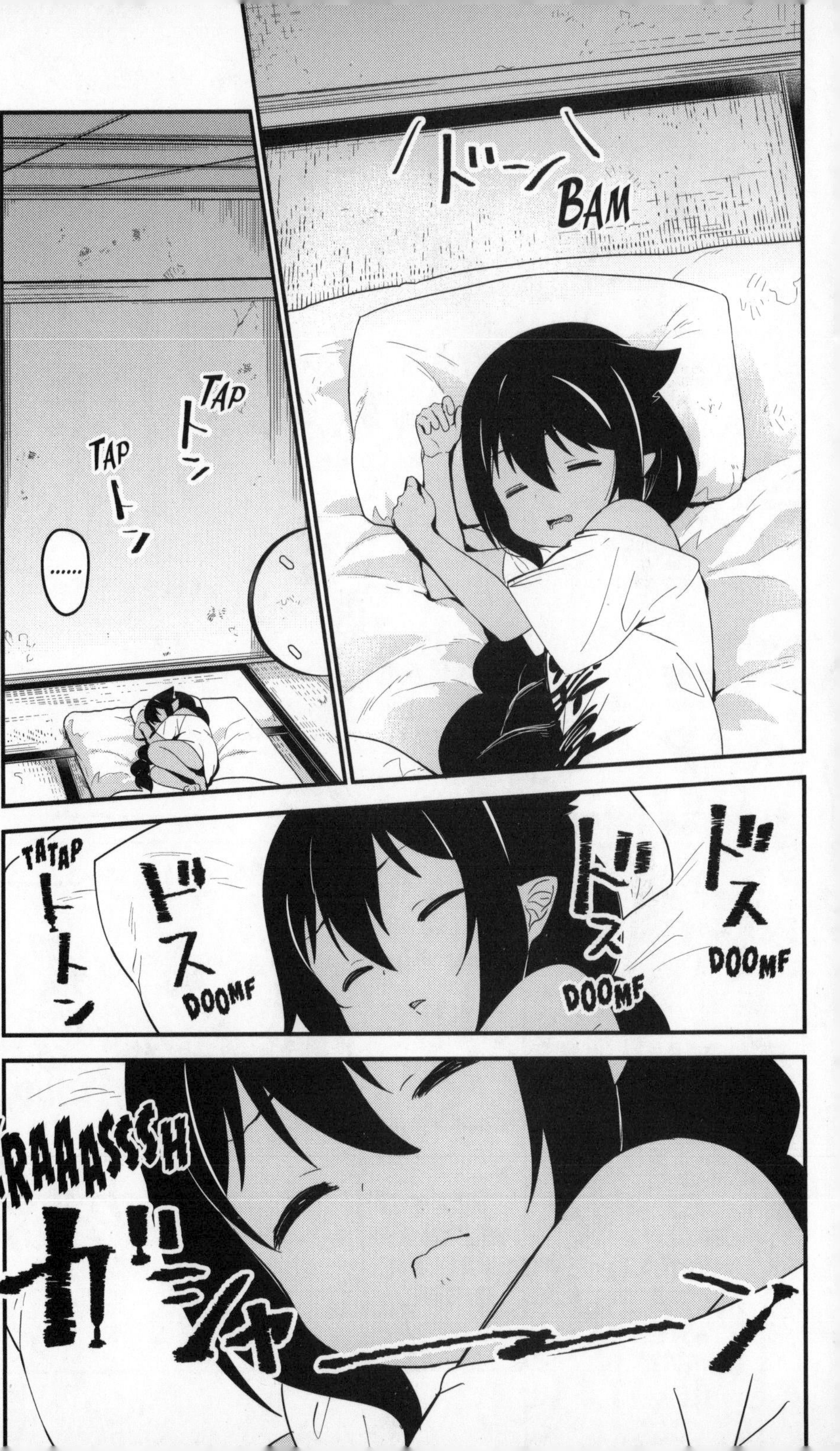
ドーン
BAM
TAP
トン
TAP
トン
……
ドス
DOOMF
ドス
DOOMF
ドス
DOOMF
TATAP
トトトン
KRAAASSSH
ガシャーン!!

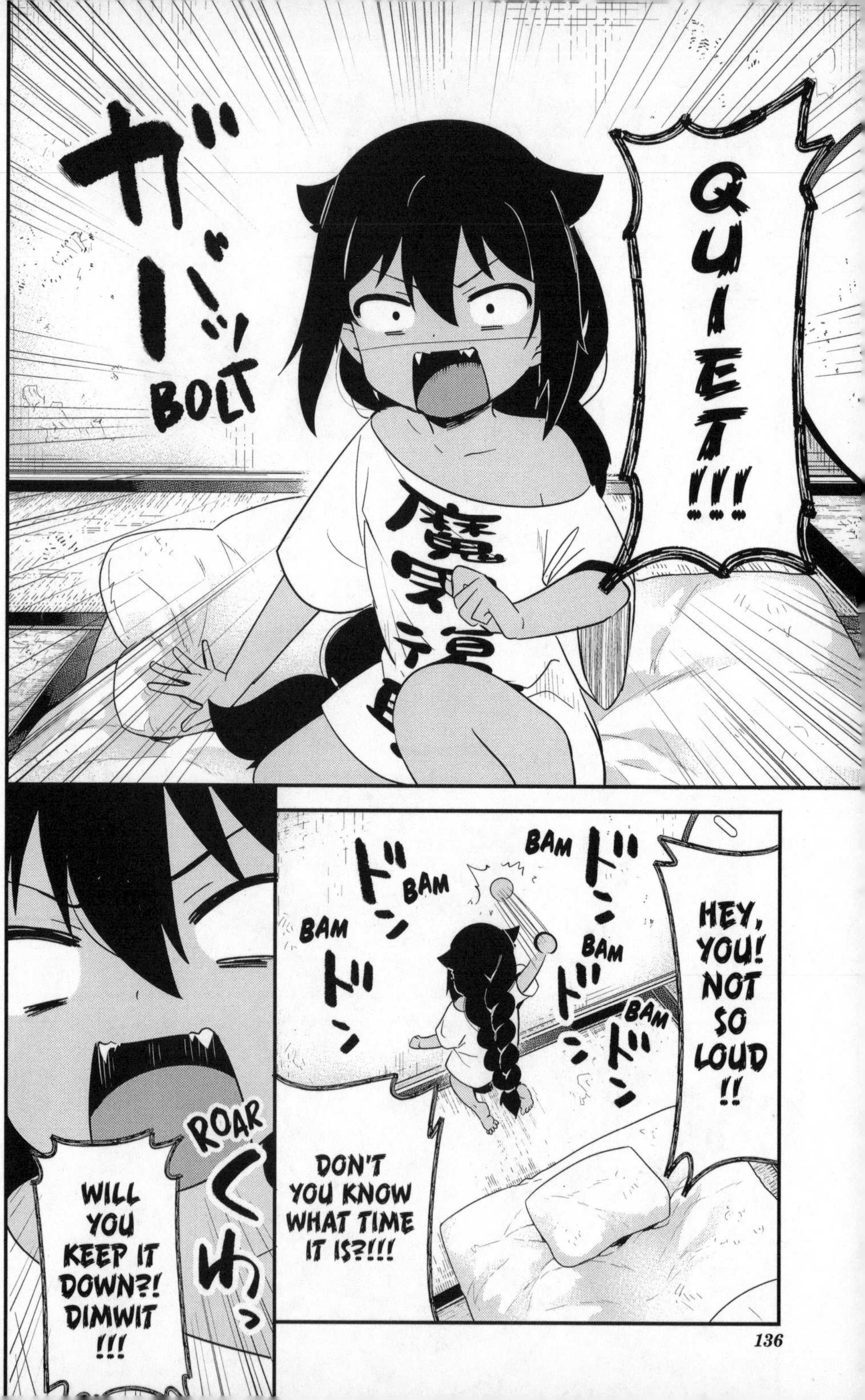
ガバーッ
BOLT
QUIET!!!
HEY, YOU! NOT SO LOUD!!
BAM
BAM
BAM
BAM
BAM
BAM
DON'T YOU KNOW WHAT TIME IT IS?!!!
ROAR
WILL YOU KEEP IT DOWN?! DIMWIT!!!

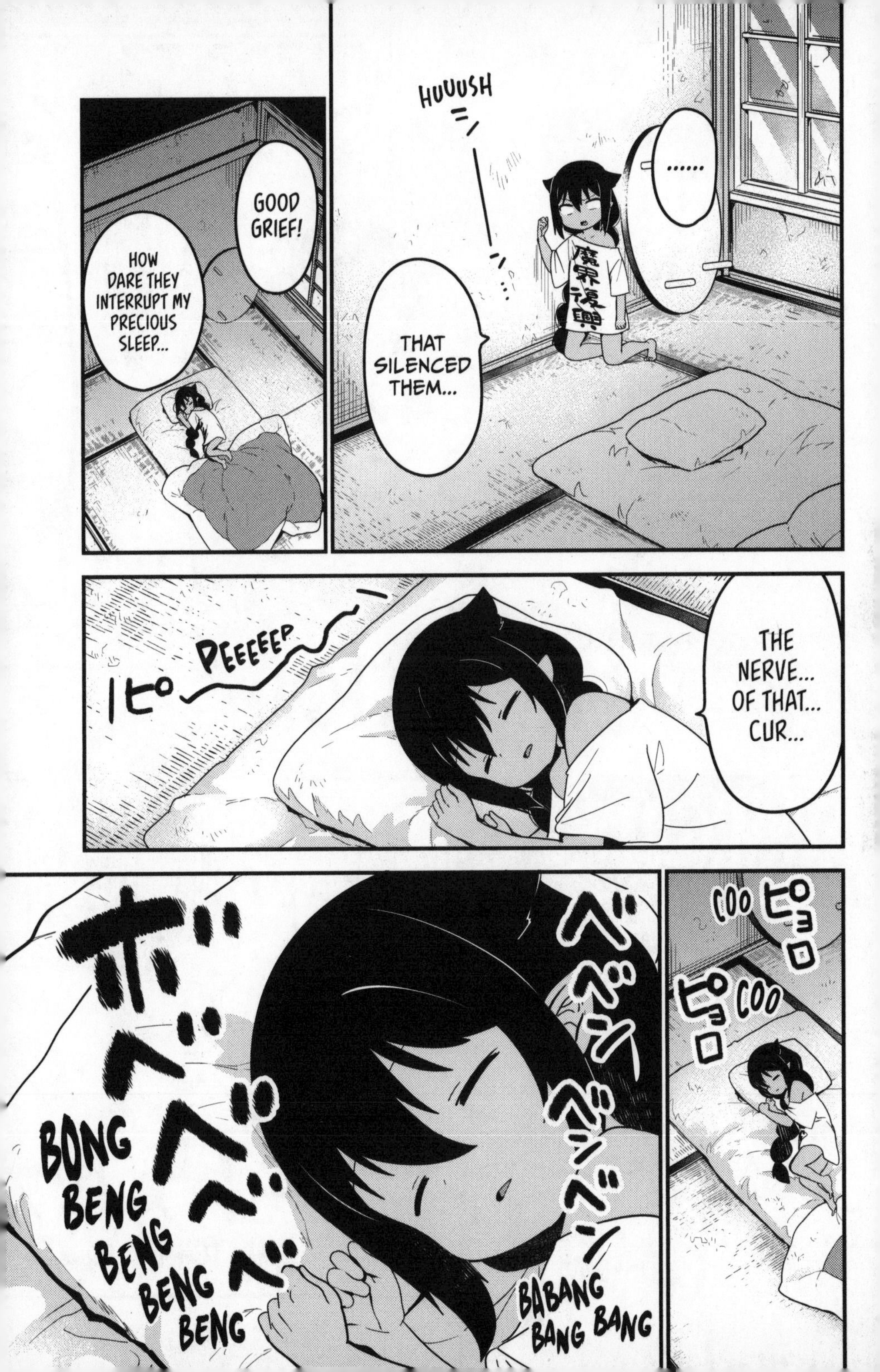
HUUUSH
......
魔界復興
THAT SILENCED THEM...
GOOD GRIEF!
HOW DARE THEY INTERRUPT MY PRECIOUS SLEEP...
THE NERVE... OF THAT... CUR...
ピ〜
PEEEEEP
ピョロ
COO
ピョロ
COO
BABANG BANG BANG
BONG BENG BENG BENG BENG

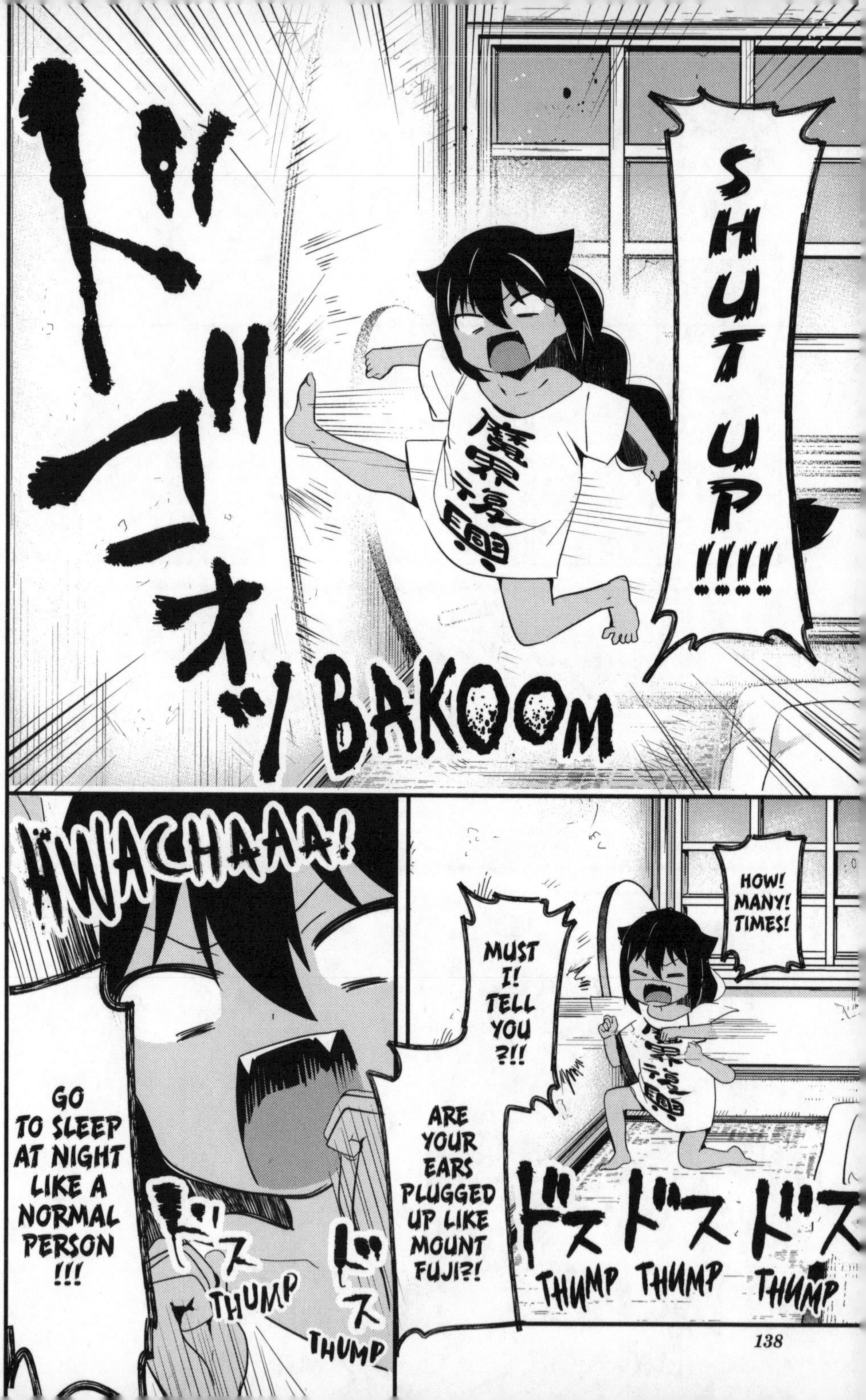
SHUT UP!!!!
魔界復興
ドゴォッ
BAKOOM
HOW! MANY! TIMES!
MUST I! TELL YOU?!!
ドスドスドス
THUMP THUMP THUMP
ARE YOUR EARS PLUGGED UP LIKE MOUNT FUJI?!
HWACHAAA!
GO TO SLEEP AT NIGHT LIKE A NORMAL PERSON!!!
ドス
THUMP
ドス
THUMP

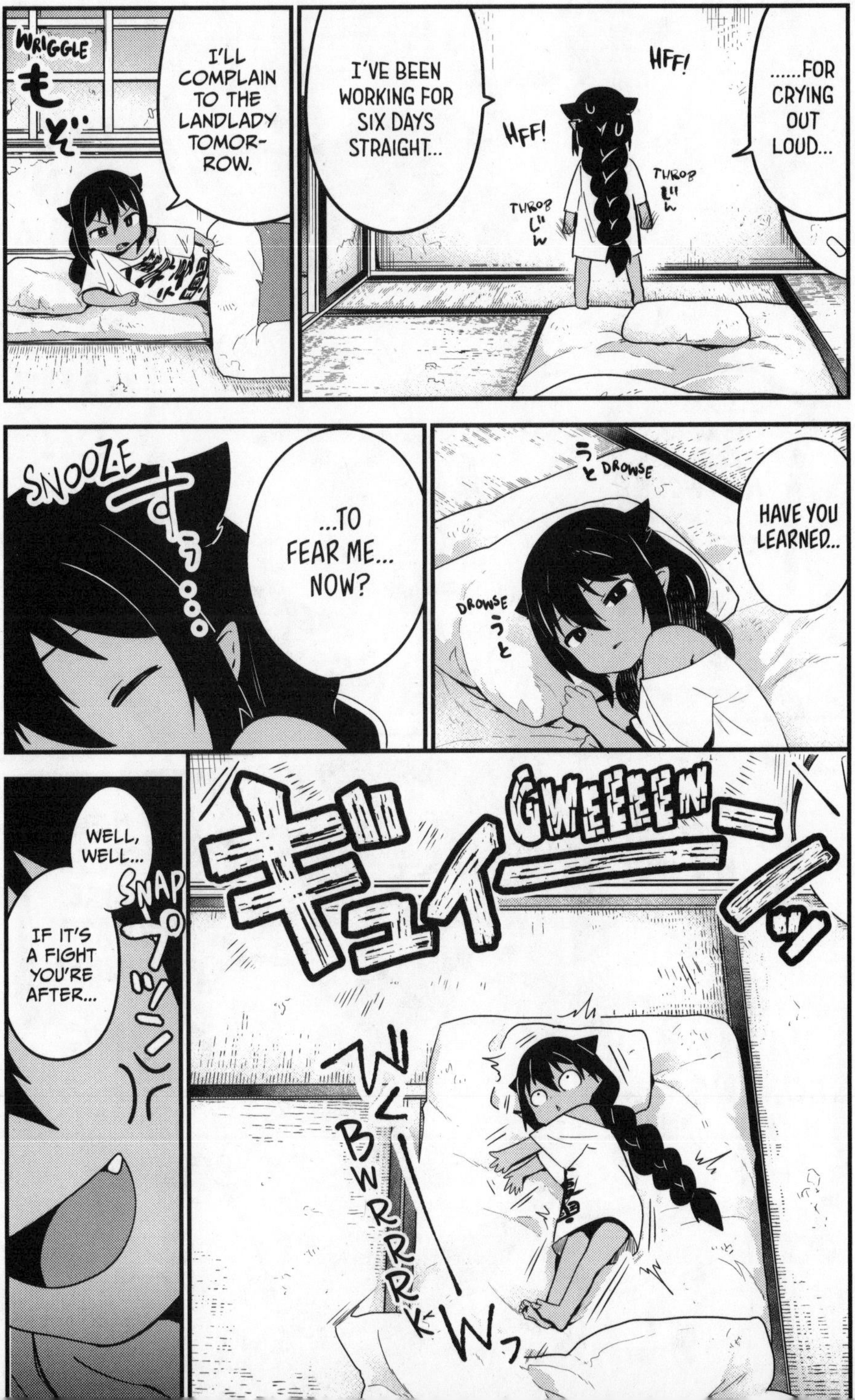
......FOR CRYING OUT LOUD...
HFF!
HFF!
THROB じん
THROB じん
I'VE BEEN WORKING FOR SIX DAYS STRAIGHT...
WRIGGLE もぞ
I'LL COMPLAIN TO THE LANDLADY TOMOR-ROW.
HAVE YOU LEARNED...
DROWSE うと
DROWSE うと
...TO FEAR ME... NOW?
SNOOZE すぅ
GWEEEEN ギュイーン
BWRRRRK
WELL, WELL...
SNAP
IF IT'S A FIGHT YOU'RE AFTER...

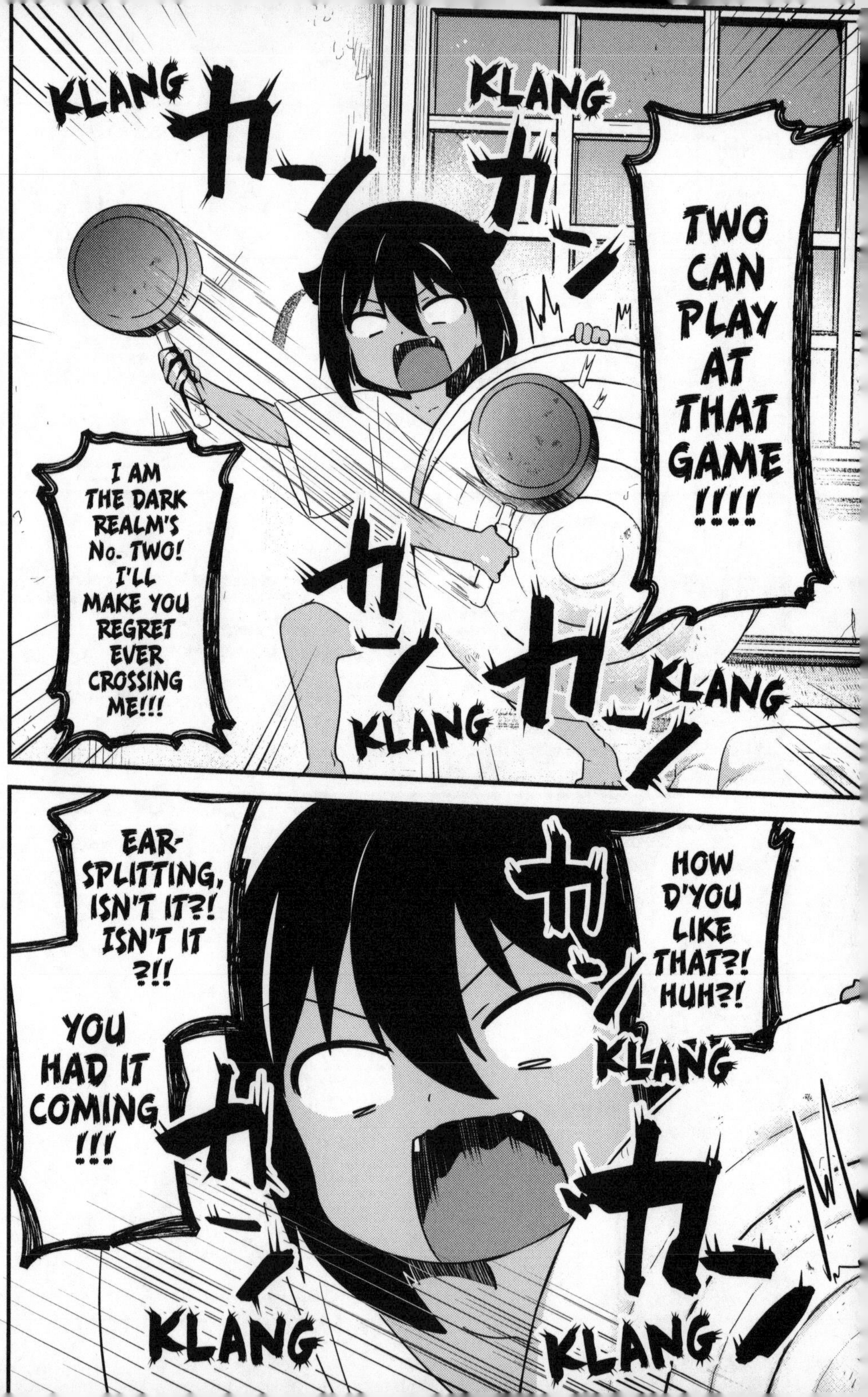
KLANG
TWO CAN PLAY AT THAT GAME!!!!!
KLANG
I AM THE DARK REALM'S No. TWO! I'LL MAKE YOU REGRET EVER CROSSING ME!!!
KLANG
KLANG
HOW D'YOU LIKE THAT?! HUH?!
EAR-SPLITTING, ISN'T IT?! ISN'T IT ?!!
KLANG
YOU HAD IT COMING!!!
KLANG
KLANG

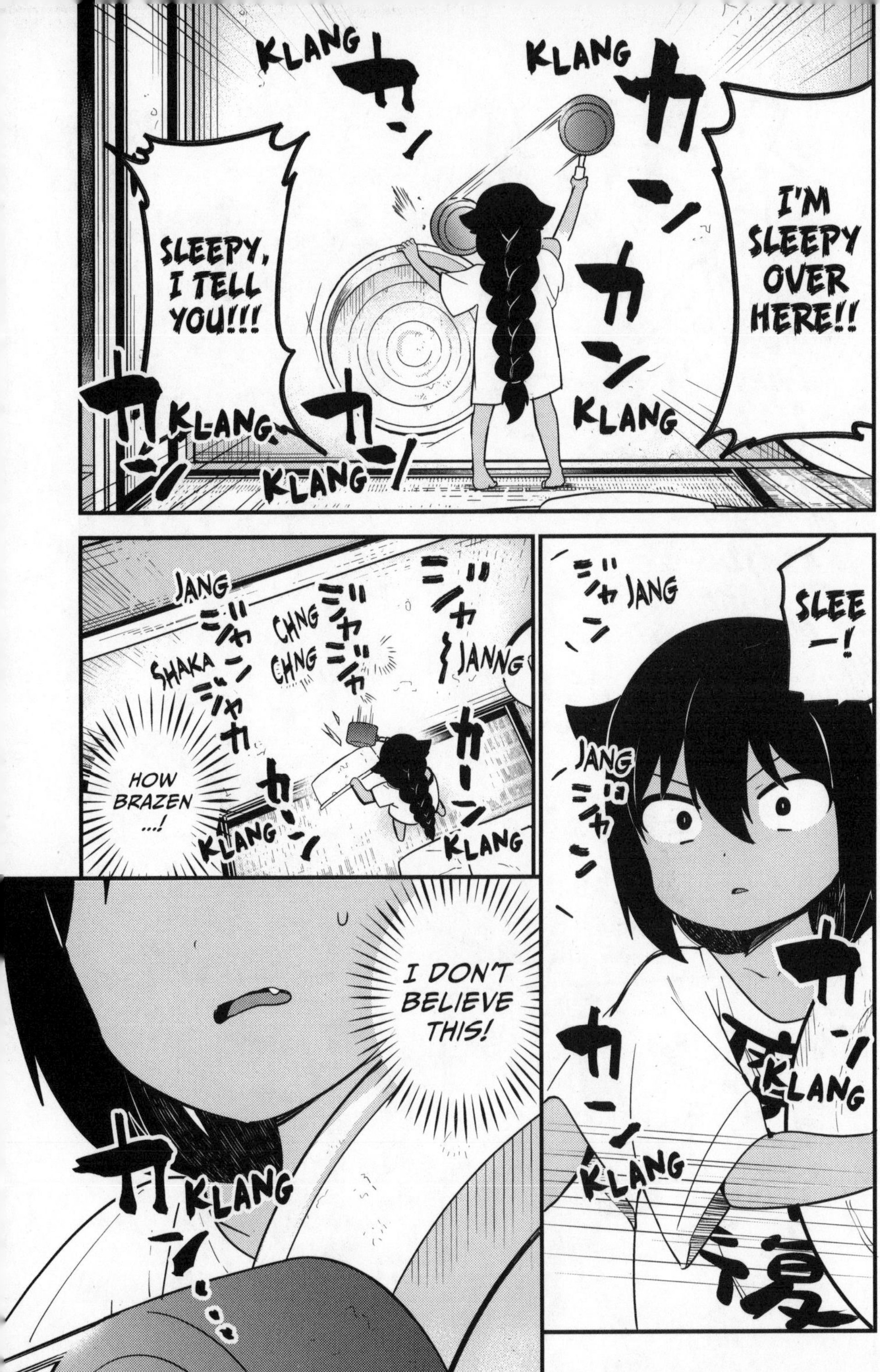
KLANG
I'M SLEEPY OVER HERE!!
KLANG
SLEEPY, I TELL YOU!!!
KLANG
KLANG
KLANG
KLANG
JANG
SLEE—!
JANG
KLANG
KLANG
JANNG
CHNG CHNG
JANG
SHAKA
HOW BRAZEN ...!
KLANG
KLANG
I DON'T BELIEVE THIS!
KLANG
...

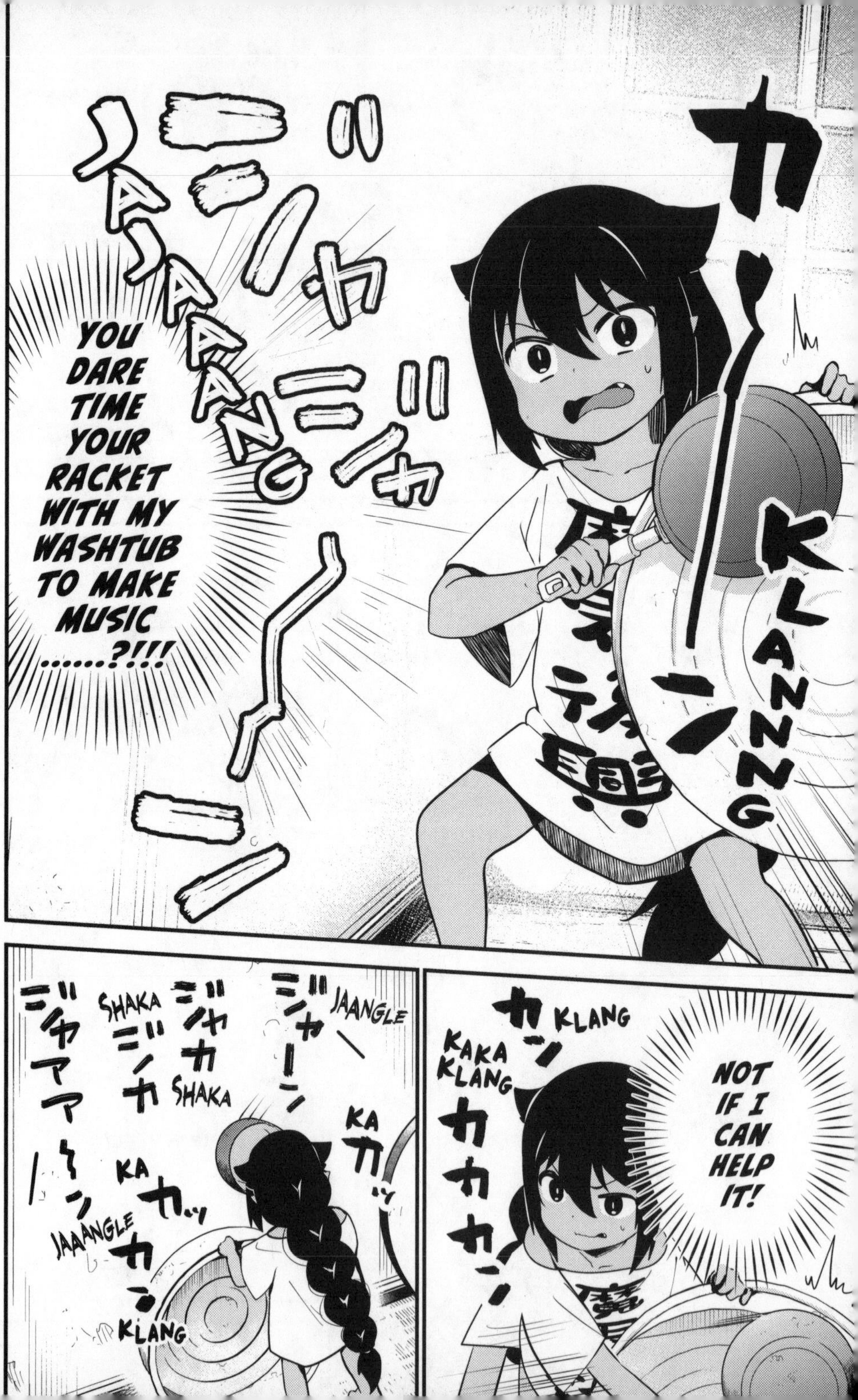
KLANNNG
JAAAAANG
YOU DARE TIME YOUR RACKET WITH MY WASHTUB TO MAKE MUSIC ......?!!!
KLANG
KAKA KLANG
NOT IF I CAN HELP IT!
JAANGLE
SHAKA
SHAKA
KA
KA
JAAANGLE
KLANG

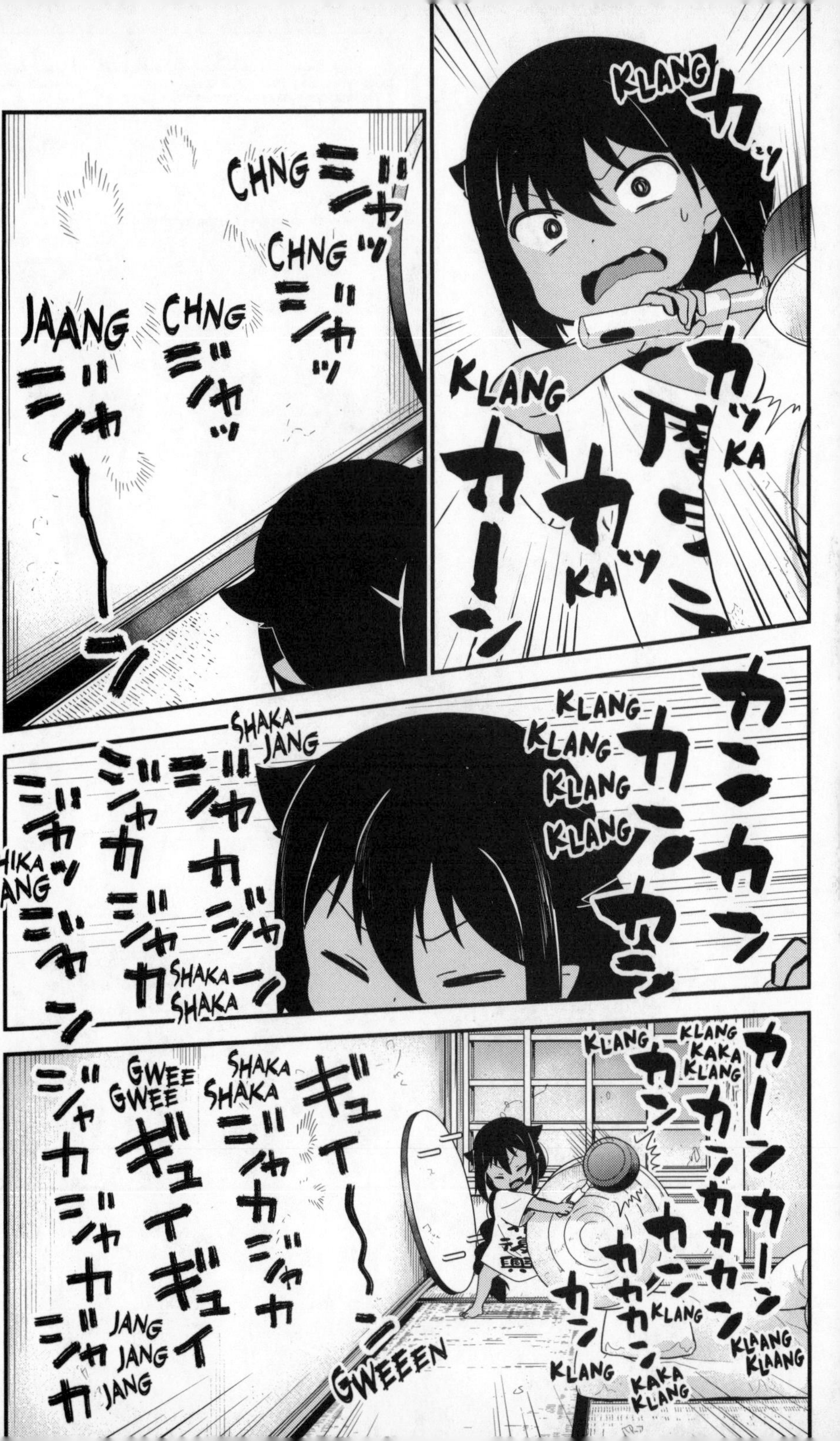
KLANG
KLANG
KA
KA
CHNG
CHNG
CHNG
JAANG
KLANG
KLANG
KLANG
KLANG
SHAKA JANG
SHAKA SHAKA
CHIKA JANG
KLANG
KLANG KAKA KLANG
KLAANG KLAANG
KLANG
KLANG
KAKA KLANG
GWEEEN
SHAKA SHAKA
GWEE GWEE
JANG JANG JANG

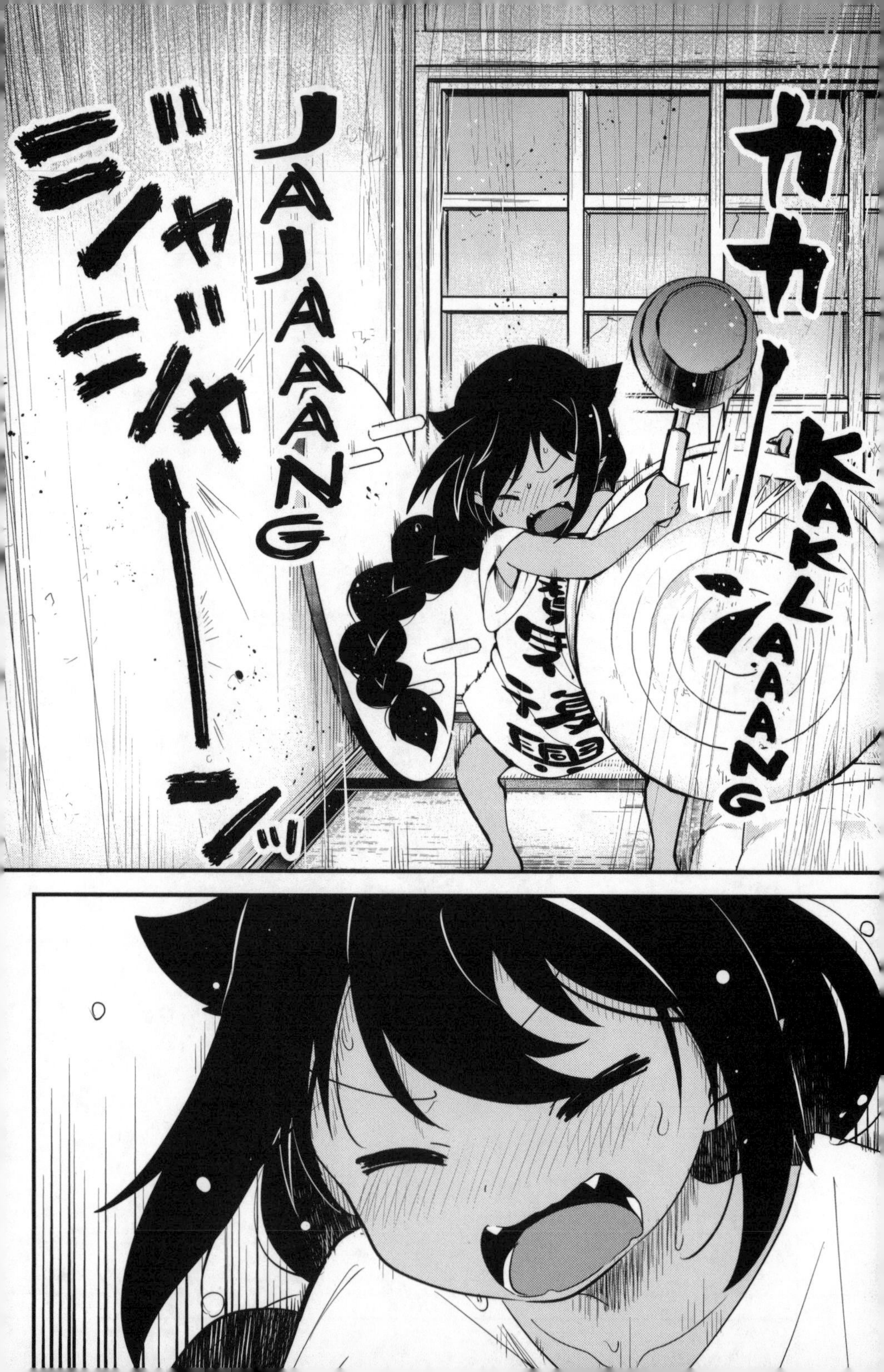

カカ
KAKLAAAANG
JAJAAAANG

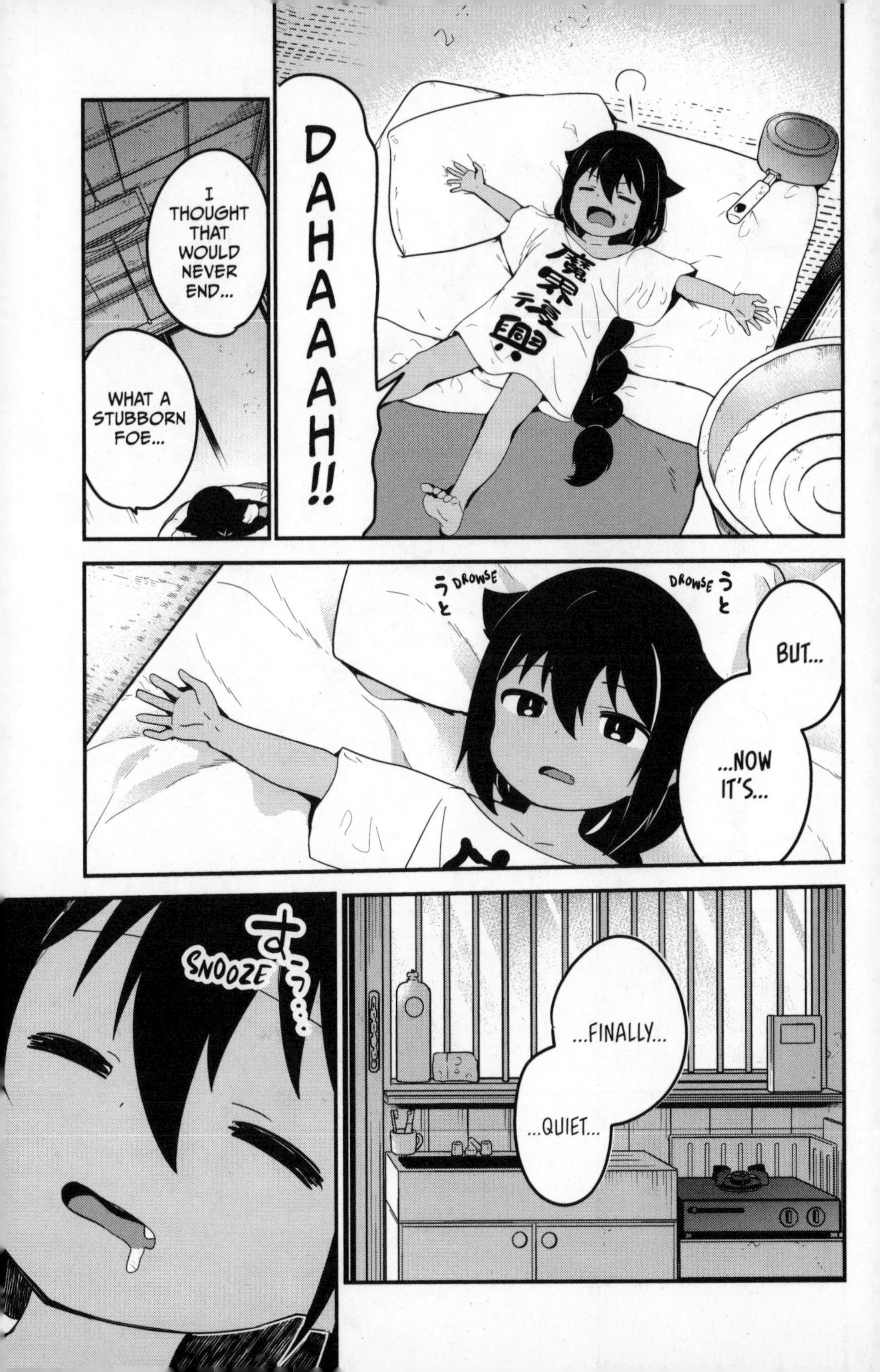
DAHAAAAH!!
I THOUGHT THAT WOULD NEVER END...
WHAT A STUBBORN FOE...
うと DROWSE
DROWSE うと
BUT...
...NOW IT'S...
...FINALLY...
...QUIET...
すー...
SNOOZE

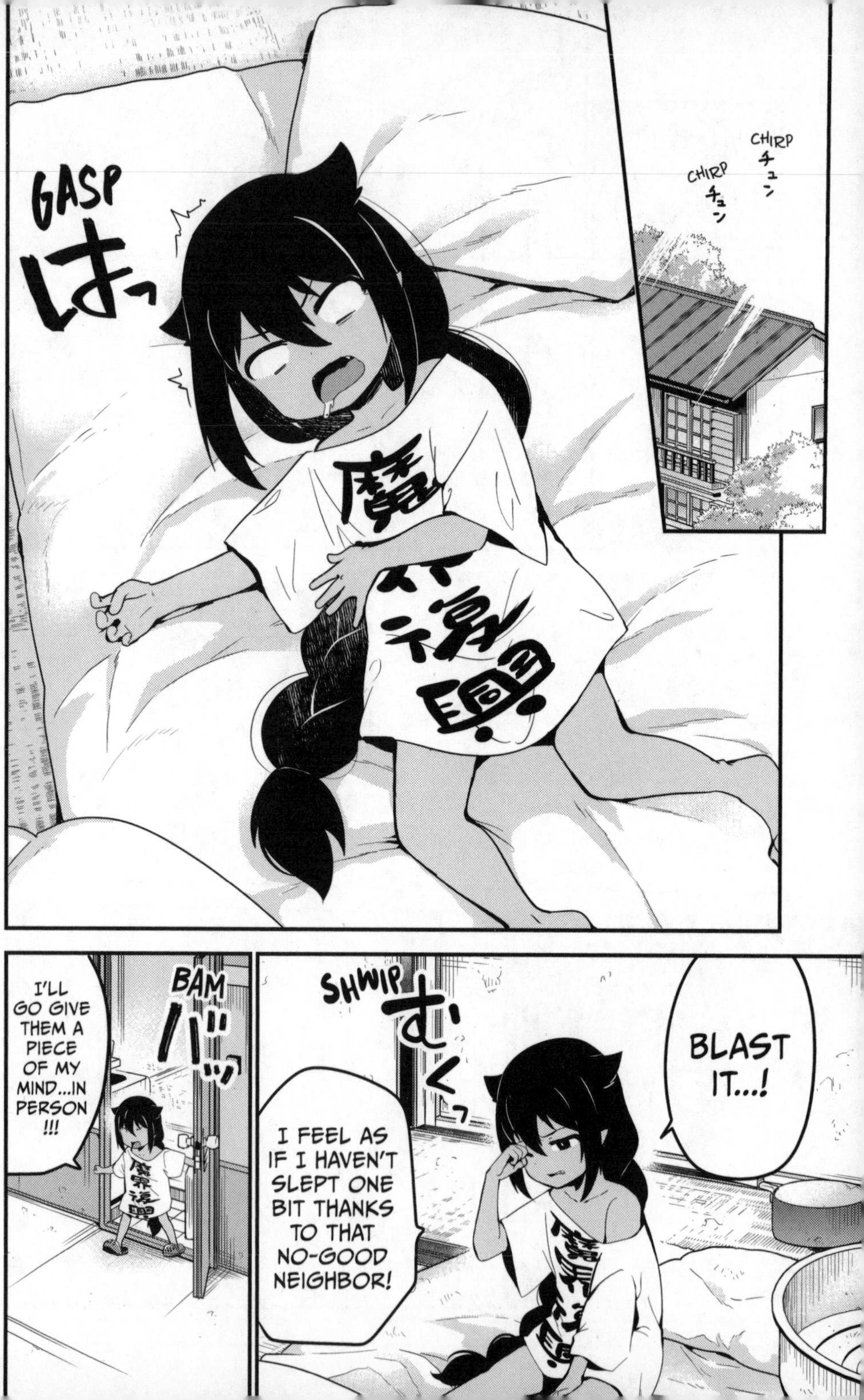
CHIRP チュン
CHIRP チュン
GASP はっ
BLAST IT...!
SHWIP すくっ
I FEEL AS IF I HAVEN'T SLEPT ONE BIT THANKS TO THAT NO-GOOD NEIGHBOR!
BAM バッ
I'LL GO GIVE THEM A PIECE OF MY MIND...IN PERSON!!!

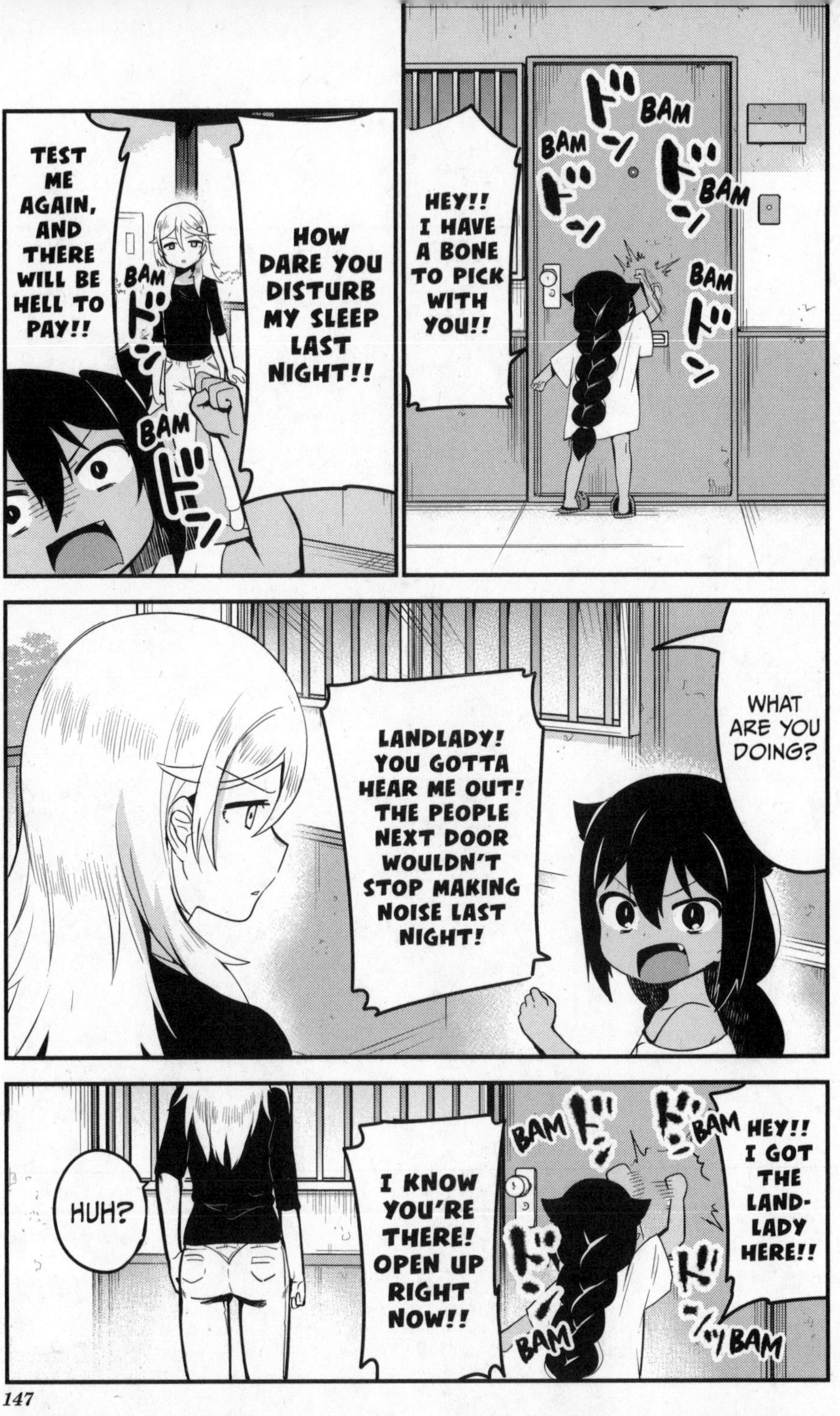
HEY!! I HAVE A BONE TO PICK WITH YOU!!
BAM
BAM
BAM
BAM
HOW DARE YOU DISTURB MY SLEEP LAST NIGHT!!
TEST ME AGAIN, AND THERE WILL BE HELL TO PAY!!
BAM
BAM
WHAT ARE YOU DOING?
LANDLADY! YOU GOTTA HEAR ME OUT! THE PEOPLE NEXT DOOR WOULDN'T STOP MAKING NOISE LAST NIGHT!
HEY!! I GOT THE LAND-LADY HERE!!
BAM
BAM
BAM
BAM
I KNOW YOU'RE THERE! OPEN UP RIGHT NOW!!
HUH?

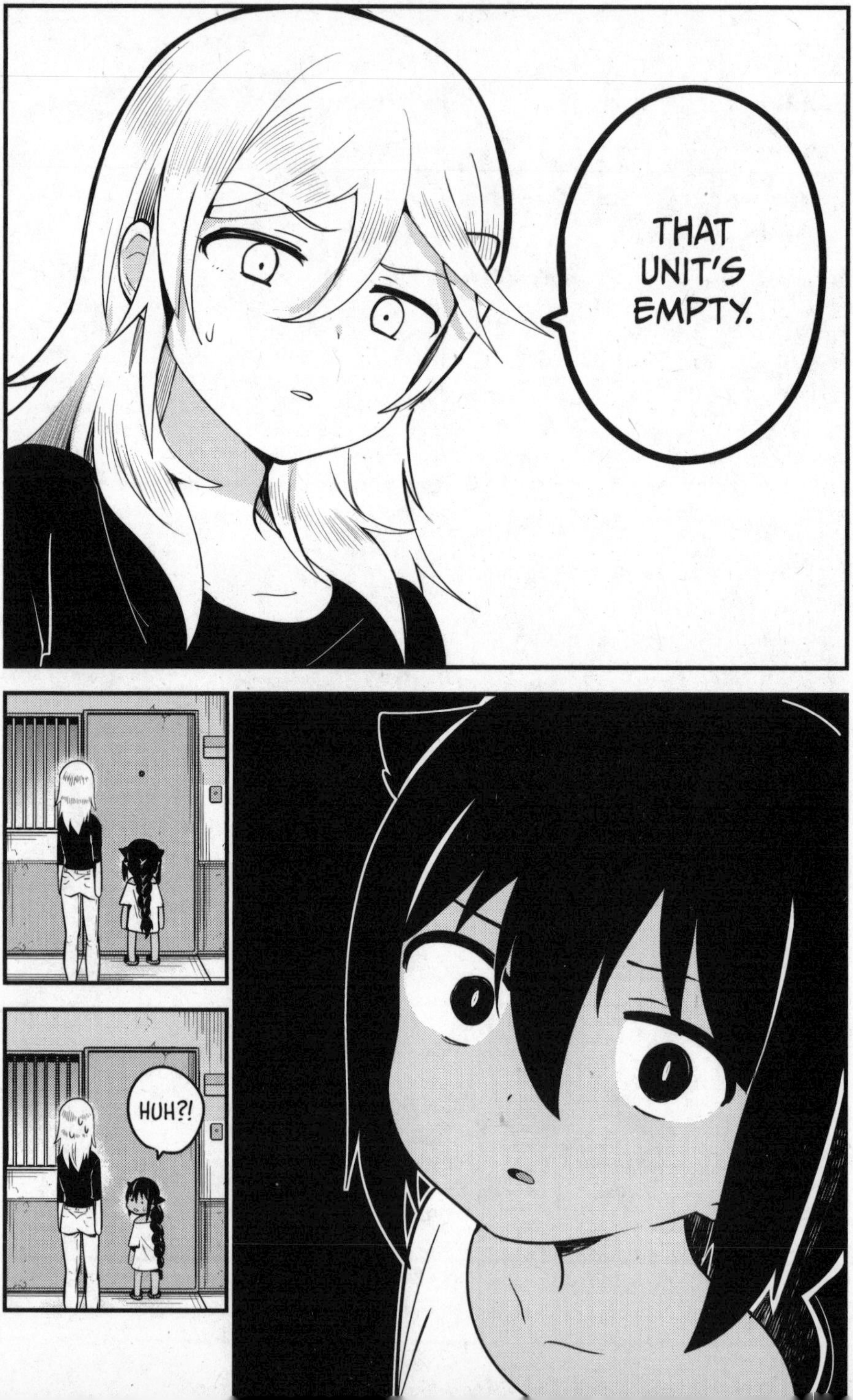
THAT UNIT'S EMPTY.
HUH?!

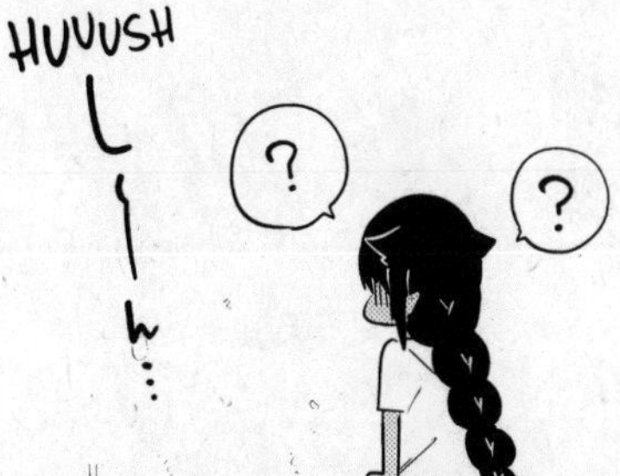
HUUUSH
しーん…
?
?

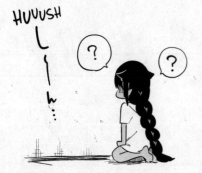

The GREAT JAHY Will NOT Be DEFEATED!

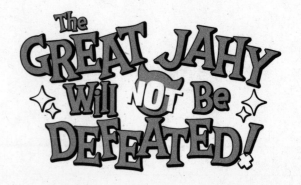

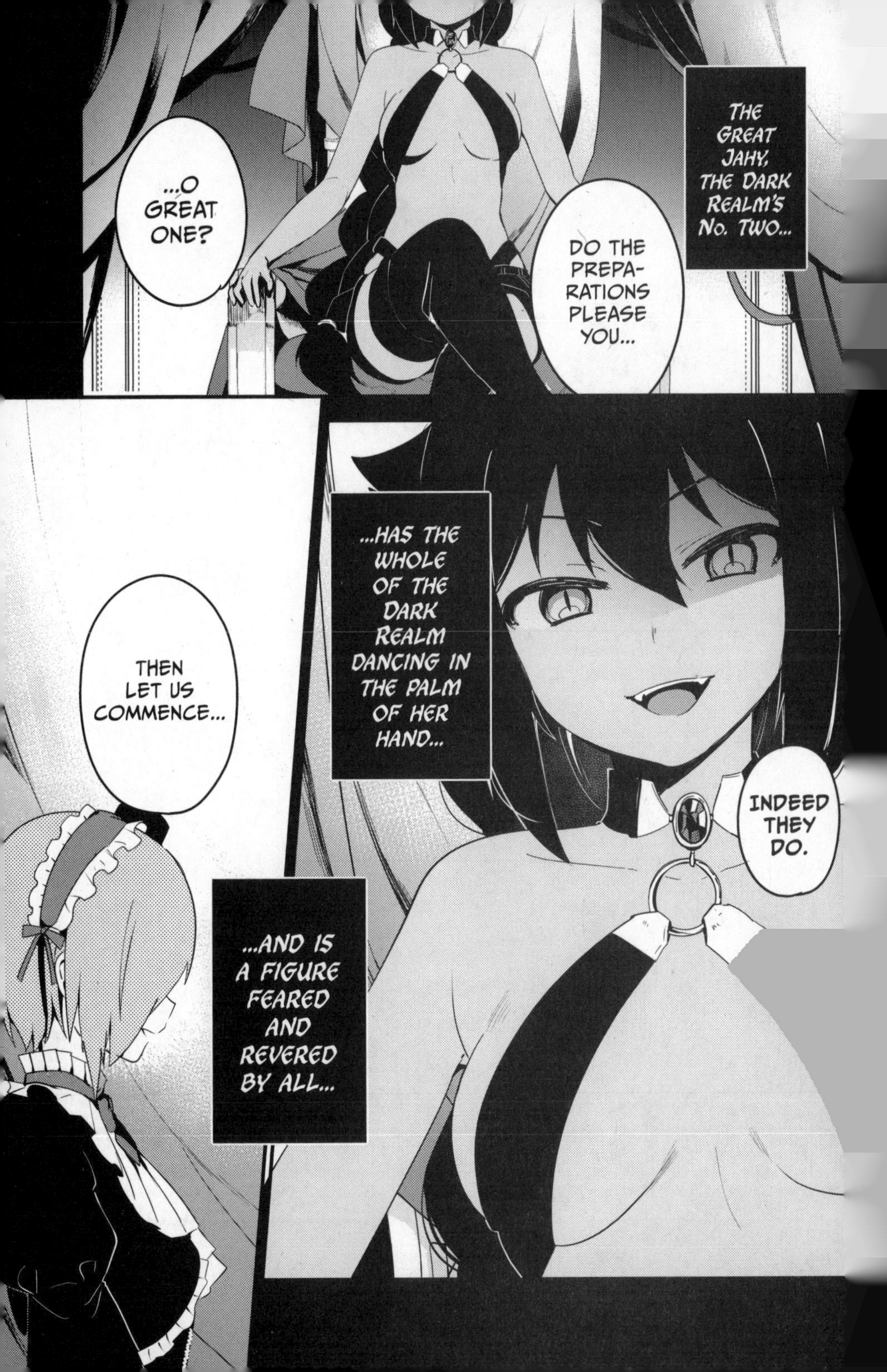
THE GREAT JAHY, THE DARK REALM'S No. TWO...
DO THE PREPA-RATIONS PLEASE YOU...
...O GREAT ONE?
...HAS THE WHOLE OF THE DARK REALM DANCING IN THE PALM OF HER HAND...
INDEED THEY DO.
...AND IS A FIGURE FEARED AND REVERED BY ALL...
THEN LET US COMMENCE...

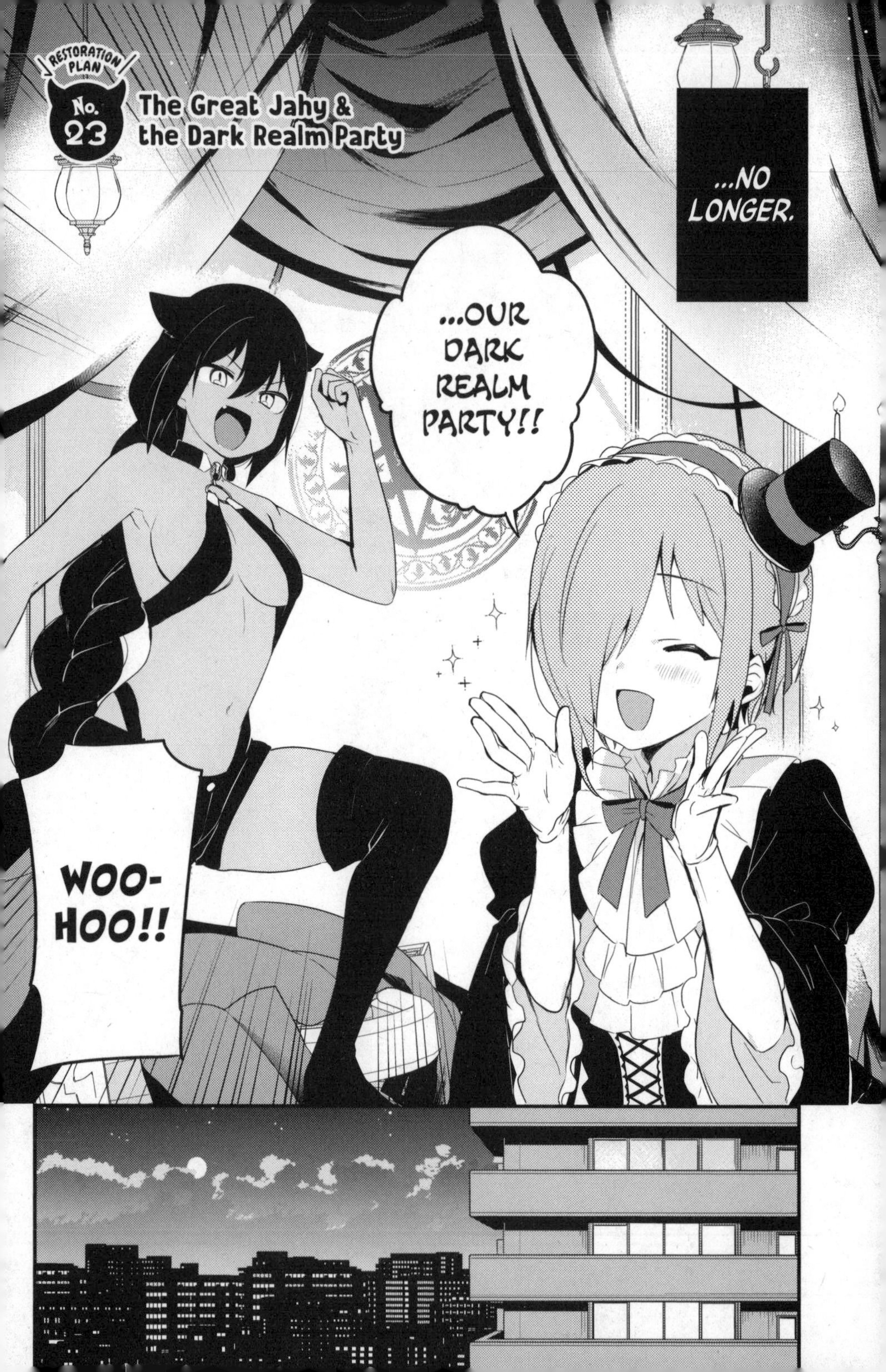
RESTORATION PLAN No. 23
The Great Jahy & the Dark Realm Party
...NO LONGER.
...OUR DARK REALM PARTY!!
WOO-HOO!!

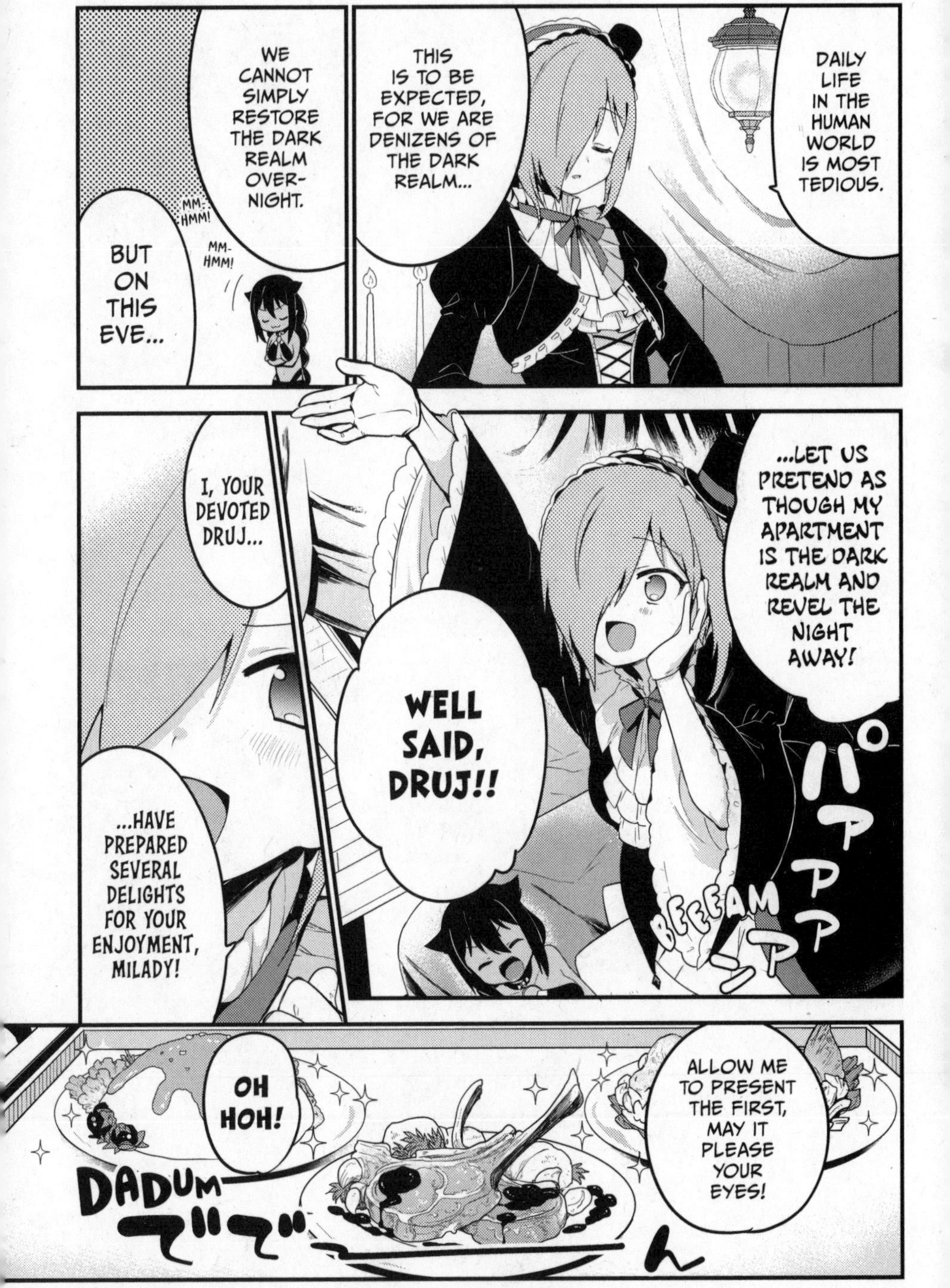
DAILY LIFE IN THE HUMAN WORLD IS MOST TEDIOUS.
THIS IS TO BE EXPECTED, FOR WE ARE DENIZENS OF THE DARK REALM...
WE CANNOT SIMPLY RESTORE THE DARK REALM OVER-NIGHT.
MM-HMM!
MM-HMM!
BUT ON THIS EVE...
...LET US PRETEND AS THOUGH MY APARTMENT IS THE DARK REALM AND REVEL THE NIGHT AWAY!
WELL SAID, DRUJ!!
BEEEAM
I, YOUR DEVOTED DRUJ...
...HAVE PREPARED SEVERAL DELIGHTS FOR YOUR ENJOYMENT, MILADY!
ALLOW ME TO PRESENT THE FIRST, MAY IT PLEASE YOUR EYES!
OH HOH!
DADUM

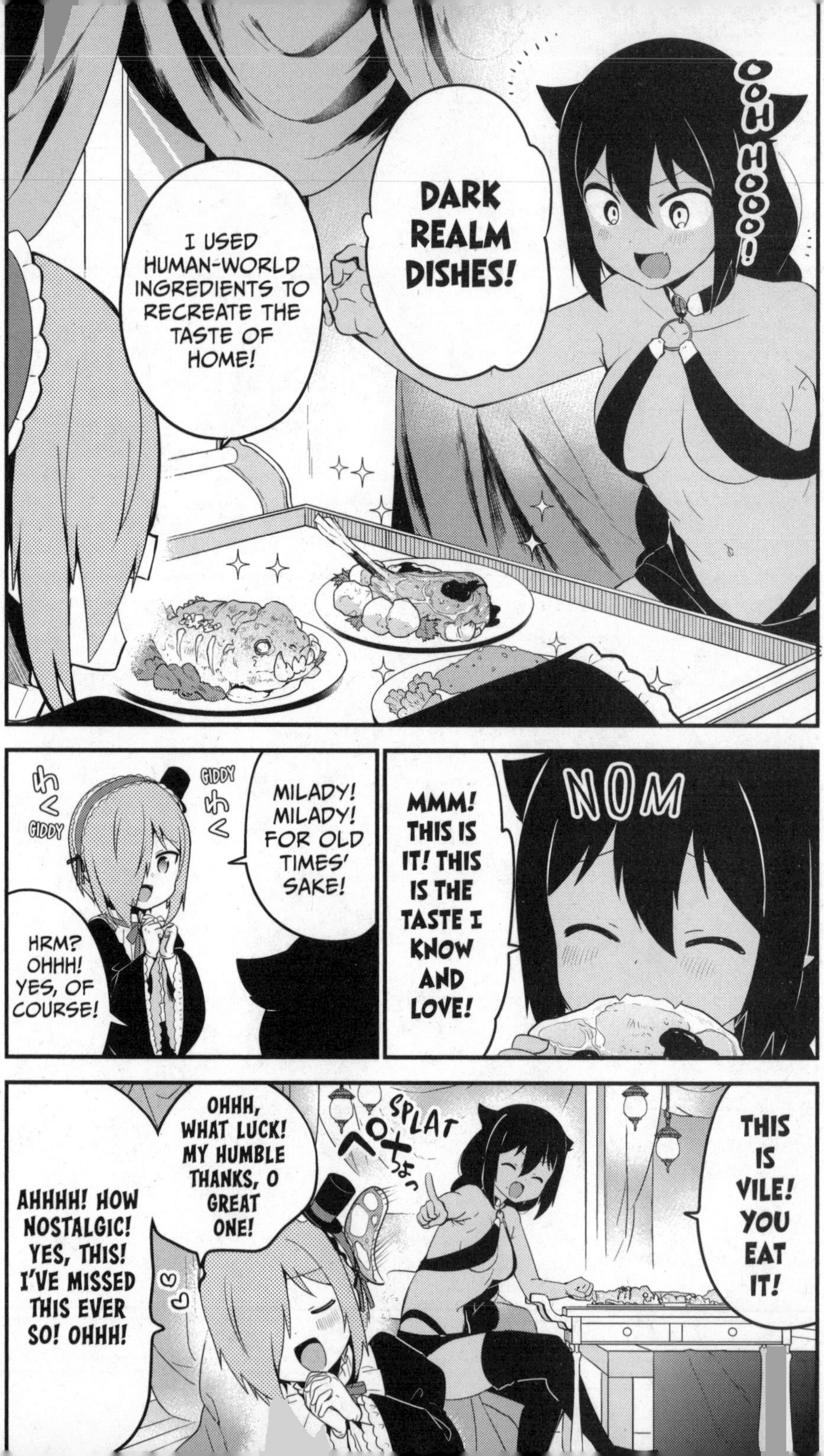
OOH HOOOO!
DARK REALM DISHES!
I USED HUMAN-WORLD INGREDIENTS TO RECREATE THE TASTE OF HOME!
NOM
MMM! THIS IS IT! THIS IS THE TASTE I KNOW AND LOVE!
GIDDY
わく
MILADY! MILADY! FOR OLD TIMES' SAKE!
わく
GIDDY
HRM? OHHH! YES, OF COURSE!
THIS IS VILE! YOU EAT IT!
SPLAT
OHHH, WHAT LUCK! MY HUMBLE THANKS, O GREAT ONE!
AHHHH! HOW NOSTALGIC! YES, THIS! I'VE MISSED THIS EVER SO! OHHH!

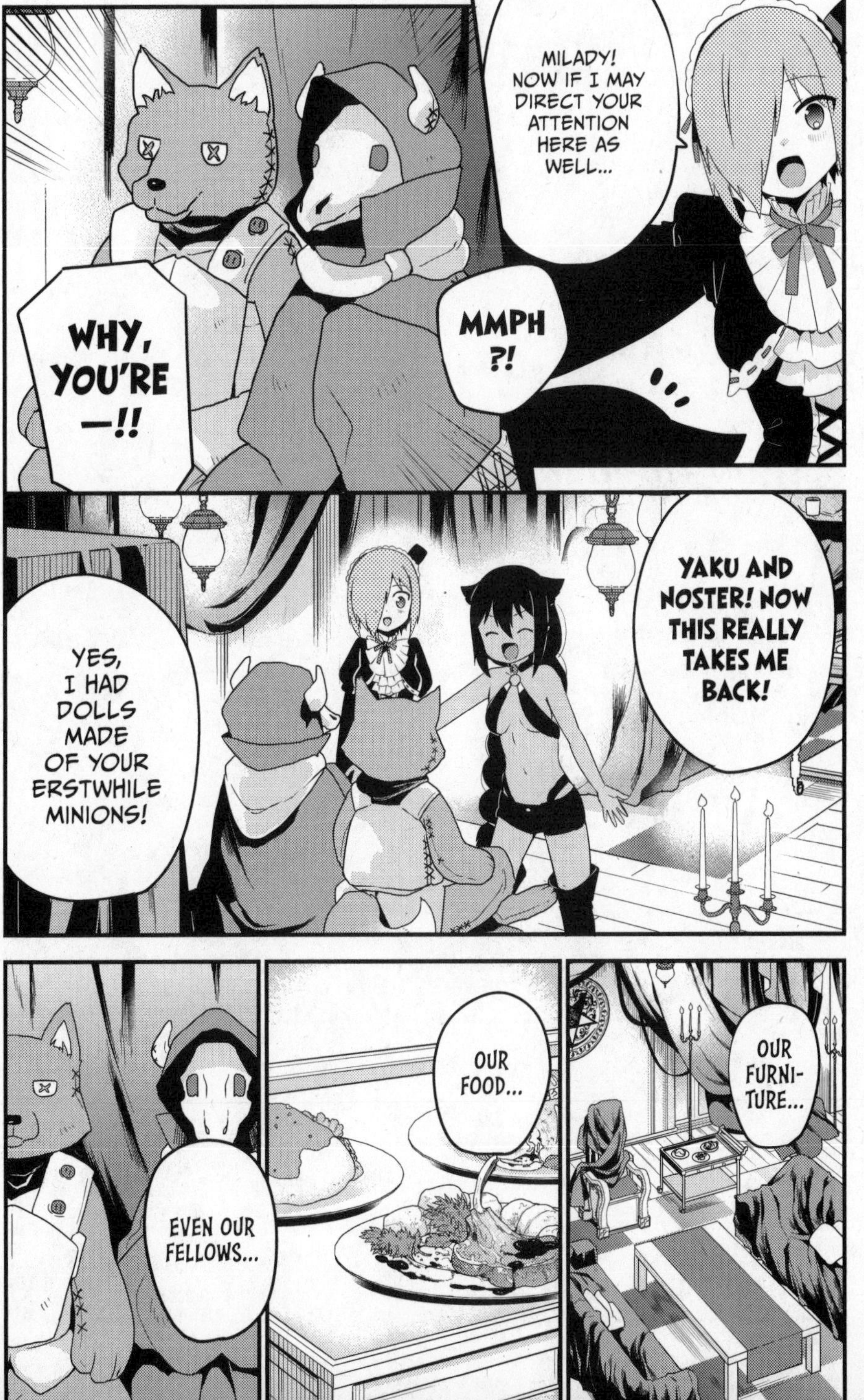
MILADY! NOW IF I MAY DIRECT YOUR ATTENTION HERE AS WELL...
MMPH ?!
...
WHY, YOU'RE —!!
YAKU AND NOSTER! NOW THIS REALLY TAKES ME BACK!
YES, I HAD DOLLS MADE OF YOUR ERSTWHILE MINIONS!
OUR FURNI-TURE...
OUR FOOD...
EVEN OUR FELLOWS...

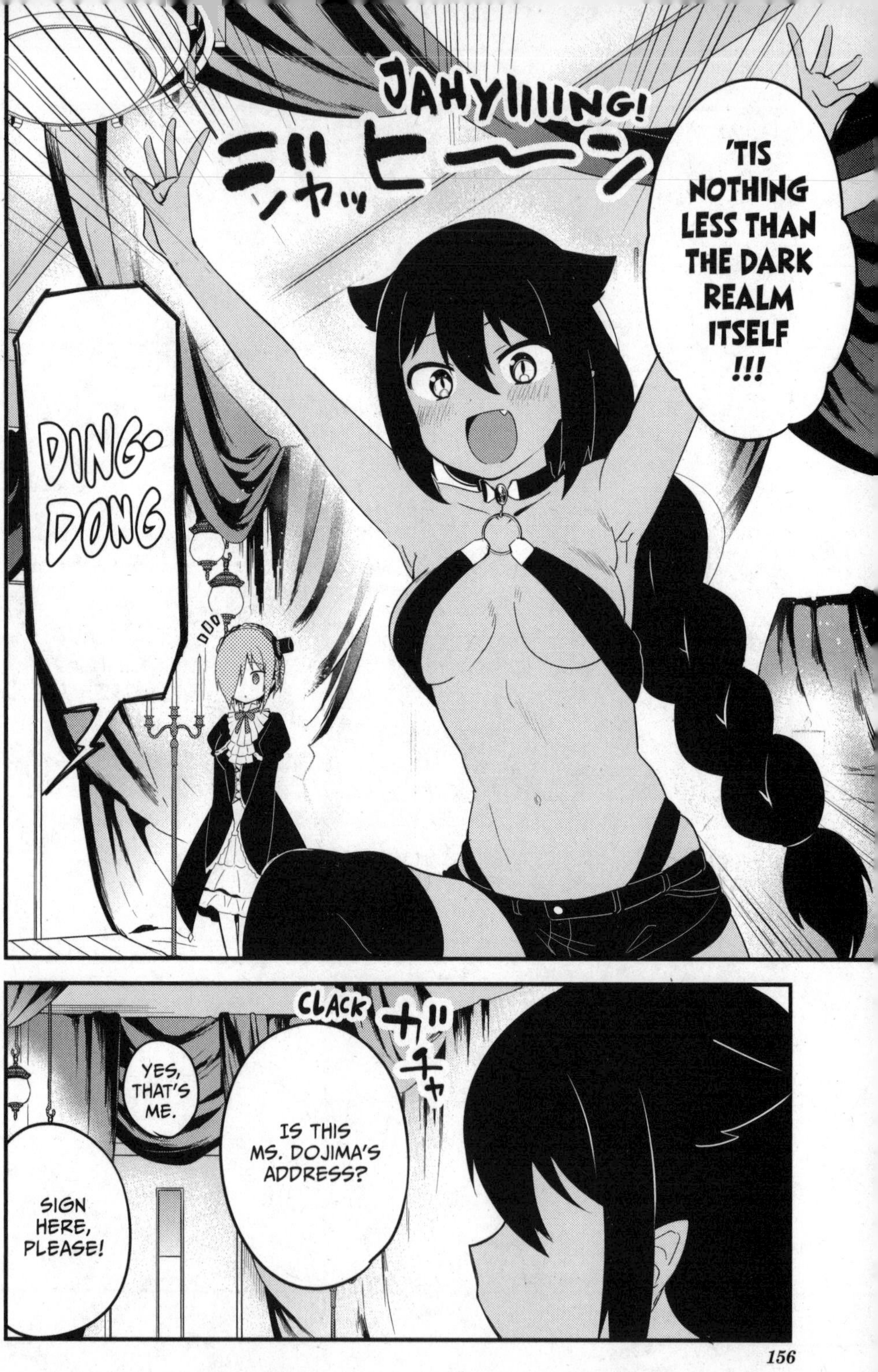
JAHYIIIING!
ジャッヒ〜〜ン
'TIS NOTHING LESS THAN THE DARK REALM ITSELF!!!
DING-DONG
CLACK
ガチャ
IS THIS MS. DOJIMA'S ADDRESS?
YES, THAT'S ME.
SIGN HERE, PLEASE!

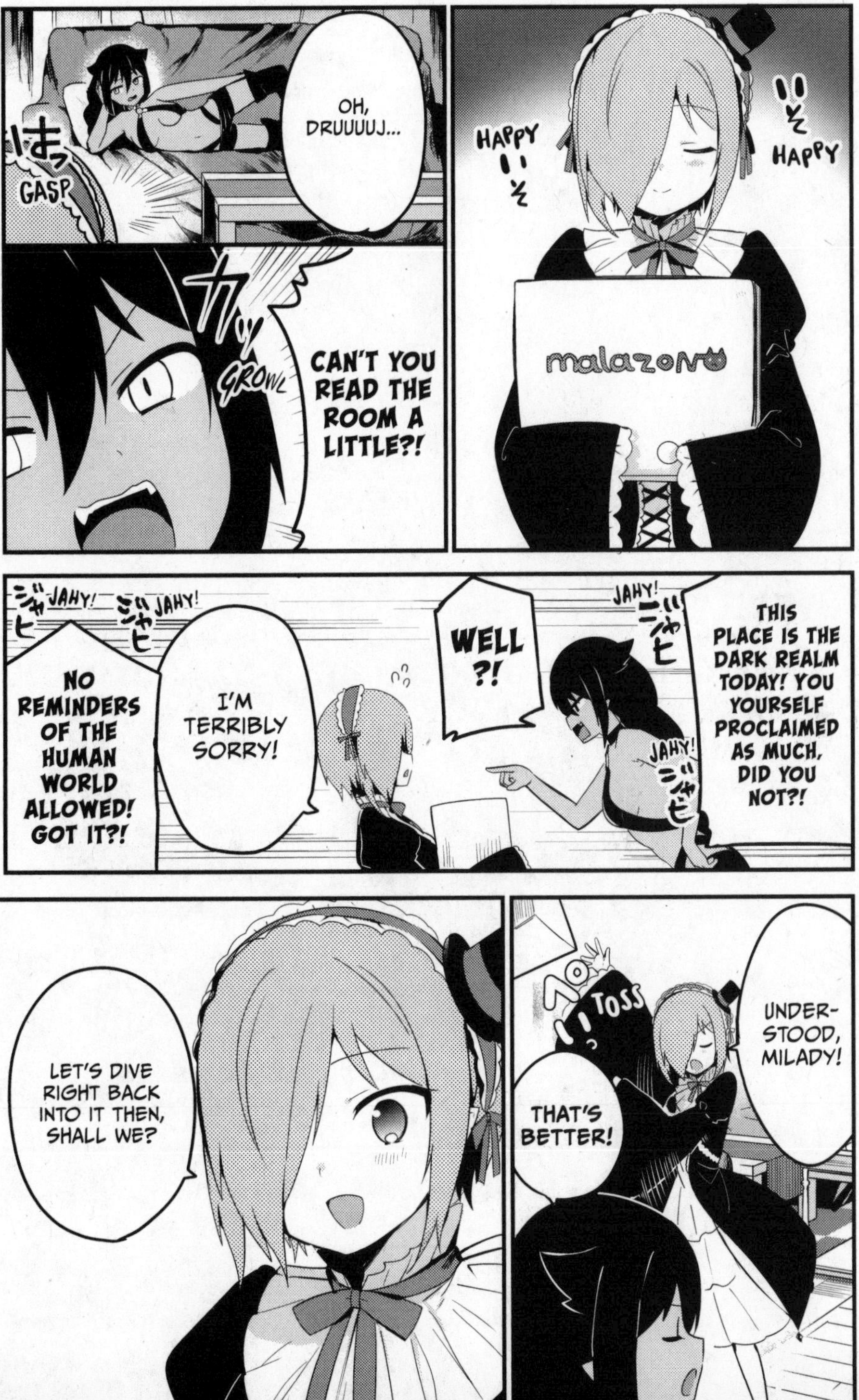

HAPPY
HAPPY
malazon
OH, DRUUUUJ...
GASP
CAN'T YOU READ THE ROOM A LITTLE?!
GROWL
JAHY!
THIS PLACE IS THE DARK REALM TODAY! YOU YOURSELF PROCLAIMED AS MUCH, DID YOU NOT?!
JAHY!
WELL?!
I'M TERRIBLY SORRY!
JAHY!
JAHY!
NO REMINDERS OF THE HUMAN WORLD ALLOWED! GOT IT?!
UNDER-STOOD, MILADY!
TOSS
THAT'S BETTER!
LET'S DIVE RIGHT BACK INTO IT THEN, SHALL WE?

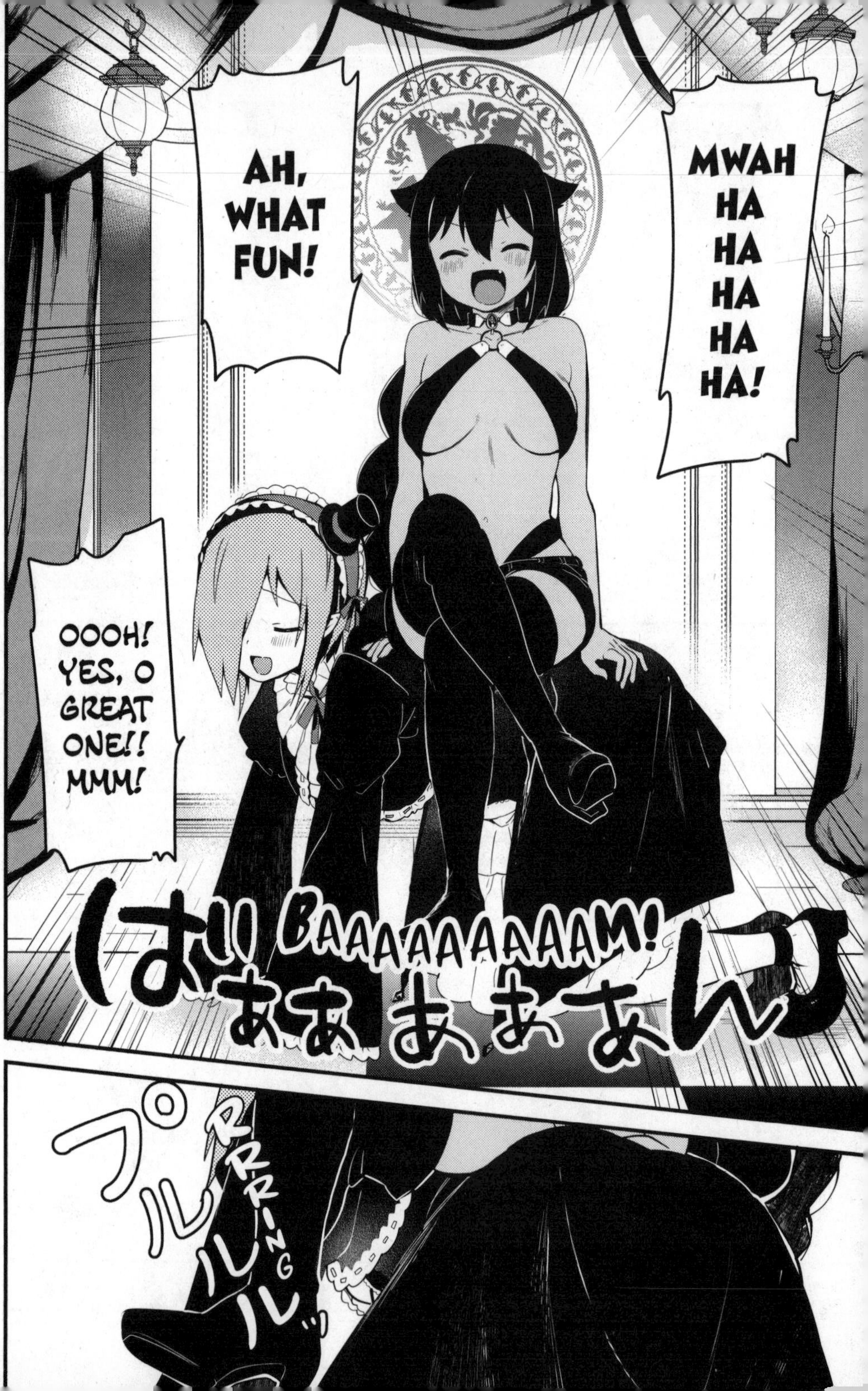
MWAH HA HA HA HA HA!
AH, WHAT FUN!
OOOH! YES, O GREAT ONE!! MMM!
BAAAAAAAAAM!
はああああん
RRRING
プルルルッ

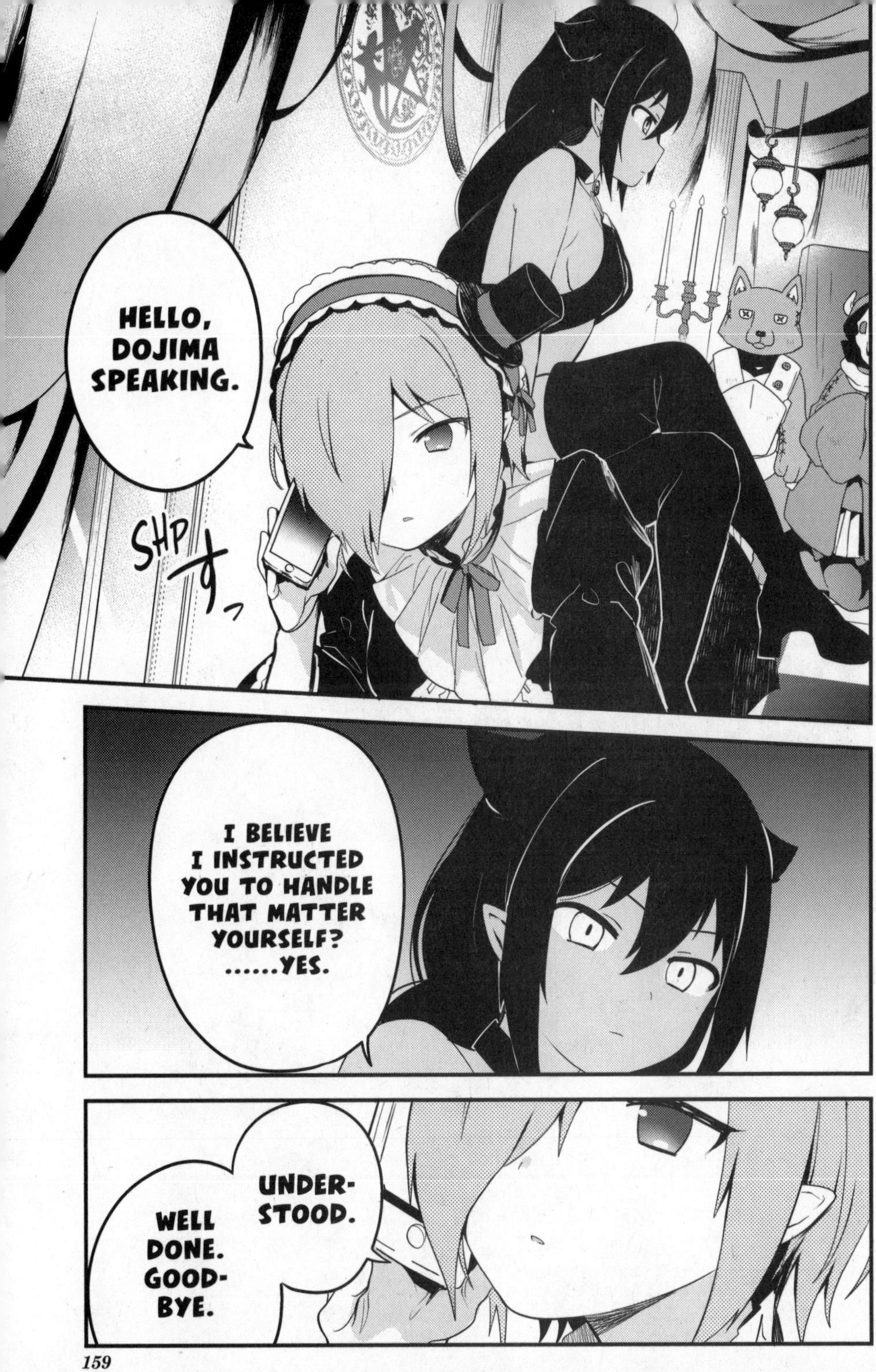
HELLO, DOJIMA SPEAKING.
SHP す
I BELIEVE I INSTRUCTED YOU TO HANDLE THAT MATTER YOURSELF? ......YES.
UNDER-STOOD.
WELL DONE. GOOD-BYE.

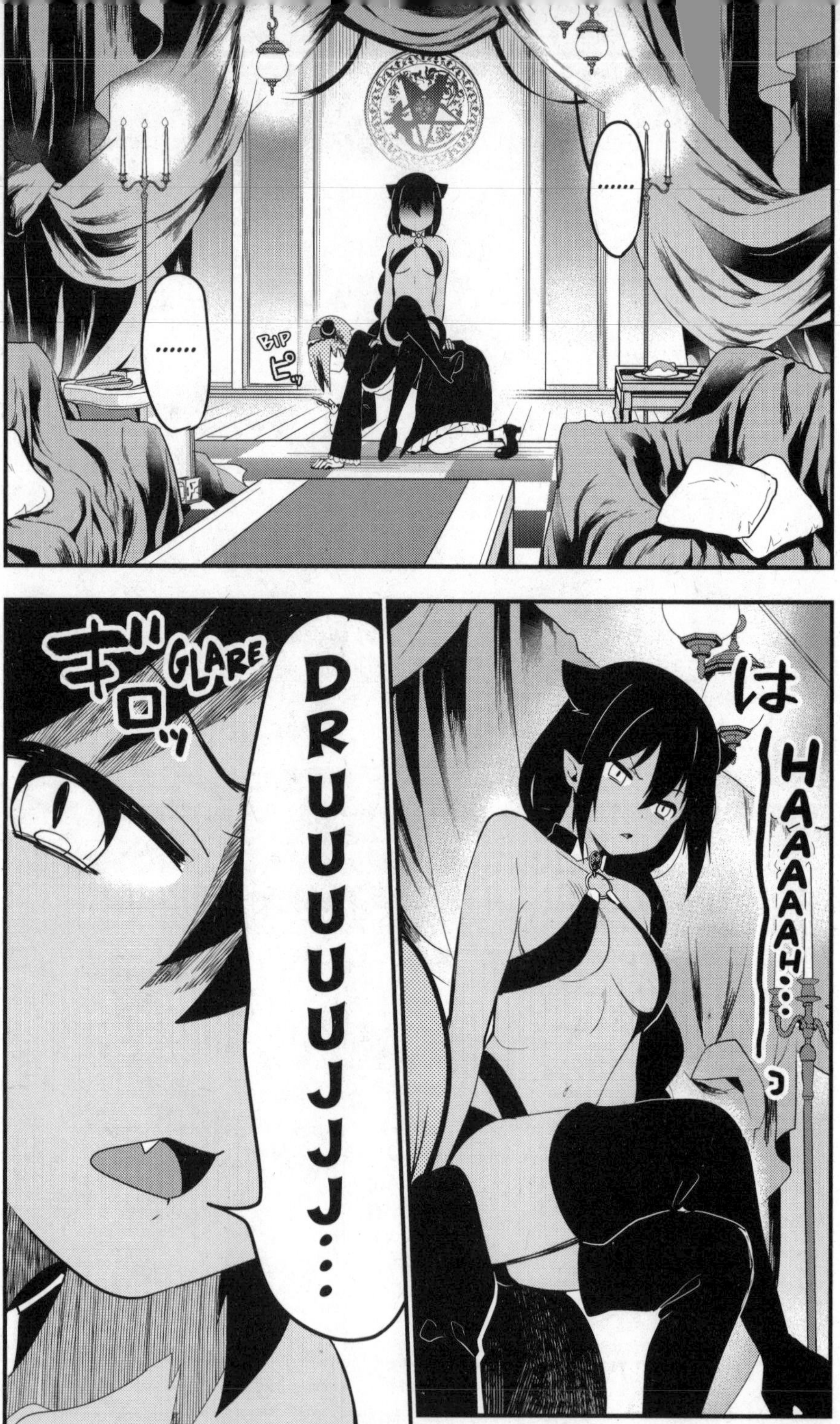
......
......
BIP
ピッ
は
HAAAAAH...っ
ギロッ
GLARE
DRUUUUUJJJ...

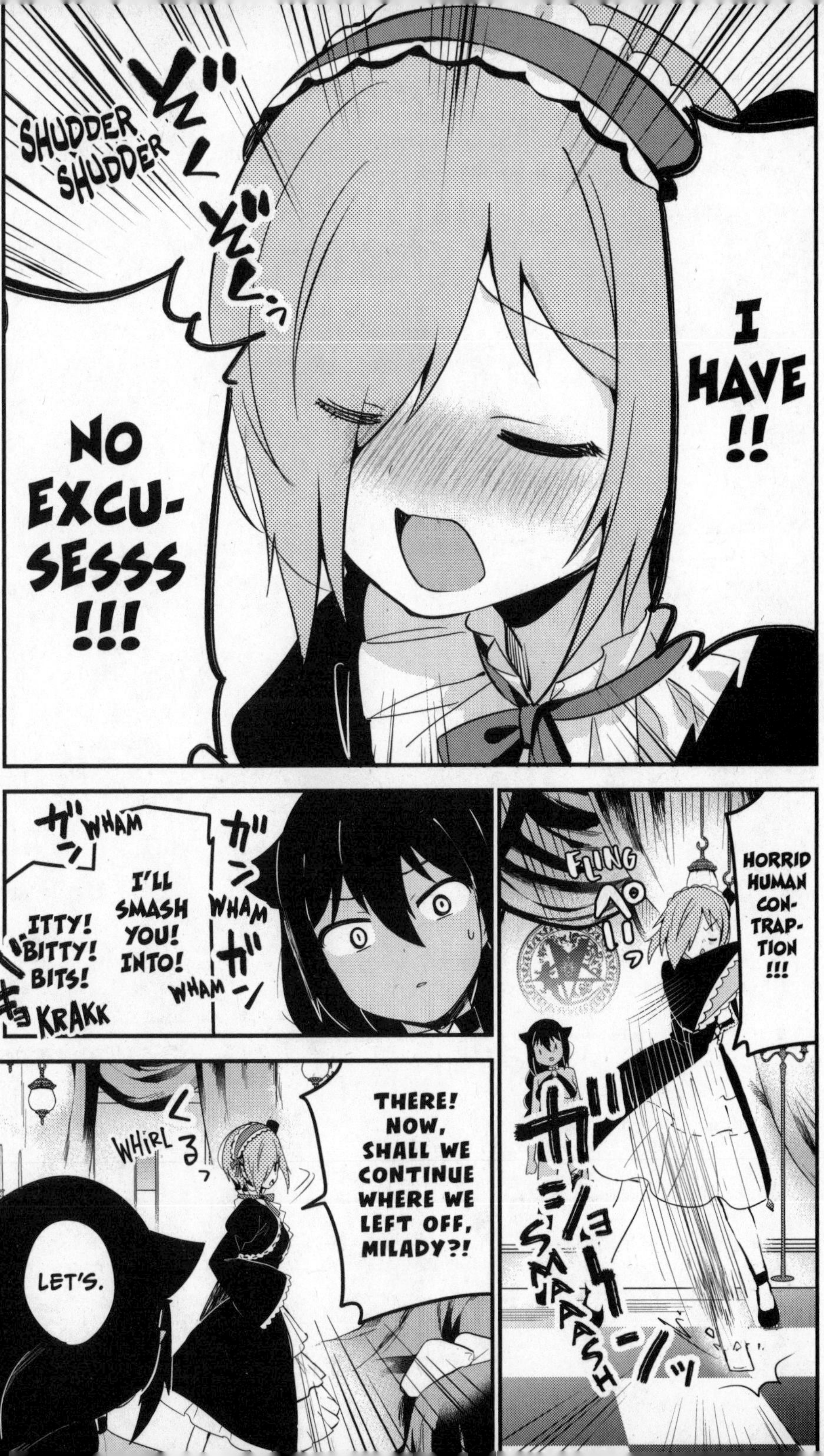
SHUDDER SHUDDER
I HAVE!!
NO EXCU-SESSSS!!!
FLING
HORRID HUMAN CON-TRAP-TION!!!
WHAM
WHAM
WHAM
I'LL SMASH YOU! INTO!
ITTY! BITTY! BITS!
KRAKK
SMAAASH
THERE! NOW, SHALL WE CONTINUE WHERE WE LEFT OFF, MILADY?!
WHIRL
LET'S.

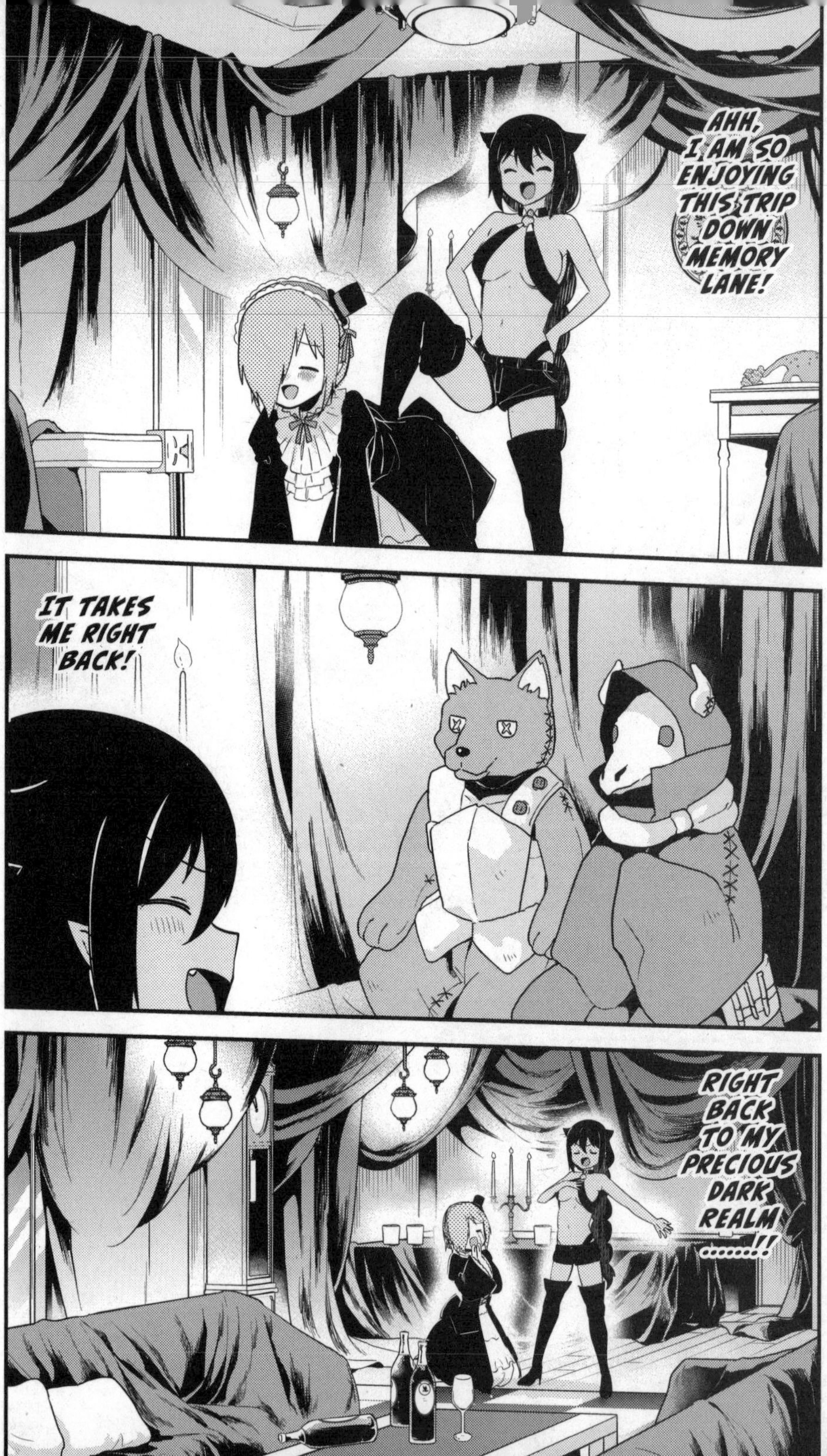
AHH, I AM SO ENJOYING THIS TRIP DOWN MEMORY LANE!
IT TAKES ME RIGHT BACK!
RIGHT BACK TO MY PRECIOUS DARK REALM ....!!

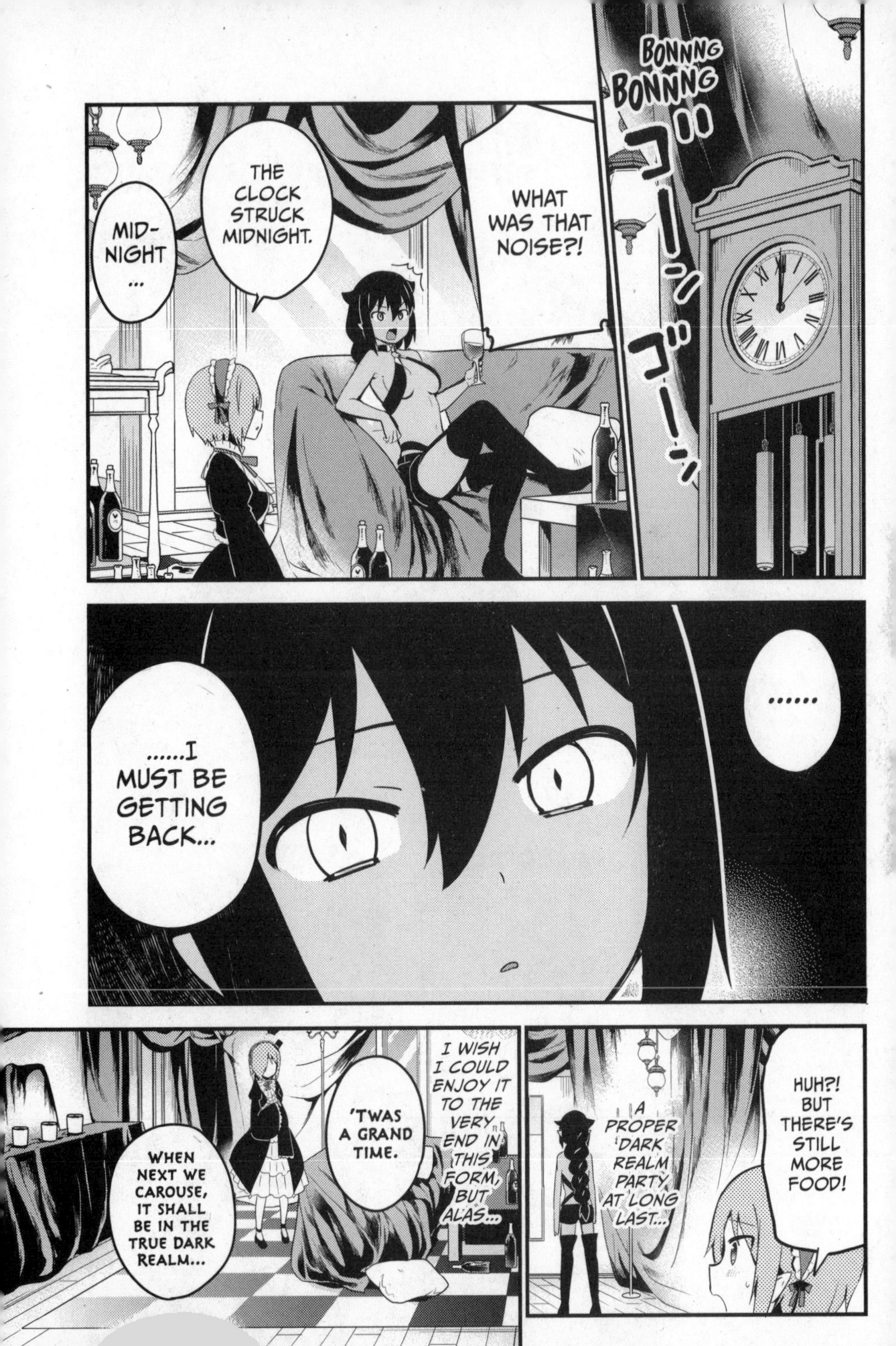
BONNNG
BONNNG
WHAT WAS THAT NOISE?!
THE CLOCK STRUCK MIDNIGHT.
MID-NIGHT...
......
......I MUST BE GETTING BACK...
HUH?! BUT THERE'S STILL MORE FOOD!
A PROPER DARK REALM PARTY AT LONG LAST...
I WISH I COULD ENJOY IT TO THE VERY END IN THIS FORM, BUT ALAS...
'TWAS A GRAND TIME.
WHEN NEXT WE CAROUSE, IT SHALL BE IN THE TRUE DARK REALM...

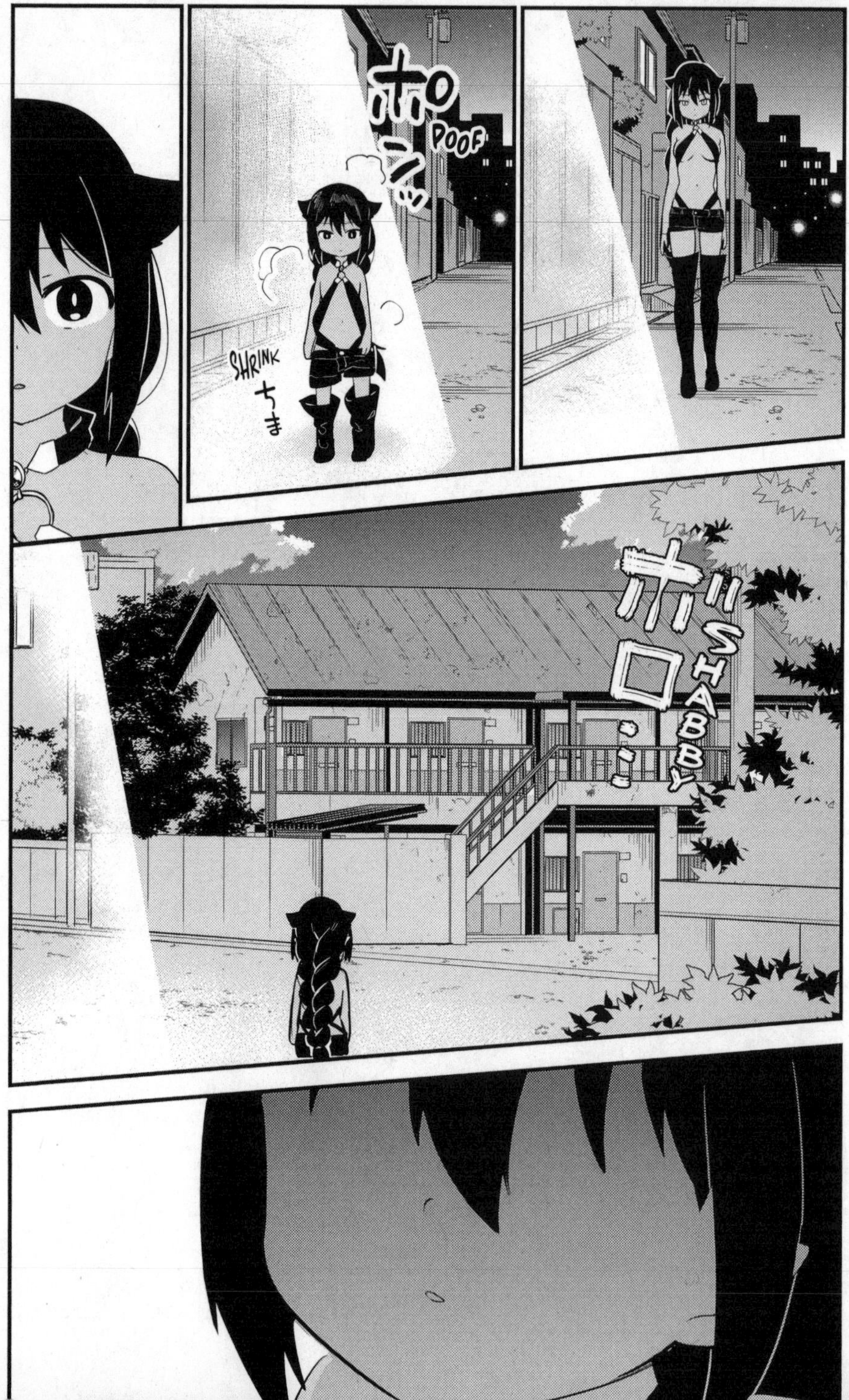
ポンッ
POOF
SHRINK
ちま
ボロ…
SHABBY

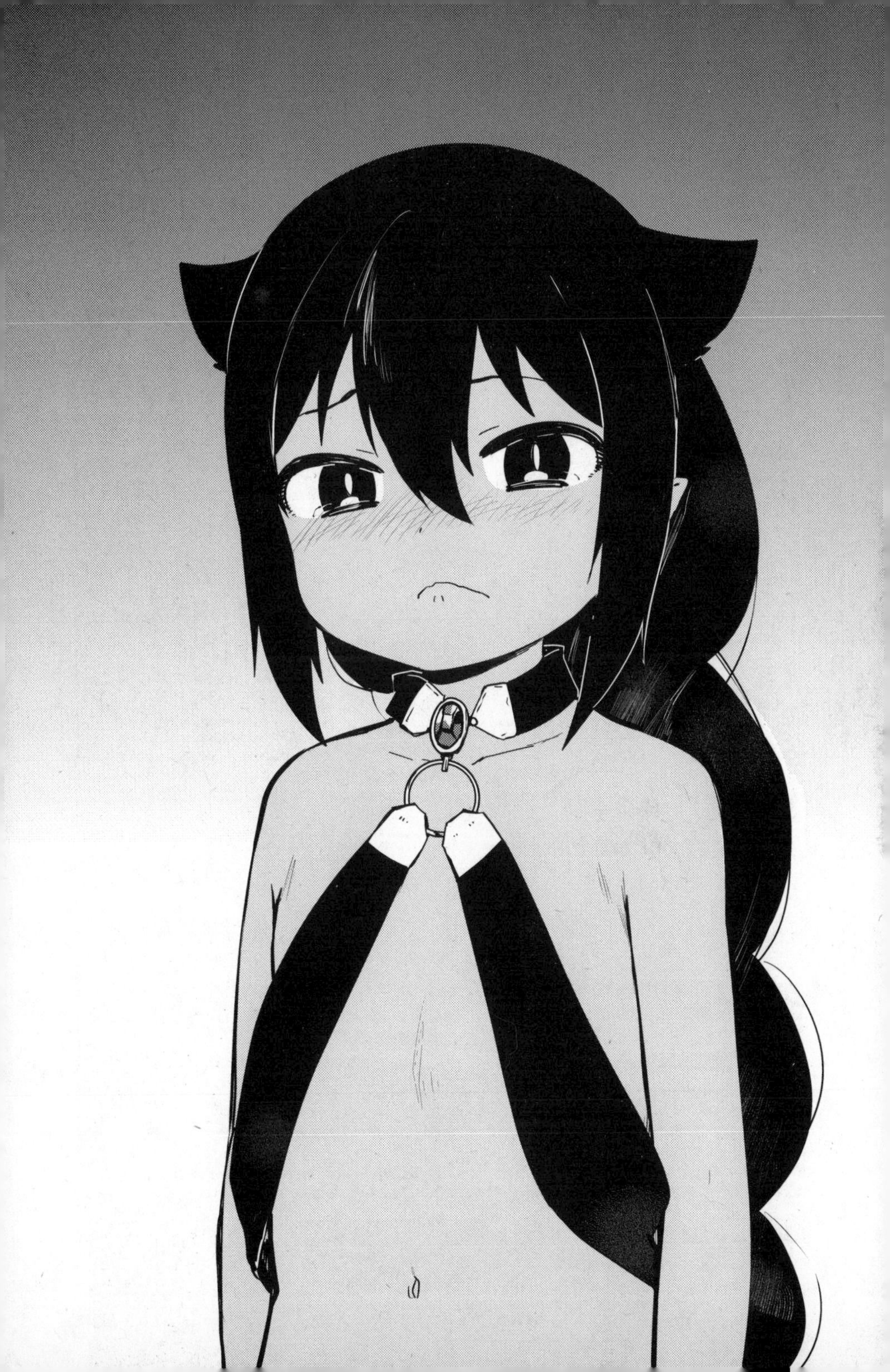

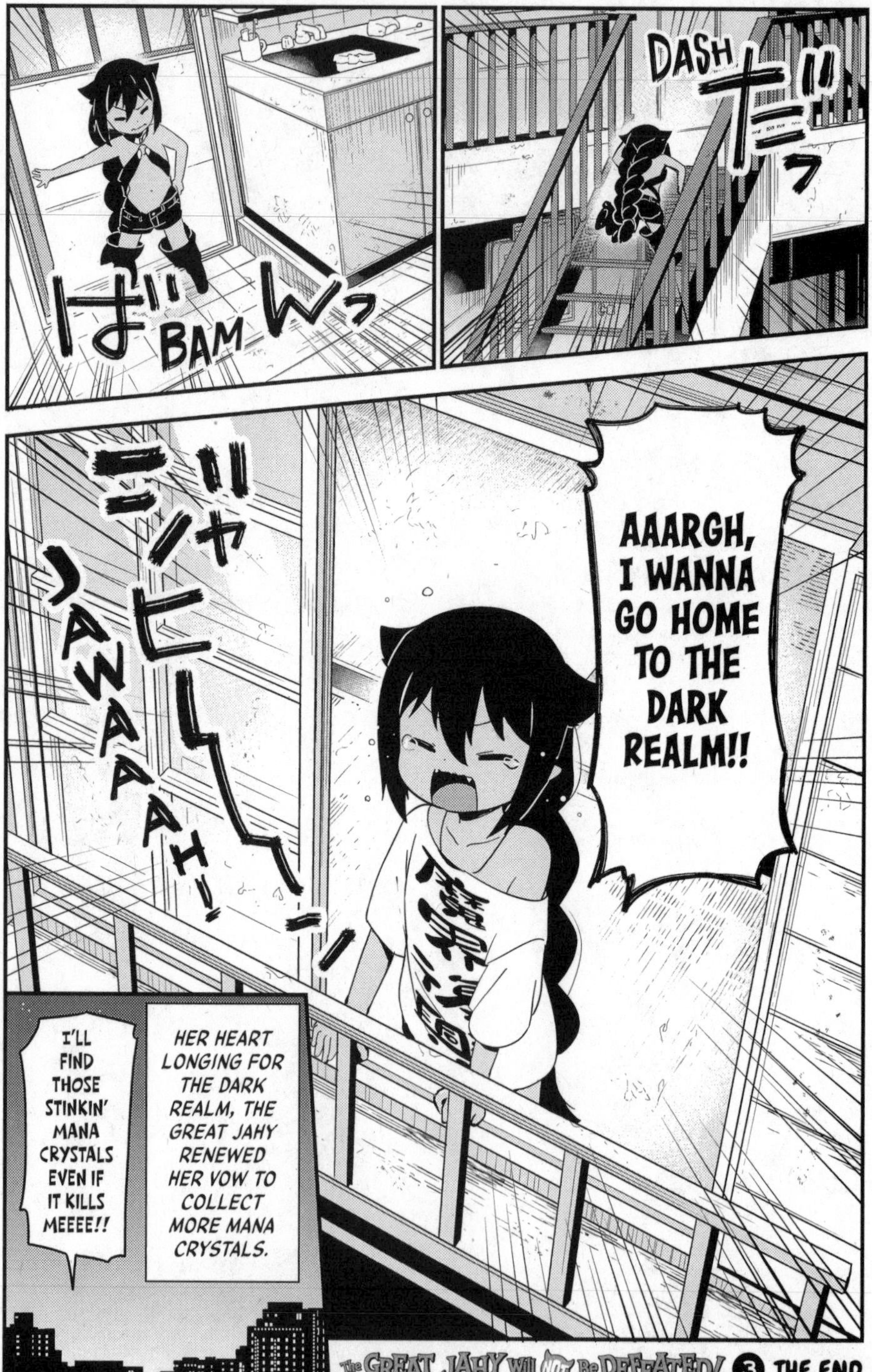
DASH
BAM
AAARGH, I WANNA GO HOME TO THE DARK REALM!!
AWAAAAH!!
HER HEART LONGING FOR THE DARK REALM, THE GREAT JAHY RENEWED HER VOW TO COLLECT MORE MANA CRYSTALS.
I'LL FIND THOSE STINKIN' MANA CRYSTALS EVEN IF IT KILLS MEEEE!!
The GREAT JAHY Will NOT Be DEFEATED! 3 THE END

GREAT JAHY DOLL
(HANDMADE)

The GREAT JAHY Will NOT Be DEFEATED!

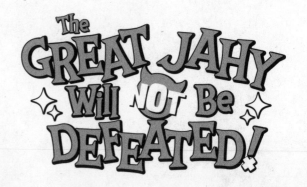

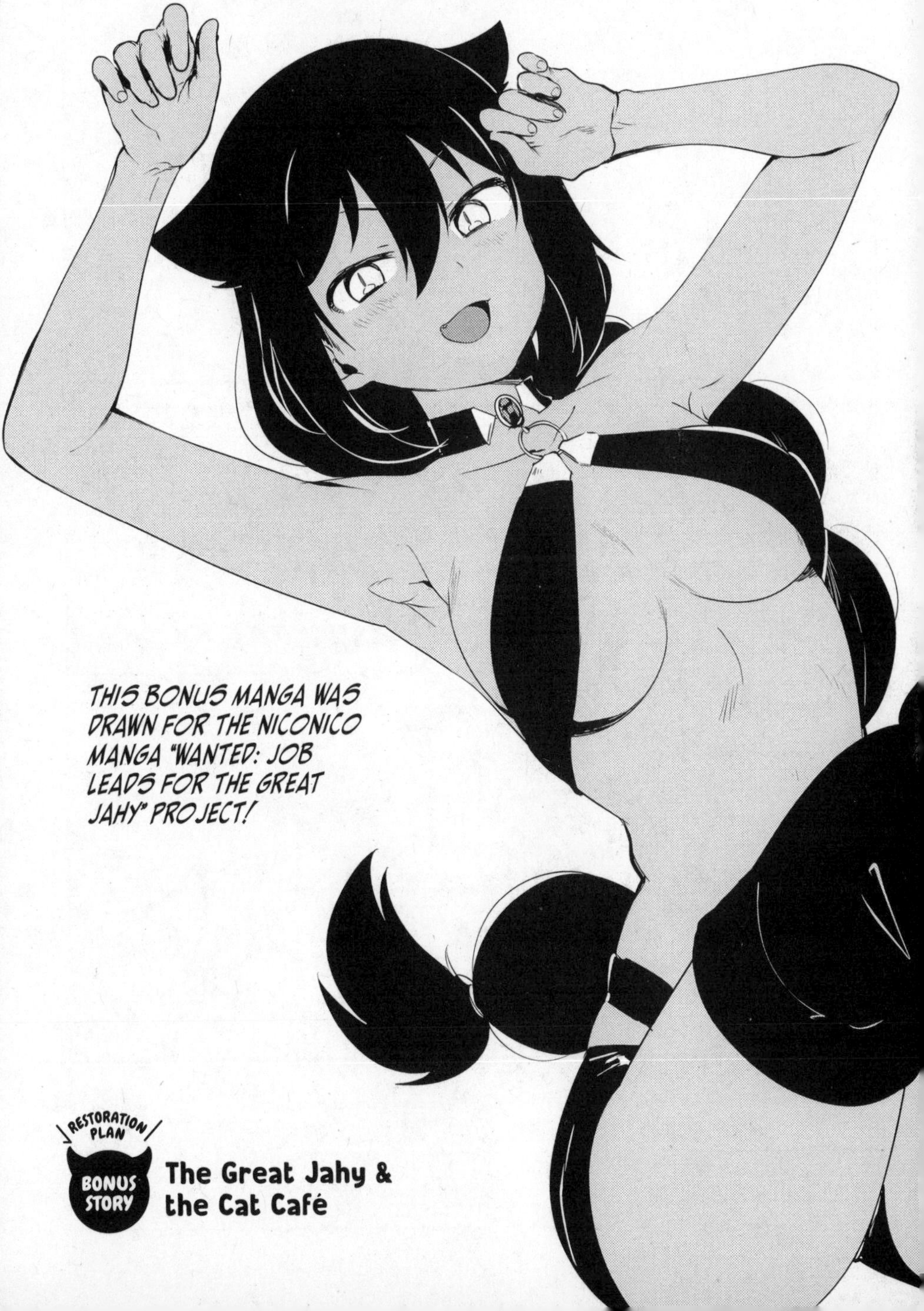
THIS BONUS MANGA WAS DRAWN FOR THE NICONICO MANGA "WANTED: JOB LEADS FOR THE GREAT JAHY" PROJECT!

RESTORATION PLAN

BONUS STORY

The Great Jahy & the Cat Café

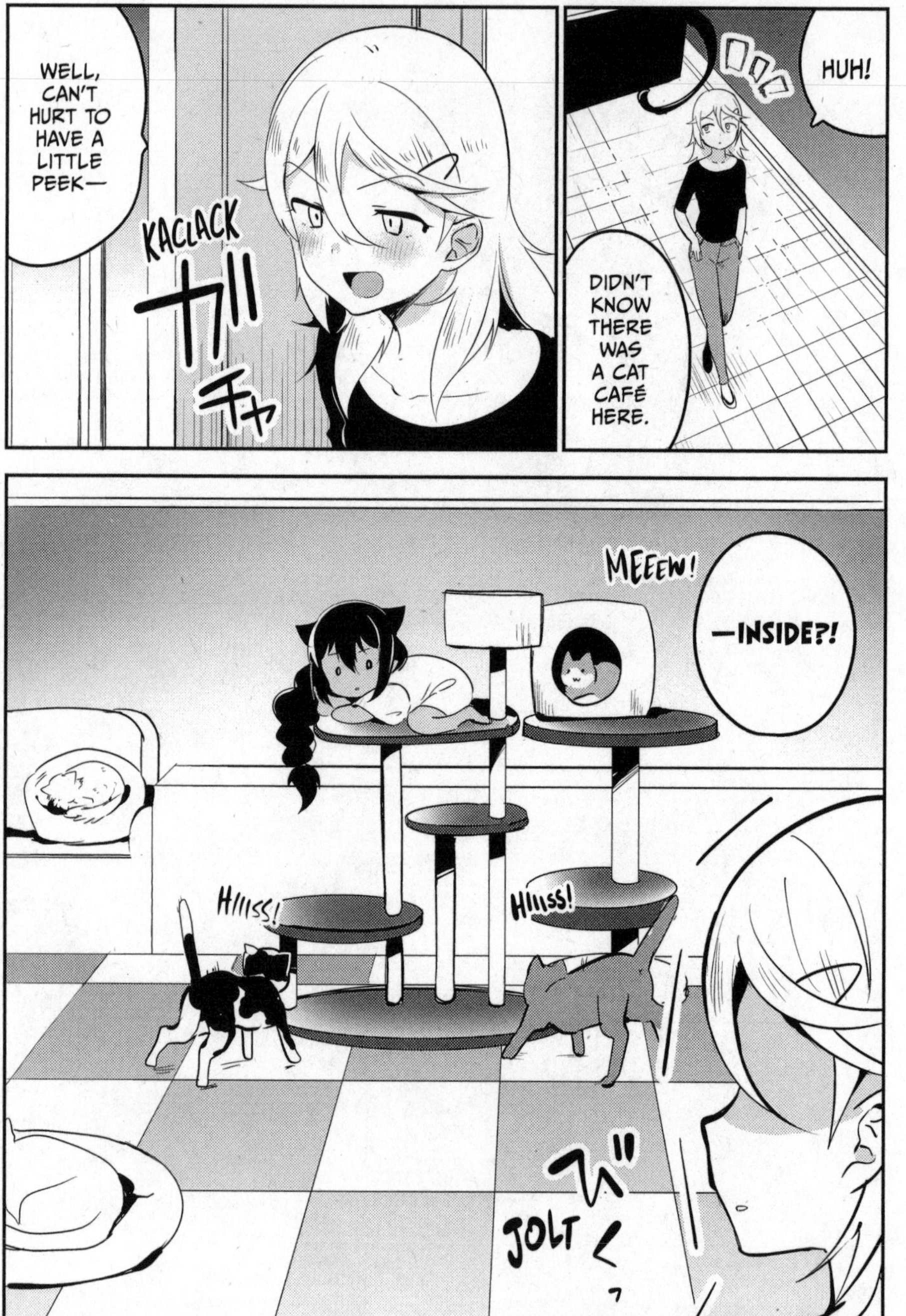
HUH!
DIDN'T KNOW THERE WAS A CAT CAFÉ HERE.
WELL, CAN'T HURT TO HAVE A LITTLE PEEK—
KACLACK
ガチャ
—INSIDE?!
MEEEW!
HIIISS!
HIIISS!
JOLT
びくっ

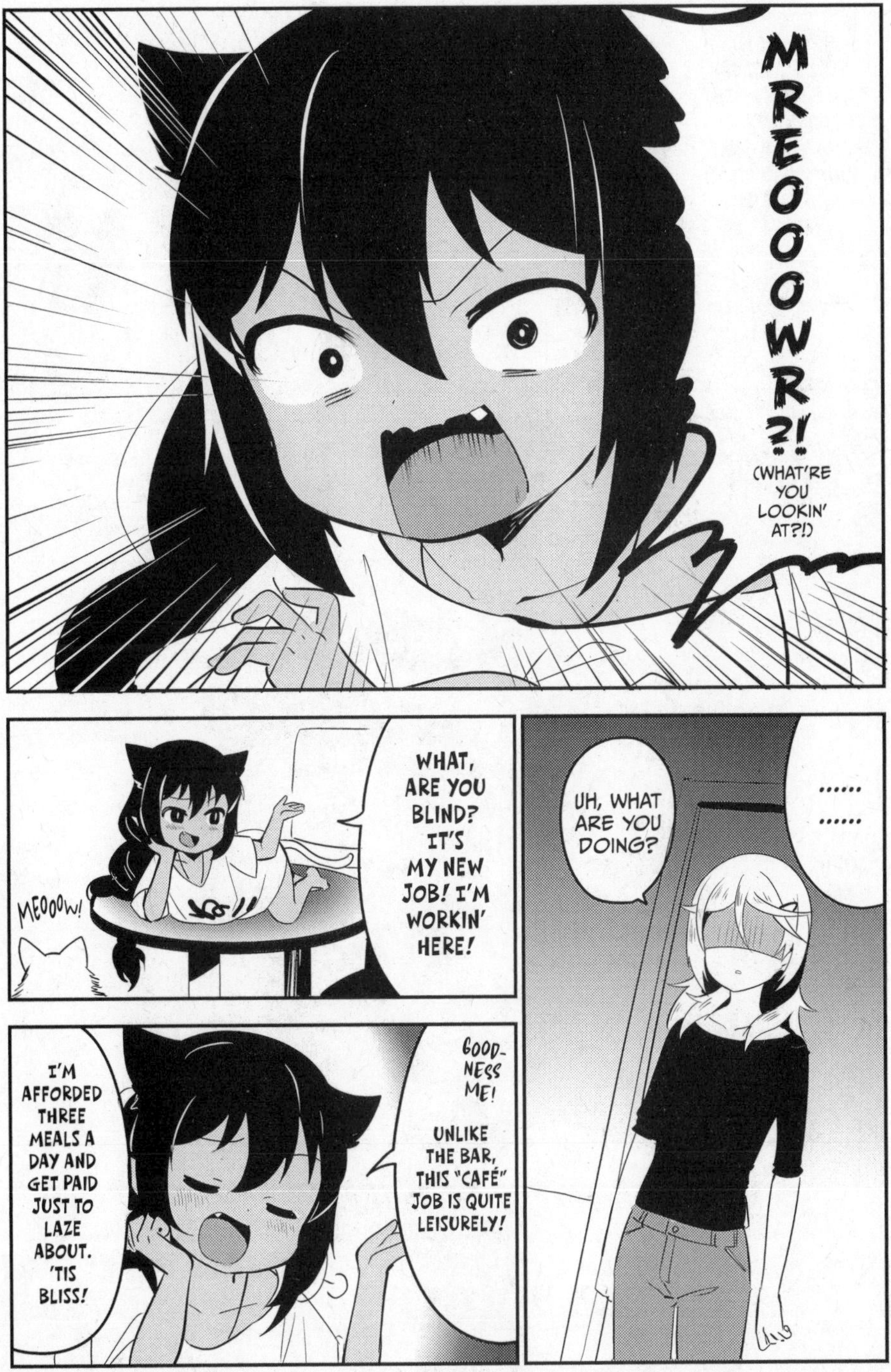
MREOOOWR?!
(WHAT'RE YOU LOOKIN' AT?!)
......
......
UH, WHAT ARE YOU DOING?
WHAT, ARE YOU BLIND? IT'S MY NEW JOB! I'M WORKIN' HERE!
MEOOOW!
GOOD-NESS ME!
UNLIKE THE BAR, THIS "CAFÉ" JOB IS QUITE LEISURELY!
I'M AFFORDED THREE MEALS A DAY AND GET PAID JUST TO LAZE ABOUT. 'TIS BLISS!

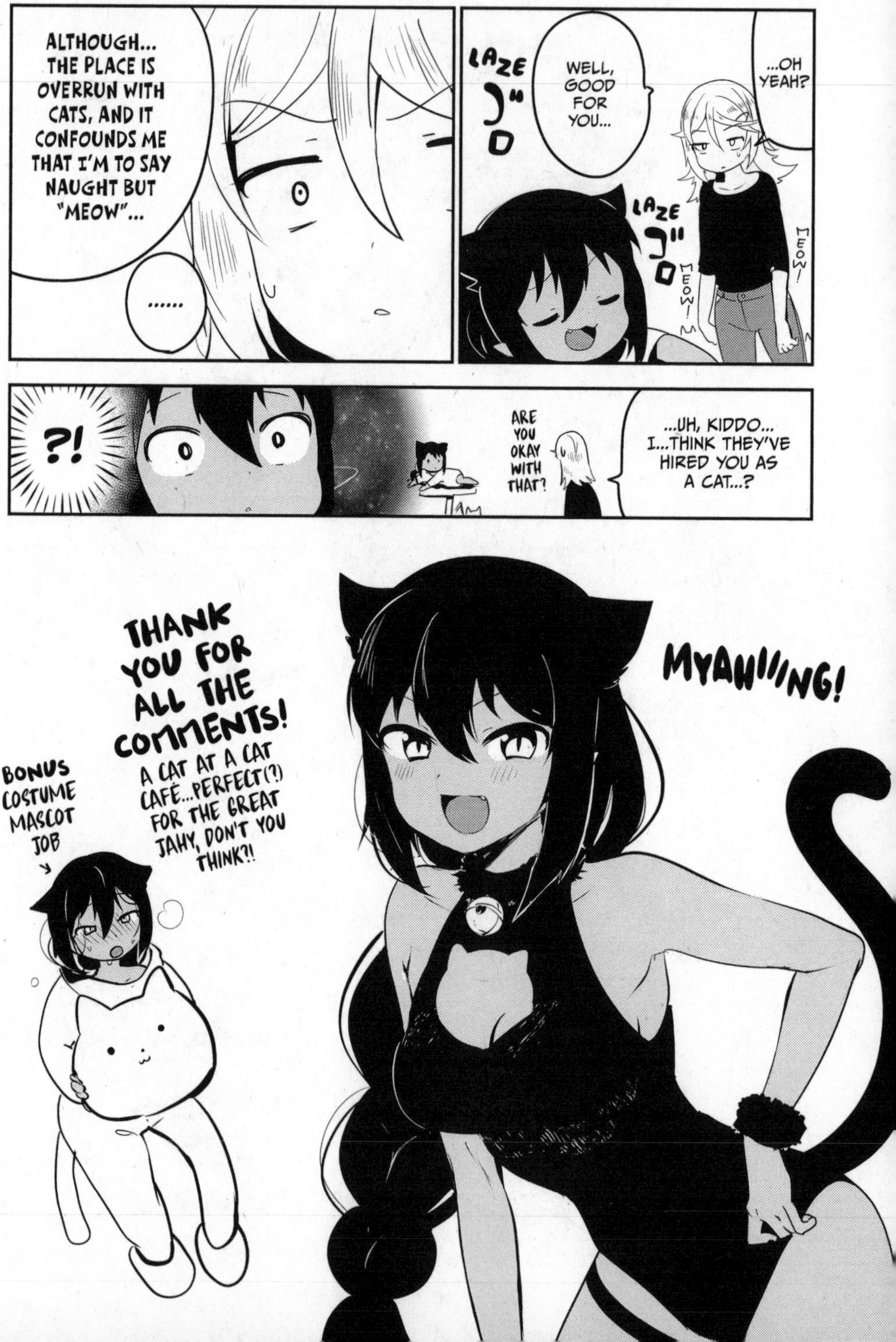
...OH YEAH?
WELL, GOOD FOR YOU...
LAZE
LAZE
MEOW!
MEOW!
ALTHOUGH... THE PLACE IS OVERRUN WITH CATS, AND IT CONFOUNDS ME THAT I'M TO SAY NAUGHT BUT "MEOW"...
......
...UH, KIDDO... I...THINK THEY'VE HIRED YOU AS A CAT...?
ARE YOU OKAY WITH THAT?
?!
MYAHIIING!
THANK YOU FOR ALL THE COMMENTS!
A CAT AT A CAT CAFÉ...PERFECT(?) FOR THE GREAT JAHY, DON'T YOU THINK?!
BONUS COSTUME MASCOT JOB

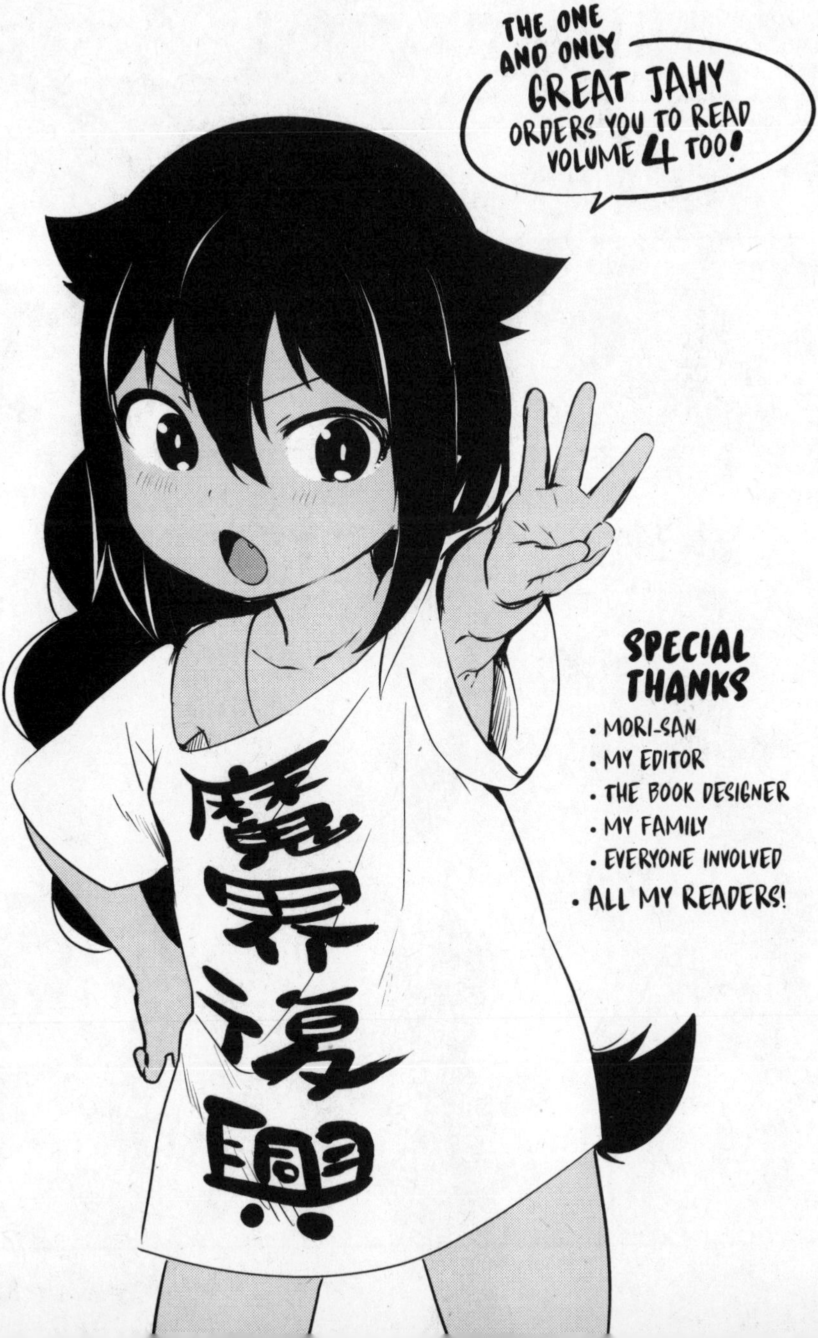
THE ONE AND ONLY GREAT JAHY ORDERS YOU TO READ VOLUME 4 TOO!
魔界復興
SPECIAL THANKS
• MORI-SAN
• MY EDITOR
• THE BOOK DESIGNER
• MY FAMILY
• EVERYONE INVOLVED
• ALL MY READERS!

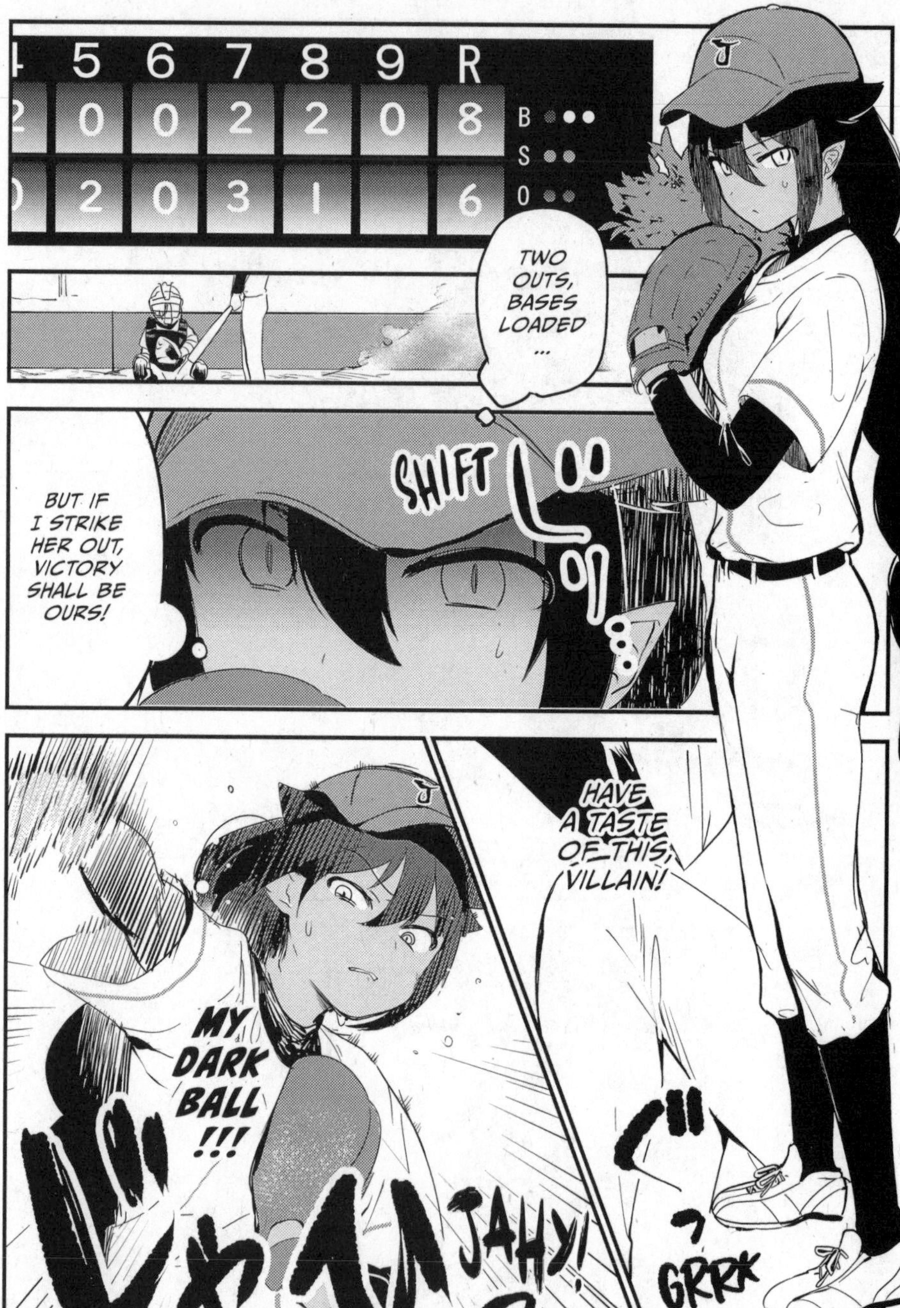
TWO OUTS, BASES LOADED ...
4 5 6 7 8 9 R
2 0 0 2 2 0 8
0 2 0 3 1 6
B
S
O
SHIFT
BUT IF I STRIKE HER OUT, VICTORY SHALL BE OURS!
HAVE A TASTE OF THIS, VILLAIN!
GRRK
MY DARK BALL!!!
JAHY!

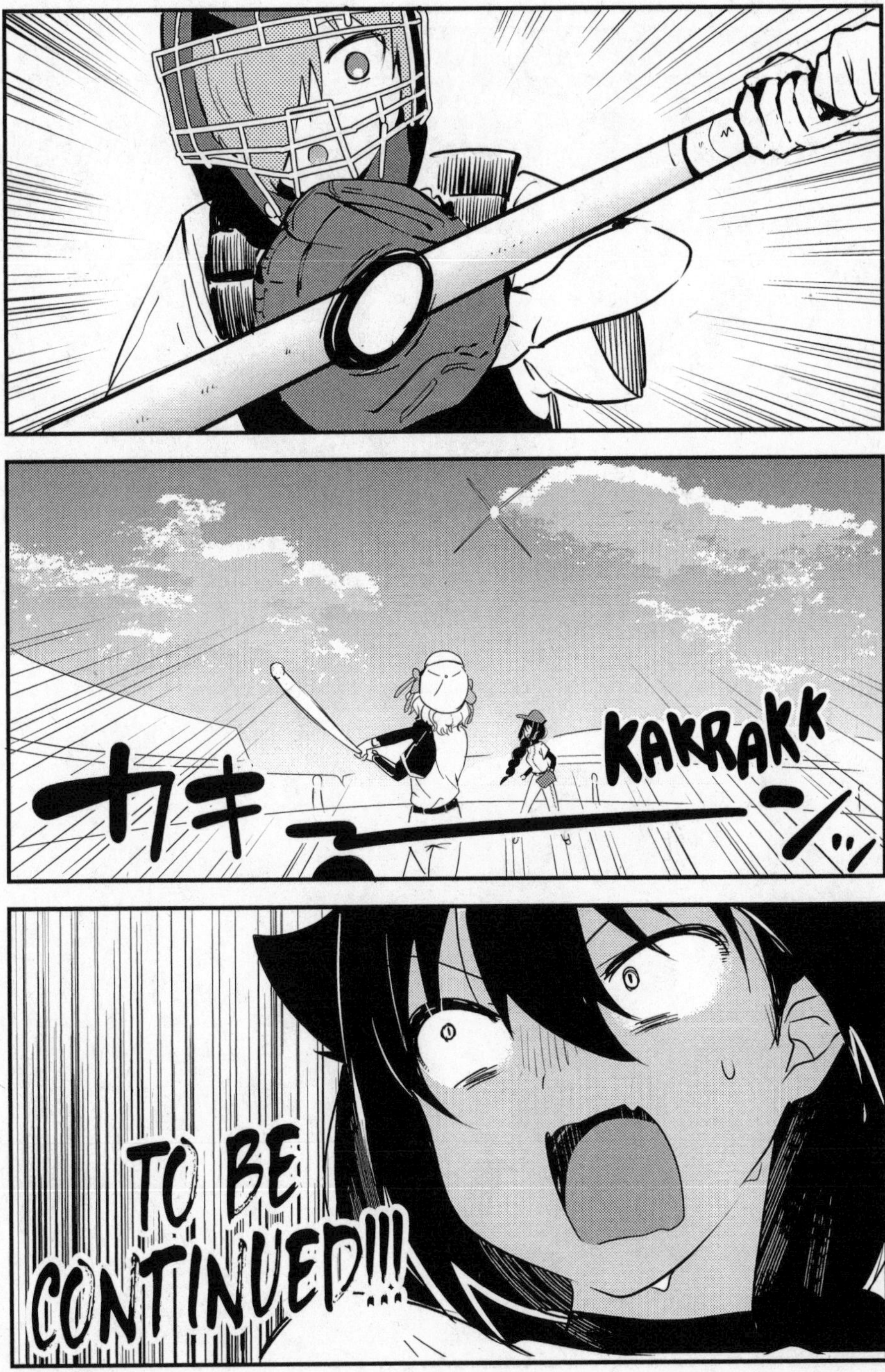
カキーンッ
KAKRAKK
TO BE CONTINUED!!!

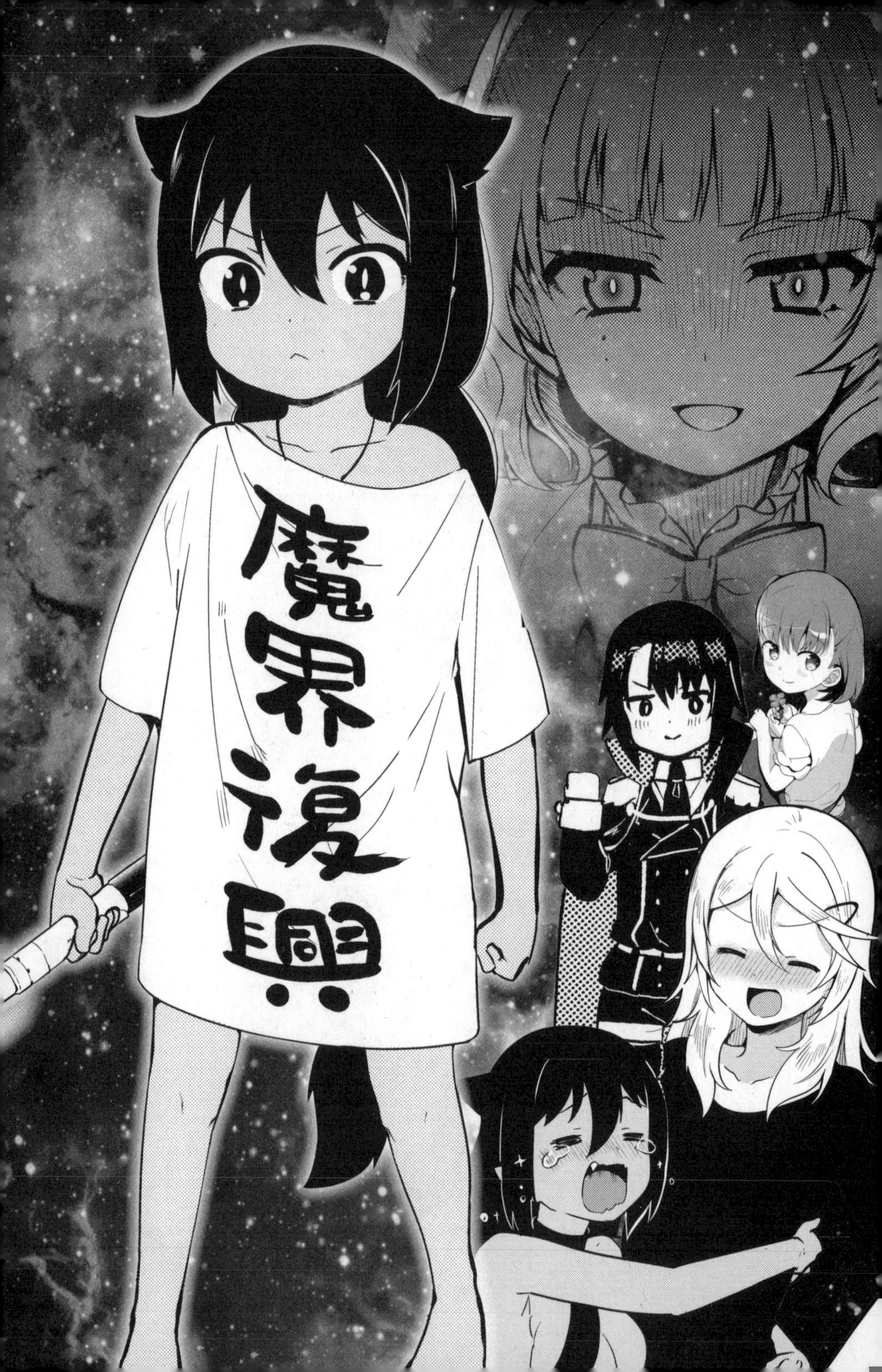
魔界復興

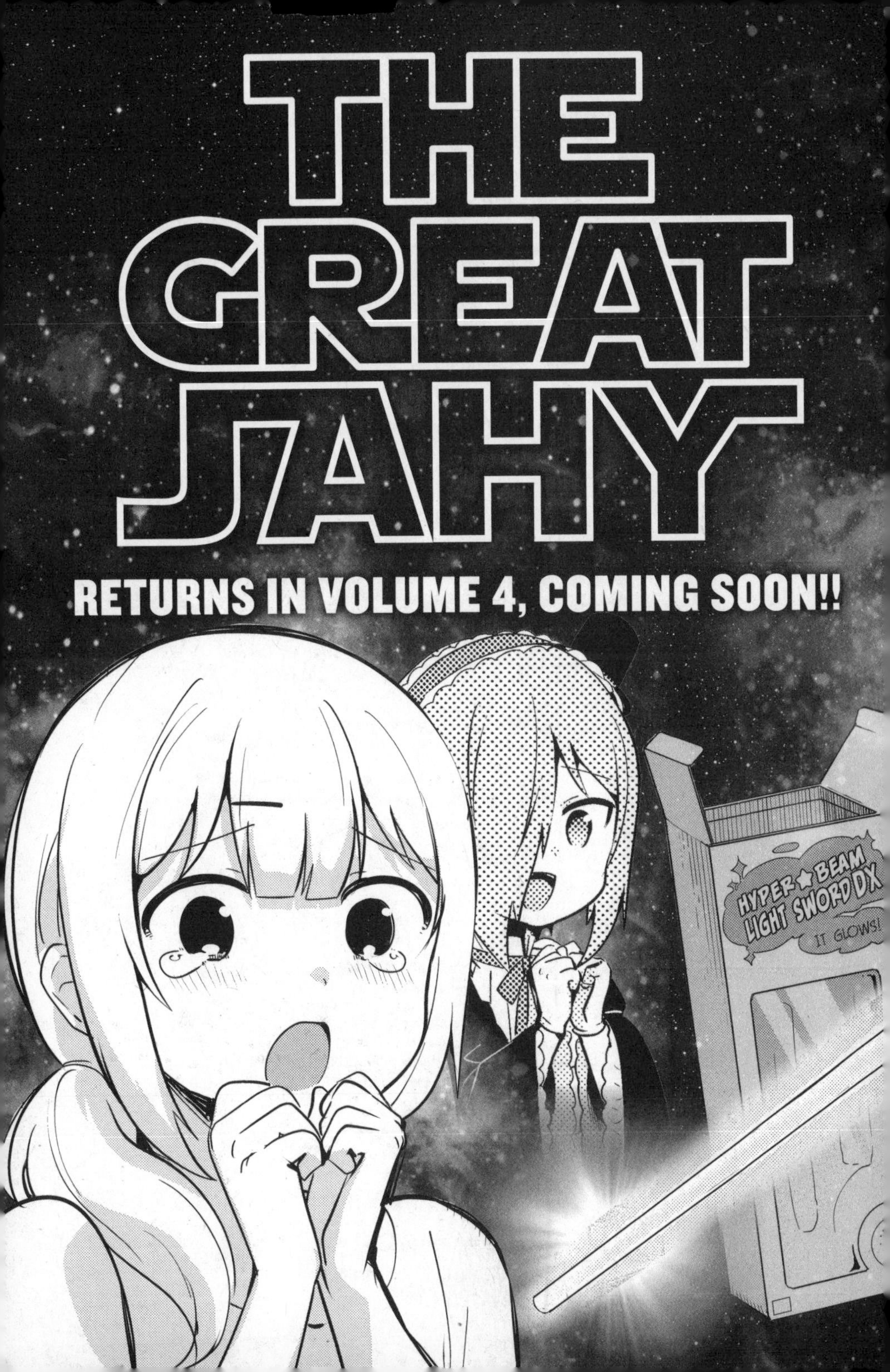
THE GREAT JAHY
RETURNS IN VOLUME 4, COMING SOON!!
HYPER★BEAM LIGHT SWORD DX
IT GLOWS!

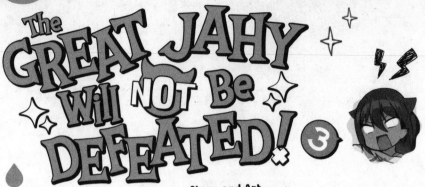

The GREAT JAHY Will NOT Be DEFEATED! 3

Story and Art
Wakame Konbu

Translation: **Amanda Haley**   Lettering: **Ken Kamura**

Cover Design: **Andrea Miller**   Editor: **Tania Biswas**

THE GREAT JAHY WILL NOT BE DEFEATED! Volume 3
© 2018 Wakame Konbu/SQUARE ENIX CO., LTD.
First published in Japan in 2018 by SQUARE ENIX CO., LTD.
English translation rights arranged with
SQUARE ENIX CO., LTD. and SQUARE ENIX, INC.
English translation © 2022 by SQUARE ENIX CO., LTD.

ISBN: 978-1-64609-078-5

Library of Congress Cataloging-in-Publication Data
is on file with the publisher.

Printed in the U.S.A.
First printing, July 2022
10 9 8 7 6 5 4 3 2 1

SQUARE ENIX
MANGA & BOOKS

www.square-enix-books.com